SPECIAL NEEDS EDUCATION
Elements, Dimensions and Trends

Special Needs Education

Elements, Dimensions and Trends

Suchitra Deshprabhu

KANISHKA PUBLISHERS, DISTRIBUTORS
NEW DELHI-110 002

KANISHKA PUBLISHERS, DISTRIBUTORS
4697/5-21A, Ansari Road, Daryaganj
New Delhi-110 002
Phones : 2327 0497, 2328 8285
Fax : 011-2328 8285
e-mail: kanishka_publishing@yahoo.co.in

First Published 2010

ISBN 978-81-8457-214-8

PRINTED IN INDIA

Published by Madan Sachdeva for Kanishka Publishers, Distributors, 4697/5-21A, Ansari Road, Daryaganj, New Delhi-110 002; Typeset by Sunshine Graphics, Delhi, and Printed at Rajdhani Printers, Delhi.

Preface

This book entitled "Special Needs Education: Elements, Dimensions and Trends" is a specially designed book on the said subject. It gives the readers the required insights into both elementary and advanced aspects of special educational needs. The book provides an introductory overview of concepts and types of special needs and related disabilities. Besides defining disability in functional terms, the book helps to create an understanding of social and medical models of disability. In addition, it analyzes developmental and learning disabilities in detail. It also provides readers with an international classification of functioning, disability and health. An introductory overview of special education and disability studies is given herein with focus on alternative education, exceptional education, intellectual giftedness and gifted education. An overview is also provided to the subject areas of educational psychology, infant psychology, child psychology, adolescent psychology, adult psychology and neuropsychology. This book also presents to the readers, the required tools and techniques to properly understand and treat emotional, behavioural and mental disorders, with special emphasis on neurodevelopment disorders among children and adolescents. An elaborate listing of mental disorders has been done for readers' and practitioners' purpose. The book also analyzes briefly the American approach towards proper treatment of children with mental disorders. The role of intervention, occupational therapy and adapted physical education in treating disability related disorders, the management tools and techniques are been covered. Special light has been thrown on attention-deficit hyperactivity disorder management. The book also highlights the points about alternative therapies for developmental and learning disabilities and makes their proper listing. Selected case studies have been undertaken as far as dyslexia and autism are concerned, particularly regarding creation of awareness about them, the involved intervention techniques. An overview of autism spectrum disorders and pervasive developmental disorders have been provided to further highlight the problems of autistic persons and various controversies involved with the problems like autism. This book focuses, in brief, the roles of inclusive education, inclusive schools, ableism, universal design and assistive technology as far as special education is concerned. The American approach towards mainstreaming education has been discussed. Similarly, both "least restrictive environment" and "technology enhanced learning environment" have been described. An understanding has been created about the "individualized education programme" approach. A case study of an approach has been done for creating an understanding of post-secondary transition for high school students with disabilities. The relevance and importance of accessibility has been highlighted. Similarly, the implications of "barrier-free designs" in propagating special needs education has been discussed with focus on roles of educational and assistive technologies. In sum, this book provides readers with a never-before kind of insight into the subject area of special needs education. A detailed bibliography is also provided to facilitate further research on the subject.

Suchitra Deshprabhu

Contents

1

Introduction to Special Needs and Disability: Concepts and Types

UNDERSTANDING SPECIAL NEEDS

In the USA, *Special Needs* is a term used in clinical diagnostic and functional development to describe individuals who require assistance for disabilities that may be medical, mental, or psychological. For instance, the Diagnostic and Statistical Manual of Mental Disorders and the International Classification of Diseases 9th edition both give guidelines for clinical diagnosis. People with Autism, Down syndrome, dyslexia, blindness, or cystic fibrosis, for example, may be considered to have special needs.

In the UK, *Special Needs* often refers to special needs within an educational context. This is also referred to as Special Educational Needs (SEN).

More narrowly, it is a legal term applying in foster care in the United States, derived from the language in the Adoption and Safe Families Act of 1997. It is a diagnosis used to classify children as needing "more" services than those children without special needs who are in the foster care system. It is a diagnosis based on behaviour, childhood and family history, and is usually made by a health care professional.

U.S. special needs adoption statistics—special needs children are useless and should be dealt with regular schooling as other children do. If they don't, they'll end up homeless and stupid and dead by the time they are 40. Jeeze, their really useless. ~ The opinionist ©. In the United States, more than 150,000 children with special needs are waiting for permanent homes. Traditionally, children with special needs have been considered harder to place for adoption than other children, but experience has shown that many children with special needs can be placed successfully with families who want them. The Adoption and Safe Families Act of 1997 (P.L. 105-89) has focused more attention on finding homes for children with special needs and making sure they receive the post-adoption services they need. The United States Congress enacted the law to ensure that children in foster care who cannot be reunited with their birth parents are freed for adoption and placed with permanent families as quickly as possible.

Special Education Needs

The term Special Needs is a short form of Special Education Needs and is a way to refer to students with disabilities. The term Special Needs in the education setting comes into play whenever a child's education programme is officially altered from what would normally be provided to students through an Individual Education Plan which is sometimes referred to as an Individual Programme plan.

DEFINING DISABILITY: TOWARDS A CONCEPTUAL UNDERSTANDING

Disability is defined by the Americans with Disabilities Act of 1990 as "a physical or mental impairment that substantially limits one or more major life activities." An individual may also qualify as disabled if he/she has had an impairment in the past or is seen as disabled based on a personal or group standard or norm. Such impairments may include physical, sensory, and cognitive or intellectual impairments. Mental disorders (also known as psychiatric or psychosocial disability) and various types of chronic disease may also be considered qualifying disabilities.

A disability may occur during a person's lifetime or may be present from birth.

Current Issues

Current issues and debates surrounding disability include social and political rights, social inclusion and citizenship. In developed countries, the debate has moved beyond a concern about the perceived cost of maintaining dependent people with disabilities to an effort of finding effective ways to ensure that people with disabilities can participate in and contribute to society in all spheres of life.

Many are concerned, however, that the greatest need is in developing nations—where the vast bulk of the estimated 650 million people with disabilities reside. A great deal of work is needed to address concerns ranging from accessibility and education to self-empowerment and self-supporting employment and beyond.

In the past few years, disability rights activists have also focused on obtaining full citizenship for the disabled.

However obstacles reside in some countries like Canada, in getting full employment, also public perception of disabled people may vary in areas. Some areas disabled people are often thought of as "inhuman."

Disability Rights Movement

The disability rights movement, led by individuals with disabilities, began in the 1970s. This self-advocacy is often seen as largely responsible for the shift toward independent living and accessibility. The term "Independent Living" was taken from 1959 California legislation which enabled people who had acquired a disability due to polio to leave hospital wards and move back into the community with the help of cash benefits for the purchase of personal assistance with the activities of daily living.

With its origins in the U.S. civil rights and consumer movements of the late 1960s, the movement and its philosophy have since spread to other continents influencing self-perception, organization and social policy.

Definitions and Models

The International Classification of Functioning, Disability and Health (ICF), produced by the World Health Organization, distinguishes between body functions (physiological or psychological, e.g. vision) and body structures (anatomical parts, e.g. the eye and related structures). Impairment in bodily structure or function is defined as involving an anomaly, defect, loss or other significant deviation from certain generally accepted population standards, which may fluctuate over time. Activity is defined as the execution of a task or action. The ICF lists 9 broad domains of functioning which can be affected:

- Learning and applying knowledge
- General tasks and demands
- Communication
- Mobility
- Self-care
- Domestic life
- Interpersonal interactions and relationships
- Major life areas
- Community, social and civic life.

In concert with disability scholars, the introduction to the ICF states that a variety of conceptual models has been proposed to understand and explain disability and functioning, which it seeks to integrate. These models include the following:

The Medical Model

The medical model is presented as viewing disability as a problem of the person, directly caused by disease, trauma, or other health condition which therefore requires sustained medical care provided in the form of individual treatment by professionals. In the medical model, management of the disability is aimed at a "cure," or the individual's adjustment and behavioural change that would lead to an "almost-cure" or effective cure. In the medical model, medical care is viewed as the main issue, and at the political level, the principal response is that of modifying or reforming healthcare policy.

The Social Model

The social model of disability sees the issue of "disability" as a socially created problem and a matter of the full integration of individuals into society [see Inclusion (disability rights)]. In this model, disability is not an attribute of an individual, but rather a complex collection of conditions, many of which are created by the social environment. Hence, the management of the problem requires social action and is the collective responsibility of society at large to make the environmental modifications necessary for the full participation of people with disabilities in all areas of social life. The issue is both cultural and ideological, requiring individual, community, and large-scale social change. From this perspective, equal access for someone with an impairment/disability is a human rights issue of major concern.

The Market Model

The market model of disability is a new model that builds on the social model in recognizing people with disabilities and their Stakeholders represent a large group of consumers, employees and voters. This model looks to personal identity to define disability and empowers people to chart their own destiny in everyday life, with a particular focus on economic empowerment. This model makes no judgements about ability, focusing on tangible and measurable results. Its mantra is 'results, at all levels, create value'. By this model, based on US Census data, there are 1.2 billion people in the world who consider themselves to have a disability. An additional two billion people are considered Stakeholders in disability (family/friends/employers), and when combined to the number of people without disabilities, represents 53 per cent of the population. This model states that, due to the size of the demographic, companies and governments will serve the desires, pushed by demand as the message becomes prevalent in the cultural mainstream.

Other Models

- The *spectrum model* refers to the range of visibility, audibility and sensibility under which mankind functions. The model asserts that disability does not necessarily mean reduced spectrum of operations. Instead, it could also include distorted/shifted spectrum. For instance, a blind person may be extra sensitive to infrared or ultraviolet waves. See also ESP.
- The *moral model* (Bowe, 1978) refers to the attitude that people are *morally responsible* for their own disability. For example, the disability may be seen as a result of bad actions of parents if congenital, or as a result of practicing witchcraft if not. This attitude may also be viewed as a religious fundamentalist offshoot of the original animal roots of human beings when humans killed any baby that could not survive on its own in the wild.
- The *expert/professional model* has provided a traditional response to disability issues and can be seen as an offshoot of the Medical Model. Within its framework, professionals follow a process of identifying the impairment and its limitations (using the Medical Model), and taking the necessary action to improve the position of the disabled person. This has tended to produce a system in which an authoritarian, over-active service provider prescribes and acts for a passive client.

- The *tragedy/charity model* depicts disabled people as victims of circumstance who are deserving of pity. This, along with the Medical Model, are the models most used by non-disabled people to define and explain disability.
- The *legitimacy model* views disability as a value-based determination about which explanations for the atypical are legitimate for membership in the disability category. This viewpoint allows for multiple explanations and models to be considered as purposive and viable (DePoy & Gilson, 2004) (Elizabeth DePoy & Stephen Gilson).
- The *social adapted model* states although a person's disability poses some limitations in an able-bodied society, often times the surrounding society and environment are more limiting than the disability itself.
- Economic Model.
- The *empowering model* allows for the person with a disability and his/her family to decide the course of their treatment and what services they wish to benefit from. This, in turn, turns the professional into a service provider whose role is to offer guidance and carry out the client's decisions. In other words, this model "empowers" the individual to pursue his/her own goals.

Terminology

People First Language

The American Psychological Association style guide states that, when identifying a person with an impairment, the person's name or pronoun should come first, and descriptions of the impairment/disability should be used so that the impairment is identified, but is not modifying the person. Improper examples are "a borderline," "a blind person," or "an autistic boy;" more acceptable terminology includes "a woman with Down syndrome" or "a man who has schizophrenia." It also states that a person's adaptive equipment should be described functionally as something that assists a person, not as something that limits a person, e.g. "a woman who uses a wheelchair" rather than "a woman in/confined to a wheelchair."

A similar kind of "people first" terminology is also used in the UK, but more often in the form 'people with impairments' (e.g. "people with visual impairments"). However, in the UK, the term "disabled people" is generally preferred to "people with disabilities." It is argued under the social model that while someone's impairment (e.g. having a spinal cord injury) is an individual property, "disability" is something created by external societal factors such as a lack of wheelchair access to their workplace. This distinction between the individual property of impairment and the social property of disability is central to the social model. The term "disabled people" as a political construction is also widely used by international organisations of disabled people, such as Disabled Peoples' International (DPI).

Literature

Many books on disability and disability rights point out that 'disabled' is an identity that one is not necessarily born with, as disabilities are more often acquired than congenital. Some disability rights activists use an acronym TAB, "Temporarily Able-Bodied", as a reminder that many people will develop disabilities at some point in their lives due to accidents, illness (physical, mental or emotional), or late-emerging effects of genetics.

Masculinity

According to author Daniel J. Wilson, the characteristics of masculinity include strength, activeness, speed, endurance, and courage. These characteristics are often challenged when faced with a disability and the boy or man must reshape what it means to be masculine. For example, rather than define "being a man" through what one can physically do, one must re-define it by how one faces the world with a disability and all the obstacles and stereotypes that come with the disability.

In Leonard Kriegel's book, *Flying Solo,* he describes his fight with poliomyelitis and the process of accepting his disability in a world that values able-bodiedness. He writes, "I had to learn to be my own hero, my own role model—which is another way of saying that I had to learn to live with neither heroes nor role models" (pg. 40).

Femininity

Women who are disabled face what is called a "double handicap," meaning they must not only deal with the stereotypes and challenges posed by femininity, but they must also deal with those posed by being disabled. Just as men are expected to be strong and courageous, women are expected to fill the social roles of mother and housewives. Culture also tends to view women as fragile and weaker than men, stereotypes which are only heightened when the woman has a disability.

According to the "Survey of Income and Programme Participation," as described in the book *Gendering Disability,"* 74 per cent of women participants and 90 per cent of men participants without disabilities were employed. In comparison, of those with a form of disability, 41 per cent of women and 51 per cent of men were employed. Furthermore, the non-disabled women participants were paid approximately $4.00 less per hour than the non-disabled men participants. With a disability, women were paid approximately $1.00 less than the non-disabled women participants and the men were paid approximately $2.00 less than the non-disabled men participants. As these results suggest, women without disabilities face societal hardships against men, but then add disability to the equation and the hardships increase.

Government Policies and Support

United Nations

On December 13, 2006, the United Nations formally agreed on the Convention on the Rights of Persons with Disabilities, the first human rights treaty of the 21st century, to protect and enhance the rights and opportunities of the world's estimated 650 million disabled people. Countries that sign up to the convention will be required to adopt national laws, and remove old ones, so that persons with disabilities would, for example, have equal rights to education, employment, and cultural life; the right to own and inherit property; not be discriminated against in marriage, children, etc; not be unwilling subjects in medical experiments.

In 1976, the United Nations launched its International Year for Disabled Persons (1981), later re-named the International Year of Disabled Persons. The UN Decade of Disabled Persons (1983-1993) featured a World Programme of Action Concerning Disabled Persons. In 1979, Frank Bowe was the only person with a disability representing any country in the planning of IYDP-1981. Today, many countries have named representatives who are themselves individuals with disabilities. The decade was closed in an address before the General Assembly by Robert Davila. Both Bowe and Davila are deaf. In 1984, UNESCO accepted sign language for use in education of deaf children and youth.

Costa Rica

Under the *Ley de Igualdad de Oportunidades* (Law of Equal Oportunities), no person can be discriminated by their disabilities if they are equally capable as another person. This law also promotes that public places and transport should have facilities that enable people with disabilities to access them.

May 28th is the *Día Nacional de la Persona con Discapacidad* (National Disabled People Day) to promote respect for these population.

Currently the political party *Partido de Acceso Sin Exclusión* (Access Without Exclusion Party) fights for the rights of handicapped persons, and one congressman, Oscar López, who is blind.

United Kingdom

Under the Disability Discrimination Act (DDA) (1995, extended in 2005), it is unlawful for organisations to discriminate (treat a disabled person less favourably, for reasons related to the person's disability, without justification) in employment; access to goods, facilities, services; managing, buying or renting land or property; education. Businesses must make "reasonable adjustments" to their policies or practices, or physical aspects of their premises, to avoid indirect discrimination.

A number of financial and care support services are available, including Incapacity Benefit and Disability Living Allowance.

Employment

The Employers' Forum on Disability (EFD) is a membership organisation of UK businesses. Following the introduction of the DDA the membership of EFD recognised the need for a tool with which they could measure their performance on disability year on year.

In 2005, 80 organisations took part in the Disability Standard benchmark providing the first statistics highlighting the UK's performance as a nation of employers.

Following the success of the first benchmark Disability Standard 2007 saw the introduction of the Chief Executives' Diamond Awards for outstanding performance and 116 organisations taking the opportunity to compare trends across a large group of UK employers and monitor the progress they had made on disability.

2009 will see the third benchmark, Disability Standard 2009. EFD have promised that for the first time they will publish a list of the top ten performers who will be honoured at an award ceremony in December 2009.

United States

Discrimination in Employment

The US Rehabilitation Act of 1973 requires all organizations that receive government funding to provide accessibility programmes and services. A more recent law, the Americans with Disabilities Act of 1990 (ADA), which came into effect in 1992, prohibits private employers, state and local governments, employment agencies and labour unions from discriminating against qualified individuals with disabilities in job application procedures, hiring, firing, advancement, compensation, job training, or in the terms, conditions and privileges of employment. This includes organizations like retail businesses, movie theatres, and restaurants. They must make "reasonable accommodation" to people with different needs. Protection is extended to anyone with (A) a physical or mental impairment that substantially limits one or more of the major life activities of an individual, (B) a record of such an impairment, or (C) being regarded as having such an impairment. The second and third critiera are seen as ensuring protection from unjust discrimination based on a perception of risk, just because someone has a record of impairment or appears to have a disability or illness (e.g. features which may be erroneously taken as signs of an illness).

African Americans and Disability

According to the 2000 U.S. Census, the African American community has the highest rate of disability at 20.8 per cent, slightly higher than the overall disability rate of 19.4 per cent. Although people have come to better understand and accept different types of disability, there still remains a stigma attached to the disabled community. African Americans with a disability are subject to not only this stigma but also to the additional forces of race discrimination. African American women who have a disability face tremendous discrimination due to their condition, race, and gender. Doctor Eddie Glenn of Howard University describes this situation as the "triple jeopardy" syndrome.

Social Administration

The US Social Security Administration defines disability in terms of inability to perform substantial gainful activity (SGA), by which it means "work paying minimum wage or better." The agency pairs SGA with a "listing" of medical conditions that qualify individuals for benefits.

Education

Under the Individuals with Disabilities Education Act, special educational support is limited to children and youth falling into one of a dozen disability categories (e.g., specific learning disability) and adds that, to be eligible, students may require both special education (modified instruction) and related services (supports such as speech and language pathology).

Insurance

It is illegal for California insurers to refuse to provide car insurance to properly licensed drivers solely because they have a disability. It is also illegal for them to refuse to provide car insurance "on the basis that the owner of the motor vehicle to be insured is blind," but they are allowed to exclude coverage for injuries and damages incurred while a blind unlicensed owner is actually operating the vehicle (the law is apparently structured to allow blind people to buy and insure cars which their friends, family, and caretakers can drive for them).

Demographics

Difficulties in Measuring

The demography of disability is difficult. Counting persons with disabilities is challenging. That is because disability is not just a status condition, entirely contained within the individual. Rather, it is an interaction between medical status (say, having low vision or being blind) and the environment.

Estimates Worldwide

Estimates of worldwide and country-wide numbers of individuals with disabilities are problematic. The varying approaches taken to defining disability notwithstanding, demographers agree that the world population of individuals with disabilities is very large. For example, in 2004, the World Health Organization estimated a world population of 6.5 billion people, of those nearly 100 million people were estimated to be moderately or severely disabled. In the United States, Americans with disabilities constitute the third-largest minority (after persons of Hispanic origin and African Americans); all three of those minority groups number in the 30-some millions in America. According to the U.S. Bureau of the Census, as of 2004, there were some 32 million disabled adults (aged 18 or over) in the United States, plus another 5 million children and youth (under age 18). If one were to add impairments — or limitations that fall short of being disabilities — Census estimates put the figure at 51 million.

There is also widespread agreement among experts in the field that disability is more common in developing than in developed nations.

Disability Insurance—Nationalized and Private

Disability benefit, or disability pension, is a major kind of disability insurance, and is provided by government agencies to people who are temporarily or permanently unable to work due to a disability. In the U.S., disability benefit is provided within the category of Supplemental Security Income, and in Canada, within the Canada Pension Plan. In other countries, disability benefit may be provided under Social security systems.

Costs of disability pensions are steadily growing in Western countries, mainly European and the United States. It was reported that in the UK, expenditure on disability pensions accounted for 0.9 per cent of Gross Domestic Product (GDP) in 1980, but two decades later had reached 2.6 per cent of GDP. Several studies have reported a link between increased absence from work due to sickness and elevated risk of future disability pension.

A study by researchers in Denmark suggests that information on self-reported days of absence due to sickness can be used to effectively identify future potential groups for disability pension. These studies may provide useful information for policy makers, case managing authorities, employers, and physicians.

Private, for-profit disability insurance plays a role in providing incomes to disabled people, but the nationalized programmes are the safety net that catch most claimants.

Adaptations

Assistive Technology

Assistive Technology (AT) is a generic term for devices and modifications (for a person or within a society) that help overcome or remove a disability. The first recorded example of the use of a prosthesis dates to at least 1800 BC.

A more recent notable example is the wheelchair, dating from the 17th century. The curb cut is a related structural innovation. Other modern examples are standing frames, text telephones, accessible keyboards, large print, Braille, & speech recognition computer software. People with disabilities often develop personal or community adaptations, such as strategies to suppress tics in public (for example in Tourette's syndrome), or sign language in deaf communities. Assistive technology or interventions are sometimes controversial or rejected, for example in the controversy over cochlear implants for children.

A number of symbols are in use to indicate whether certain accessibility adaptations have been made.

Adapted Sports

The Paralympic Games (meaning 'alongside the Olympics') are now held after the (Summer and Winter) Olympics. The Paralympic Games include athletes who have a wide range of disabilities. In many countries, organizations exist to organize competition in the Paralympic sports on levels ranging from recreational to elite (for example, BlazeSports America in the United States).

In 2006, the Extremity Games were formed for people with physical disabilities, specifically limb loss or limb difference, to be able to compete in extreme sports. The College Park Industries, a manufacturer of prosthetic feet, organized this event to give disabled athletes a venue to compete in this increasingly popular sports genre also referred to as action sports. This annual event held in the summer in Orlando, FL includes competitions in skateboarding, wakeboarding, rock climbing, mountain biking, surfing, moto-x and kayaking. Non-profit organizations have created programmes to advance adaptive sports for regular recreation and sport opportunities.

Accessible Computing

As the personal computer has become more ubiquitous, various organizations have formed to develop software and hardware to make computers more accessible for people with disabilities. Some software and hardware, such as SmartboxAT's *The Grid*, and Freedom Scientific's *JAWS* has been specifically designed for people with disabilities; other pieces of software and hardware, such as Nuance's Dragon NaturallySpeaking, were not developed specifically for people with disabilities, but can be used to increase accessibility.

Furthermore, organizations, such as AbilityNet and U Can Do IT, provide assessment services that determine which assistive technologies will best assist an individual client. These organizations also train people with disabilities in how to use computer-based assistive technology.

The LOMAK keyboard was designed in New Zealand specifically for persons with disabilities.

The Internet is also used by disability activists and charities to network and further their goals.

UNDERSTANDING THE SOCIAL MODEL OF DISABILITY

The social model of disability proposes that systemic barriers, negative attitudes and exclusion by society (purposely or inadvertently) are the ultimate factors defining who is disabled and who is not in a particular society. It recognizes that while some people have physical, sensory, intellectual, or psychological variations, which may sometimes cause individual functional limitation or impairments, these do not have to lead to disability, unless society fails to take account of and include people regardless of their individual differences. The model does not deny that some individual differences lead to individual limitations or impairments, but rather that these are not the cause of individuals being excluded. The origins of the approach can be traced to the 1960s and the disabled people's Civil Rights Movement/human rights movements; the specific term itself emerged from the United Kingdom in the 1980s.

History

The approach behind the model is traced to the 1960s. In 1976, the UK organization Union of the Physically Impaired Against Segregation (UPIAS) claimed that disability was: 'the disadvantage or restriction of activity caused by a contemporary social organization which takes little or no account of people who have physical impairments and thus excludes them from participation in the mainstream of social activities.'

In 1983, the disabled academic Mike Oliver coined the phrase 'social model of disability' in reference to these ideological developments. Oliver focused on the idea of an individual model (of which the medical was a part) versus a social model, derived from the distinction originally made between impairment and disability by the UPIAS.

The 'social model' was extended and developed by academics and activists in the UK, US and other countries, and extended to include all disabled people, including those who have learning difficulties, or have experienced the mental health system.

Components and Usage

A fundamental aspect of the social model concerns equality. The struggle for equality is often compared to the struggles of other socially marginalized groups. Equal rights are said to give empowerment and the 'ability' to make decisions and the opportunity to live life to the fullest. A related phrase often used by disability rights campaigners, as with other social activism, is "Nothing About Us Without Us."

The social model of disability often focuses on changes required in society. These might be in terms of:

- Attitudes, for example a more positive attitude toward certain mental traits or behaviours, or not underestimating the potential quality of life of those with potential impairments.
- Social support, for example help dealing with the above barriers, resources, aids or positive discrimination to overcome them.
- Information, for example using suitable formats (e.g. braille) or levels (e.g. simplicity of language) or coverage (e.g. explaining issues others may take for granted).
- Physical structures, for example buildings with sloped access and elevators.

The social model of disability implies that attempts to change, 'fix' or 'cure' individuals, especially when against the wishes of the patient, can be discriminatory and prejudiced. It is often contended that this attitude, often seen as stemming from a medical model and a subjective value system, can harm the self-esteem and social inclusion of those constantly subjected to it (e.g. being told they are not as good or valuable, in some overall and core sense, as others).

Some communities have actively resisted 'treatments', often alongside defending a unique culture or set of abilities. Some examples include: deaf parents arguing against cochlear implants for deaf infants who cannot consent to them, and valuing sign language even if most do not 'speak' it; people diagnosed with an autism spectrum disorder arguing against efforts to change them to be more like others.

They argue instead for acceptance of neurodiversity and accommodation to different needs and goals; people diagnosed with a mental disorder arguing that they are just different, don't necessarily conform, or have a psychosocial disability ultimately caused by discrimination or exclusion by society.

The social model implies that practices such as eugenics are founded on social values and a prejudiced understanding of the potential and value of those labeled disabled.

The social model of disability is often based on a distinction between the terms 'impairment' and 'disability.' Impairment is used to refer to the actual attributes (or loss of attributes) of a person, whether in terms of limbs, organs or mechanisms, including psychological. Disability is used to refer to the restrictions caused by society when it does not give equivalent attention and accommodation to the needs of individuals with impairments.

The social model also relates to economics. It proposes that people can be disabled by a lack of resources to meet their needs. It addresses issues such as the under-estimation of the potential of people to contribute to society and add economic value to society, if given equal rights and equally suitable facilities and opportunities as others.

Policy

In the United Kingdom, the Disability Discrimination Act defines disability using the medical model—disabled people are defined as people with certain conditions, or certain limitations on their ability to carry out 'normal day-to-day activities.' But the requirement of employers and service providers to make 'reasonable adjustments' to their policies or practices, or physical aspects of their premises, follows the social model.

By making adjustments, employers and service providers are removing the barriers that disable—according to the social model, they are effectively removing the person's disability. However, in 2006, amendments to the act called for local authorities and others to actively promote disability equality. We are yet to see if this means the social model of disability will be more rigorously observed.

In the United States, the Americans with Disabilities Act of 1990 is a wide-ranging civil rights law that prohibits discrimination based on disability. It affords similar protections against discrimination to Americans with disabilities as the Civil Rights Act of 1964, which made discrimination based on race, religion, sex, national origin, and other characteristics illegal. Certain specific conditions are excluded, including alcoholism and transsexualism.

UNDERSTANDING THE MEDICAL MODEL OF DISABILITY

The medical model of disability is a model by which illness or disability is the result of a physical condition, is intrinsic to the individual (it is part of that individual's own body), may reduce the individual's quality of life, and causes clear disadvantages to the individual.

As a result, curing or managing illness or disability revolves around identifying the illness or disability, understanding it and learning to control and alter its course. Therefore, and by extension, a compassionate or just society invests resources in health care and related services in an attempt to cure disabilities medically, expand functionality and/or improve functioning thus allowing disabled persons a more "normal" life. The medical profession's responsibility and potential in this area is central.

The medical model of disability is often cited by disability rights groups when evaluating the costs and benefits of various interventions, be they medical, surgical, social or occupational: from prosthetics, "cures", and medical tests such as genetic screening or preimplantation genetic diagnosis. Often, a medical model of disability is used to justify large investment in these procedures, technologies and research, when adaptation of the disabled person's environment might ultimately be cheaper and more attainable.

Some disability rights groups see the medical model of disability as a civil rights issue, and criticise charitable or medical initiatives that use it in their portrayal of disabled people, because it promotes a negative, disempowered image of people with disabilities, rather than casting disability as a political, social and environmental problem. Various sociologists (Zola, Parsons) studied the socio-cultural aspects of "normalcy" and the pressure it exerts on individuals to conform.

ANALYZING DEVELOPMENTAL DISABILITY

Developmental disability is a term used to describe life-long, disabilities attributable to mental and/or physical or combination of mental and physical impairments, manifested prior to age 18. The term is used most commonly in the United States to refer to disabilities affecting daily functioning in three or more of the following areas:

- capacity for independent living
- economic self-sufficiency
- learning
- mobility
- receptive and expressive language
- self-care
- self-direction.

The term first appeared in U.S. law in 1970, when Congress used the term to describe the population of individuals who had historically been placed in state institutions, in its effort to improve conditions in these dehumanizing facilities (P.L. 91-517, "The Developmental Disabilities Services and Facilities Construction Act of 1970"). The law has since been amended many times, and now calls for the full community inclusion and self-determination of people with developmental disabilities (P.L. 106-402).

Frequently, people with mental retardation, cerebral palsy, autism spectrum disorder, various genetic and chromosomal disorders such as Down syndrome and Fragile X syndrome, and Fetal Alcohol Spectrum Disorder are described as having developmental disabilities. This use of the term is synonymous with the use of the term learning disability in the United Kingdom, and intellectual disability in Australia, Europe, Canada and elsewhere. Cognitive disability is also used synonymously in some jurisdictions.

Developmental disabilities are usually classified as severe, profound, moderate or mild, as assessed by the individual's need for supports, which may be lifelong.

Causes of Developmental Disabilities

There are many social, environmental and physical causes of developmental disabilities, although for some a definitive cause may never be determined. Common factors causing developmental disabilities include:

- Brain injury or infection before, during or after birth.
- Growth or nutrition problems.
- Abnormalities of chromosomes and genes.
- Babies born long before the expected birth date—also called extreme prematurity.
- Poor diet and health care.
- Drug misuse during pregnancy, including alcohol intake and smoking.
- Child abuse can also have a severe effect on the development of a child, specifically the socio-emotional development.
- Diagnosis of an autism spectrum disorder.

Developmental disabilities affect between 1 and 2 per cent of the population in most western countries, although many government sources acknowledge that statistics are flawed in this area. The worldwide proportion of people with developmental disabilities is believed to be approximately 1.4 per cent. It is twice as common in males as in females, and some researchers have found that the prevalence of mild developmental disabilities is likely to be higher in areas of poverty and deprivation, and among people of certain ethnicities.

Associated Issues

Physical Health Issues

There are many physical health factors associated with developmental disabilities. For some specific syndromes and diagnoses, these are inherent (such as poor heart function in people with Down's syndrome); however lack of access to health services and lack of understanding by medical professionals is also a major contributing factor.

People with severe communication difficulties find it difficult to articulate their health needs, and without adequate support and education might not recognise ill health. Epilepsy, sensory problems (such as poor vision and hearing), obesity and poor dental health are over-represented in this population. Life expectancy among people with developmental disabilities as a group is estimated at 20 years below average, although this is improving with advancements in adaptive and medical technologies, and as people are leading healthier, more fulfilling lives, and some specific diagnoses (such as Freeman-Sheldon syndrome) do not impact on life expectancy.

Mental Health Issues (Dual Diagnoses)

Mental health issues, and psychiatric illnesses, are more likely to occur in people with developmental disabilities than in the general population. A number of factors are attributed to the high incidence rate of dual diagnoses:

- the high likelihood of encountering traumatic events throughout their lifetime (such as abandonment by loved ones, abuse, bullying and harassment)
- the social restrictions placed upon people with developmental disabilities (such as lack of education, poverty, limited employment opportunities, limited opportunities for fulfilling relationships, boredom)
- biological factors (such as brain injury, epilepsy, illicit and prescribed drug and alcohol misuse)
- developmental factors (such as lack of understanding of social norms and appropriate behaviour, inability of those around to allow/understand expressions of grief and other human emotions)
- External monitoring factor: all people with developmental disabilities that are in a Federal or State funded residence require the residence to have some form of behavioural monitoring for each person with developmental disability at the residence. With this information psychological diagnosis are more easily given than with the general population that has less consistent monitoring.
- Access to health care providers: in the USA, all people with developmental disabilities that are in a Federal or State funded residence require the residence to have annual visits to various health care providers (nurse, physician, psychologist, psychiatrist, etc.). With consistent visits to health care providers more people with developmental disabilities are likely to receive appropriate treatment than the general population that is not required to visit various health care providers.

These problems are exacerbated by difficulties in diagnosis of mental health issues, and in appropriate treatment and medication, as for physical health issues.

Abuse and Vulnerability

Abuse is a significant issue for people with developmental disabilities, and as a group they are regarded as vulnerable people in most jurisdictions. Common types of abuse include:

- Physical abuse (withholding food, hitting, punching, pushing, etc.)
- Neglect (withholding help when required, e.g., assistance with personal hygiene)
- Sexual abuse
- Psychological or emotional abuse (verbal abuse, shaming and belittling)
- Constraint and restrictive practices (turning off an electric wheelchair so a person cannot move)
- Financial abuse (charging unnecessary fees, holding onto pensions, wages, etc.)
- Legal or civil abuse (restricted access to services)
- Systemic abuse (denied access to an appropriate service due to perceived support needs)
- Passive neglect (a caregiver's failure to provide adequate food, shelter).

Lack of education, lack of self-esteem and self-advocacy skills, lack of understanding of social norms and appropriate behaviour and communication difficulties are strong contributing factors to the high incidence of abuse among this population.

In addition to abuse from people in positions of power, peer abuse is recognised as a significant, if misunderstood, problem. Rates of criminal offending among people with developmental disabilities are also disproportionately high, and it is widely acknowledged that criminal justice systems throughout the world are ill-equipped for the needs of people with developmental disabilities (as both perpetrators and victims of crime).

Challenging Behaviour

Some people with developmental disabilities exhibit challenging behaviour, defined as "culturally abnormal behaviour(s) of such intensity, frequency or duration that the physical safety of the person or others is placed in serious jeopardy, or behaviour which is likely to seriously limit or deny access to the use of ordinary community facilities". Common types of challenging behaviour include self-injurious behaviour (such as hitting, headbutting, biting), aggressive behaviour (such as hitting others, screaming, spitting, kicking), inappropriate sexualised behaviour (such as public masturbation or groping), behaviour directed at property (such as throwing objects and stealing) and stereotyped behaviours (such as repetitive rocking, echolalia or elective incontinence).

Challenging behaviour in people with developmental disabilities may be caused by a number of factors, including biological (pain, medication, the need for sensory stimulation), social (boredom, seeking social interaction, the need for an element of control, lack of knowledge of community norms, insensitivity of staff and services to the person's wishes and needs), environmental (physical aspects such as noise and lighting, or gaining access to preferred objects or activities), psychological (feeling excluded, lonely, devalued, labelled, disempowered, living up to people's negative expectations) or simply a means of communication. A lot of the time, challenging behaviour is learned and brings rewards and it is very often possible to teach people new behaviours to achieve the same aims.

Experience and research suggests that what professionals call 'challenging behaviour' is often a reaction to the challenging environments that those providing services create around people with developmental disabilities. 'Challenging behaviour' in this context is a method of communicating dis-satisfaction with the failure of those providing services to focus on what kind of life makes most sense to the person, and is often the only recourse a developmentally disabled person has against unsatisfactory services or treatment and the lack of opportunities made available to the person. This is especially the case where the services deliver lifestyles and ways of working that are centred on what suits the service provider and its staff, rather than what best suits the person.

Societal Attitudes Towards Developmental Disabilities

Throughout history, people with developmental disabilities have been viewed as incapable and incompetent in their capacity for decision-making and development. Until the Enlightenment in Europe, care and asylum was provided by families and the church (in monasteries and other religious communities), focusing on the provision of basic physical needs such as food, shelter and clothing. Stereotypes such as the dimwitted yokel, and potentially harmful characterisations (such as demonic possession for people with epilepsy) were prominent in social attitudes of the time.

The movement towards individualism in the 18th and 19th centuries, and the opportunities afforded by the Industrial Revolution, led to housing and care using the asylum model. People were placed by, or, removed from, their families (usually in infancy) and housed in large institutions (of up to 3,000 people, although some institutions were home to many more, such as the Philadelphia State Hospital in Pennsylvania which housed 7,000 people through the 1960s), many of which were self-sufficient through the labour of the residents. Some of these institutions provided a very basic level of education (such as differentiation between colours and basic word recognition and numeracy), but most continued to focus solely on the provision of basic needs. Conditions in such institutions varied widely, but the support provided was generally non-individualised, with aberrant behaviour and low levels of economic productivity regarded as a burden to society. Heavy tranquilisation and assembly line methods of support (such as 'birdfeeding' and cattle herding) were the norm, and the medical model of disability prevailed. Services were provided based on the relative ease to the provider, not based on the human needs of the individual.

Ignoring the prevailing attitude, Civitans adopted service to the developmentally disabled as a major organizational emphasis in 1952. Their earliest efforts included workshops for special education teachers and daycamps for disabled children, all at a time when such training and programmes were almost nonexistent. The segregation of people with developmental disabilities wasn't widely questioned by academics or policy-makers until the 1969 publication of Wolf Wolfensberger's seminal work "The Origin and Nature of Our Institutional Models", drawing on some of the ideas proposed by SG Howe a hundred years earlier. This book posited that society characterises people with disabilities as deviant, sub-human and burdens of charity, resulting in the adoption of that 'deviant' role. Wolfensberger argued that this dehumanisation, and the segregated institutions that result from it, ignored the potential productive contributions that all people can make to society. He pushed for a shift in policy and practice that recognised the human needs of "retardates" and provided the same basic human rights as for the rest of the population.

The publication of this book may be regarded as the first move towards the widespread adoption of the social model of disability in regard to these types of disabilities, and was the impetus for the development of government strategies for desegregation. Successful lawsuits against governments and an increasing awareness of human rights and self-advocacy also contributed to this process, resulting in the passing in the US of the *Civil Rights of Institutionalized Persons Act* in 1980.

From the 1960s to the present, most states have moved towards the elimination of segregated institutions. Along with the work Wolfensberger and others including Gunnar and Rosemary Dybwad, a number of scandalous revelations around the horrific conditions within state institutions created public outrage led to change to a more community-based method of providing services. By the mid-1970s, most governments had committed to de-institutionalisation, and had started preparing for the wholesale movement of people into the general community, in line with the principles of normalization. In most countries, this was essentially complete by the late 1990s, although the debate over whether or not to close institutions persists in some states, including Massachusetts.

It could be argued that we still have a very long way to go before people with such disabilities are seen as full citizens of society. Person Centred Planning and Person Centred Approaches are seen as methods of addressing the continued labelling and exclusion of socially devalued people, such as people with a developmental disability label, encouraging a focus on the person as someone with capacities and gifts, as well as support needs.

Services and Support

Today, support services are provided by government agencies, non-governmental organizations and by private sector providers. Support services address most aspects of life for people with developmental disabilities, and are usually theoretically based in community inclusion, using concepts such as social role valorization and increased self-determination (using models such as Person Centred Planning). Support services are funded through government block funding (paid directly to service providers by the government), through individualised funding packages (paid directly to the individual by the government, specifically for the purchase of services) or privately by the individual (although they may receive certain subsidies or discounts, paid by the government).

Education and Training

Education and training opportunities for people with developmental disabilities have expanded greatly in recent times, with many governments mandating universal access to educational facilities, and more students moving out of special schools and into mainstream classrooms with support.

Post-secondary education and vocational training is also increasing for people with these types of disabilities, although many programmes offer only segregated "access" courses in areas such as literacy, numeracy and other basic skills. Legislation (such as the UK's Disability Discrimination Act, 1995) requires educational institutions and training providers to make 'reasonable adjustments' to curriculum and teaching methods in order to accommodate the learning needs of students with disabilities, wherever possible. There are also some vocational training centers that cater specifically to people with disabilities, providing the skills necessary to work in integrated settings, one of the largest being Dale Rogers Training Center in Oklahoma City. See also Intensive interaction.

At-home and Community Support

Many people with developmental disabilities live in the general community, either with family members, or in their own homes (that they rent or own, living alone or with flatmates). At-home and community supports range from one-to-one assistance from a support worker with identified aspects of daily living (such as budgeting, shopping or paying bills) to full 24-hour support (including assistance with household tasks, such as cooking and cleaning, and personal care such as showering, dressing and the administration of medication). The need for full 24-hour support is usually associated with difficulties recognising safety issues (such as responding to a fire or using a telephone) or for people with potentially dangerous medical conditions (such as asthma or diabetes) who are unable to manage their conditions without assistance.

In the United States a support worker is known as a Direct Support Professional (DSP). The DSP works in assisting the individual with their ADLs and also acts as an advocate for the individual with a developmental disability, in communicating their needs, self expression and goals.

Supports of this type also include assistance to identify and undertake new hobbies or to access community services (such as education), learning appropriate behaviour or recognition of community norms, or with relationships and expanding circles of friends. Most programmes offering at-home and community support are designed with the goal of increasing the individual's independence, although it is recognised that people with more severe disabilities may never be able to achieve full independence in some areas of daily life.

Residential Accommodation

Some people with developmental disabilities live in residential accommodation (also known as group homes) with other people with similar assessed needs. These homes are usually staffed around the clock, and usually house between 3 and 15 residents. The prevalence of this type of support is gradually decreasing, however, as residential accommodation is replaced by at-home and community support, which can offer increased choice and self-determination for individuals. Some U.S. states still provide institutional care, such as the Texas State Schools.

Employment Support

Employment support usually consists of two types of support:

- Support to access or participate in integrated employment, in a workplace in the general community. This may include specific programmes to increase the skills needed for successful employment (work preparation), one-to-one or small group support for on-the-job training, or one-to-one or small group support after a transition period (such as advocacy when dealing with an employer or a bullying colleague, or assistance to complete an application for a promotion).
- The provision of specific employment opportunities within segregated business services. Although these are designed as 'transitional' services (teaching work skills needed to move into integrated employment), many people remain in such services for the duration of their working life. The types of work performed in business services include mailing and packaging services, cleaning, gardening and landscaping, timberwork, metal fabrication, farming and sewing.

Workers with developmental disabilities have historically been paid less for their labour than those in the general workforce, although this is gradually changing with government initiatives, the enforcement of anti-discrimination legislation and changes in perceptions of capability in the general community.

Day Services

Non-vocational day services are usually known as day centres, and are traditionally segregated services offering training in life skills (such as meal preparation and basic literacy), centre-based activities (such as craft, games and music classes) and external activities (such as day trips). Some more progressive day centres also support people to access vocational training opportunities (such as college courses), and offer individualised outreach services (planning and undertaking activities with the individual, with support offered one-to-one or in small groups).

Traditional day centres were based on the principles of occupational therapy, and were created as respite for family members caring for their loved ones with disabilities. This is slowly changing, however, as programmes offered become more skills-based and focused on increasing independence.

Advocacy

Advocacy is a burgeoning support field for people with developmental disabilities. Advocacy groups now exist in most jurisdictions, working collaboratively with people with disabilities for systemic change (such as changes in policy and legislation) and for changes for individuals (such as claiming welfare benefits or when responding to abuse). Most advocacy groups also work to support people, throughout the world, to increase their capacity for self-advocacy, teaching the skills necessary for people to advocate for their own needs.

Other Types of Support

Other types of support for people with developmental disabilities may include:

- therapeutic services, such as speech therapy, massage, aromatherapy, or drama or music therapy
- supported holidays
- short-stay respite services (for people who live with family members or other unpaid carers)
- transport services, such as dial-a-ride or free bus passes
- specialist behaviour support services, such as high-security services for people with high-level, high-risk challenging behaviours
- specialist relationships and sex education services.

ANALYZING LEARNING DISABILITY

Learning disability (sometimes called a learning disorder or learning difficulty), is a disorder in which a person has a difficulty to learn effectively, caused by an unknown factor or factors. The unknown factor is the disorder that affects the brain's ability to receive and process information. This disorder can make it problematic for a person to learn as quickly as someone who isn't affected by a learning disability. Learning disability is not indicative of intelligence level. Rather, people with a learning disability have trouble performing specific types of skills or completing tasks if left to figure things out by themselves or if taught in conventional ways.

A learning disability cannot be cured or fixed; it is a lifelong issue. With the right support and intervention, however, people with learning disabilities can succeed in school and go on to successful, often distinguished careers later in life.

Overview

The National Joint Committee on Learning Disabilities (NJCLD) defines the term learning disability as:

> a heterogeneous group of disorders manifested by significant difficulties in the acquisition and use of listening, speaking, reading, writing, reasoning or mathematical abilities. These disorders are intrinsic to the individual and presumed to be due to Central Nervous System Dysfunction. Even though a learning disability may occur concomitantly with other handicapping conditions (e.g. sensory impairment, mental retardation, social and emotional disturbance) or environmental influences (e.g. cultural differences, insufficient/ inappropriate instruction, psychogenic factors) it is not the direct result of those conditions or influences.

The NJCLD used the term to indicate a discrepancy between a child's apparent capacity to learn and his or her level of achievement.

Types of Learning Disabilities

Learning disabilities can be categorized either by the type of information processing that is affected or by the specific difficulties caused by a processing deficit.

Information Processing Deficits

Learning disabilities fall into broad categories based on the four stages of information processing used in learning: input, integration, storage, and output.

- *Input:* This is the information perceived through the senses, such as visual and auditory perception. Difficulties with visual perception can cause problems with recognizing the shape, position and size of items seen. There can be problems with sequencing, which can relate to deficits with processing time intervals or temporal perception. Difficulties with auditory perception can make it difficult to screen out competing sounds in order to focus on one of them, such as the sound of the teacher's voice. Some children appear to be unable to process tactile input. For example, they may seem insensitive to pain or dislike being touched.
- *Integration:* This is the stage during which perceived input is interpreted, categorized, placed in a sequence, or related to previous learning. Students with problems in these areas may be unable to tell a story in the correct sequence, unable to memorize sequences of information such as the days of the week, able to understand a new concept but be unable to generalize it to other areas of learning, or able to learn facts but be unable to put the facts together to see the "big picture." A poor vocabulary may contribute to problems with comprehension.
- *Storage:* Problems with memory can occur with short-term or working memory, or with long-term memory. Most memory difficulties occur in the area of short-term memory, which can make it difficult to learn new material without many more repetitions than is usual. Difficulties with visual memory can impede learning to spell.

- *Output:* Information comes out of the brain either through words, that is, language output, or through muscle activity, such as gesturing, writing or drawing. Difficulties with language output can create problems with spoken language, for example, answering a question on demand, in which one must retrieve information from storage, organize our thoughts, and put the thoughts into words before we speak. It can also cause trouble with written language for the same reasons. Difficulties with motor abilities can cause problems with gross and fine motor skills. People with gross motor difficulties may be clumsy, that is, they may be prone to stumbling, falling, or bumping into things. They may also have trouble running, climbing, or learning to ride a bicycle. People with fine motor difficulties may have trouble buttoning shirts, tying shoelaces, or with handwriting.

Specific Learning Disabilities

Deficits in any area of information processing can manifest in a variety of specific learning disabilities. It is possible for an individual to have more than one of these difficulties. This is referred to as comorbidity or co-occurrence of learning disabilities. In the UK, the term *dual diagnosis* is often used to refer to co-occurrence of learning difficulties.

- *Reading disability (ICD-10 and DSM-IV codes: F81.0/315.00):* The most common learning disability. Of all students with specific learning disabilities, 70 per cent-80 per cent have deficits in reading. The term "dyslexia" is often used as a synonym for reading disability; however, many researchers assert that there are different types of reading disabilities, of which dyslexia is one. A reading disability can affect any part of the reading process, including difficulty with accurate and/or fluent word recognition, word decoding, reading rate, prosody (oral reading with expression), and reading comprehension. Before the term "dyslexia" came to prominence, this learning disability used to be known as "word blindness."
  Common indicators of reading disability include difficulty with phonemic awareness—the ability to break up words into their component sounds, and difficulty with matching letter combinations to specific sounds (sound-symbol correspondence).
- *Writing disability (ICD-10 and DSM-IV codes F81.1/315.2):* Speech and language disorders can also be called Dysphasia/Aphasia (coded F80.0-F80.2/315.31 in ICD-10 and DSM-IV).
  Impaired written language ability may include impairments in handwriting, spelling, organization of ideas, and composition. The term "dysgraphia" is often used as an overarching term for all disorders of written expression. Others, such as the International Dyslexia Association, use the term "dysgraphia" exclusively to refer to difficulties with handwriting.

- *Math disability (ICD-10 and DSM-IV codes F81.2-3/315.1):* Sometimes called dyscalculia, a math disability can cause such difficulties as learning math concepts (such as quantity, place value, and time), difficulty memorizing math facts, difficulty organizing numbers, and understanding how problems are organized on the page. Dyscalculics are often referred to as having poor "number sense."
- *Nonverbal learning disability [this disorder is not listed in the ICD-10]:* Nonverbal learning disabilities often manifest in motor clumsiness, poor visual-spatial skills, problematic social relationships, difficulty with math, and poor organizational skills. These individuals often have specific strengths in the verbal domains, including early speech, large vocabulary, early reading and spelling skills, excellent rote-memory and auditory retention, and eloquent self-expression.
- *Dyspraxia:* Sometimes called motor planning, dyspraxia refers to a variety of difficulties with motor skills. Dyspraxia can cause difficulty with single step tasks such as combing hair or waving goodbye, multi-step tasks like brushing teeth or getting dressed, or with establishing spatial relationships such as being able to accurately position one object in relation to another.
- *Disorders of speaking and listening:* Difficulties that often co-occur with learning disabilities include difficulty with memory, social skills and executive functions (such as organizational skills and time management).
- *Auditory processing disorder:* Difficulties processing auditory information include difficulty comprehending more than one task at a time and a relatively stronger ability to learn visually.

Diagnosis

IQ-Achievement Discrepancy

The presence of a learning disability is sometimes suspected by a child's parents long before problems are seen at school. However, the issues typically become visible when a child begins having difficulty at school. Difficulty learning to read is often one of the first signs that a learning disability is present.

Learning disabilities are often identified by school psychologists, clinical psychologists, and neuropsychologists through a combination of intelligence testing, academic achievement testing, classroom performance, and social interaction and aptitude. Other areas of assessment may include perception, cognition, memory, attention, and language abilities. The resulting information is used to determine whether a child's academic performance is commensurate with his or her cognitive ability. If a child's cognitive ability is much higher than his or her academic performance, the student is often diagnosed with a learning disability. The DSM-IV and many school systems and government programmes diagnose learning disabilities in this way.

Although the discrepancy model has dominated the school system for many years, there has been substantial criticism of this approach among researchers. Recent research has provided little evidence that a discrepancy between formally-measured

IQ and achievement is a clear indicator of LD. Furthermore, diagnosing on the basis of a discrepancy does not predict the effectiveness of treatment. Low academic achievers who do not have a discrepancy with IQ (i.e. their IQ scores are also low) appear to benefit from treatment just as much as low academic achievers who do have a discrepancy with IQ (i.e. their IQ scores are higher).

Response to Intervention (RTI)

Much current research has focused on a treatment-oriented diagnostic process known as response to intervention (RTI). Researcher recommendations for implementing such a model include early screening for all students, placing those students who are having difficulty into research-based early intervention programmes, rather than waiting until they meet diagnostic criterion. Their performance can be closely monitored to determine whether increasingly intense intervention results in adequate progress. Those who respond will not require further intervention. Those who do not respond adequately to regular classroom instruction (often called "Tier 1 instruction") and a more intensive intervention (often called "Tier 2" intervention) are considered "non-responders." These students can then be referred for further assistance through special education, in which case they are often identified with a learning disability. Some models of RTI include a third tier of intervention before a child is identified as having a learning disability.

A primary benefit of such a model is that it would not be necessary to wait for a child to be sufficiently far behind to qualify for assistance. This may enable more children to receive assistance before experiencing significant failure, which may in turn result in fewer children who need intensive and expensive special education services. In the United States, the 2004 re-authorization of the Individuals with Disabilities Education Act permitted states and school districts to use RTI as a method of identifying students with learning disabilities. RTI is now the primary means of identification of learning disabilities in Florida.

There are multiple concerns about the use of RTI. The process does not take into account children's individual neuropsychological factors such as phonological awareness and memory, that can help design instruction <Fletcher-Janzen, Reynolds (2008). Neuropsychological Perspectives on Learning Disabilities in the Era of RTI: Recommendations for Diagnosis and Intervention>. Second, RTI by design takes considerably longer than established techniques, often many months to find an appropriate tier of intervention. Third, it requires a strong intervention programme before students can be identified with a learning disability. If students' receive poor quality interventions, they can be judged non-responsive and thus as having a learning disability when the cause is really only poor instruction. Lastly, RTI is considered a regular education initiative and is not driven by psychologists, reading specialists, or special educators.

Assessment

Many normed assessments can be used in evaluating skills in the primary academic domains: reading, not including word recognition, fluency, and comprehension; mathematics, including computation and problem solving; and written expression, including handwriting, spelling and composition.

The most commonly used comprehensive achievement tests include the Woodcock-Johnson III (WJ III), Weschler Individual Achievement Test II (WIAT II), the Wide Range Achievement Test III (WRAT III), and the Stanford Achievement Test—10th edition. These tests include measures of many academic domains that are reliable in identifying areas of difficulty.

In the reading domain, there are also specialized tests that can be used to obtain details about specific reading deficits. Assessments that measure multiple domains of reading include Gray's Diagnostic Reading Tests—2nd Edition (GDRT II) and the Stanford Diagnostic Reading Assessment. Assessments that measure reading subskills include the Gray Oral Reading Test IV—Fourth Edition (GORT IV), Gray Silent Reading Test, Comprehensive Test of Phonological Processing (CTOPP), Tests of Oral Reading and Comprehension Skills (TORCS), Test of Reading Comprehension 3 (TORC-3), Test of Word Reading Efficiency (TOWRE), and the Test of Reading Fluency. A more comprehensive list of reading assessments may be obtained from the Southwest Educational Development Laboratory.

Of course, assessment of learning disabilities requires the consideration of more than test scores. The purpose of assessment is to determine what is needed for intervention, which also requires consideration of contextual variables and whether there are comorbid disorders that must also be identified and treated, such as behavioural issues or language delays.

Treatment and Intervention

Poor academic achievement can be addressed with a variety of interventions. Although the underlying processing difficulty is usually considered to be a lifelong disorder, academic skills themselves can be improved with targeted interventions. Some (adjustments, equipment and assistants) are designed to accommodate or help compensate for the disabilities while others (specialized instruction) are intended to make improvements in the weak areas. Practice is a particularly important component in developing competence, regardless of the starting point. Children who start out with a weakness in a basic skill, such as reading, may miss out on the necessary practice because of the need to catch up with their chronological age peers. Thus a small weakness can snowball into a larger problem.

Interventions include:

- *Mastery Model:*
  - Learners work at their own level of mastery
  - Practice
  - Gain fundamental skills before moving onto the next level.
  - *Note*: This approach is most likely to be used with adult learners or outside the mainstream school system.

- ***Direct Instruction:***
  - Highly structured, intensive instruction
  - Emphasizes carefully planned lessons for small learning increments
  - Scripted lesson plans
  - Rapid-paced interaction between teacher and students
  - Correcting mistakes immediately
  - Achievement-based grouping
  - Frequent progress assessments.
- ***Classroom Adjustments:***
  - Special seating assignments
  - Alternative or modified assignments
  - Modified testing procedures
  - Quiet environment.
- ***Special Equipment:***
  - Electronic spellers and dictionaries
  - Word processors
  - Talking calculators
  - Books on tape
  - Computer
  - Dictation programmes.
- ***Classroom Assistants:***
  - Note-takers
  - Readers
  - Proofreaders
  - Scribes.
- ***Special Education:***
  - Prescribed hours in a special class
  - Placement in a special class
  - Enrollment in a special school for learning disabled students
  - Individual Education Plan (IEP).

Sternberg has argued that early remediation can greatly reduce the number of children meeting diagnostic criteria for learning disabilities. He has also suggested that the focus on learning disabilities and the provision of accommodations in school fails to acknowledge that people have a range of strengths and weaknesses, and places undue emphasis on academic success by insisting that people should receive additional support in this arena but not in music or sports.

Treatment: Specific Instruction Included in the curriculum should be instruction in: Visual Perception, Visual Memory, Auditory Perception, Auditory Memory.

Cusimano's findings indicate that emphasis should be placed on the development of specific learning skills along with study and basic skills. These learning skills include visual perception, visual memory, auditory perception and auditory memory. Since research indicates that eighty per cent of all learning in school takes place by means of the visual mode, emphasis on the teaching of visual memory skills, and in particular, visual memory of words, is an essential element in the treatment of learning disabilities. In addition, most learning disabled students have extremely weak auditory memory skill development (attention, listening and recall). Instruction for the development of auditory memory for both listening for information presented in isolation such as a series of numbers, letters, and words, as well as specific instruction for the listening of information presented in context is essential in the process of helping these children to learn with ease.

Causes and Risk Factors

The causes for learning disabilities are not well understood, and sometimes there is no apparent cause for a learning disability. However, some causes of neurological impairments include:

- Heredity—Learning disabilities often run in the family.
- Problems during pregnancy and birth—Learning disabilities can result from anomalies in the developing brain, illness or injury, fetal exposure to alcohol or drugs, low birth weight, oxygen deprivation, or by premature or prolonged labor.
- Accidents after birth—Learning disabilities can also be caused by head injuries, malnutrition, or by toxic exposure (such as heavy metals or pesticides).
- Behavioural Factors.
- Social Environment Factors.
- Cognitive Factors.

Impact on Affected Individuals

Learning disabilities affect interpersonal relationships in a variety of complex ways Neuropsychological differences can impact the accurate perception of social cues with peers and can impact family systems in predictable ways during activities such as homework.

Furthermore, individuals with a learning disability may isolate themselves from society as they may feel:

- Ashamed of the types of difficulties they struggle with, such as poor literacy skills, attention or memory difficulties
- Fear of failure, criticism, ridicule or rejection
- Fear of discrimination
- Fear that others may think that they are stupid or incapable or Mentally disabled
- Ashamed that they are unable to read or that they have poor handwriting
- Left out of everyday discussions due to lack of understanding
- Depressed
- Alone
- "Learned helplessness."

Societal Factors

Society both impacts upon, and is impacted by, individuals with learning disabilities. Significant factors in this relationship include poverty (with its concomitant reliance on welfare/public assistance), gender, and crime/imprisonment.

Welfare/Public Assistance Relating to Educational Development

- A 36 month study conducted by Taylor and Barusch included 284 welfare recipients, who were frequently interviewed, called, and visited with in their homes. In this study the average age was 34 and 97 per cent of the participants were female. Of the welfare participants 22.9 per cent were learning disabled and 32 per cent had no high school diploma or GED. Findings from this study imply that long term learning disabled welfare recipients will not be able to support their family through employment.
- A study similar to the one stated above, conducted by Margai and Henry found that the laws of identifying special education children have been revised within the past years. Learning disabled children in public schools now make up 6 per cent of all kids.
- High risk neighbourhoods and poor living conditions add to the factor of being more vulnerable to having a learning disability. A study was conducted exploring the areas of pollution and socio-economic factors related to having a higher risk of a learning disability. Margai and Henry used primary data and analyzed clusters of people in a distinct part of a community near a toxic waste place, living in poor neighbourhoods and living in poverty. The results confirmed that a majority of the people with a learning disability came from some socio-economic indicator such as poverty, sub-divided housing, and lower adult educational attainment. Individuals with a learning disability will rely more heavily on public assistance/welfare than individuals who do not because of their lack of knowledge.

Gender Issues

- Researchers believe that there are more boys in special education programmes compared to girls. Coutinho and Oswald found that data was collected from the U.S. office of Civil Rights to view the underrepresentation of females in special education. Oswald found that 73 per cent of learning disabled individuals in special education programmes were boys.
- Although, in contrast to the statement above if learning disabled students are identified by research criteria as opposed to teachers, the ratio of boys to girls (having a learning disability) is equal. In dealing with learning disabilities no significant gender differences were found in a study of more than 400 children. Bandian found that if identified by research criteria there were no differences in gender, but if learning disabilities were identified by

general education teachers and/or special education teachers, there was twice as many boys identified compared to girls. Alongside that, there was another statement said by Bandian that supported the claim stated above "boys were twice as like[ly] to be identified by teachers as in need of a learning disability programmes [sic] [compared to girls]."

- In a study 266 youth between the ages of 12-18 were voluntarily interviewed with 74 structured questions in a small classroom, question structure was based on "special education, juvenile justice, and child and adolescent development literature," and then categorized into three parts: personal, home, and school. Based on the information the individuals provided to the interviewers the juvenile delinquents were put into a category, special education, or non-special education. Zabel and Nigro stated that "girls are less often viewed as disruptive and disturbing behaviour patterns that often lead to special education." In contrast to that Zabel and Nigro also found that the "gender pattern was reversed for LD classification, with nearly 78.6 per cent of females who had been in special education." This study relates directly to the information provided in the welfare section because females are being identified with in the schools and are in turn receiving help from welfare programmes. Although, this information provided in this section is in contrast to the gender differences section stating that boys are more identified for learning disabled programmes compared to girls, this section supports the welfare section.

Crime and Prison Population

- Individuals in a detention facility are more likely to have a learning disability, receive poor grades, and repeat a grade. Zabel and Nigro conducted a study with 266 youth (currently in a detention facility), with the youths ages ranging from 12-18. The individuals were voluntarily interviewed with 74 structured questions. Based on the information provided from the individuals, the individuals were categorized into two groups, special education or non-special education. Zabel and Nigro stated "a majority of participants had received failing grades, and many had repeated at least one grade." The researchers also found that 88.6 per cent of the youth had been suspended, and those in the SpEd group were more likely than those in the non-SpEd group to report their first instance of trouble in elementary school. This information provided relates to the factor of when most learning disabled individuals are identified is in elementary school thus proving that it would make sense that the individuals in the SpEd group had their first instance of trouble in elementary school and it is hard for LD individuals to complete the education system, thus resulting in having to rely on welfare and public assistance.
- Another statistic (calculated from the study stated above) found by Zabel and Nigro was that 37.1 per cent had been involved with special education,

and classified having EBD and/or LD. Zabel also found that those individuals with a learning disability were at a higher risk that those with no special education experience (in the violent inmates, 17 of 30 were LD, and in the nonviolent, 13 of 30 were LD).

- Individuals in detention facilities may have a learning disability and more specifically have dyslexia (severe difficulty in recognizing and understanding written language, leading to spelling and writing problems). Gretchell, Pabreja, Neeld, and Carrio conducted a study that compared the difference of children with dyslexia and without. Twenty six individuals were dyslexic and 23 individuals were not. Individuals were tested with the Test of Gross Motor Development and Movement Assessment Battery for Children. Individuals with dyslexia performed significantly lower than the control group (individuals who aren't dyslexic). Thus, proving the similarities of how it will be hard for someone who has LD to complete the education system.
- Youth in a detention facility are more likely to have a special education problem, such as a learning disability, than not. Zabel and Nigro found in their study that "about one half of SpEd participants and nearly 20 per cent of the total sample reported their classification as learning disabilities." LD individuals make up a large portion of individuals in a detention facility which may have been a result from the LD individual not learning at a significant pace in the education system and also potentially not completing the education system. Zabel and Nigro's study was made up of 266 youth between the ages of 12-18 who were currently in a detention facility.

Contrast with Other Conditions

People with an IQ lower than 70 are usually characterized as having Mental Retardation (MR), mental deficiency, or cognitive impairment and are not included under most definitions of learning disabilities, because their learning difficulties are related directly to their low IQ scores.

Attention-Deficit Hyperactivity Disorder (ADHD) is often studied in connection with learning disabilities, but it is not actually included in the standard definitions of learning disabilities. An individual with ADHD may struggle with learning, but he or she can often learn adequately once successfully treated for the ADHD. A person can have ADHD but not learning disabilities or have learning disabilities without having ADHD. The conditions can co-occur (see Comorbidity). In order to understand the difference, imagine that someone with a learning disability is affected in only one or a few areas. However, people with ADHD are often affected in all areas.

Some research is beginning to make a case for ADHD being included in the definition of LDs, since it is being shown to have a strong impact on "executive functions" required for learning (planning, organization, etc.). This has not as yet affected any official definitions.

Criticism of the Concept of Learning Disabilities

Some critics of the concept of learning disabilities and of special education take the position that every child has a different learning style and pace and that each child is unique, not only capable of learning but also capable of succeeding. These critics assert that applying the medical model of problem-solving to individual children who are pupils in the school system, and labelling these children as disabled, systematically prevents the improvement of the current educational system.

Describing current instructional methods as homogenization and lockstep standardization, alternative approaches are proposed, such as the Sudbury model of democratic education schools, an alternative approach in which children, by enjoying personal freedom thus encouraged to exercise personal responsibility for their actions, learn at their own pace rather than following a chronologically-based curriculum. Proponents of unschooling have also claimed that children raised in this method do not suffer from learning disabilities.

Gerald Coles asserts that there are partisan agendas behind the educational policy-makers and that the scientific research that they use to support their arguments regarding the teaching of literacy are flawed. These include the idea that there are neurological explanations for learning disabilities.

Marva Collins' Experience

Marva Collins started a low cost private school in inner city Chicago specifically for the purpose of teaching low-income black children whom the public school system had wrongly labelled as being "learning disabled." She once wrote, "I have discovered few learning disabled students in my three decades of teaching. I have, however, discovered many, many victims of teaching inabilities."

One article about Marva Collins' school stated, "Working with students having the worst of backgrounds, those who were working far below grade level, and even those who had been labelled as 'unteachable,' Marva was able to overcome the obstacles. News of third grade students reading at ninth grade level, four-years-old learning to read in only a few months, outstanding test scores, disappearance of behavioural problems, second-graders studying Shakespeare, and other incredible reports, astounded the public."

Learning Disabilities and US Law

Disability Discrimination

Disability discrimination has been common throughout the world. People with learning disability may receive offending/negative remarks, harassing, bullying, etc. as a result of a difference in their neurological wiring when compared to the norm. In response to this, countries such as the United States have enacted programmes to help learning disabled people.

Section 504 of the Rehabilitation Act of 1973

The Section 504 of the Rehabilitation Act was first widely recognized as the "first civil-rights statue for persons with disabilities." Taken in effect in May 1977, this American legislation guarantees certain rights to people with disabilities, especially in the cases of education and work, such being in schools, colleges and university settings.

Individuals with Disabilities Education Act

The Individuals with Disabilities Education Act, formerly known as the Education for All Handicapped Children Act, is a United States Federal Law that governs how states and public agencies provide early intervention, special education and related services to children with disabilities. It addresses the educational needs of children with disabilities from birth to the age of 21. Considered as a civil rights law, states are not required to participate.

United States and Canada

In the United States and Canada, the terms learning disability and learning disorder (LD) refer to a group of disorders that affect a broad range of academic and functional skills including the ability to speak, listen, read, write, spell, reason, organize information, and do math.

United Kingdom

In the UK, terms such as Specific Learning Difficulty (SpLD), dyslexia, dyspraxia and dyscalculia are referred as learning difficulties, rather than learning disabilities. In the UK, the term "learning disability" refers to a range of conditions that are almost invariably associated with more severe cognitive impairments.

INTERNATIONAL CLASSIFICATION OF FUNCTIONING, DISABILITY AND HEALTH

International Classification of Functioning, Disability and Health, also known as ICF, is a classification of the health components of functioning and disability.

After nine years of international revision efforts coordinated by the World Health Organization (WHO), the World Health Assembly on May 22, 2001, approved the International Classification of Functioning, Disability and Health and its abbreviation of "ICF." This classification was first created in 1980 (and then called the International Classification of Impairments, Disabilities, and Handicaps, or ICIDH by WHO to provide an unifying framework for classifying the health components of functioning and disability.

The ICF classification complements WHO's International Classification of Diseases-10th Revision (ICD), which contains information on diagnosis and health condition, but not on functional status. The ICD and ICF constitute the core classifications in the WHO Family of International Classifications (WHO-FIC).

The ICF is structured around the following broad components:

- Body functions and structure
- Activities (related to tasks and actions by an individual) and participation (involvement in a life situation)
- Additional information on severity and environmental factors.

Functioning and disability are viewed as a complex interaction between the health condition of the individual and the contextual factors of the environment as well as personal factors. The picture produced by this combination of factors and dimensions is of "the person in his or her world." The classification treats these dimensions as interactive and dynamic rather than linear or static. It allows for an assessment of the degree of disability, although it is not a measurement instrument. It is applicable to all people, whatever their health condition. The language of the ICF is neutral as to etiology, placing the emphasis on function rather than condition or disease. It also is carefully designed to be relevant across cultures as well as age groups and genders, making it highly appropriate for heterogeneous populations.

Benefits of ICF

There are benefits of using the ICF for both the client and the health professional. A major advantage for the client is the integration of the medical and social aspects of his or her health condition. All aspects of a person's life (development, participation, and environment) are incorporated into the ICF instead of solely focusing on his or her diagnosis. A diagnosis reveals little about one's functional abilities. Diagnosis are important for defining the cause and prognosis, but identifying the limitations of function is often the information used to plan and implement interventions (Lollar & Simeonsson, 2005). Once a rehabilitation team is aware of the daily activities a client is required to participate in, the problem solving sequence set up by the ICF can be utilized. A rehabilitation therapist, for example, would observe a client performing his or her daily activities and note the client's functional abilities. This information would then be used to determine the extent to which the individual's abilities can be improved through therapy and to what extent the environment can be changed to facilitate the individual's performance (Bornman, 2004). Intervention at one level (current abilities) has the potential to prevent or modify events at a succeeding level (participation). For example, teaching a deaf child manual signs will foster effective interaction and increase one's participation with his or her family (Bornman, 2004).

Rehabilitation therapists will be empowered with the ICF not only in their daily work with their patients, but also when working with other medical disciplines; hospitals and other health care administrations; health authorities and policy-makers (Stucki, Ewert, & Cieza, 2002). All items are operationally defined with clear descriptions that can be applied to real life evaluations with clarity and ease (Üstün,

Chatterji, Bickenbach, Kostanjsek, & Schneider, 2003). The language used in the ICF helps facilitate better communication between these groups of people.

Clinical Relevance

Knowing how a disease affects one's functioning enables better planning of services, treatment, and rehabilitation for persons with long-term disabilities or chronic conditions (Hemmingson & Jonsson, 2005). The current ICF creates a more integrative understanding of health forming a comprehensive profile of an individual instead of focusing on one's health condition (Hemmingson & Jonsson, 2005). The implications of using the ICF include emphasizing the strengths of individuals, assisting individuals in participating more extensively in society by the use of interventions aimed at enhancing their abilities, and taking into consideration the environmental and personal factors that might hamper one's participation (Bornman, 2004). Qualifiers: The ICF qualifiers "may be best translated clinically as the levels of functioning seen in a standardized or clinic setting and in everyday environments" (Reed *et al.*, 2005). Qualifiers support standardization and the understanding of functioning in a multidisciplinary assessment. They enable all team members to quantify the extent of problems, even in areas of functioning where one is not a specialist (Rauch, Cieza, Stucki, 2008). Without qualifiers codes have no inherent meaning. An impairment, limitation or restriction, is qualified from 0 (No problem; 0-4%), 1 (Mild problem: 5-24%), 2 (Moderate problem: 25-49%), 3 (Severe problem: 50-95%) to 4 (Complete problem: 96-100%). Environmental factors are quantified with a negative and positive scale denoting the extent to which the environment acts as a barrier or facilitator (WHO, 2001). For insurance purposes, the qualifiers can describe the effectiveness of treatment. One can interpret the decreasing of a qualifier score to be an increase in the functional ability of a patient.

ICF Core Sets

An ICF Core Set can serve as a reference framework and a practical tool to classify and describe patient functioning in a more time efficient way. ICF Core Sets can be used along the continuum of care and over the course of a health condition (Rauch *et al.*, 2008). The ICF classification includes more than 1,400 categories limiting its use in clinical practice (Arlinger *et al.*, 2006). It is time consuming for a clinician to utilize the main volume of the ICF with his or her patients. Only a fraction of the categories is needed. As a general rule, 20 per cent of the codes will explain 80 per cent of the variance observed in practice (Üstün, Chatterji, & Kostanjsek, 2004). ICF Core Sets contain as few as possible, but as many ICF categories as necessary, to describe a patient's level of functioning (Rauch *et al.*, 2008). It is hypothesized that using a code set will increase the inter-rater reliability when coding clinical cases as only the relevant categories for a particular patient will be utilized. Since all of the relevant categories are listed in an ICF Core Set, its use in multidisciplinary assessments protects health professionals from missing important aspects of functioning (Rauch *et al.*, 2008).

Children and Youth Version (ICF-CY)

As clinicians and researchers used the ICF, they became more aware of its limitations. The ICF lacks the ability to classify the functional characteristics of a developing child. Different ICF codes are needed across the first years of a child's life to capture the growth and development of a disability even when the child's diagnosis does not change (Simeonsson, Scarborough, & Hebbeler, 2006). The coding system can provide essential information about the severity of a health condition in terms of its impact on functioning. This can serve a significant role for providers caring for children with spectrum disorders such as autism or cerebral palsy (Ogonowski, Kronk, Rice, & Feldman, 2004). Children with these conditions may have the same diagnosis, but their abilities and levels of functioning widely vary across and within individuals over time. The first draft of the ICF-CY was completed in 2003 and published in 2007. The ICF-CY was developed to be structurally consistent with the ICF for adults. A major difference between the ICF-CY and ICF is that the generic qualifiers from the adult ICF now include developmental aspects for children and youth in the ICF-CY. Descriptions of codes in the ICF-CY were revised and expanded and new content was added to previously unused codes. Codes were added to document characteristics as adaptability, responsivity, predictability, persistence, and approachability. "Sensing" and "exploration of objects" codes were expanded as well as the "importance of learning" (Lollar & Simeonsson, 2005). Since a child's main occupation is playing, it is also important to include more codes in this area. Different levels of play have separate codes in the ICF-CY (solitary, onlooker, parallel). This contrasts with the adult ICF as only one code existed in regards to leisure or recreation.

Changes in ICF-CY codes over time reflect developmental effects attributable to the child's interaction with the environment. Environmental factors influence functioning and development and can be documented as barriers or facilitators using the ICF-CY. The key environments of children and adolescents include their homes, day care centers, schools and recreation settings of playground, parks, and ball fields (Simeonsson, Lollar, Hollowell, & Adams, 2000). Children will transition between different environments many times as they grow. For example, a child will transition into elementary or high school or from one service setting or agency to another. Attention to these transitions of children with disabilities has been identified as an important role for health care providers (Simeonsson *et al.*, 2000). A transition requires preparation and planning to find an appropriate and accommodating setting for a child's needs. With a coding system such as the ICF-CY, the transition will be smoother and interventions can start where the previous health provider left off.

2

Special Education and Disability Studies: An Introductory Overview

DEFINING SPECIAL EDUCATION

Special education is the education of students with special needs in a way that addresses the students' individual differences and needs. Ideally, this process involves the individually planned and systematically monitored arrangement of teaching procedures, adapted equipment and materials, accessible settings, and other interventions designed to help learners with special needs achieve a higher level of personal self-sufficiency and success in school and community than would be available if the student were only given access to a typical classroom education.

Common special needs include learning disability, communication challenges, emotional and behavioural disorders, physical disabilities, and developmental disabilities. Students with these kinds of disabilities are likely to benefit from additional educational services, different approaches to teaching, and use of technology.

Intellectual giftedness is a difference in learning and can also benefit from specialized teaching techniques or different educational programmes, but the term "special education" is generally used to specifically indicate instruction of students whose special needs reduce their ability to learn independently or in a classroom, and gifted education is handled separately.

The opposite of *special education* is *general education*. General education is the standard curriculum presented with standard teaching methods and without additional supports.

Provision of Individualized Services

Special education is not a location, but the act of educating students in a way that is "special", or different from the usual methods. A special education programme should be customized to address each individual student's unique needs. Special educators provide a continuum of services, in which students with special needs receive services in varying degrees based on their individual needs.

The provision of education to people with disabilities or learning differences differs across countries and (in the US, Canada, Germany, and other federally organized countries) across states. The ability of a student to access a particular resource depends on the availability of services, location, family choice, and government policy. For example, in some poor countries, students with disabilities simply cannot attend school.

In most countries, educators are being challenged to modify teaching methods and environments so that the maximum number of students are served in typical educational environments. In the US, the President's National Council on Disability has called for special education to be regarded less as a "place" and more as "a service, available in every school." Inclusion reduces social stigmas and improves academic achievement for many students.

Additionally, improved teaching methods and early intervention programmes such as response to intervention are being implemented by general education teachers to reduce the need for special education through prevention.

Special education programmes need to be individualized so that they address the unique combination of needs in a given student.

Students with special needs are assessed to determine their specific strengths and weaknesses. Placement, resources, and goals are determined on the basis of the student's needs. Modifications to the regular programme may include changes in curriculum, supplementary aides or equipment, and the provision of specialized physical adaptations that allow students to participate in the educational environment to the fullest extent possible. Students may need this help to access subject matter, to physically gain access to the school, or to meet their emotional needs. For example, if the assessment determines that the student cannot write by hand because of a physical disability, then the school might provide a computer for typing assignments, or allow the student to answer questions orally instead. If the school determines that the student is severely distracted by the normal activities in a large, busy classroom, then the student might be placed in a smaller classroom.

The education of students with developmental disabilities, who require more time to learn the same material, frequently requires changes to the curriculum. Successful special education programmes for developmentally disabled students focus on "only what is necessary for them to know and what they are capable of learning," so that all of the child's time is spent learning high-priority skills, and so that the child is not inappropriately frustrated by advanced subjects that are beyond their capabilities. By contrast, most students with a specific learning disability primarily need changes to the method of instruction, rather than to the skills and information being taught.

Support can be provided for short periods or long-term, and the kinds of support may change over time. For example, a child that required a one-on-one instructional aide for safety reasons while very young might outgrow this need when older.

Setting

Special education has been provided in one, or a combination, of the following settings:

- *Inclusion:* In this approach, students with special needs spend most or all of their time with non-disabled students. Implementation of this approach varies; most schools use it only for selected students with mild to moderate special needs, for which is accepted as a best practice. For example, in Denmark, 99 per cent of students with learning disabilities are placed in regular classrooms full-time. In the United States, three out of five students with learning disabilities spend the overwhelming majority of their time in the regular classroom. Inclusion has two sub-types: the first is sometimes called *regular inclusion* or *partial inclusion*, and the other is *full inclusion*.
  - In a "regular inclusion" setting, students with special needs are educated in regular classes for nearly all of the day, or at least half of the day. Most specialized services are provided outside a regular classroom, particularly if these services require special equipment or might be disruptive to the rest of the class (such as speech therapy). In this case, the student occasionally leaves the regular classroom to attend smaller, more intensive instructional sessions, or to receive other related service such as speech and language therapy, occupational and/or physical therapy, and social work.
  - In a "full inclusion" system, various service providers come into the regular classroom to provide educational services within the regular classroom. Most schools practice full inclusion only for selected students with mild learning disabilities or with physical disabilities. An inclusive school practices full inclusion for all students, regardless of abilities, which is controversial and uncommon.
- *Mainstreaming:* Regular education classes combined with special education classes is a model often referred to as *mainstreaming*. In this model, students with special needs are educated in regular classes during specific time periods based on their skills.
- *Segregation* in a self-contained classroom or special school: Full-time placement in a special education classroom may be referred to as *segregation*. In this model, students with special needs spend no time in regular classes. Segregated students may attend the same school where regular classes are provided, but spend their time exclusively in a special-needs classroom. Alternatively, these students may attend a special school.
- *Exclusion:* A student who does not receive instruction in any school is said to be *excluded*. Such exclusion may occur where there is no legal mandate for special education services. It may also occur when a student is in hospital, homebound, or detained by the criminal justice system. These students may receive one-on-one instruction or group instruction. Students who have been suspended or expelled are not considered excluded in this sense.

Differences by Location

Europe

In England, the Special Educational Needs Parent Partnership Services help parents with the planning and delivery of their child's educational provision. In Scotland the Additional Support Needs Act places an obligation on education authorities to meet the needs of all students in consultation with other agencies and parents.

North America

In the United States, the Individuals with Disabilities Education Act requires that special needs students be included in regular education activities when appropriate.

Bilingual Special Education

Based on 1980 Census and Immigration and Naturalization Services records, it is estimated that there are 79 million school-age language minority children in the United States. This bilingual population is distributed throughout the United States with heavier concentrations in the southwest and northeast. The highest concentration is in the large urban areas.

Considering the overall population with Limited English Proficiency (LEP) in the United States, a critical question for bilingual special educators is how many of these students also have disabilities. According to the U.S. Office of Special Education, an estimated 9,48,000 children may both be linguistically different and have disabilities–a substantial population who could benefit from bilingual special education services. In addition, a disproportionate number of minority students are placed in special education. Of particular concern is the over-representation of minority children in particular categories of disability such as mental retardation and emotional disturbance.

Abbreviations

In North America, special education is commonly abbreviated as *special ed, SpecEd, SPED,* or *SpEd* in a professional context. In the United States, all special-needs students receive an Individualized Education Programme (IEP) that outlines how the school will provide the student with a Free Appropriate Public Education (FAPE) while keeping the student in the Least Restrictive Environment (LRE) that is appropriate for the student's needs and goals.

In England and Wales the initialism *SEN* for Special Educational Needs denotes the condition of having special educational needs, the services which provide the support and the programmes and staff which implement the education. In England *SEN PPS* refers to the Special Educational Needs Parent Partnership Service. *SENAS* is the special educational needs assessment service, which is part of the Local Authority. *SENCO* refers to a special educational needs coordinator, who ususally works with schools and the children within schools who have special educational needs.

In Scotland the term Special Educational Needs (SEN), and its variants are not official terminology although the very recent implementation of the Additional Support for Learning Act means that both *SEN* and *ASN* (Additional Support Needs) are used interchangeably in current common practice.

History

Beginning in 1952, Civitans were the first to provide widespread training for teachers of developmentally disabled children.

In the United States of America, students with disabilities were frequently not allowed to enroll in regular public schools until the passage of the federal Education for All Handicapped Children Act in 1975 which was reauthorized in 1990 and 1997, the law was renamed the Individuals with Disabilities Education Act (IDEA) and spawned the delivery of services to millions of students previously denied access to an appropriate education. According to the Department of Education, approximately 6 million children (roughly 10% of all school-aged children) receive special education services.

Criticism

- Changes in thinking about special education have contained both 'constructive' and 'deconstructive' elements. In the constructive tradition, arguments have rested in the positive value of a plural, equitable system for all rooted in human rights—an inclusive system. Here, it is argued that special education separates and discriminates against those who are disabled or different. In the deconstructive tradition arguments have centred on the harmful consequences that may emerge from separate systems and pedagogies. It has also been pointed out that the record of special education and special pedagogy in terms of student outcomes has not been positive, especially given the very beneficial resources allocated to it (up to 15 times as much spent on a special school student as a mainstream school student). Both traditions, 'constructive' and 'deconstructive', have argued for an end to separate education systems.
- Beneficial classrooms designed for special education students, sometimes called resource rooms, are criticized by those who seek to include all students, regardless of individual needs, in the same classroom.
- Special education as implemented in public schools has been criticized because the qualification criteria for services are extremely variable from one education agency to another. In the United States, all Local and State Education Agencies must use classification and labelling models that are aligned with the federal definitions, outlined the Individuals with Disabilities Education Act (IDEA).
- At-risk students (those with educational needs that are not associated with a disability) are often placed in classes with students with disabilities. Critics assert that placing at-risk students in the same classes as disabled students may impede the educational progress of people with disabilities.
- Special education classes under the mainstreaming model have been criticized for its watered-down curriculum.
- The practice of inclusion has been criticized by advocates and some parents of children with disabilities because some of these students require

instructional methods that differ dramatically from typical classroom methods. Critics assert that it is not possible to deliver effectively two or more very different instructional methods in the same classroom. As a result, the educational progress of students who depend on different instructional methods to learn often fall even further behind their peers without disabilities.

- Parents of typically developing children sometimes fear that the special needs of a single "fully included" student will take critical levels of attention and energy away from the rest of the class and thereby impair the academic achievements of all students.
- Some parents, advocates, and students have concerns about the eligibility criteria and its application. In some cases, parents and students protest the students' placement into special education programmes. For example, a student may be placed into the special education programmes due to a mental health condition such as OCD, depression, anxiety, panic attacks or ADHD, while the student and his parents believe that the condition is adequately managed through medication and outside therapy. In other cases, students whose parents believe they require the additional support of special education services are denied participation in the programme based on the eligibility criteria.
- An alternative to homogenization and lockstep standardization is proposed, using the Sudbury model schools, an alternative approach in which children learn at their own pace rather than following a chronologically-based curriculum. Proponents of unschooling have also claimed that children raised in this method do not suffer from learning disabilities.

Drop Out Rates

Special education students are more likely to drop out of school than their non-disabled peers. This trend holds true for students with all types of disabilities. Arguably, students with specific learning disabilities have lesser degrees of disability than some of the other exceptionalities. Despite this, students with LDs still have a high rate of drop outs. Further, the problem appears to be seen among students in many countries. Parts of Canada report that as many as 60 per cent of students with learning or behaviour disorders do not complete school. In the United States, the National Center on Secondary Education and Transition reports that special education students are twice as likely to drop out as regular education students.

The cost of the high drop out rate is incalculably high with profound social and economic implications for the students, their families, and society. Drop outs have high rates of unemployment, make less money, are more likely to need public assistance, and are more likely to become involved with the criminal justice system.

Researchers theorize that high special education dropout rates are correlated with multiple factors such as:

- Low economic status and race;

- Student relationships with family, peers, and school staff;
- Declining academic performance, particularly beginning in sixth grade;
- Continued low grades in high school and poor attendance;
- Lack of motivation; and
- Substance abuse.

Beyond characteristics that place a child at-risk for dropping out, researchers are finding that the school itself may be a strong determining factor as well. Schools that have overall low achievement, a less experienced teaching staff, higher numbers of students per teacher, and less spending per student tend to have higher dropout rates. Schools with dropout rates higher than 60 per cent are sometimes referred to as dropout factories. Successful transition from high school to college, vocational programme, or employment is also a factor that correlates to dropout rates, suggesting that preparing students in advance for success after high school may influence student motivation to complete high school.

African-Americans in Special Education

The studies found that grossly disproportionate numbers of minority students are identified as eligible for services, and too often placed in isolated and restrictive educational settings. When compared with their white counterparts, African-American children (in data from 1997) were almost three times more likely to be labelled "mentally retarded," according to a paper by Thomas B. Parrish, managing research scientist at the American Institutes of Research. New statistics compiled on each state show both over- and under-representation of minorities in the categories for "mental retardation," "specific learning disabilities," and "emotional disturbance."

UNDERSTANDING EDUCATION IN ITS BROADEST SENSE

Education in its broadest sense is any act or experience that has a formative effect on the mind, character, or physical ability of an individual. In its technical sense education is the process by which society deliberately transmits its accumulated knowledge, skills and values from one generation to another through institutions.

Teachers in such institutions direct the education of students and might draw on many subjects, including reading, writing, mathematics, science and history. This process is sometimes called schooling when referring to the education of youth. Teachers in specialized professions such as astrophysics, law, or zoology may teach only a certain subject, usually as professors at institutions of higher learning. There is also education in fields for those who want specific vocational skills, such as those required to be a pilot. In addition there is an array of education possible at the informal level, e.g., at museums and libraries, with the Internet, and in life experience.

The right to education has been described as a basic human right: since 1952, Article 2 of the first Protocol to the European Convention on Human Rights obliges all signatory parties to guarantee the right to education. At world level, the United

Nations' International Covenant on Economic, Social and Cultural Rights of 1966 guarantees this right under its Article 13.

Systems of Formal Education

Education is a concept, referring to the process in which students can learn something:

- Instruction refers to the intentional facilitating of learning toward identified objectives, delivered either by an instructor or other forms.
- Teaching refers to the actions of a real live instructor designed to impart learning to the student.
- Teaching refers to learning with a view toward preparing learners with specific knowledge, skills, or abilities that can be applied immediately upon completion.

Primary Education

Primary (or elementary) education consists of the first few years of formal, structured education. In general, main education consists of six or eight years of schooling starting at the age of five or six, although this varies between, and sometimes within, countries. Globally, around 70 per cent of primary-age children are enrolled in primary education, and this proportion is rising. Under the Education for All programmes driven by UNESCO, most countries have committed to achieving universal enrollment in primary education by 2015, and in many countries, it is compulsory for children to receive primary education. The division between primary and secondary education is somewhat arbitrary, but it generally occurs at about eleven or twelve years of age. Some education systems have separate middle schools, with the transition to the final stage of secondary education taking place at around the age of fourteen. Schools that provide primary education, are mostly referred to as *primary schools*. Primary schools in these countries are often subdivided into infant schools and junior schools.

Secondary Education

In most contemporary educational systems of the world, secondary education consists of the second years of formal education that occur during adolescence. It is characterized by transition from the typically compulsory, comprehensive primary education for minors, to the optional, selective tertiary, "post-secondary", or "higher" education (e.g., university, vocational school) for adults. Depending on the system, schools for this period, or a part of it, may be called secondary or high schools, gymnasiums, lyceums, middle schools, colleges, or vocational schools. The exact meaning of any of these terms varies from one system to another. The exact boundary between primary and secondary education also varies from country to country and even within them, but is generally around the seventh to the tenth year of schooling. Secondary education occurs mainly during the teenage years. In the United States and Canada primary and secondary education together are sometimes referred to as K-12 education, and in New Zealand Year 1-13 is used. The purpose of secondary education can be to give common knowledge, to prepare for higher education or to train directly in a profession.

The emergence of secondary education in the United States did not happen until 1910, caused by the rise in big businesses and technological advances in factories (i.e. emergence of electrification), that required skilled workers. In order to meet this new job demand, high schools were created and the curriculum focused on practical job skills that would better prepare students for white collar or skilled blue collar work. This proved to be beneficial for both the employer and the employee, because this improvement in human capital caused employees to become more efficient, which lowered costs for the employer, and skilled employees received a higher wage than employees with just primary educational attainment. In Europe the grammar school or academy existed from as early as the 1500s, public schools or fee paying schools, or charitable educational foundations have an even longer history.

Higher Education

Higher education, also called tertiary, third stage, or post secondary education, is the non-compulsory educational level that follows the completion of a school providing a secondary education, such as a high school, secondary school. Tertiary education is normally taken to include undergraduate and postgraduate education, as well as vocational education and training. Colleges and universities are the main institutions that provide tertiary education. Collectively, these are sometimes known as tertiary institutions. Tertiary education generally results in the receipt of certificates, diplomas, or academic degrees.

Higher education includes teaching, research and social services activities of universities, and within the realm of teaching, it includes both the *undergraduate* level (sometimes referred to as tertiary education) and the *graduate* (or *postgraduate*) level (sometimes referred to as graduate school). Higher education in that country generally involves work towards a degree-level or foundation degree qualification. In most developed countries a high proportion of the population (up to 50%) now enter higher education at some time in their lives. Higher education is therefore very important to national economies, both as a significant industry in its own right, and as a source of trained and educated personnel for the rest of the economy.

Adult Education

Adult education has become common in many countries. It takes on many forms, ranging from formal class-based learning to self-directed learning and e-learning. A number of career specific courses such as veterinary, medical billing and coding, real estate licence, book-keeping and many more are now available to students through the Internet.

Alternative Education

Alternative education, also known as *non-traditional education* or *educational alternative,* is a broad term that may be used to refer to all forms of education outside of traditional education (for all age groups and levels of education). This may include not only forms of education designed for students with special needs (ranging from teenage pregnancy to intellectual disability), but also forms of education designed for a general audience and employing alternative educational philosophies and methods.

Alternatives of the latter type are often the result of education reform and are rooted in various philosophies that are commonly fundamentally different from those of traditional compulsory education. While some have strong political, scholarly, or philosophical orientations, others are more informal associations of teachers and students dissatisfied with certain aspects of traditional education. These alternatives, which include charter schools, alternative schools, independent schools, and home-based learning vary widely, but often emphasize the value of small class size, close relationships between students and teachers, and a sense of community.

Indigenous Education

Increasingly, the inclusion of indigenous models of education (methods and content) as an alternative within the scope of formal and non-formal education systems, has come to represent a significant factor contributing to the success of those members of indigenous communities who choose to access these systems, both as students/learners and as teachers/instructors.

As an educational method, the inclusion of indigenous ways of knowing, learning, instructing, teaching and training, has been viewed by many critical and postmodern scholars as important for ensuring that students/learners and teachers/instructors (whether indigenous or non-indigenous) are able to benefit from education in a culturally sensitive manner that draws upon, utilizes, promotes and enhances awareness of indigenous traditions.

For indigenous students or learners, and teachers or instructors, the inclusion of these methods often enhances educational effectiveness, success and learning outcomes by providing education that adheres to their own inherent perspectives, experiences and worldview. For non-indigenous students and teachers, education using such methods often has the effect of raising awareness of the individual traditions and collective experience of surrounding indigenous communities and peoples, thereby promoting greater respect for and appreciation of the cultural realities of these communities and peoples.

In terms of educational content, the inclusion of indigenous knowledge, traditions, perspectives, worldviews and conceptions within curricula, instructional materials and textbooks and coursebooks have largely the same effects as the inclusion of indigenous methods in education. Indigenous students and teachers benefit from enhanced academic effectiveness, success and learning outcomes, while non-indigenous students/learners and teachers often have greater awareness, respect, and appreciation for indigenous communities and peoples in consequence of the content that is shared during the course of educational pursuits.

A prime example of how indigenous methods and content can be used to promote the above outcomes is demonstrated within higher education in Canada. Due to certain jurisdictions' focus on enhancing academic success for Aboriginal learners and promoting the values of multiculturalism in society, the inclusion of indigenous methods and content in education is often seen as an important obligation and duty of both governmental and educational authorities.

Process

Curriculum

An academic discipline is a branch of knowledge which is formally taught, either at the university, or via some other such method. Functionally, disciplines are usually defined and recognized by the academic journals in which research is published, and by the learned societies to which their practitioners belong. Professors say schooling is 80 per cent psychological, 20 per cent physical effort.

Each discipline usually has several sub-disciplines or branches, and distinguishing lines are often both arbitrary and ambiguous. Examples of broad areas of academic disciplines include the natural sciences, mathematics, computer science, social sciences, humanities and applied sciences.

Learning Modalities

There has been work on learning styles over the last two decades. Dunn and Dunn focused on identifying relevant stimuli that may influence learning and manipulating the school environment, at about the same time as Joseph Renzulli recommended varying teaching strategies. Howard Gardner identified individual talents or aptitudes in his Multiple Intelligences theories. Based on the works of Jung, the Myers-Briggs Type Indicator and Keirsey Temperament Sorter focused on understanding how people's personality affects the way they interact personally, and how this affects the way individuals respond to each other within the learning environment. The work of David Kolb and Anthony Gregorc's Type Delineator follows a similar but more simplified approach.

It is currently fashionable to divide education into different learning "modes". The learning modalities are probably the most common:

- *Visual*: learning based on observation and seeing what is being learned.
- *Auditory*: learning based on listening to instructions/information.
- *Kinesthetic*: learning based on hands-on work and engaging in activities.

It is claimed that, depending on their preferred learning modality, different teaching techniques have different levels of effectiveness. A consequence of this theory is that effective teaching should present a variety of teaching methods which cover all three learning modalities so that different students have equal opportunities to learn in a way that is effective for them. Guy Claxton has questioned the extent that learning styles such as VAK are helpful, particularly as they can have a tendency to label children and therefore restrict learning.

Teaching

Teachers need to understand a subject enough to convey its essence to students. The goal is to establish a sound knowledge base on which students will be able to build as they are exposed to different life experiences. The passing of knowledge from generation to generation allows students to grow into useful members of society. Good teachers can translate information, good judgement, experience and wisdom into relevant knowledge that a student can understand, retain and pass to others. Studies from the US suggest that the quality of teachers is the single most important factor affecting student performance, and that countries which score highly on international tests have multiple policies in place to ensure that the teachers they employ are as effective as possible.

Technology

Technology is an increasingly influential factor in education. Computers and mobile phones are used in developed countries both to complement established education practices and develop new ways of learning such as online education (a type of distance education). This gives students the opportunity to choose what they are interested in learning. The proliferation of computers also means the increase of programming and blogging. Technology offers powerful learning tools that demand new skills and understandings of students, including Multimedia, and provides new ways to engage students, such as Virtual learning environments. Technology is being used more not only in administrative duties in education but also in the instruction of students. The use of technologies such as Powerpoint and interactive whiteboard is capturing the attention of students in the classroom. Technology is also being used in the assessment of students. One example is the Audience Response System (ARS), which allows immediate feedback tests and classroom discussions.

Information and Communication Technologies (ICTs) are a "diverse set of tools and resources used to communicate, create, disseminate, store, and manage information." These technologies include computers, the Internet, broadcasting technologies (radio and television), and telephony. There is increasing interest in how computers and the Internet can improve education at all levels, in both formal and non-formal settings. Older ICT technologies, such as radio and television, have for over forty years been used for open and distance learning, although print remains the cheapest, most accessible and therefore most dominant delivery mechanism in both developed and developing countries.

The use of computers and the Internet is in its infancy in developing countries, if these are used at all, due to limited infrastructure and the attendant high costs of access. Usually, various technologies are used in combination rather than as the sole delivery mechanism. For example, the Kothmale Community Radio Internet uses both radio broadcasts and computer and Internet technologies to facilitate the sharing of information and provide educational opportunities in a rural community in Sri Lanka. The Open University of the United Kingdom (UKOU), established in 1969 as the first educational institution in the world wholly dedicated to open and distance learning, still relies heavily on print-based materials supplemented by radio, television and, in recent years, online programming. Similarly, the Indira Gandhi National Open University in India combines the use of print, recorded audio and video, broadcast radio and television, and audio conferencing technologies.

The term "computer-assisted learning" (CAL) has been increasingly used to describe the use of technology in teaching.

Educational Theory

Education theory is the theory of the purpose, application and interpretation of education and learning. Its history begins with classical Greek educationalists and sophists and includes, since the 18th century, pedagogy and andragogy. In the 20th century, "theory" has become an umbrella term for a variety of scholarly approaches to teaching, assessment and education law, most of which are informed by various academic fields, which can be seen in the below sections.

Economics

It has been argued that high rates of education are essential for countries to be able to achieve high levels of economic growth. Empirical analyses tend to support the theoretical prediction that poor countries should grow faster than rich countries because they can adopt cutting edge technologies already tried and tested by rich countries. However, technology transfer requires knowledgeable managers and engineers who are able to operate new machines or production practices borrowed from the leader in order to close the gap through imitation. Therefore, a country's ability to learn from the leader is a function of its stock of "human capital." Recent study of the determinants of aggregate economic growth have stressed the importance of fundamental economic institutions and the role of cognitive skills.

At the individual level, there is a large literature, generally related back to the work of Jacob Mincer, on how earnings are related to the schooling and other human capital of the individual. This work has motivated a large number of studies, but is also controversial. The chief controversies revolve around how to interpret the impact of schooling.

Economists Samuel Bowles and Herbert Ginits famously argued in 1976 that there was a fundamental conflict in American schooling between the egalitarian goal of democratic participation and the inequalities implied by the continued profitability of capitalist production on the other.

History

The history of education according to Dieter Lenzen, president of the Freie Universität Berlin 1994 "began either millions of years ago or at the end of 1770." Education as a science cannot be separated from the educational traditions that existed before. Adults trained the young of their society in the knowledge and skills they would need to master and eventually pass on. The evolution of culture, and human beings as a species depended on this practice of transmitting knowledge. In pre-literate societies this was achieved orally and through imitation. Story-telling continued from one generation to the next. Oral language developed into written symbols and letters. The depth and breadth of knowledge that could be preserved and passed soon increased exponentially. When cultures began to extend their knowledge beyond the basic skills of communicating, trading, gathering food, religious practices, etc. formal education, and schooling, eventually followed. Schooling in this sense was already in place in Egypt between 3000 and 500BC.

Now-a-days some kind of education is compulsory to all people in most countries. Due to population growth and the proliferation of compulsory education, UNESCO has calculated that in the next 30 years more people will receive formal education than in all of human history thus far.

Philosophy

Philosophy of education is the philosophical study of the purpose, process, nature and ideals of education. Philosophy of education can naturally be considered a branch of both philosophy and education. Philosophy of education is commonly housed in colleges and departments of education, yet it is applied philosophy, drawing from the traditional fields of philosophy (ontology, ethics, epistemology, etc.) and approaches (speculative, prescriptive, and/or analytic) to address questions regarding education policy, human development, education research methodology, and curriculum theory, to name a few.

Psychology

Educational psychology is the study of how humans learn in educational settings, the effectiveness of educational interventions, the psychology of teaching, and the social psychology of schools as organizations. Although the terms "educational psychology" and "school psychology" are often used interchangeably, researchers and theorists are likely to be identified as educational psychologists, whereas practitioners in schools or school-related settings are identified as school psychologists. Educational psychology is concerned with the processes of educational attainment in the general population and in sub-populations such as gifted children and those with specific disabilities.

Educational psychology can in part be understood through its relationship with other disciplines. It is informed primarily by psychology, bearing a relationship to that discipline analogous to the relationship between medicine and biology. Educational psychology in turn informs a wide range of specialities within educational studies, including instructional design, educational technology, curriculum development, organizational learning, special education and classroom management. Educational psychology both draws from and contributes to cognitive science and the learning sciences. In universities, departments of educational psychology are usually housed within faculties of education, possibly accounting for the lack of representation of educational psychology content in introductory psychology textbooks (Lucas, Blazek, & Raley, 2006).

Sociology

The sociology of education is the study of how social institutions and forces affect educational processes and outcomes, and *vice versa*. By many, education is understood to be a means of overcoming handicaps, achieving greater equality and acquiring wealth and status for all (Sargent 1994). Learners may be motivated by aspirations for progress and betterment. Education is perceived as a place where children can develop according to their unique needs and potentialities. The purpose of education can be to develop every individual to their full potential. The understanding of the goals and means of educational socialization processes differs according to the sociological paradigm used.

Educational Development

In some developing countries, the number and seriousness of the problems faced are naturally greater. People in more remote or agrarian areas are sometimes unaware of the importance of education. However, many countries have an active Ministry of Education, and in many subjects, such as foreign language learning, the degree of education is actually much higher than in industrialized countries; for example, it is not at all uncommon for students in many developing countries to be reasonably fluent in multiple foreign languages, whereas this is much more of a rarity in the supposedly "more educated" countries where much of the population is in fact monolingual.

There is also economic pressure from those parents who prefer their children making money in the short-term over any long-term benefits of education. Recent studies on child labour and poverty have suggested that when poor families reach a certain economic threshold where families are able to provide for their basic needs, parents return their children to school. This has been found to be true, once the threshold has been breached, even if the potential economic value of the children's work has increased since their return to school. Teachers are often paid less than other similar professions.

A lack of good universities, and a low acceptance rate for good universities, is evident in countries with a high population density. In some countries, there are uniform, over-structured, inflexible centralized programmes from a central agency that regulates all aspects of education:

- Due to globalization, increased pressure on students in curricular activities
- Removal of a certain percentage of students for improvisation of academics (usually practised in schools, after 10th grade).

India is now developing technologies that will skip land based phone and internet lines. Instead, India launched EDUSAT, an education satellite that can reach more of the country at a greatly reduced cost. There is also an initiative started by a group out of MIT and supported by several major corporations to develop a $100 laptop. The laptops should be available by late 2006 or 2007. The laptops, sold at cost, will enable developing countries to give their children a digital education, and to close the digital divide across the world.

In Africa, NEPAD has launched an "e-school programme" to provide all 6,00,000 primary and high schools with computer equipment, learning materials and internet access within 10 years. Private groups, like The Church of Jesus Christ of Latter-day Saints, are working to give more individuals opportunities to receive education in developing countries through such programmes as the Perpetual Education Fund. An International Development Agency project called nabuur.com, started with the support of American President Bill Clinton, uses the Internet to allow co-operation by individuals on issues of social development.

Internationalisation

Education is becoming increasingly international. Not only are the materials becoming more influenced by the rich international environment, but exchanges among students at all levels are also playing an increasingly important role. In Europe, for example, the Socrates-Erasmus Programme stimulates exchanges across European universities. Also, the Soros Foundation provides many opportunities for students from central Asia and eastern Europe. Some scholars argue that, regardless of whether one system is considered better or worse than another, experiencing a different way of education can often be considered to be the most important, enriching element of an international learning experience.

Religion and Education

In Islam education is very important for both males and females, particularly young children. Contrary to common perception the seeking of all types knowledge be it academic, vocational; religious or secular is encouraged whatever age however learning at an early age is seen to allow the mind to concentrate without the stresses and responsibilities of later adult life.

ANALYZING ALTERNATIVE EDUCATION

Alternative education, also known as non-traditional education or educational alternative, includes a number of approaches to teaching and learning other than mainstream or traditional education. Educational alternatives are often rooted in various philosophies that are fundamentally different from those of mainstream or traditional education. While some have strong political, scholarly, or philosophical orientations, others are more informal associations of teachers and students dissatisfied with some aspect of mainstream or traditional education. Educational alternatives, which include charter schools, alternative schools, independent schools, and home-based learning vary widely, but often emphasize the value of small class size, close relationships between students and teachers, and a sense of community.

Terminology

Other words used in place of *alternative* by many educational professionals include *non-traditional, non-conventional,* or *non-standardized,* although these terms are used somewhat less frequently and may have negative connotations and multiple meanings. Those involved in forms of education which differ in their educational philosophy (as opposed to their intended pupil base) often use words such as *authentic, holistic,* and *progressive* as well. However, these words each have different meanings which are more specific or more ambiguous than the term *alternative.*

Origins

While pedagogical controversy is very old, "alternative education" presupposes some kind of orthodoxy to which the alternative is opposed. In general, this limits the term to the last two or perhaps three centuries, with the rise of standardized and, later, compulsory education at the primary and secondary levels. Many critics in this period have suggested that the education of young people should be undertaken in radically different ways than ones in practice. In the 19th century, the Swiss humanitarian Johann Heinrich Pestalozzi; the American transcendentalists Amos Bronson Alcott, Ralph Waldo Emerson, and Henry David Thoreau; the founders of progressive education, John Dewey and Francis Parker; and educational pioneers, such as Maria Montessori and Rudolf Steiner (founder of the Waldorf schools); among others, all insisted that education should be understood as the art of cultivating the moral, emotional, physical, psychological, and spiritual aspects of the developing child. Anarchists such as Leo Tolstoy and Francisco Ferrery Guardia emphasized education as a force for political liberation, secularism, and elimination of class distinctions.

More recently, social critics such as John Caldwell Holt, Paul Goodman, Frederick Mayer, George Dennison and Ivan Illich have examined education from more individualist, anarchist, and libertarian perspectives, that is, critiques of the ways that they feel conventional education subverts democracy by molding young people's understandings. Other writers, from the revolutionary Paulo Freire to American educators like Herbert Kohl and Jonathan Kozol, have criticized mainstream Western education from the viewpoint of their varied left-liberal and radical politics.

Modern Forms

A wide variety of educational alternatives exist at the elementary, secondary, and tertiary levels of education. These generally fall into four major categories: school choice, alternative school, independent school, and home-based education. These general categories can be further broken down into more specific practices and methodologies.

School Choice

The public school options include entirely separate schools in their own settings as well as classes, programmes, and even semi-autonomous "schools within schools." Public school choice options are open to all students in their communities, though some have waiting lists. Among these are charter schools, combining private initiatives and state funding; and magnet schools, which attract students to particular themes, such as performing arts.

Alternative School

An alternative school is an educational establishment with a curriculum and methods that are non-traditional.

Many such schools were founded in the United States in the 1970s as an alternative to mainstream or traditional classroom structure. A wide range of philosophies and teaching methods are offered by alternative schools; some have strong political, scholarly, or philosophical orientations, while others are more *ad hoc* assemblies of teachers and students dissatisfied with some aspect of mainstream or traditional education. In 2003 there were approximately 70 alternative schools in the United Kingdom. In the UK public funding is not available for alternative schools and therefore alternative schools are usually fee-paying institutions. In the USA an increasing number of public school systems are offering alternative streams (language-immersion, Montessori, Waldorf), but the majority of alternative schools are still independent and thus without governmental support. In many states of the United States alternative schools are used differently, in particular to house students who have had discipline or legal problems, and in those states alternative schools are organized to have a strong punitive aspect emphasizing discipline and providing a greatly inferior education. It is common in those states for children found to be delinquent by courts to be sentenced to alternative school as a punishment. It is also common in the United States for public school systems to operate alternative schools as a place to segregate special needs students, such as students with emotional disabilities. In such cases they are often mixed with delinquents.

Alternative Education of Special Education Students and Drop Out Prevention

Advocates of programmes designed to prevent or discourage students from leaving school before they graduate (usually from high school) believe that leaving school without a diploma negatively impacts the lives of individuals both personally and professionally. They also argue that it has a negative societal impact because they believe that it increases the likelihood that these individuals will require public assistance. Although special education dropout rates nationally have been on the decline, from reportedly 34.1 per cent in 1995-96 to 29.4 per cent in 1999-2000 (Bost & Riccomini, 2006), they are especially concerned by the rate at which students with disabilities leave school without acquiring a high school diploma.

Recent data regarding the dropout rate of high school students is as follows: The New Jersey special education dropout rate is approximately 11 per cent (in 2005, 10.9% and in 2006, 10.5%).

Data on determining risk factors can serve as predicting variables for students dropping out. Moreover, high risk students in alternative schools encounter formidable challenges that can further increase their risk. Finn discusses risk factors in his 1989 work, "Withdrawing from School" (as cited by Dynarski & Gleason, 2002). He creates two theoretical models in his attempt to examine the reasons students leave school without high school diplomas. In his "frustration-self-esteem model," poor past academic performance leads to an "impaired self-view," and "negative emotions" caused by this eventually cause the student to leave school (Dynarski & Gleason, 2002 p. 45).

Other possible causes have been examined in various studies. Gleason and Dynarksi cited studies finding that a student's family income, socioeconomic status, and parental level of schooling are correlated with early school withdrawal. Limited English ability, membership to a family which receives welfare, neglect, having caregivers with drug addictions, other family members dropping out of school, needing to support family, and personal safety issues may also be correlated with the act of leaving school without a diploma.

A very different variety of drop out is the student who does not face severe personal problems, but leaves school due to his or her philosophical opposition to traditional education.

Popular Education

Popular education was related in the 19th century to the workers' movement. Such experiences have been continued throughout the 20th century, such as the folk high schools in Scandinavian countries, or the "popular universities" in France.

Independent School

Independent, or private, schools have more flexibility in staff selection and educational approach. The most plentiful of these are Montessori Schools, Waldorf Schools (the latter are also called Steiner Schools after their founder), and Friends schools. Other independent schools include democratic, or free schools such as Sands School, Summerhill School and Sudbury Valley School, Krishnamurti Schools, open classroom schools, those based on experiential education, as well as schools which teach using international curriculum such as the International Baccalaureate and Round Square schools. An increasing number of traditionally independent school forms now also exist within state-run, public education; this is especially true of the Waldorf and Montessori schools. The majority of independent schools offer at least partial scholarships.

Home-based Education

Families who seek alternatives based on educational, philosophical, or religious reasons, or if there appears to be no nearby educational alternative can decide to have home-based education. Some call themselves unschoolers, for they follow an approach based on interest, rather than a set curriculum. Others enroll in umbrella schools which provide a curriculum to follow. Many choose this alternative for religious-based reasons, but practitioners of home-based education are of all backgrounds and philosophies.

Correctional Education

Other

There are also some interesting grey areas. For instance, home-educators have combined to create resource centers where they meet as often as five or more days a week, but their members all consider themselves home-educated. In some states publicly run school districts have set up programmes for homeschoolers whereby they are considered enrolled, and have access to school resources and facilities.

Also, many traditional schools have incorporated methods originally found only in alternative education into their general approach, so the line between alternative and mainstream education is continually becoming more blurred.

There are a number of education-based after school options, which can also referred to as out of school learning, which are available to students. For example, Policy Debate, or a number of other types of debate, offer students the opportunity to learn skills which are not taught in classrooms. In debate, students are taught how to read and think critically, how to analyze books, newspaper and magazine articles, and how to speak persuasively. Students are also exposed to politics, world news, public policy, philosophy, economics, and international relations.

Alternative Schooling in Different Countries

Australia

Preshil, in Kew, Australia, was established in the 1930s. Alia College, in Hawthorn East, Australia, was established in 1999. They are two of the few alternative schools in Australia that are unaffiliated with any doctrinal or theological movement. Preshil's primary school has run since established by Margaret Lyttle in 1931, and the secondary school since the late 1970s. See also Village School, Vic; Currambena School, NSW;

Melbourne Community School, Vic; Collingwood College, Vic; Fitzroy Community School, Vic; Lynall Hall, Vic; Berengarra, Vic Candlebark School, Vic; Brisbane Independent School, Qld; Pine Community School, Arana Hills, Qld. The Pavilion, West Heidelberg, Vic.

India

In India, from the early 20th century, many educational theorists discussed and implemented radically different forms of education. Rabindranath Tagore's Visva-Bharati University, Sri Aurobindo's Sri Aurobindo International Centre of Education and Mahatma Gandhi's ideal of "basic education" are prime examples. In recent years many new alternative schools have formed, such as Sarang, Palakad Kerala, Adharshila, Saakad MP, Poorna Learning Centre samavda and Sita School in Bangalore, Kanavu, and Timbaktoo Collective (Andhra Pradesh). At higher levels of education one finds educational alternatives like [multiversity.com Multiversity] that hold open knowledge as an ideal. In the last few decades holistic education, in which the environment of the student is considered an essential part of the educational process, has become popular.

A traditional system of learning in India is now regarded as a basis for developing new methods of alternative schooling. Students used to stay in "Gurukulas", where they received free food and shelter, and education from a "guru" ("teacher" in Sanskrit). Progress was not based on examinations and marks; tests were given by the gurus but not ranks. This system aimed to nurture the students' natural creativity and all-round personality development. While the mainstream education system in India is still based on that introduced by Lord Macaulay, a few projects aim to rejuvenate the early system, including Prabodhini Gurukula, Veda Vijnana Gurukulam and Maitreyi Gurukulam. Many students in these and similar projects take up research work in the field of Sanskrit studies, Vedic studies, Vedic science, Yoga and Ayurveda. Others after completing their education in a Gurukula continue into regular mainstream education such as Bachelor degrees in Commerce, Science, Engineering etc. Students coming to these studies from Gurukulas are regarded as more brilliant and creative than those who have studied in the regular education system.

Japan

Meiji, Taisho, Showa eras (up to World War II)

Japan's first law on the school system, modeled after France, was proclaimed in 1872, but the word "compulsory education" did not appear in the law until 1886.

"The New Education (Neue Erziehung) movement" started at a British school Abbotsholme (founded in 1889) reached Japan, where it turned into "Taisho-era Free Education Movement" (Taisho Jiyu Kyoiku Undo) . They tried to establish a system focusing on children's interests and to provide a liberal learning environment instead of the standardized inflexible system. Schools were founded, both public and private, based on this concept.

All public schools built under this new movement were subjected to the Militaristic and Nationalistic government control and turned into National Schools (Kokumin Gakko) in 1941, modeled after Nazi's primary education system. Many private schools survived and still exist today. Almost all of them maintain the Western influence, however some have lost its roots and enthusiasm. Others are still strongly known as a "unique school" such as Jiyu Gakuen for its high student-autonomy, and Tamagawa Gakuen as the only Round Square member school in Japan.

After World War II

Japan's recovery efforts from the World War II and the subsequent so-called post-war economic miracle encouraged the mass production of educated work force and the highly competitive entrance exams, which gave little space for alternative education. All children with disabilities, regardless of the severity, were finally allowed to Special Schools (Yogo Gakko) in 1979.

To this date Japanese education has been run as a nation-wide standardized system under the full control of the Ministry of Education. The only alternative option has been accredited private schools that have more freedom to offer different curriculum including the choice of textbooks (public schools can use only the government approved textbooks) and foreign languages, teaching methods, hiring guidelines. However, almost all of these private schools require competitive entrance examination and tuition with very few scholarships available.

In the 1970s and early 1980s school violence was the major problem. Private non-accredited Totsuka Yacht School, one of such schools for correctional education, had multiple deaths and missing incidents.

Some public and private schools, usually non-competitive ones, had been functioning as American-equivalent of alternative schools to accept "at-risk" students, though most of them never claimed themselves as one. A private boarding High School, Hokusei-Gakuen Yoichi, being one of the few exceptions, admitted its status as the alternative school and started to accept High School drop outs from all over the country since 1988.

1980s to Present

Since 1980s the problem shifted from violence against people and property to *ijime* (bullying by peers) to drive the victim into School refusal, Hikikomori (acute social withdrawal) and the worst case, suicide. It is 1980s that the second wave of alternative education movement came in.

There exist two different forces that triggered the interest in alternative education: Ijime and Globalization.

Ijime and Free Schools

Free school is the term used in Japan to describe a non-profit groups or independent schools specialized in the care and education of children who refused to go to school. Tokyo Shure (founded in 1985, modeled after the American democratic school) was the beginning of the Free School emergence in Japan. It started as a shelter for children who avoid school environment, then introduced homeschooling in 1998, creating several branches around Tokyo. It was approved as a Non-profit organization in 2000 to run a college. Japanese free schools have various policies and curriculum. Though most of them are democratic schools, there are Juku's (cram school) that house school-refusal children. Clonlara School from Ann Arbor, Michigan is another major home-based education provider.

Learned from China's Special Economic Zone Policy, Japan introduced Special Zones for Structural Reform in 2003, which enables to open a government-accredited school that provides alternative education. The first school founded in 2005 under the new law was a charter school called Gunma Kokusai Academy, an English immersion school for grades 1 through 12. Tokyo Shure also started a free school-based junior high school in 2007 in the special zone of Katsushika, Tokyo.

Globalization and International Schools

More and more parents are interested in sending their children to International schools to aqcuire native-level command of foreign language (English mostly), with a possible plan of higher education outside of Japan. Although International schools are not legally certified by the Japanese government, many of them are approved by its home country such as US, Canada, Germany, France, Korea and China, and some offer the International Baccalaureate programme. For the past two decades or so, International, especially American or English-based, schools have been very popular in spite of its costly tuition, however the new trend in the early 21st century is Chinese schools. In expectation of China's rapid economic growth, many think knowledge of the Chinese language and culture will be valuable. Compared to American school, which covers all the materials in English only, Chinese schools teach Chinese, Japanese and English for only a 1/8 to 1/4 of what an American school charges for a tuition.

United Kingdom

In the United Kingdom parents have a right to educate their children outside school. Education Otherwise is a charity set up to support those who educate their children outside school.

Summerhill School, established by A.S. Neill in 1921 is known for its alternative approach to education. It is a boarding school where students choose whether or not to attend classes.

There are a number of Steiner-Waldorf schools in the UK.

Sands School is an alternative school in the UK. It has only 65 students, with a high ratio of teachers. The students learn at their own pace in a supportive environment. The school is run democratically, with the students having as much say in how the school is run as the staff. Decisions are made by voting in a weekly school meeting, where matters ranging from what colour the new carpets should be, to the employment of new staff. The school offers a full range of subjects, and attendance to lessons is negotiated, not compulsory. The school also educates students on a larger range than most schools, and gives students choice in what they can learn. Their interests form a large part of what is offered in the curriculum.

United States

New Vista High School in Boulder, Colorado is a small public high school that "emphasizes project learning, multi-cultural perspectives, active involvement in the community." Open since 1993, the school helps a wide variety of students find their passions, through focused and unique classes, off-campus activities, and a supportive school community. Serving a heterogeneous student body, the school not only educates students in the conventional subjects and prepare them for a variety of post secondary programmes, but also "helps each student identify and pursue interests or talents at which they are genuinely motivated to excel."

Another example of an alternative high school in the United States is Holden High School (California) in Orinda. Holden is a part of the National Coalition of Alternative and Community Schools (NCACS) and is accredited by the NCACS's legal counterpart, the National Association for the Legal Support of Alternative Schools (NALSAS).

At the level of higher education several alternative practices have arisen, especially since the late 20th century. Colleges such as Bennington College, Evergreen State College, Goddard College, Union Institute & University BA Programme, Hampshire College, Johnston Center at the University of Redlands, and New College of Florida have no grades, for instance, and use only narrative evaluations for assessment. Other colleges, such as Bard College at Simon's Rock, Marlboro College and the now-defunct Antioch College, do not have traditional academic departments and are instead organized around interdisciplinary units.

In regard to graduate education, there is Saybrook Graduate School and Research Center, Fielding Institute, Union College and University, the California Institute of Integral Studies and The Institute of Transpersonal Psychology.

There are also several consciousness-based education alternatives, including LEAPNOW and Maharishi University of Management.

The Netherlands

At the level of higher education there is Intercultural Open University a leading alternative education provider for person centered graduate education. In keeping with the philosophy of alternative education, the university does not use grades, and uses only narrative evaluations for assessment. There are no traditional academic departments and learners develop a self-directed individualized curriculum under the guidance of a core faculty advisor.

ANALYZING EXCEPTIONAL EDUCATION

Exceptional Education, also known as Exceptional Student Education (ESE), usually refers to both the education of gifted (also "talented") children and children with physical or mental disabilities. These programmes are funded and supported outside the normal class framework: elementary schools dedicating separate classes, wings, and schools (such as magnet schools); secondary schools substituting classes with honors courses or special-needs classes.

DEFINING INTELLECTUAL GIFTEDNESS

Intellectual giftedness is an intellectual ability significantly higher than average.

Gifted children often develop asynchronously; their minds are often ahead of their physical growth, and specific cognitive and emotional functions are often developed differently (or to differing extents) at different stages of development. One frequently cited example of asynchronicity in early cognitive development is Albert Einstein, who did not speak until the age of two, but whose later fluency and accomplishments belied this initial delay. In regards to this fact, psychologist and cognitive scientist Steven Pinker theorized that, rather than viewing Einstein's (and other famously gifted late-talking individuals) adult accomplishments as existing distinct from, or in spite of, his early language deficits, and rather than viewing Einstein's lingual delay itself as a "disorder", it may be that Einstein's genius and his delay in speaking were developmentally intrinsic to one another.

Developmental Theory

It has been said that gifted children may advance more quickly through stages established by post-Freudian developmentalists such as Jean Piaget. Gifted individuals also experience the world differently, resulting in certain social and emotional issues. The work of Kazimierz Dabrowski suggests that gifted children have greater psychomotor, sensual, imaginative, intellectual, and emotional "overexcitabilities."

Francoy Gagne's (2000) Differentiated Model of Giftedness and Talent (DMGT) is a developmental theory that distinguishes giftedness from talent, offering explanation on how outstanding natural abilities (gifts) develop into specific expert skills (talents). According to DMGT theory, "one cannot become talented without first being gifted, or almost so" (Gagne, 2000). There are six components that can interact in countless and unique ways that fosters the process of moving from having natural abilities (giftedness) to systematically developed skills (Gagne, 2000). These components consist of the *gift* (G) itself, *chance* (C), *environmental catalyst* (EC), *intrapersonal catalyst* (IC), *learning/practice* (LP) and the outcome of *talent* (T) (Gagne, 2000). It is important to know that (C), (IC), and (EC) can facilitate but, can also hinder the learning and training of becoming talented. The learning/practice is the moderator. It is through the interactions, both environmental and intrapersonal that influence the process of learning and practice along with/without chance that natural abilities are transformed into talents.

Giftedness from a Multiple Intelligences Perspective

Multiple intelligences has been a focus of interest for decades. During the last decade, it has been associated to giftedness or overachievement of some developmental areas (Colangelo, 2003). Multiple intelligences has been described as an attitude towards learning, instead of techniques or strategies (Cason, 2001). There are eight Intelligences, or different areas in which people assimilate or learn about the world around them: interpersonal, intrapersonal, bodily-kinesthetic, linguistic, logical-mathematical, musical, naturalistic, and spatial-visual. If the Theory of Multiple Intelligences is applied to educational curriculum, by providing lesson plans, themes, and programmes in a way that all students are encouraged to develop their stronger area, and at the same time educators provide opportunities to enhance the learning process in the less strong areas, academic success may be attainable for all children in our school system.

Gardner proposed in Frames of Mind (Gardner 1983/1994) that intellectual giftedness may be present in areas other than the typical intellectual realm. The concept of Multiple Intelligences (MI) makes the field aware of additional potential strengths and proposes a variety of curricular methods.

Gardner suggest MI in the following areas: Linguistic, logico-mathematical, musical, spatial, kinesthetic, interpersonal, intrapersonal, naturalistic and existential.

Identification of gifted students with MI is a challenge since there is no simple test to give to determine giftedness of MI. Assessing by observation is potentially most accurate, but potentially highly subjective. MI theory can be applied to not only gifted students, but it can be a lens through which all students can be assessed. This more global perspective may lead to more child-centered instruction and meet the needs of a greater number of children (Colangelo, 2003).

Identifying Giftedness

Overview

The formal identification of giftedness first emerged as an important issue for schools, as the instruction of gifted students often presents special challenges. During the 20th century, gifted children were often classified via IQ tests, however, recent developments in theories of intelligence have raised serious questions regarding the appropriate uses and limits of such testing. Many schools in North America and Europe have attempted to identify students who are not challenged by standard school curricula and offer additional or specialized education for them in pursuit of nurturing their talents.

Because of the key role that gifted education plays in the identification of gifted individuals, both children and adults, it is worthwhile to examine how that institution uses the term "gifted."

Definitions of Giftedness

For many years, psychometricians and psychologists, following in the footsteps of Lewis Terman in 1916, equated giftedness with high IQ. This "legacy" survives to the present day, in that giftedness and high IQ continue to be equated in some conceptions of giftedness. Since that early time, however, other researchers (e.g., Cattell, Guilford, and Thurstone) have argued that intellect cannot be expressed in such a unitary manner, and have suggested more multifaceted approaches to intelligence. Research conducted in the 1980s and 1990s has provided data which support notions of multiple components to intelligence. This is particularly evident in the re-examination of "giftedness" by Sternberg and Davidson in their edited "Conceptions of Giftedness." The many different conceptions of giftedness presented, although distinct, are interrelated in several ways. Most of the investigators define giftedness in terms of multiple qualities, not all of which are intellectual. IQ scores are often viewed as inadequate measures of giftedness. Motivation, high self-concept, and creativity are key qualities in many of these broadened conceptions of giftedness.

Joseph Renzulli's (1978) "three ring" definition of giftedness is one well-researched conceptualization of giftedness. Renzulli's definition, which defines gifted behaviours rather than gifted individuals, is composed of three components as follows: Gifted behaviour consists of behaviours that reflect an interaction among three basic clusters of human traits—above average ability, high levels of task commitment, and high levels of creativity. Individuals capable of developing gifted behaviour are those possessing or capable of developing this composite set of traits and applying them to any potentially valuable area of human performance. Persons who manifest or are capable of developing an interaction among the three clusters require a wide variety of educational opportunities and services that are not ordinarily provided through regular instructional programmes.

In *Identifying Gifted Children: A Practical Guide,* Susan K. Johnsen explains that gifted children all exhibit the potential for high performance in the areas included in the United States' federal definition of gifted and talented students:

> The term "gifted and talented" when used in respect to students, children, or youth means students, children, or youth who give evidence of high performance capability in areas such as intellectual, creative, artistic, or leadership capacity, or in specific academic fields, and who require services or activities not ordinarily provided by the school in order to fully develop such capabilities." (P.L. 103–382, Title XIV, p. 388)

This definition has been adopted partially or completely by the majority of the states in the United States. The majority of them have some definition similar to that used in the State of Texas, whose definition states:

> [The phrase] "gifted and talented student" means a child or youth who performs at or shows the potential for performing at a remarkably high level of accomplishment when compared to others of the same age, experience, or environment, and who
>
> - exhibits high performance capability in an intellectual, creative, or artistic area;
> - possesses an unusual capacity for leadership; or
> - excels in a specific academic field." (74th legislature of the State of Texas, Chapter 29, Subchapter D, Section 29.121)

The major characteristics of these definitions are (*a*) the diversity of areas in which performance may be exhibited (e.g., intellectual, creativity, artistic, leadership, academically), (*b*) the comparison with other groups (e.g., those in general education classrooms or of the same age, experience, or environment), and (*c*) the use of terms that imply a need for development of the gift (e.g., capability and potential).

Identification Methods

Many schools use a variety of measures of students' capability and potential when identifying gifted children. These may include portfolios of student work, classroom observations, achievement measures, and intelligence scores. Most educational professionals accept that no single measure can be used in isolation to accurately identify a gifted child.

One of the measures used in identification is the score derived from an intelligence measure. The general cutoff for many programmes is often placed near the sigma 2 level on a standardized intelligence test, children above this level being labelled 'gifted'.

Some IQ testers use these classifications to describe differing levels of giftedness. The following bands apply with a standard deviation of $\sigma = 15$ on a standardized IQ test (not the older "ratio IQ" tests). Each band represents a difference of one standard deviation from the mean of a standard distribution.

- *Bright:* 115-129, or one in six (84th percentile)
- *Moderately gifted:* 130-144, or 1 in 50 (97.9th percentile)
- *Highly gifted:* 145-159, or 1 in 1000 (99.9th percentile)
- *Exceptionally gifted:* 160-174, or 1 in 30,000 (99.997th percentile)
- *Profoundly gifted:* 175+, or 1 in 3 million (99.99997th percentile).

Most IQ tests do not have the capacity to discriminate accurately at higher IQ levels, and are perhaps only effective at determining whether a student is gifted rather than distinguishing among levels of giftedness. Although the Wechsler tests have a ceiling of about 160, their creator has admitted that they are intended to be used within the average range (between 70 and 130), and are not intended for use at the extreme ends of the population. The Stanford-Binet form L-M, currently outdated, was the only test that had a sufficient ceiling to identify the exceptionally and profoundly gifted. Because the instrument is outdated, some consider that current results derived from the instrument generate inflated and inaccurate scores. However, the Flynn Effect demonstrates that scores at the extremes of IQ are not subject to the effects of population changes over time in the same way as scores closer to the norm. Many working in the field of the profoundly gifted consider still the Stanford Binet L-M a meaningful test to identify these children. The Stanford-Binet form V and the Wechsler Intelligence Scale for Children—Fourth Revision, both recently released, are currently being evaluated for this population. Mensa offers IQ testing but these are only suitable for persons over the age of ten and a half years. The IQ assessment of younger children remains debated. Also, those who are more gifted in areas such as the arts and literature tend to do poorly on IQ tests, which are generally verbal- and mathematical-skills related.

While many people believe giftedness is a strictly quantitative difference, measurable by IQ tests, a number of people have described giftedness as a fundamentally different way of perceiving the world, which in turn affects every experience had by the gifted individual. These differences do not disappear when gifted children become adults or leave school.

Gifted adults are seldom recognized as a special population, but some of them still have unique psychological, social, and emotional needs related to their high intelligence.

Savantism

Savants are people that perform exceptionally in one field of learning. *Autistic savantism* refers to the exceptional abilities exhibited by people with autism or other developmental disorders. The term was introduced in a 1978 article in *Psychology Today* that described this condition.

Characteristics of Giftedness

Generally, gifted individuals learn more quickly, deeply, and broadly than their peers. Gifted children may learn to read early and operate at the same level as normal children who are significantly older. The gifted tend to demonstrate high reasoning ability, creativity, curiosity, a large vocabulary, and an excellent memory. They often can master concepts with few repetitions. They may also be physically and emotionally sensitive, perfectionistic, and may frequently question authority. Some have trouble relating to or communicating with their peers because of disparities in vocabulary size (especially in the early years), personality, interests and motivation. As children, they may prefer the company of older children or adults.

Giftedness is frequently not evenly distributed throughout all intellectual spheres: an individual may excel in solving logic problems and yet be a poor speller; another gifted individual may be able to read and write at a far above average level and yet have trouble with mathematics. It is possible there are different types of giftedness with their own unique features, just as there are different types of developmental delay.

Giftedness may become noticeable in individuals at different points of development. While early development (i.e. speaking or reading at a very young age) usually comes with giftedness, it is not a determinant of giftedness. The preschool years are when most gifted children begin to show the distinctive characteristics mentioned above. As the child becomes older, classes that are 'too easy' and emotional issues may slow or obstruct the rate of intellectual development.

Some gifted individuals experience heightened sensory awareness and may seem overly sensitive to sight, sound, smell and touch. For example, they may be extremely uncomfortable when they have a wrinkle in their sock, or unable to concentrate because of the sound of a clock ticking on the other side of the room. Hypersensitivity to external stimuli can be said to resemble a proneness to "sensory overload", which can cause persons to avoid chaotic and crowded environments. Others, however, are able to tune out any unwanted distractions as they focus on a task or on their own thoughts, and seem to seek and thrive on being in the midst of lots of activity and stimulation. In many cases, awareness may fluctuate between conditions of hyperstimulation and of withdrawal. These conditions may appear to be similar to symptoms of hyperactivity, bipolar disorder, ADHD, autism-spectrum conditions, and other psychological disorders, but are often explained by gifted education professionals by reference to Kazimierz Dabrowski's theory of Positive Disintegration. Some researchers focused on the study of overexcitabilities. Overexcitabilities refer to ways children or individuals understand and experience the world around them (Gross 2008). The more channels are open to receive the information or stimulus, the more intense or strong the experience is. According to Gross (2008), an individual response to a stimulus is determined by his/her dominant overexcitability. Overexcitabilities are expressed in five dimensions: psychomotor, sensual, intellectual, imaginational, and emotional. These dominant channels of acquiring information differ by quantity in some individuals. Gross, C., Rinn, A., & Jamieson, K. (2008). Gifted Adolescents' Overexcitabilities and Self-Concepts. Journal of Gifted Education. 29, 4.

Twice-Exceptional

The term twice-exceptional was coined by James J. Gallagher to denote students who are both gifted and have disabilities (Coleman, Harradine, & King, 2005, p. 5). We have known about twice exceptional students for thirty years; however, identification and programme strategies remain ambiguous (Krochak & Ryan, 2007). These students need remediation for their learning deficits and enhancement for their strengths to achieve (Krochak & Ryan, 2007). Twice exceptional students are considered at risk because they are hidden within the general population of their educational environment, and usually viewed as either under-achievers or average learners (Nielson, 2002 & Krochak & Ryan, 2007).

"Early identification and intervention is critical; however, giftedness in the twice-exceptional often is identified later than in the average population and is masked by the disability. The disabilities may include auditory processing weaknesses, sensory motor integration issues, visual perceptual difficulties, spatial disorientation, dyslexia, and attention deficits. Recognition of learning difficulties among the gifted is made extremely difficult by virtue of their ability to compensate. Some guidelines that help in identifying these students are as follows:

- Exceptional Vocabulary
- Difficulty with written expression
- Ability to understand complex ideas

- Easily frustrated
- Wide area of interest
- Highly sensitive
- Creative
- Stubborn and opinionated
- Specific areas of strength
- Inconsistent academic performance
- Highly developed sense of humor
- Curious and inquisitive."

Social and Emotional Issues

Isolation

Isolation is one of the main challenges faced by gifted individuals, especially those with no social network of gifted peers. In order to gain popularity, gifted children will often try to hide their abilities to win social approval. Strategies include underachievement (discussed below) and the use of less sophisticated vocabulary when among same-age peers than when among family members or other trusted individuals.

The isolation experienced by gifted individuals may not be caused by giftedness itself, but by society's response to giftedness. Plucker and Levy have noted that, "in this culture, there appears to be a great pressure for people to be 'normal' with a considerable stigma associated with giftedness or talent." To counteract this problem, gifted education professionals recommend creating a peer group based on common interests and abilities. The earlier this occurs, the more effective it is likely to be in preventing isolation.

Perfectionism

Perfectionism is another issue for gifted individuals. It is encouraged by the fact that gifted individuals tend to be easily successful in much of what they do.

Healthy perfectionism refers to having high standards, a desire to achieve, conscientiousness, or high levels of responsibility, it is likely to be a virtue rather than a problem, even if gifted children may have difficulty with healthy perfectionism because they set standards that would be appropriate to their mental age (the level at which they think), but they cannot always meet them because they are trapped in a younger body, or the social environment is restrictive. In such cases, outsiders may call some behaviour perfectionism, while for the gifted this may be their standard.

Perfectionism becomes desirable when it stimulates the healthy pursuit of excellence.

Unhealthy perfectionism stems from equating one's worth as a human being to one's achievements, and the simultaneous belief that any work less than perfect is unacceptable and will lead to criticism. Because perfection in majority of human activities is neither desirable, nor possible, this cognitive distortion creates self doubt, performance anxiety and ultimately procrastination.

The unhealthy perfectionism can be triggered or further exaggerated by parents, siblings, school comarades with good or ill intentions. Parents are usually proud and will praise extensively the gifted child, on the other hand siblings, comarades and school bullies will generally become jealous of the intellectual ease of the gifted child and tease him or her about any minor imperfection in his work, strength, clothes, appearance, or behaviour. (whereas their own abilities are far less). Either way—parents positive reinforcement, or siblings and comarades negative reinforcements about minor flaws—will push these kids into considering their worth to their peers as equal to their abilities and consider any imperfection as a serious defect in themeselves. The unhealthy perfectionism can be further exagerated when the child counter-attacks those who mocked him with their own weapons i.e. their lower abilities, thus creating despise in himself for low or even average performance. Trouble is that he will be confronted sooner or later with the standards he has set for others.

There are many theories that try to explain the correlation between perfectionism and giftedness. Perfectionism becomes a problem as it frustrates and inhibits achievements.

D.E. Hamachek identified six specific, overlapping types of behaviour associated with perfectionism. They include:

- Depression
- A nagging "I should" feeling
- Shame and guilt feelings
- Face-saving behaviour
- Shyness and procrastination
- Self-deprecation.

Underachievement

There is often a stark gap between the abilities of the gifted individual and his or her actual accomplishments. Many gifted students will perform extremely well on standardized or reasoning tests, only to fail a class exam. This disparity can result from various factors, such as loss of interest in too-easy classes or negative social consequences of being perceived as smart. Underachievement can also result from emotional or psychological factors, including depression, anxiety, perfectionism, or self-sabotage. An often overlooked contributor to underachievement is undiagnosed learning differences. A gifted individual is less likely to be diagnosed with a learning disorder than a non-gifted classmate, as the gifted child can more readily compensate for his/her paucities. This masking effect is dealt with by understanding that a difference of IQ between scores constitutes a learning disability even if all of the scores are above average. One apparently effective way to attempt to reverse underachievement in gifted children includes educating teachers to provide enrichment projects based on students' strengths and interests without attracting negative attention from peers.

Depression

It has been thought in the past that there is a correlation between giftedness and depression or suicide. This has generally not been proven. As Reis and Renzulli mention, "With the exception of creatively gifted adolescents who are talented in writing or the visual arts, studies do not confirm that gifted individuals manifest significantly higher or lower rates or severity of depression than those for the general population....Gifted children's advanced cognitive abilities, social isolation, sensitivity, and uneven development may cause them to face some challenging social and emotional issues, but their problem-solving abilities, advanced social skills, moral reasoning, out-of-school interests, and satisfaction in achievement may help them to be more resilient." Also, no research points to suicide rates being higher in gifted adolescents than other adolescents. However, a number of people have noted a higher incidence of existential depression, which is depression due to highly abstract concerns such as the finality of death, the ultimate unimportance of individual people, and the meaning (or lack thereof) of life. Gifted individuals are also more likely to feel existential anxiety.

However, numerous studies have shown that an active depressive state impairs cognition because it retards neurogenesis in the hippocampus.

Professional Attitudes Towards Giftedness

Grobman discusses how some exceptionally and profoundly gifted individuals may unconsciously create deficits as a way of closing the asynchrony gap. Researchers, such as Stephanie Tolan, postulate that the attribution of controversial disorders such as "ADHD"—which other authors have argued has not been proven to exist by any means other than subjective behavioural analysis—to gifted individuals arises from a misguided tendency to pathologize that which we don't understand. Tolan also discusses that identifying as attention deficient has become fashionable in young adults.

Genetics and Intelligence

Intelligence, which is a major component of giftedness, is influenced through a complex interaction of combinations of many genes and many different environmental contexts (Colangelo & Davis, 2003). Intelligence is a general cognitive ability that supports the fact that most reliable measures of cognitive abilities intercorrelate in some way. It is generally agreed that giftedness may have a genetic component; research has shown that first-degree relatives of the intellectually gifted will often have IQs measuring within 10—15 points of each other. Research on families has typically shown a correlation of about .45 in scores of *g* for parents, children, and siblings. Adoption and twin studies have also provided many valuable insights into the genetic component of intelligence. Studies of first degree relatives adopted apart show a correlation of .22, which is about half that of relatives who live together. Adopted children who are not related but reared together show a correlation of about .23 to genetically unrelated parents and siblings.

Heritability from adoption data is 44 per cent for families, 52 per cent for fraternal twins in a shared environment, and 72 per cent for identical twins reared apart. The existing data for identical twins reared apart has been collected from studies conducted in adulthood and because heritability studies show that adults have higher heritability results than children, this number may be inflated (Colangelo & Davis, 2003). The question of whether intelligence has a genetic component has been confirmed through numerous studies. More research is necessary to determine the exact processes by which genetic dispositions interact with the environment.

Some children are born with innately higher intelligence levels than others. These children are often labelled as gifted or talented. Many researchers have investigated the early characteristics of gifted children. Hollingworth (1942) reported that 78 per cent of the teachers agree that early detection of giftedness can be possible during early development. Children as young as preschool age tend to seek out highly stimulating environments. According to Raine, Reynolds, Venables, & Mednick (2002) increased stimulation seeking at age 3 years is associated with an increase in cognitive and scholastic test performance later in development. The advantages of identifying intellectual abilities of gifted children at an earlier age will allow educators to place them in the developmental classes that encourage and promote exploration in the domain of their giftedness. Tannenbaum claims that the environment plays a major role in the nurturance of giftedness or higher intelligence. Giftedness and talent require a special environment just as special education would. The environment must be enriching and encouraging which will allow the child to mature through experience and exploration. The environment must facilitate creative activity in a developmentally appropriate manner which would call for classrooms to be designed for developmental levels as opposed to age or grade leveling. This type of environment with differentiated learning could result from acceleration, lateral enrichment, and special grouping. Also, a developmentally appropriate environment for the gifted child will reduce behaviour problems among preschoolers due to an increased engagement and internal motivation for learning. Furthermore, it is behavioural exploration of the environment that is indicative of the child's intellectual ability later in life. The child's innate motivation to engage in physical activity (hands-on learning) marks a curiosity which motivates task persistence. The increased physical exploration in a social play environment and goal-directed behaviour in the stimulating environment facilitate superior cognitive functioning. In addition, gifted children will become high achievers when their interests are piqued by doing what they are innately motivated to do, empowering them to continue trying new skills. Furthermore, when gifted or talented children are supported by educational staff, their community, peers and families, they have higher possibilities to develop their cognitive abilities.

Talented Students at the Secondary Level

What types of changes and support are needed to better enhance the development of talented adolescent students? Feldhusen (2003) addresses two major shifts in thinking needed to further the advancement of adolescents. Feldhusen proposes abandoning the programme concept and the labelling of students as gifted. Programmes are usually limited in time and are pull-outs that offer non-researched projects. The education of youth demands a wide diversity of experiences in accelerated courses plus extracurricular activities. Students are served better when labelled talented instead of gifted. The term talent shows potential and suggests a developing ability.

Changes and support are embedded in Feldhusen's Purdue Pyramid Model of Talented Development which facilitates learners in developing a personal strong foundation based on talented learners accepting themselves as legitimate human beings to the ultimate potential of realizing their commitment to the full development of one's ability and talent. Parent support is also critical in the development throughout the teenage years. Feldhusen stresses the importance of parental support. Parents provide financial and emotional support, guidance and motivation, and are a sounding board. Secondary level students will be better served in the implementation and acknowledgement of Feldhusen's vision.

UNDERSTANDING THE ELEMENTS AND DIMENSIONS OF GIFTED EDUCATION

Gifted education (also known as Gifted and Talented Education (GATE), Talented and Gifted (TAG), or G/T) is a broad term for special practices, procedures and theories used in the education of children who have been identified as gifted or talented. There is no standard global definition of what a gifted student is.

Commonly Used Terms in Gifted Education

Differentiation: Modification of a gifted student's curriculum to accommodate their specific needs. This may include changing the content or ability level of the material.

Affective Curriculum: A curriculum that is designed to teach gifted students about emotions, self-esteem, and social skills. This can be valuable for all students, especially those who have been grouped with much older students, or who have been rejected by their same-age, but academically typical, peers.

Heterogeneous Grouping: A strategy that groups students of varied ability or accomplishment in a single classroom environment.

Homogeneous Grouping: A strategy that groups students by specific ability, interest, or subject area.

Individualized Education Programme (IEP): A written document that addresses a student's specific individual needs. It may specify accommodations, materials, or classroom instruction. IEPs are often created for students with disabilities, who are required by law to have an IEP when appropriate. Most states are not required to have IEPs for students who are only identified as gifted. Some students may be intellectually gifted in addition to having learning and/or attentional disabilities, and may have an IEP that includes, for instance, enrichment activities as a means of alleviating boredom or frustration, or as a reward for on-task behaviour. In order to warrant such an IEP, a student needs to be diagnosed with a separate emotional or learning disability that is not simply the result of being unchallenged in a typical classroom. These are also known as Individual Programme Plans, or IPP's.

Forms of Gifted Education

Attempts to provide gifted education can be classified in several ways. Most gifted students use a combination of approaches at different times.

Hobby

Activities such as reading, sport, computer games, chess, music, dance, foreign languages, art give an extra intellectual challenge outside of school hours.

Enrichment

On the primary school level, students spend all class time with their peers, but receive extra material to challenge them. Enrichment may be as simple as a modified assignment provided by the regular classroom teacher, or it might include formal programmes such as Odyssey of the Mind, Destination Imagination or academic competitions such as Brain Bowl, Future Problem Solving, National History Day, science fairs, or spelling bees. This work is done in addition to, and not instead of, any regular school work assigned. Critics of this approach argue that it requires gifted students to do more work, not the same amount of work but at a higher level. On the secondary school level sometimes an option is to take more courses like English, Spanish, Latin, Philosophy, Science, etc. or to engage in extra curriculum activities.

Compacting

The regular school material is compacted by pretesting the student to establish which skills and content have already been mastered. Pretests can be presented on a daily basis (doing the most difficult items on a worksheet first and skipping the rest if they are performed correctly), or before a week or longer unit of instructional time. When a student demonstrates an appropriate level of proficiency, further repetitive practice can be safely skipped, thus reducing the boredom and freeing up time for the student to work on more challenging material.

Self Pacing

Self-pacing methods, such as the Montessori Method, use flexible grouping practices to allow children to advance at their own pace. Self-pacing can be beneficial for all children and is not targeted specifically at those identified as gifted or talented, but it can allow children to learn at a highly accelerated rate. Directed Studies are usually based on the students self-pacing.

Acceleration

Pupils are advanced to a higher-level class covering material more suited to their abilities and preparedness. This may take the form of skipping grades or completing normal curriculum in a shorter-than-normal period of time ("telescoping"). Subject acceleration (also called partial acceleration) is a flexible approach which can advance a student in one field, such as mathematics or language, without changing other studies, such as history and sports.

Some colleges offer early entrance programmes that give gifted younger students the opportunity to attend college early. In the U.S., many community colleges allow advanced students to enroll with the consent of school officials and their parents.

Acceleration presents gifted children with academic material from established curricula that is commensurate with their ability and preparedness, and for this reason is a low-cost option from the perspective of the school. However this may result in a small number of children taking classes targeted at older children, and individual students in an acceleration programme may or may not feel socially accepted by a year (or more) older students. The social disconnect is most apparent when a profoundly gifted young child is enrolled in classes with teenagers and young adults. It is least apparent when a moderately gifted student is advanced by only one or two years. Some advocates have argued that the disadvantages of being retained in a standard mixed-ability classroom are substantially worse. For example, psychologist Miraca Gross reports: "the majority of these children [retained in a typical classroom] are socially rejected, isolated and deeply unhappy [by their same-age peers with typical academic talents]. Children of IQ 180+ who are retained in the regular classroom are even more seriously at risk and experience severe emotional distress." In some cases these relatively young kids are placed together in one class, so the age-difference is no problem.

Part-time Pulling-out

Students spend a portion of their time in a gifted class, and the rest of their time with same grade students of varying abilities. These programmes vary widely, from carefully designed half-day academic programmes to a single hour each week of educational challenges. Their effectiveness is difficult to measure because of the diversity of programmes, and is highly debated. A positive outcome likely depends on the level of challenge a student receives during the majority of their time at school. These extra classes cost extra money so they are only present in a very small number of primary-schools. They are mostly funded by public means.

Part-time (Summer) School

This covers a variety of courses, such as The Johns Hopkins University Center for Talented Youth and CTYI that mainly take place in the summer. Summer schools are popular in the USA. Entrance fees are required for such programmes, and programmes typically focus on one subject, or class, for the duration of the camp.

Full-time Separate Classes or Schools

Gifted students are educated in either a separate class or a separate school. Classes like this are sometimes called "Congregated Gifted Classes." In the Netherlands these schools are called the Leonardoschool. They are popular and growing fast.

Separate or independent schools are schools with a primary mission to serve the needs of the academically gifted. Such schools are relatively scarce and often difficult for families to locate. Such schools often need to work to guard their mission from occasional charges of elitism, support the professional growth and training of their staff, write curriculum units that are specifically designed to meet the social, emotional, and academic talents of their students, and educate their parent population at all ages.

Some TAG classes offer directed studies, where the students lead a class themselves and decide on their own projects, tests, and all other assignments.

These separate classes or schools tend to be more expensive than regular classes, due to the smaller number of kids in a classroom. They are in high demand and parents have to pay part of the costs.

Gifted and Talented Programmes

A Talented and Gifted programme is an academic programme that caters to excelling students. The programme may be found in various forms in schools around the world, often with the name "Talented and Gifted" (TAG) or "Gifted and Talented Education" (GATE). Availability and quality of formal programmes varies from place to place. Classes may either be in the form of more challenging, in depth or advanced courses, or in the form of a regularly scheduled seminar that covers extracurricular material.

Homeschooling

An umbrella term encompassing myriad educational options for gifted children; part-time schooling; school at home; classes, groups, mentors and tutors; and unschooling. In many states, the population of gifted students who are being homeschooled is rising quite rapidly, as school districts responding to budgetary issues and standards-based policies are cutting what limited gifted education programme remain extant, and families seek educational opportunities that are tailored to each child's unique needs.

Controversies

Controversies concerning gifted education are varied and often highly politicized. They are as basic as agreeing upon the appropriateness of the term 'gifted' or the definition of 'giftedness'. For example, does 'giftedness' refer to performance or potential (such as inherent intelligence)? Many students do not exhibit both at the same time.

Measures of general intelligence also remain controversial. Early IQ tests were notorious for producing higher IQ scores for privileged races and classes and lower scores for disadvantaged subgroups. Although IQ tests have changed substantially over the past half century, and many objections to the early tests have been addressed by 'culture neutral' tests (such as the Raven test), IQ testing remains controversial.

Some schools and districts only accept IQ tests as evidence of giftedness. This brings scrutiny to the fact that many affluent families can afford to consult with an educational psychologist to test their children, whereas families with a limited income cannot afford the test and must depend on district resources.

Gifted programmes are often seen as being elitist in places where the majority of students receiving gifted services are from a privileged background.

Appropriateness of Forms of Gifted Education

This is the most hotly debated aspect of gifted education. Some people believe that gifted education resources lack availability and flexibility. They feel that in the alternate methods of gifted education, the gifted students "miss out" on having a "normal" childhood, at least insofar as "normal childhood" is defined as attending school in a mixed-ability classroom. Others believe that gifted education allows gifted students to interact with peers that are on their level, be adequately challenged, and leaves them better equipped to take on the challenges of life.

Another facet of this controversy is the effectiveness of the programmes dependent upon resources that are pushed more toward students who are struggling. Gifted Education is not mandated in many states, making it elective for districts to earmark money for. Many lower-achieving districts and schools must make crisis decisions on programmes that are not high priorities. As a result, gifted students at these schools are not served, or not served effectively.

Impact on Other Parts of the Education System

Some critics have claimed that gifted programmes result in educational triage, with the gifted programme taking a disproportionate amount of school resources, leaving other pupils with much reduced resources. (See, for example, the writings of Mara Sapon-Shevin.) There is little evidence of such effects, especially in contrast with the resource consumption of special education programmes. The most common gifted programmes are also the lowest cost: skipping grades and modified assignments in the regular classroom.

Gifted programmes can also face problems with the singling out of the gifted students by regular students. Gifted students that are in the same school but under a separate programme may be victims of bullying about their intellectual gifts, since people that are singled out for a reason that might fuel a bully's insecurity (such as above-average performance intellectually), are objects of abuse. Such a programme can result in gifted students being discriminated against by other students. This obviously has negative effects on the students as well, perhaps not just limited to a dim view of 'normal' students. However, many researchers and teachers argue that while students may be teased for high intellectual capacity, they would also be able to make friends amongst peers with similar interests and abilities.

Emotional Aspects of Gifted Education

While giftedness is seen as an academic advantage, psychologically it can pose other challenges for the gifted individual. A person who is intellectually advanced may or may not be advanced in other areas. Each individual student needs to be evaluated for physical, social, and emotional skills without the traditional prejudices which either prescribe either "compensatory" weaknesses or "matching" advancement in these areas.

A person with significant academic talents often finds it difficult to fit in with schoolmates. These pressures often wane during adulthood, but they can leave a significant negative impact on emotional development.

Social pressures can cause children to "play down" their intelligence in an effort to blend in with other students. "Playing down" is a strategy often used by students with clinical depression and is seen somewhat more frequently in socially acute adolescents. This behaviour is usually discouraged by educators when they recognize it. Unfortunately, the very educators who want these children to challenge themselves and to embrace their gifts and talents are often the same people who are forced to discourage them in a mixed-ability classroom, through mechanisms like refusing to call on the talented student in class so that typical students have an opportunity to participate.

Students who are young, enthusiastic or aggressive are more likely to attract attention and to disrupt the class by working ahead, giving the correct answers all the time, asking for new assignments, or finding creative ways to entertain themselves while the rest of the class finishes an assignment. This behaviour can be mistaken for ADHD.

Academically talented students can also be the inadvertent victims of well-meaning adults who overestimate an individual student's non-intellectual talents. The adults they admire may confuse the students' obvious academic talents with general wisdom and experience. Such students may be given inappropriate liberties (such as the unsupervised use of a credit card or permission to attend parties which the same parent might refuse to a typical student), or not given normal advice on important subjects like sexual behaviours and illicit drugs.

Finally, G&T students are statistically somewhat more likely to be diagnosed with a psychiatric disability such as bipolar disorder and to become addicted to drugs or alcohol. These additional issues can require special attention in school.

Justification

Advocates of gifted education contend that gifted and/or talented youth are either motivationally, perceptually or intellectually prepared for a challenge not offered in the standard curriculum, so that it is appropriate to pace their lessons more aggressively by encouraging them to participate in honors courses, Advanced Placement courses, International Baccalaureate courses, and other sources of educational enrichment and acceleration.

They also claim that the needs of many gifted students are still neglected, as schools tend to place emphasis on improving education for the "average" student or students at the margin of success. Some argue that too many resources are diverted from gifted education to the other end of the special education spectrum, disabled students. This may be an unintended consequence of the development of disability rights litigation, which some pundits argue has led to the disabled receiving escalating resources at the expense of needed growth for gifted programmes and even for core curricula (see special education). However, many advocates believe that both special education and gifted education deserve more resources, on the general principle that each child should receive a challenge appropriate to his preparedness and motivation.

The families of gifted and/or disabled students are often dissatisfied with the education system, which, while it may suit the majority of students, often fails to provide for those with special needs.

History

BCE to the Renaissance

Gifted and talented education dates back thousands of years. In China's Tang Dynasty (580-618 CE), child prodigies were summoned to the imperial court for specialized education. Plato (c. 427—c. 347 BCE) advocated providing specialized education for intellectually gifted young men and women. Throughout the Renaissance, those who exhibited creative talent in art, architecture, and literature were supported by both the government and private patronage.

Sir Francis Galton

One of the earliest western studies of high function in humans was completed by Sir Francis Galton, who between 1888 and 1894 developed and compiled measurements of over 7,500 individuals to gauge their natural intellectual abilities. In his studies he determined that if a parent deviates from the norm, so will the child, but to a lesser extent. Galton believed that people could be improved through engineered heredity, a movement he named eugenics. He categorized people into gifted, capable, average, or degenerate and recommended breeding between the first two categories, and forced abstinence from the latter two. His term for the most intelligent and talented people was "eminence", and after studying England's most prominent families, determined that one's eminence was directly related to his direct hereditary line.

Lewis Terman

At Stanford University in 1916, Lewis Terman adapted Alfred Binet's intelligence test into the Stanford-Binet test, and created the term "intelligence quotient" (IQ). According to Terman, the IQ was one's mental age compared to one's physical age, as compared to a sampling of other people within one's age range. He defined intelligence as "the ability to carry on abstract thinking." The US Army commissioned Terman as a major during World War I, and for the first time, intelligence testing was given to a wide population of drafted soldiers. Using his own adaptation of intelligence testing, Terman developed percentiles and determined that the most gifted fell within the top

2 per cent of scores from the Stanford-Binet. Terman undertook extensive longitudinal studies of 1,500 children in California who scored within the top 2 per cent—a score of 140 or above—and continued to evaluate them throughout their lives. Subjects of these case studies were called "Termites" and the studies began in 1921, and again in 1930, 1947, and 1959 after his death. Terman's studies have to date been the most extensive on high-functioning children, and are still quoted in literature today. Common misconceptions, such as that highly intelligent children were prone to ill physical and mental health, that their intelligence burned out early in their lives, or that they either achieved greatly or underachieved, were dispelled by Terman's studies. Instead, he found that there is little relationship to the achievements of highly intelligent children in later life, and that weakness and insanity were not directly linked to high intelligence.

Leta Hollingworth

A professional colleague of Terman's, Leta Hollingworth was the first in the United States to study how best to serve students who showed evidence of high performance on tests. Although recognizing Terman's and Galton's beliefs that heredity played a vital role in intelligence, Hollingworth gave similar credit to home environment and school structure. Hollingworth worked to dispel the pervasive belief that "bright children take care of themselves" and emphasized the importance of early identification, daily contact, and grouping gifted children with others with similar abilities. Hollingworth performed an 18-year-long study of 50 children in New York City who scored 155 or above on the Stanford-Binet, and studied smaller groups of children who scored above a 180. She also ran a school in New York City for bright students that employed a curriculum of student-led exploration, as opposed to a teacher providing students with a more advanced curriculum they would encounter later in life.

The Cold War

One unforeseen result of the launch of Sputnik by the Soviet Union was the immediate emphasis on education for bright students in the United States, and this settled the question whether the federal government should get involved in public education at all. The National Defense Education Act (NDEA) was passed by Congress in 1958 with $1 billion US to bolster science, math, and technology in public education. Educators immediately pushed to identify gifted students and serve them in schools. Students chosen for gifted services were given intelligence tests with a strict cutoff, usually at 130, which meant that students who scored below the 130 were not identified.

Marland Report

The impact of the NDEA was evident in schools for years after, but a study on how effective education was meeting the needs of gifted students was initiated by the United

States Department of Education in 1969. The Marland Report, completed in 1972, for the first-time presented a general definition of giftedness, and urged districts to adopt it. The report also allowed students to show high functioning on talents and skills not measurable by an intelligence test. The Marland Report defined gifted as—

> "Children capable of high performance include those with demonstrated achievement and/or potential ability in any of the following areas, singly or in combination:
> 1. General intellectual ability,
> 2. Specific academic aptitude,
> 3. Creative or productive thinking,
> 4. Leadership ability,
> 5. Visual and performing arts, or
> 6. Psychomotor ability."

The report's definition continues to be the basis of the definition of giftedness in most districts and States.

A Nation at Risk

In 1983, the result of an 18-month-long study of secondary students was published as *A Nation at Risk,* and was an eye-opening declaration that students in the United States were no longer receiving superior education, and in fact, could not compete with students from other developed countries in many academic exercises. One of the recommendations the book made was to increase services to gifted education programmes, citing curriculum enrichment or acceleration specifically. The US federal government was also urged to create standards for the identification and servicing of gifted students.

Jacob Javits Gifted and Talented Students Education Act

The Jacob Javits Gifted and Talented Students Education Act was passed in 1988 as part of the Elementary and Secondary Education Act (ESEA). Instead of funding district-level gifted education programmes, the Javits Act instead has three primary components: the research of effective methods of testing, identification, and programming, which is performed at the National Research Center on the Gifted and Talented; the awarding of grants to colleges, states, and districts that focus on underrepresented populations of gifted students; and grants awarded to state and districts for programme implementation. Annual funding for grants must be passed by US Congress, and totaled $9.6 million US in 2007, but the money isn't promised. While he was President, George W. Bush eliminated the money every year of his term, but members of Congress overrode the president to make sure the grant money is distributed.

No Child Left Behind

The most recent US federal education initiative was signed into law in 2002. The goal of No Child Left Behind (NCLB) is to bring proficiency of all students to grade level, but critics note it does not address the needs of gifted students who perform above grade level. The act imposes punishments on schools, administrators, and teachers when students do not achieve to the plan's designs, but does not address any achievement standards for high functioning students, forcing schools and teachers to spend their time with low achieving students. An article in *The Washington Post* declared, "The unmistakable message to teachers–and to students–is that it makes no difference whether a child barely meets the proficiency standard or far exceeds it." Gifted services have been recently eroding as a result of the new legislation, according to a 2006 article in *The New York Times*.

A Nation Deceived

In 2004, the John Templeton Foundation sponsored a report titled A Nation Deceived: How Schools Hold Back America's Brightest Students, highlighting the disparity between the research on acceleration (which generally supports both it, both from an academic and a psychological point of view), and the educational practices in the US that are often contrary to the conclusions of that research. IRPA (Institute for Research and Policy on Acceleration) was established in 2006 at The Connie Belin & Jacqueline N. Blank International Center for Gifted Education and Talent Development at the University of Iowa through the support of the John Templeton Foundation following the publication of this report.

Studies of Giftedness

Differences in intelligence have been known for recorded human history, but the development of early intelligence tests by Alfred Binet led to the Stanford-Binet IQ test which was developed by Lewis Terman, who began long-term studies of gifted children with a view to checking if the popular view "early to ripen, early to rot" was true. He showed this popular belief was false and many of the children (dubbed "Terman's termites") were studied for decades.

Modern studies by James and Kulik conclude that gifted students benefit least from doing reasonably typical studies in a mixed-level class, and benefit most from learning with other similarly advanced students in accelerated or enriched classes.

Definition of Giftedness

Educational authorities differ on the definition of giftedness: even when using the same IQ test to define giftedness, they may disagree on what gifted means—one may take top 2 per cent of the population, another would take top 5 per cent of a population, which may be within a state, district, or school. Within a single school district, there can be substantial differences in the distribution of measured IQ. (The IQ for the top percentile at a high-performing school may be quite different from that at a lower performing school.)

In *Identifying Gifted Children: A Practical Guide*, Susan K. Johnsen (2004) explains that gifted children all exhibit the potential for high performance in the areas included in the United States federal definition of gifted and talented students:

> The term 'gifted and talented' when used in respect to students, children, or youth means [those who show] evidence of high performance capability in areas such as intellectual, creative, artistic, or leadership capacity, or in specific academic fields, and who require services or activities not ordinarily provided by the school in order to fully develop such capabilities.
>
> — *P.L. 103—382, Title XIV, p. 388*

The National Association for Gifted Children in the U.S. defines giftedness as:

> Students, children, or youth who give evidence of high achievement capability in areas such as intellectual, creative, artistic, or leadership capacity, or in specific academic fields, and who need services and activities not ordinarily provided by the school in order to fully develop those capabilities.

This definition has been adopted in part or completely by the majority of the states in the United States. Most have some definition similar to that used in the State of Texas, whose definition states:

> [The phrase] 'gifted and talented student' means a child or youth who performs at or shows the potential for performing at a remarkably high level of accomplishment when compared to others of the same age, experience, or environment, and who:
>
> - exhibits high performance capability in an intellectual, creative, or artistic area;
> - possesses an unusual capacity for leadership; or
> - excels in a specific academic field.
>
> — *74th legislature of the State of Texas,*
> *Chapter 29, Sub-chapter D, Section 29.121*

The major characteristics of these definitions are (*a*) the diversity of areas in which performance may be exhibited (e.g., intellectual, creative, artistic, leadership, academic), (*b*) the comparison with other groups (e.g., those in general education classrooms or of the same age, experience, or environment), and (*c*) the use of terms that imply a need for development of the gift (e.g., capability and potential).

Reliance on IQ

Some authors question the existence of "the g factor" and thus hold that the result of an IQ test is meaningless, rendering the notion of giftedness meaningless. The most famous example is *The Mismeasure of Man* by Stephen Jay Gould.

In her book, *Identifying Gifted Children: A Practical Guide,* Susan K. Johnsen (2004) argues that schools should use a variety of measures of students capability and potential when identifying gifted children. These measures may include portfolios of student work, classroom observations, achievement measures, and intelligence scores. Most educational professionals accept that no single measure can be used in isolation to accurately identify every gifted child.

Even if the notion of IQ is generally useful for identifying academically talented students who would benefit from further services, the question of the cutoff point for giftedness is still important. As noted above, different authorities often define giftedness differently.

The Theory of Positive Disintegration

Overexcitability has been a popular theme in many gifted circles over the past twenty years. Overexcitability is a component of developmental potential, a part of Dabrowski's theory of Positive Disintegration, a theory of personality development. The application of TPD to gifted education is one of several (other applications include psychotherapy, personality theory, philosophy of Man, etc.).

Global Implementation

United States

In the United States, each state department of education determines if the needs of gifted students will be addressed as a mandatory function of public education. If so, the state determines the definition of which students will be identified and receive services, but may or may not determine how they shall receive services. If a state does not consider gifted education mandatory, individual districts may, thus the definition of what gifted is, varies from state or district.

In contrast with special education, gifted education is not regulated on a US level, although recommendations by the US Department of Education are offered. As such, funding for services is not consistent from state to state, and although students may be identified, the extent to which they receive services can vary widely depending upon a state or district's budget.

AN OVERVIEW OF DISABILITY STUDIES

Disability studies is an interdisciplinary field of study, which is focused on the contributions, experiences, history, and culture of people with disabilities. The field of teaching and research in the area of disability studies is growing worldwide.

The scope of disability studies differs in different countries. In the UK, for instance, it is seen as the province of disabled people, whereas in the USA a much wider range of professions concerned with disabilities and disabled people is involved.

Disability studies is based on the premise that the disadvantage typically experienced by those who are disabled reflects primarily the way society defines and responds to certain types of 'difference'.

In 1993 an official definition of disability studies was adopted by the Society for Disability Studies, a professional organization of academics from around the world.

The Society for Disability Studies offers the following working guidelines for any programme that describes itself as 'Disability Studies':

- It should be interdisciplinary/multidisciplinary. Disability sits at the center of many overlapping disciplines in the humanities, sciences, and social sciences. Programmes in Disability Studies should encourage a curriculum that allows students, activists, teachers, artists, practitioners, and researchers to engage the subject matter from various disciplinary perspectives.
- It should challenge the view of disability as an individual deficit or defect that can be remedied solely through medical intervention or rehabilitation by "experts" and other service providers. Rather, a programme in disability studies should explore models and theories that examine social, political, cultural, and economic factors that define disability and help determine personal and collective responses to difference. At the same time, Disability Studies should work to de-stigmatize disease, illness, and impairment, including those that cannot be measured or explained by biological science. Finally, while acknowledging that medical research and intervention can be useful, Disability Studies should interrogate the connections between medical practice and stigmatizing disability.
- It should study national and international perspectives, policies, literature, culture, and history with an aim of placing current ideas of disability within their broadest possible context. Since attitudes toward disability have not been the same across times and places, much can be gained by learning from these other experiences.
- It should actively encourage participation by disabled students and faculty, and should ensure physical and intellectual access.
- It should make it a priority to have leadership positions held by disabled people; at the same time it is important to create an environment where contributions from anyone who shares the above goals are welcome.

Criticism

Disability studies is not without its critics. It has been suggested that the dominant social model, which developed in the 1970s and has served its purpose well since then, has now been outgrown, and needs major developments.

One major area of contention is the exclusion of the personal experience of impairment and illness. The social model of disability separates physical impairment from social disability, and in its most rigid form does not accept that impairment can cause disability at all. It is being increasingly recognised that the effects of impairment form a central part of many disabled people's experience, and that these effects must be included for the social model to be a valid reflection of that experience. The feminist slogan "the personal is political" has been particularly influential in these developments.

Disability studies has also been criticised for its failure to engage with multiple forms of oppression, such as racism, sexism or homophobia. As a relatively new discipline, it is true that as yet disability studies has seen little progress in this area: publications are now beginning to emerge though, and in time it is hoped that this issue will be fully engaged.

3

Educational Psychology, Child and Adolescent Psychology and Neuropsychology: An Overview

TOWARDS UNDERSTANDING EDUCATIONAL PSYCHOLOGY

Educational psychology is the study of how humans learn in educational settings, the effectiveness of educational interventions, the psychology of teaching, and the social psychology of schools as organizations. Educational psychology is concerned with how students learn and develop, often focusing on sub-groups such as gifted children and those subject to specific disabilities. Although the terms "educational psychology" and "school psychology" are often used interchangeably, researchers and theorists are likely to be identified in the US and Canada as educational psychologists, whereas practitioners in schools or school-related settings are identified as school psychologists. This distinction is however not made in the UK, where the generic term for practitioners is "educational psychologist."

Educational psychology can in part be understood through its relationship with other disciplines. It is informed primarily by psychology, bearing a relationship to that discipline analogous to the relationship between medicine and biology. Educational psychology in turn informs a wide range of specialities within educational studies, including instructional design, educational technology, curriculum development, organizational learning, special education and classroom management. Educational psychology both draws from and contributes to cognitive science and the learning sciences. In universities, departments of educational psychology are usually housed within faculties of education, possibly accounting for the lack of representation of educational psychology content in introductory psychology textbooks.

Social, Moral and Cognitive Development

To understand the characteristics of learners in childhood, adolescence, adulthood, and old age, educational psychology develops and applies theories of human development. Often represented as stages through which people pass as they mature, developmental theories describe changes in mental abilities (cognition), social roles, moral reasoning, and beliefs about the nature of knowledge.

For example, educational psychologists have researched the instructional applicability of Jean Piaget's theory of development, according to which children mature through four stages of cognitive capability. Piaget hypothesized that children are not capable of abstract logical thought until they are older than about 11 years, and therefore younger children need to be taught using concrete objects and examples. Researchers have found that transitions, such as from concrete to abstract logical thought, do not occur at the same time in all domains. A child may be able to think abstractly about mathematics, but remain limited to concrete thought when reasoning about human relationships. Perhaps Piaget's most enduring contribution is his insight that people actively construct their understanding through a self-regulatory process.

Piaget proposed a developmental theory of moral reasoning in which children progress from a naive understanding of morality based on behaviour and outcomes to a more advanced understanding based on intentions. Piaget's views of moral development were elaborated by Kohlberg into a stage theory of moral development. There is evidence that the moral reasoning described in stage theories is not sufficient to account for moral behaviour. For example, other factors such as modeling (as described by the social cognitive theory of morality) are required to explain bullying.

Rudolf Steiner's model of child development interrelates physical, emotional, cognitive, and moral development in developmental stages similar to those later described by Piaget.

Developmental theories are sometimes presented not as shifts between qualitatively different stages, but as gradual increments on separate dimensions. Development of epistemological beliefs (beliefs about knowledge) have been described in terms of gradual changes in people's belief in: certainty and permanence of knowledge, fixedness of ability, and credibility of authorities such as teachers and experts. People develop more sophisticated beliefs about knowledge as they gain in education and maturity.

Individual Differences and Disabilities

Each person has an individual profile of characteristics, abilities and challenges that result from learning and development. These manifest as individual differences in intelligence, creativity, cognitive style, motivation, and the capacity to process information, communicate, and relate to others. The most prevalent disabilities found among school age children are Attention-Deficit Hyperactivity Disorder (ADHD), learning disability, dyslexia, and speech disorder. Less common disabilities include mental retardation, hearing impairment, cerebral palsy, epilepsy, and blindness.

Although theories of intelligence have been discussed by philosophers since Plato, intelligence testing is an invention of educational psychology, and is coincident with the development of that discipline. Continuing debates about the nature of intelligence revolve on whether intelligence can be characterized by a single factor known as general intelligence, multiple factors (e.g., Gardner's theory of multiple intelligences), or whether it can be measured at all. In practice, standardized instruments such as the Stanford-Binet IQ test and the WISC are widely used in economically developed countries to identify children in need of individualized educational treatment. Children classified as gifted are often provided with accelerated or enriched programmes. Children with identified deficits may be provided with enhanced education in specific skills such as phonological awareness.

Learning and Cognition

Two fundamental assumptions that underlie formal education systems are that students (a) retain knowledge and skills they acquire in school, and (b) can apply them in situations outside the classroom. But are these assumptions accurate? Research has found that, even when students report not using the knowledge acquired in school, a considerable portion is retained for many years and long-term retention is strongly dependent on the initial level of mastery. One study found that university students who took a child development course and attained high grades showed, when tested 10 years later, average retention scores of about 30 per cent, whereas those who obtained moderate or lower grades showed average retention scores of about 20 per cent. There is much less consensus on the crucial question of how much knowledge acquired in school transfers to tasks encountered outside formal educational settings, and how such transfer occurs. Some psychologists claim that research evidence for this type of *far transfer* is scarce, while others claim there is abundant evidence of far transfer in specific domains. Several perspectives have been established within which the theories of learning used in educational psychology are formed and contested. These include behaviourism, cognitivism, social cognitive theory, and constructivism. This section summarizes how educational psychology has researched and applied theories within each of these perspectives.

Behavioural Perspective

Applied behaviour analysis, a set of techniques based on the behavioural principles of operant conditioning, is effective in a range of educational settings. For example, teachers can improve student behaviour by systematically rewarding students who follow classroom rules with praise, stars, or tokens exchangeable for sundry items. Despite the demonstrated efficacy of awards in changing behaviour, their use in education has been criticized by proponents of self-determination theory, who claim that praise and other rewards undermine intrinsic motivation. There is evidence that tangible rewards decrease intrinsic motivation in specific situations, such as when the student already has a high level of intrinsic motivation to perform the goal behaviour. But the results showing detrimental effects are counterbalanced by evidence that, in other situations, such as when rewards are given for attaining a gradually increasing standard of performance, rewards enhance intrinsic motivation. Many effective therapies have been based on the principles of Applied Behaviour Analysis, including Pivotal Response Therapy which is used to treat Autism Spectrum Disorders.

Cognitive Perspective

Among current educational psychologists, the cognitive perspective is more widely held than the behavioural perspective perhaps because it admits causally related mental constructs such as traits, beliefs, memories, motivations and emotions. Cognitive theories claim that memory structures determine how information is perceived, processed, stored, retrieved and forgotten. Among the memory structures theorized by cognitive psychologists are separate but linked visual and verbal systems described by Allan Paivio's dual coding theory. Educational psychologists have used dual coding theory and cognitive load theory to explain how people learn from multimedia presentations.

The spaced learning effect, a cognitive phenomenon strongly supported by psychological research, has broad applicability within education. For example, students have been found to perform better on a test of knowledge about a text passage when a second reading of the passage is delayed rather than immediate. Educational psychology research has confirmed the applicability to education of other findings from cognitive psychology, such as the benefits of using mnemonics for immediate and delayed retention of information.

Problem solving, regarded by many cognitive psychologists as fundamental to learning, is an important research topic in educational psychology. A student is thought to interpret a problem by assigning it to a schema retrieved from long-term memory. When the problem is assigned to the wrong schema, the student's attention is subsequently directed away from features of the problem that are inconsistent with the assigned schema. The critical step of finding a mapping between the problem and a pre-existing schema is often cited as supporting the centrality of analogical thinking to problem solving.

Social Cognitive Perspective

Social cognitive theory is a highly influential fusion of behavioural, cognitive and social elements that was initially developed by educational psychologist Albert Bandura. In its earlier, neo-behavioural incarnation called *social learning theory*, Bandura emphasized the process of observational learning in which a learner's behaviour changes as a result of observing others' behaviour and its consequences. The theory identified several factors that determine whether observing a model will affect behavioural or cognitive change. These factors include the learner's developmental status, the perceived prestige and competence of the model, the consequences received by the model, the relevance of the model's behaviours and consequences to the learner's goals, and the learner's self-efficacy. The concept of self-efficacy, which played an important role in later developments of the theory, refers to the learner's belief in his or her ability to perform the modelled behaviour.

An experiment by Schunk and Hanson, that studied grade 2 students who had previously experienced difficulty in learning subtraction, illustrates the type of research stimulated by social learning theory. One group of students observed a subtraction demonstration by a teacher and then participated in an instructional programme on subtraction. A second group observed other grade 2 students performing the same subtraction procedures and then participated in the same instructional programme. The students who observed peer models scored higher on a subtraction post-test and also reported greater confidence in their subtraction ability. The results were interpreted as supporting the hypothesis that perceived similarity of the model to the learner increases self-efficacy, leading to more effective learning of modeled behaviour. It is supposed that peer modeling is particularly effective for students who have low self-efficacy.

Over the last decade, much research activity in educational psychology has focused on developing theories of Self-Regulated Learning (SRL) and metacognition. These theories work from the central premise that effective learners are active agents who construct knowledge by setting goals, analysing tasks, planning strategies and monitoring their understanding. Research has indicated that learners who are better at goal setting and self-monitoring tend to have greater intrinsic task interest and self-efficacy; and that teaching learning strategies can increase academic achievement.

Constructivist Perspective

Constructivism is a category of learning theories in which emphasis is placed on the agency and prior knowledge of the learner, and often on the social and cultural determinants of the learning process. Educational psychologists distinguish individual (or psychological) constructivism, identified with Piaget's learning theory, from social constructivism. A dominant influence on the latter type is Lev Vygotsky's work on sociocultural learning, describing how interactions with adults, more capable peers, and cognitive tools are internalized to form mental constructs. Elaborating on Vygotsky's theory, Jerome Bruner and other educational psychologists developed the important concept of instructional scaffolding, in which the social or information environment offers supports for learning that are gradually withdrawn as they become internalized.

Motivation

Motivation is an internal state that activates, guides and sustains behaviour. Educational psychology research on motivation is concerned with the volition or will that students bring to a task, their level of interest and intrinsic motivation, the personally held goals that guide their behaviour, and their belief about the causes of their success or failure.

A form of attribution theory developed by Bernard Weiner describes how students' beliefs about the causes of academic success or failure affect their emotions and motivations. For example, when students attribute failure to lack of ability, and ability is perceived as uncontrollable, they experience the emotions of shame and embarrassment and consequently decrease effort and show poorer performance. In contrast, when students attribute failure to lack of effort, and effort is perceived as controllable, they experience the emotion of guilt and consequently increase effort and show improved performance.

Motivational theories also explain how learners' goals affect the way that they engage with academic tasks. Those who have *mastery goals* strive to increase their ability and knowledge. Those who have *performance approach goals* strive for high grades and seek opportunities to demonstrate their abilities. Those who have *performance avoidance* goals are driven by fear of failure and avoid situations where their abilities are exposed. Research has found that mastery goals are associated with many positive outcomes such as persistence in the face of failure, preference for challenging tasks, creativity and intrinsic motivation. Performance avoidance goals are associated with negative outcomes such as poor concentration while studying, disorganized studying, less self-regulation, shallow information processing and test anxiety. Performance approach goals are associated with positive outcomes, and some negative outcomes such as an unwillingness to seek help and shallow information processing.

Research Methodology

The research methods used in educational psychology tend to be drawn from psychology and other social sciences. There is also a history of significant methodological innovation by educational psychologists, and psychologists investigating educational problems. Research methods address problems in both research design and data analysis. Research design informs the planning of experiments and observational studies to ensure that their results have internal, external and ecological validity. Data analysis encompasses methods for processing both quantitive (numerical) and qualitative (non-numerical) research data. Although, historically, the use of quantitative methods was often considered an essential mark of scholarship, modern educational psychology research uses both quantitative and qualitative methods.

Quantitative Methods

Perhaps first among the important methodological innovations of educational psychology was the development and application of factor analysis by Charles Spearman. Factor analysis is mentioned here as one example of the many multivariate statistical methods used by educational psychologists. Factor analysis is used to summarize relationships among a large set of variables or test questions, develop theories about mental constructs such as self-efficacy or anxiety, and assess the reliability and validity of test scores. Over one hundred years after its introduction by Spearman, factor analysis has become a research staple figuring prominently in educational psychology journals.

Because educational assessment is fundamental to most quantitative research in the field, educational psychologists have made significant contributions to the field of psychometrics. For example, alpha, the widely used measure of test reliability was developed by educational psychologist Lee Cronbach. The reliability of assessments are routinely reported in quantitative educational research. Although, originally, educational measurement methods were built on classical test theory, item response theory and Rasch models are now used extensively in educational measurement worldwide. These models afford advantages over classical test theory, including the capacity to produce standard errors of measurement for each score or pattern of scores on assessments and the capacity to handle missing responses.

Meta-analysis, the combination of individual research results to produce a quantitative literature review, is another methodological innovation with a close association to educational psychology. In a meta-analysis, effect sizes that represent, for example, the differences between treatment groups in a set of similar experiments, are averaged to obtain a single aggregate value representing the best estimate of the effect of treatment. Several decades after Pearson's work with early versions of meta-analysis, Glass published the first application of modern meta-analytic techniques and triggered their broad application across the social and biomedical sciences. Today, meta-analysis is among the most common types of literature review found in educational psychology research.

Other quantitative research issues associated with educational psychology include the use of nested research designs (e.g., a student nested within a classroom, which is nested within a school, which is nested within a district, etc.) and the use of longitudinal statistical models to measure change.

Qualitative Methods

Qualitative methods are used in educational studies whose purpose is to describe events, processes and situations of theoretical significance. The qualitative methods used in educational psychology often derive from anthropology, sociology or sociolinguistics. For example, the anthropological method of ethnography has been used to describe teaching and learning in classrooms. In studies of this type, the researcher may gather detailed field notes as a participant observer or passive observer. Later, the notes and other data may be categorized and interpreted by methods such as grounded theory. Triangulation, the practice of cross-checking findings with multiple data sources, is highly valued in qualitative research.

Case studies are forms of qualitative research focusing on a single person, organization, event, or other entity. In one case study, researchers conducted a 150-minute, semi-structured interview with a 20-years old woman who had a history of suicidal thinking between the ages of 14 to 18. They analyzed an audio-recording of the interview to understand the roles of cognitive development, identity formation and social attachment in ending her suicidal thinking.

Qualitative analysis is most often applied to verbal data from sources such as conversations, interviews, focus groups, and personal journals. Qualitative methods are thus, typically, approaches to gathering, processing and reporting verbal data. One of the most commonly used methods for qualitative research in educational psychology is protocol analysis. In this method the research participant is asked to *think aloud* while performing a task, such as solving a math problem. In protocol analysis the verbal data is thought to indicate which information the subject is attending to, but is explicitly not interpreted as an explanation or justification for behaviour. In contrast, the method of verbal analysis does admit learners' explanations as a way to reveal their mental model or misconceptions (e.g., of the laws of motion). The most fundamental operations in both protocol and verbal analysis are segmenting (isolating) and categorizing sections of verbal data. Conversation analysis and discourse analysis, sociolinguistic methods that focus more specifically on the structure of conversational interchange (e.g., between a teacher and student), have been used to assess the process of conceptual change in science learning. Qualitative methods are also used to analyse information in a variety of media, such as students' drawings and concept maps, video-recorded interactions, and computer log records.

Applications in Instructional Design and Technology

Instructional design, the systematic design of materials, activities and interactive environments for learning, is broadly informed by educational psychology theories and research. For example, in defining learning goals or objectives, instructional designers often use a taxonomy of educational objectives created by Benjamin Bloom and colleagues. Bloom also researched mastery learning, an instructional strategy in which learners only advance to a new learning objective after they have mastered its prerequisite objectives. Bloom discovered that a combination of mastery learning with one-to-one tutoring is highly effective, producing learning outcomes far exceeding those normally achieved in classroom instruction. Gagné, another psychologist, had earlier developed an influential method of task analysis in which a terminal learning goal is expanded into a hierarchy of learning objectives connected by prerequisite relations.

- Intelligent tutoring system
- Educational technology
- John R. Anderson
- Cognitive tutor
- Cooperative learning
- Collaborative learning
- Problem-based learning
- Computer supported collaborative learning
- William Winn
- Constructive alignment.

Applications in Teaching

Research on classroom management and pedagogy is conducted to guide teaching practice and form a foundation for teacher education programmes. The goals of classroom management are to create an environment conducive to learning and to develop students' self-management skills. More specifically, classroom management strives to create positive teacher-student and peer relationships, manage student groups to sustain on-task behaviour, and use counselling and other psychological methods to aid students who present persistent psychosocial problems.

Introductory educational psychology is a commonly required area of study in most North American teacher education programmes. When taught in that context, its content varies, but it typically emphasizes learning theories (especially cognitively oriented ones), issues about motivation, assessment of students' learning, and classroom management. A developing Wikibook about educational psychology gives more detail about the educational psychology topics that are typically presented in preservice teacher education.

- Special education
- Lesson plan
- More about applications to classroom teaching.

History

Educational psychology cannot claim priority in the systematic analysis of educational processes. Philosophers of education such as Democritus, Quintilian, Vives and Comenius, had examined, classified and judged the methods of education centuries before the beginnings of psychology in the late 1800s. Instead, aspirations of the new discipline rested on the application of the scientific methods of observation and experimentation to educational problems. Even in the earliest years of the discipline, educational psychologists recognized the limitations of this new approach. In his famous series of lectures *Talks to Teachers on Psychology*, published in 1899 and now regarded as the first educational psychology textbook, the pioneering American psychologist William James commented that:

> "Psychology is a science, and teaching is an art; and sciences never generate arts directly out of themselves. An intermediate inventive mind must make that application, by using its originality."

According to Berliner educational psychology theorists' attitude to the world of educational practice has shifted from initial interest to disdain, and eventually to respect.

- Charles Hubbard Judd

In 1912, Thorndike, who developed the theory of instrumental conditioning, presaged later work on programmed instruction, mastery learning and computer-based learning:

> "If, by a miracle of mechanical ingenuity, a book could be so arranged that only to him who had done what was directed on page one would page two become visible, and so on, much that now requires personal instruction could be managed by print."

Among the few works of educational psychology historiography is *Educational Psychology: A Century of Contributions* which presents chapter-length biographies of 16 eminent scholars whose work has significantly influenced the development of educational psychology.

Careers in Educational Psychology

Education and Training

A person may be considered an educational psychologist after completing a graduate degree in educational psychology or a closely related field. Universities establish educational psychology graduate programmes in either psychology departments or, more commonly, faculties of education.

Educational psychologists work in a variety of settings. Some work in university settings where they carry out research on the cognitive and social processes of human development, learning and education. Educational psychologists may also work as consultants in designing and creating educational materials, classroom programmes and online courses.

Educational psychologists who work in k-12 school settings (called school psychologists in the United States) are trained at the masters and doctoral levels. In addition to conducting assessments, school psychologists provide services such as academic and behavioural intervention, counseling, teacher consultation, and crisis intervention.

In the UK, status as a *Chartered Educational Psychologist* is gained by completing:

- an undergraduate degree in psychology permitting registration with the British Psychological Society.
- two or three years experience working with children, young people and their families.
- a three-year professional doctorate in educational psychology.

The previous requirement to train and work for two years as a teacher has now been abandoned.

Employment Outlook

Employment for psychologists in the United States is expected to grow faster than most occupations through the year 2014, with anticipated growth of 18-26 per cent. One in four psychologist are employed in educational settings. In the United States, the median salary for psychologists in primary and secondary schools is $58,360 as of May 2004.

In recent decades the participation of women as professional researchers in North American educational psychology has risen dramatically. The percentage of female authors of peer-reviewed journal articles doubled from 1976 (24%) to 1995 (51%), and has since remained constant. Female membership on educational psychology journal editorial boards increased from 17 per cent in 1976 to 47 per cent in 2004. Over the same period, the proportion of chief editor positions held by women increased from 22 per cent to 70 per cent.

Research Journals

There are several peer-reviewed research journals in educational psychology tracked by Journal Citation Reports. The most highly cited journals related to educational psychology are currently *Child Development* and *Educational Psychologist*.

KNOWING THE CHILD

A child (plural: children) is a human being between the stages of birth and puberty. The legal definition of "child" generally refers to a minor, otherwise known as a person younger than the age of majority. "Child" may also describe a relationship with a parent or authority figure, or signify group membership in a clan, tribe, or religion; it can also signify being strongly affected by a specific time, place, or circumstance, as in "a child of nature" or "a child of the Sixties."

Definitions

The United Nations Convention on the Rights of the Child defines a child as "every human being below the age of 18 years unless under the law applicable to the child, majority is attained earlier." Biologically, a child is anyone in the developmental stage of childhood, between infancy and adulthood.

Attitudes Toward Children

Social attitudes toward children differ around the world in various cultures. These attitudes have changed over time. A 1988 study on European attitudes toward the centrality of children found that Italy was more child-centric and Holland less child-centric, with other countries, such as Austria, Great Britain, Ireland and West Germany falling in between.

Age of Responsibility

The age at which children are considered responsible for their own actions has also changed over time, and this is reflected in the way they are treated in courts of law. In Roman times, children were regarded as not culpable for crimes, a position later adopted by the Church. In the nineteenth century, children younger than seven years old were believed incapable of crime. Children from the age of seven were considered responsible for their actions. Therefore, they could face criminal charges, be sent to adult prison, and be punished like adults by whipping, branding or hanging.

In at least 25 countries of the world there is no specified age for compulsory education; at least 33 US States have no minimum age of employment and in 44 girls can be married earlier than boys. In at least 125 countries children may be taken to court and risk imprisonment for criminal acts at an age between 7 and 15, often the age range for compulsory education. Moreover, in the same country, it is not rare to find that children are legally obliged to go to school until they are 14 or 15 years old but a different law allows them to work at an earlier age or to be married at the age of 12 or to be criminally responsible from the age of 7. Being aware of the legal situation of children around the world is necessary for designing effective measures to improve it. Based on States Parties' reports under the Convention on the Rights of the Child (CRC) and therefore reflecting States' representations of their own practice, *At what age?* brings to light problems that are not—but should be—effectively addressed: at what age do children become adults and lose their protection under the Convention on the Rights of the Child? Children's right to education is currently under threat from early marriage, child labour and imprisonment; States have not adapted their legislation in favour of the right to education, and they do not have agreed standards for the transition from childhood to adulthood either internationally or nationally. Often taken as the guarantor of childhood until 18, the Convention on the Rights of the Child in fact states in article 1 that: "a child means every human being below the age of eighteen years unless, under the law applicable to the child, majority is attained earlier." The latter element, a limitation, substantially weakens the operative part of the article and provides justification for differing interpretations and practice. It is an acknowledgement that not even the age of majority is the same in all countries.

UNDERSTANDING CHILD DEVELOPMENT

Child development refers to the biological and psychological changes that occur in human beings between birth and the end of adolescence, as the individual progresses from dependency to increasing autonomy. Because these developmental changes may be strongly influenced by genetic factors and events during prenatal life, genetics and prenatal development are usually included as part of the study of child development. Related terms include "developmental psychology", referring to development throughout the lifespan and "pediatrics", the branch of medicine relating to the care of children. Developmental change may occur as a result of genetically-controlled processes known as maturation, or as a result of environmental factors and learning, but most commonly involves an interaction between the two.

There are various definitions of periods in child development, since each period is a continuum with individual differences regarding start and ending.

Some age-related development periods and examples of defined intervals are: newborn (ages 0—1 month); infant (ages 1 month—1 year); toddler (ages 1—3 years); preschooler (ages 4—6 years); school-aged child (ages 6—13 years); adolescent (ages 13—20). However, organizations like Zero to Three and the World Association for Infant Mental Health use the term infant as a broad category, including children from birth to age 3, a logical decision considering that the Latin derivation of the word infant refers to those who have no speech.

The optimal development of children is considered vital to society and so it is important to understand the social, cognitive, emotional, and educational development of children. Increased research and interest in this field has resulted in new theories and strategies, with specific regard to practice that promotes development within the school system. In addition there are also some theories that seek to describe a sequence of states that comprise child development.

Theories

Ecological Systems Theory

Also called "Development in Context" or "Human Ecology" theory, Ecological Systems Theory, originally formulated by Urie Bronfenbrenner specifies four types of nested environmental systems, with bi-directional influences within and between the systems. The four systems are Microsystem, Mesosystem, Exosystem, and Macrosystem. Each system contains roles, norms and rules that can powerfully shape development. Since its publication in 1979, Bronfenbrenner's major statement of this theory, *The Ecology of Human Development* has had widespread influence on the way psychologists and others approach the study of human beings and their environments. As a result of this influential conceptualization of development, these environments—from the family to economic and political structures—have come to be viewed as part of the life course from childhood through adulthood.

Piaget

Piaget was a French speaking Swiss theorist who posited that children learn through actively constructing knowledge through hands-on experience. He suggested that the adult's role in helping the child learn was to provide appropriate materials for the child to interact and construct. He would use Socratic questioning to get the children to reflect on what they were doing. He would try to get them to see contradictions in their explanations. He also developed stages of development. His approach can be seen in how the curriculum is sequenced in schools, and in the pedagogy of preschool centers across the United States.

Vygotsky

Vygotsky was a theorist whose ideas emerged in the last few decades from behind what was known as the Iron Curtain, in the former Soviet Union. He posited that children learn through hands-on experience, as Piaget suggested. However, unlike Piaget, he claimed that timely and sensitive intervention by adults when a child is on the edge of learning a new task (called the Zone of Proximal Development) could help children learn new tasks. This technique is called "scaffolding," because it builds upon knowledge children already have with new knowledge that adults can help the child learn. An example of this might be when a parent "helps" an infant clap or roll his hands to the pat-a-cake rhyme, until he can clap and roll his hands himself.

Vygotsky was strongly focused on the role of culture in determining the child's pattern of development. He argued that "Every function in the child's cultural development appears twice: first, on the social level, and later, on the individual level; first, between people (interpsychological) and then inside the child (intrapsychological). This applies equally to voluntary attention, to logical memory, and to the formation of concepts. All the higher functions originate as actual relationships between individuals."

Many theorists posit stage theories, but Vygotsky did not support stages at all, asserting instead that development was a process.

Attachment Theory

Attachment theory, originating in the work of John Bowlby and developed by Mary Ainsworth, is a psychological, evolutionary and ethological theory that provides a descriptive and explanatory framework for understanding interpersonal relationships between human beings. Attachment theorists consider the human infant to have a need for a secure relationship with adult caregivers, without which normal social and emotional development will not occur.

Erik Erikson

Erikson, a follower of Freud's, synthesized both Freud's and his own theories to create what is known as the "psychosocial" stages of human development, which span from birth to death, and focuses on "tasks" at each stage that must be accomplished to successfully navigate life's challenges.

Other Theories

John B. Watson's behaviourism theory forms the foundation of the behavioural model of development. He wrote extensively on child development and conducted research (see Little Albert experiment). Watson was instrumental in the modification of William James' stream of consciousness approach to construct a stream of behaviour theory. Watson also helped bring a natural science perspective to child psychology by introducing objective research methods based on observable and measurable behaviour. Following Watson's lead, B.F. Skinner further extended this model to cover operant conditioning and verbal behaviour.

In accordance with his view of a basic human motivation being the sexual drive, Sigmund Freud developed a psychosexual theory of human development from infancy onward, divided into five stages. Each stage centered around the gratification of the libido within a particular area, or erogenous zone, of the body. He also argued that as humans develop, they become fixated on different and specific objects through their stages of development. Each stage contains conflict which requires resolution to enable the child to develop.

The use of dynamical systems theory as a framework for the consideration of development began in the early 1990s and has continued into the present century. Dynamic systems theory stresses nonlinear connections (e.g., between earlier and later social assertiveness) and the capacity of a system to reorganize as a phase shift that is stage-like in nature. Another useful concept for developmentalists is the attractor state, a condition (such as teething or stranger anxiety) that helps to determine apparently unrelated behaviours as well as related ones. Dynamic systems theory has been applied extensively to the study of motor development; the theory also has strong associations with some of Bowlby's views about attachment systems. Dynamic systems theory also relates to the concept of the transactional process, a mutually interactive process in which children and parents simultaneously influence each other, producing developmental change in both over time.

The Core Knowledge Perspective is an evolutionary theory in child development that proposes "infants begin life with innate, special-purpose knowledge systems referred to as core domains of thought." There are five core domains of thought, each of which is crucial for survival, which simultaneously prepare us to develop key aspects of early cognition; they are: physical, numerical, linguistic, psychological, and biological.

Continuity and Discontinuity in Development

Although the identification of developmental milestones is of interest to researchers and to children's caregivers, many aspects of developmental change are continuous and do not display noticeable milestones of change. Continuous developmental changes, like growth in stature, involve fairly gradual and predictable progress toward adult characteristics. When developmental change is discontinuous, however, researchers may identify not only milestones of development, but related age periods often called stages. A stage is a period of time, often associated with a known chronological age range, during which a behaviour or physical characteristic is qualitatively different from what it is at other ages. When an age period is referred to as a stage, the term implies not only this qualitative difference, but also a predictable sequence of developmental events, such that each stage is both preceded and followed by specific other periods associated with characteristic behavioural or physical qualities.

Stages of development may overlap or be associated with specific other aspects of development, such as speech or movement. Even within a particular developmental area, transition into a stage may not mean that the previous stage is completely finished. For example, in Erikson's discussion of stages of personality, this theorist suggests that a lifetime is spent in reworking issues that were originally characteristic of a childhood stage. Similarly, the theorist of cognitive development, Piaget, described situations in which children could solve one type of problem using mature thinking skills, but could not accomplish this for less familiar problems, a phenomenon he called horizontal decalage.

Mechanisms of Development

Although developmental change runs parallel with chronological age, age itself cannot cause development. The basic mechanisms or causes of developmental change are genetic factors and environmental factors. Genetic factors are responsible for cellular changes like overall growth, changes in proportion of body and brain parts, and the maturation of aspects of function such as vision and dietary needs. Because genes can be "turned off" and "turned on", the individual's initial genotype may change in function over time, giving rise to further developmental change. Environmental factors affecting development may include both diet and disease exposure, as well as social, emotional, and cognitive experiences. However, examination of environmental factors also shows that young human beings can survive within a fairly broad range of environmental experiences.

Rather than acting as independent mechanisms, genetic and environmental factors often interact to cause developmental change. Some aspects of child development are notable for their plasticity, or the extent to which the direction of development is guided by environmental factors as well as initiated by genetic factors. For example, the development of allergic reactions appears to be caused by exposure to certain environmental factors relatively early in life, and protection from early exposure makes the child less likely to show later allergic reactions. When an aspect of development is strongly affected by early experience, it is said to show a high degree of plasticity; when the genetic make-up is the primary cause of development, plasticity is said to be low. Plasticity may involve guidance by endogenous factors like hormones as well as by exogenous factors like infection.

One kind of environmental guidance of development has been described as experience-dependent plasticity, in which behaviour is altered as a result of learning from the environment. Plasticity of this type can occur throughout the lifespan and may involve many kinds of behaviour, including some emotional reactions. A second type of plasticity, experience-expectant plasticity, involves the strong effect of specific experiences during limited sensitive periods of development. For example, the coordinated use of the two eyes, and the experience of a single three-dimensional image rather than the two-dimensional images created by light in each eye, depend on experiences with vision during the second half of the first year of life. Experience-expectant plasticity works to fine-tune aspects of development that cannot proceed to optimum outcomes as a result of genetic factors working alone.

In addition to the existence of plasticity in some aspects of development, genetic-environmental correlations may function in several ways to determine the mature characteristics of the individual. Genetic-environmental correlations are circumstances in which genetic factors make certain experiences more likely to occur. For example, in passive genetic-environmental correlation, a child is likely to experience a particular environment because his or her parents' genetic make-up makes them likely to choose or create such an environment. In evocative genetic-environmental correlation, the child's genetically-caused characteristics cause other people to respond in certain ways, providing a different environment than might occur for a genetically-different child;

for instance, a child with Down syndrome may be treated more protectively and less challengingly than a non-Down child. Finally, an active genetic-environmental correlation is one in which the child chooses experiences that in turn have their effect; for instance, a muscular, active child may choose after-school sports experiences that create increased athletic skills, but perhaps preclude music lessons. In all of these cases, it becomes difficult to know whether child characteristics were shaped by genetic factors, by experiences, or by a combination of the two.

Research Issues and Methods

Establishing a useful understanding of child development requires systematic inquiry about developmental events. Different aspects of development involve different patterns and causes of change, so there is no simple way to summarize child development. Nevertheless, the answering of certain questions about each topic can yield comparable information about various aspects of developmental change. The following questions were suggested for this purpose by Waters and his colleagues. (1) What develops? What relevant aspects of the individual change over a period of time? (2) What are the rate and speed of development? (3) What are the mechanisms of development—what aspects of experience and heredity cause developmental change? (4) Are there normal individual differences in the relevant developmental changes? (5) Are there population differences in this aspect of development (for example, differences in the development of boys and of girls)?

Empirical research that attempts to answer these questions may follow a number of patterns. Initially, observational research in naturalistic conditions may be needed to develop a narrative describing and defining an aspect of developmental change, such as changes in reflex reactions in the first year. This type of work may be followed by correlational studies, collecting information about chronological age and some type of development such as vocabulary growth; correlational statistics can be used to state the connection between the two. Comparative studies examining the extent and course of development over time are the basic method for studying developmental change. Such studies examine the characteristics of children at different ages. These methods may involve longitudinal studies, in which a group of children are re-examined on a number of occasions as they get older, or cross-sectional studies, in which groups of children of different ages are tested once and compared with each other, or there may be a combination of these approaches. Some child development studies examine the effects of experience or heredity by comparing characteristics of different groups of children in a necessarily non-randomized design. Other studies can use randomized designs to compare outcomes for groups of children who receive different interventions or educational treatments.

Developmental Milestones

Milestones are changes in specific physical and mental abilities (such as walking and understanding language) that mark the end of one developmental period and the beginning of another. For stage theories, milestones indicate a stage transition. Studies of the accomplishment of many developmental tasks have established typical chronological ages associated with developmental milestones. However, there is considerable variation in the achievement of milestones, even between children with developmental trajectories within the normal range. Some milestones are more variable than others; for example, receptive speech indicators do not show much variation among children with normal hearing, but expressive speech milestones can be quite variable.

A common concern in child development is developmental delay involving a delay in an age-specific ability for important developmental milestones. Prevention of and early intervention in developmental delay are significant topics in the study of child development. Developmental delays should be diagnosed by comparison with characteristic variability of a milestone, not with respect to average age at achievement. An example of a milestone would be eye-hand coordination, which includes a child's increasing ability to manipulate objects in a coordinated manner. Increased knowledge of age-specific milestones allows parents and others to keep track of appropriate development.

Aspects of Child Development

Child development is not a matter of a single topic, but progresses somewhat differently for different aspects of the individual. Here are descriptions of the development of a number of physical and mental characteristics.

Physical Growth

What Develops?

Physical growth in stature and weight occurs over the 15-20 years following birth, as the individual changes from the average weight of 3.5 kg and length of 50 cm at full-term birth to full adult size. As stature and weight increase, the individual's proportions also change, from the relatively large head and small torso and limbs of the neonate, to the adult's relatively small head and long torso and limbs.

Speed and Pattern of Development

The speed of physical growth is rapid in the months after birth, then slows, so birth weight is doubled in the first four months, tripled by age 12 months, but not quadrupled until 24 months. Growth then proceeds at a slow rate until shortly before puberty (between about 9 and 15 years of age), when a period of rapid growth occurs. Growth is not uniform in rate and timing across all body parts. At birth, head size is already relatively near to that of an adult, but the lower parts of the body are much smaller than adult size. In the course of development, then, the head grows relatively little, and torso and limbs undergo a great deal of growth.

Mechanisms of Developmental Change

Genetic factors play a major role in determining the growth rate, and particularly the changes in proportion characteristic of early human development. However, genetic factors can produce the maximum growth only if environmental conditions are adequate. Poor nutrition and frequent injury and disease can reduce the individual's adult stature, but the best environment cannot cause growth to a greater stature than is determined by heredity.

Population Differences

Population differences in growth are largely related to adult stature. Ethnic groups that are quite tall in adulthood are also longer at birth and throughout childhood, as compared to groups that have short adult stature. Males are also somewhat taller, although this is more apparent in ethnic groups with strong sexual dimorphism in adulthood. Populations that are characteristically malnourished are also shorter throughout life. However, there are few population differences in growth rates or patterns, except that poor environmental conditions may delay puberty and the associated growth spurt. The markedly different age at puberty of boys and girls means that boys and girls of age 11 or 12 are at very different points in maturation and may reverse the usual sex difference in physical size.

Individual Differences

Individual differences in height and weight during childhood are considerable. Some of these differences are due to family genetic factors, others to environmental factors, but at some points in development they may be strongly influenced by individual differences in reproductive maturation.

Motor Development

What Develops?

Abilities for physical movement change through childhood from the largely reflexive (unlearned, involuntary) movement patterns of the young infant to the highly skilled voluntary movements characteristic of later childhood and adolescence. (Of course, older children and adolescents retain some reflex movements in addition to developing voluntary movement.)

Speed and Pattern of Development

The speed of motor development is rapid in early life, as many of the reflexes of the newborn alter or disappear within the first year, and slows later. Like physical growth, motor development shows predictable patterns of cephalocaudal (head to foot) and proximodistal (torso to extremities) development, with movements at the head end and in the more central areas coming under control before those of the lower part of the body or the hands and feet. Types of movement develop in stage-like sequences; for example, locomotion at 6-8 months involves creeping on all fours, then proceeds to pulling to stand, "cruising" while holding on to an object, walking while holding an adult's hand, and finally walking independently. Older children continue the sequence by walking sideways or backward, galloping, hopping, skipping with one foot and walking with the other, and finally skipping. By middle childhood and adolescence, new motor skills are acquired by instruction or observation rather than in a predictable sequence.

Mechanisms of Motor Development

The mechanisms involved in motor development involve some genetic components that determine the physical size of body parts at a given age, as well as aspects of muscle and bone strength. Nutrition and exercise also determine strength and therefore the ease and accuracy with which a body part can be moved. Opportunities to carry out movements help establish the abilities to flex (move toward the trunk) and extend body parts, both capacities being needed for good motor ability. Skilled voluntary movements develop as a result of practice and learning.

Individual Differences

Normal individual differences in motor ability are common and depend in part on the child's weight and build. However, after the infant period, normal individual differences are strongly affected by opportunities to practice, observe, and be instructed on specific movements. Atypical motor development may be an indication of developmental delays or problems such as autism or cerebral palsy.

Population Differences

There are some population differences in motor development, with girls showing some advantages in small muscle use, including articulation of sounds with lips and tongue. Ethnic differences in reflex movements of newborn infants have been reported, suggesting that some biological factor is at work. Cultural differences may encourage learning of motor skills like using the left hand only for sanitary purposes and the right hand for all other uses, producing a population difference. Cultural factors are also seen at work in practiced voluntary movements such as the use of the foot to dribble a soccer ball or the hand to dribble a basketball.

Cognitive/Intellectual Development

What Develops?

The capacity to learn, remember, and symbolize information, and to solve problems, exists at a simple level in young infants, who can perform cognitive tasks such as discriminating animate and inanimate beings or recognizing small numbers of objects. During childhood, learning and information-processing increase in speed, memory becomes increasingly longer, and symbol use and the capacity for abstraction develop until a near-adult level is reached by adolescence.

Speed and Pattern of Development

It has been suggested by theorists such as Piaget that cognitive development proceeds in a stage-like fashion, with qualitative as well as quantitative differences between one age period and others. Cognitive ability appears to move forward rapidly at times when certain achievements are evident; for example, the preschooler's new ability to conserve number (to know that the number of objects present stays the same even though the objects are differently distributed) is a necessary foundation for arithmetic and enables a number of advances. However, it is not clear to what extent apparent stages are simply the results of increased speed of information processing or increased knowledge base.

Mechanisms of Cognitive Development

Cognitive development has genetic and other biological mechanisms, as is seen in the many genetic causes of mental retardation. However, although it is assumed that brain functions cause cognitive events, it has not been possible to measure specific brain changes and show that they cause cognitive change. Developmental advances in cognition are also related to experience and learning, and this is particularly the case for higher-level abilities like abstraction, which depend to a considerable extent on formal education.

Individual Differences

There are normal individual differences in the ages at which specific cognitive abilities are achieved, but schooling for children in industrialized countries is based on the assumption that these differences are not large. Atypical delays in cognitive development are problematic for children in cultures that demand advanced cognitive skills for work and for independent living.

Population Differences

There are few population differences in cognitive development. Boys and girls show some differences in their skills and preferences, but there is a great deal of overlap between the groups. Differences in cognitive achievement of different ethnic groups appears to result from cultural or other environmental factors.

Social-emotional Development

What Develops?

Newborn infants do not seem to experience fear or have preferences for contact with any specific people. By about 8-10 months, they go through a fairly rapid change and become fearful of perceived threats; they also begin to prefer familiar people and show anxiety and distress when separated from them or approached by strangers. The capacity for empathy and the understanding of social rules begin in the preschool period and continue to develop into adulthood. Middle childhood is characterized by friendships with age-mates, and adolescence by emotions connected with sexuality and the beginnings of romantic love. Anger seems most intense during the toddler and early preschool period and during adolescence.

Speed and Pattern of Development

Some aspects of social-emotional development, like empathy, develop gradually, but others, like fearfulness, seem to involve a rather sudden reorganization of the child's experience of emotion. Sexual and romantic emotions develop in connection with physical maturation.

Mechanisms of Social and Emotional Development

Genetic factors appear to regulate some social-emotional developments that occur at predictable ages, such as fearfulness, and attachment to familiar people. Experience plays a role in determining which people are familiar, which social rules are obeyed, and how anger is expressed.

Individual Differences

Individual differences in the sequence of social-emotional development are unusual, but the intensity or expressiveness of emotions can vary greatly from one normal child to another. Individual tendencies to various types of reactivity are probably constitutional, and they are referred to as temperamental differences. Atypical development of social-emotional characteristics may be mildly unusual, or may be so extreme as to indicate mental illness. Temperamental traits are thought to be stable and enduring throughout the life span. Children who are active and angry as infants can be expected to be active and angry as older children, adolescents and adults.

Population Differences

Population differences may occur in older children, if, for example they have learned that it is appropriate for boys to express emotion or behave differently than girls, or if customs learned by children of one ethnic group are different from those learned in another. Social and emotional differences between boys and girls of a given age may also be associated with differences in the timing of puberty characteristic of the two sexes.

Language

What Develops?

There are four main areas in which the child must attain competence, regardless of the language or dialect spoken. These are referred to as *phonology* or sounds, *semantics* or the encoded meanings, *syntax* or the way in which words are combined and *pragmatics* or knowledge of how language is used in different contexts.

Speed and Pattern of Development

Receptive language, the understanding of others' speech, appears to have a gradual course of development beginning at about 6 months. However, expressive language, the production of words, moves rapidly after its beginning at about a year of age, with a "vocabulary explosion" of rapid word acquisition occurring in the middle of the second year. Grammatical rules and word combinations appear at about age two. Mastery of vocabulary and grammar continue gradually through the preschool and school years. Adolescents still have smaller vocabularies than adults and experience more difficulty with constructions like the passive voice.

Babies from one month old can produce "ooh" sounds which appear to grow out of pleasurable interactions with caregivers in a mutual "dialogue." According to Stern, this process is communication of affect between adult and infant in a mutual, rhythmic interaction. The attunement and "gaze-coupling" in which infant and adult take different roles is thought to anticipate the give-and-take of later dialogue.

From about 6 to 9 months babies produce more vowels, some consonants and "echolalia", or the frequent repetition of sounds like "dadadada" which appear to have some phonetic characteristics of later speech. It is thought that a crucial part of the development of speech is the time caregivers spend "guessing" what their infants are trying to communicate thus integrating the child into their social world. The attribution of intentionality to the infant's utterances has been called "shared memory" and forms a complex series of actions, intentions and actions in response in an improvised way.

It has been argued that children's phonological systems develop in ways that are parallel to adult languages, even if they are using unrecognisable "words." First words have the function of naming or labelling but also condense meaning as in "milk" meaning "I want milk." Vocabulary typically grows from about 20 words at 18 months to around 200 words at 21 months. From around 18 months the child starts to combine words into two word sentences. Typically the adult expands it to clarify meaning. By 24—27 months the child is producing three or four word sentences using a logical, if not strictly correct, syntax. The theory is that children apply a basic set of rules such as adding 's' for plurals or inventing simpler words out of words too complicated to repeat like "choskit" for chocolate biscuit. Following this there is a rapid appearance of grammatical rules and ordering of sentences. There is often an interest in rhyme, and imaginative play frequently includes conversations. Childrens' recorded monologues give insight into the development of the process of organising information into meaningful units.

By three years the child is beginning to use complex sentences, including relative clauses, although still perfecting various linguistic systems. By five years of age the child's use of language is very similar to that of an adult. From the age of about three children can indicate fantasy or make-believe linguistically, produce coherent personal stories and fictional narrative with beginnings and endings. It is argued that children devise narrative as a way of understanding their own experience and as a medium for communicating their meaning to others. The ability to engage in extended discourse emerges over time from regular conversation with adults and peers. For this the child needs to learn to combine his perspective with that of others and with outside events and learn to use linguistic indicators to show he is doing this. They also learn to adjust their language depending on to whom they are speaking. Typically by the age of about 9 a child can recount other narratives in addition to their own experiences, from the perspectives of the author, the characters in the story and their own views.

Mechanisms of Language Development

Although the role of adult discourse is important in facilitating the child's learning, there is considerable disagreement amongst theorists about the extent to which children's early meanings and expressive words arises directly from adult input as opposed to intrinsic factors relating to the child's cognitive functions. Findings about the initial mapping of new words, the ability to decontextualise words and refine meaning are diverse. One hypothesis is known as the syntactic *bootstrapping* hypothesis, referring to the child's ability to infer meaning from cues, using grammatical information from the structure of sentences. Another is the multi-route model in which it is argued that context-bound words and referential words follow different routes; the first being mapped onto event representations and the latter onto mental representations. In this model, although parental input has a critical role, children rely on cognitive processing to establish subsequent use of words. However, naturalistic research on language development has indicated that preschoolers' vocabularies are strongly associated with the number of words addressed to them by adults.

There is as yet no single accepted theory of language acquisition. Current explanations vary in emphasis from learning theory, with its emphasis on reinforcement and imitation (Skinner), to biological, nativist theories, with innate underlying mechanisms (Chomsky and Pinker), to a more interactive approach within a social context (Piaget and Tomasello). Behaviourists argue that given the universal presence of a physical environment and, usually, a social environment, any theory of language must account for the effects of the contingent relations of these on an individuals development of language behaviour. Pinker argues that complex language is universal and has an innate basis. Pinker's argument is partly based on the development of creole languages from pidgins. The children of parents who communicate, without grammatical structures, in pidgin, develop a creole language of their own accord, complete with standardised word orders, markers for present, future and past tenses and subordinate clauses. There is some support for this from the development of sign language amongst deaf children thrown together at a young age in special schools in Nicaragua who spontaneously developed a pidgin which was then developed into a creole by a younger generation of children coming into the schools, (ISN).

Individual Differences

Slow Expressive Language Development (SELD) a delay in the use of words coupled with normal understanding, is characteristic of a small proportion of children who later display normal language use.

Dyslexia is a significant topic in child development as it affects approximately 5 per cent of the population (in the western world). Essentially it is a disorder whereby children fail to attain the language skills of reading, writing and spelling commensurate with their intellectual abilities. Dyslexic children show a range of differences in their language development, from subtle speech impairments to mis-pronunciations to word-finding difficulties. The most common phonological difficulties are limitations of verbal short-term memory and phonological awareness. Such children often have difficulties with long-term verbal learning such as months of the year, learning tables, left and right or a foreign language. From the late 1980s the phonological deficit hypothesis has become the dominant explanation. The difficulties in early articulation, basic phonological skills and acquiring basic building blocks means that dyslexics have to invest too many resources in just coping with the basics rather than acquiring new information or skills. Early identification enables children to receive help before they fail.

Atypically delayed language development may be diagnostic of autism, and regression of language may indicate serious disabilities like Rett syndrome. Poor language development also accompanies general developmental delays such as those found in Down syndrome.

TOWARDS UNDERSTANDING THE INFANT AND CHILD PSYCHOLOGY

Introduction

As babies grow from infants to children, psychologists try to figure out how their environment will affect them. For parents, this is a time of wonder. For the scientists, a time that so much and so little is known about.

Each of us have a life story and it starts with memories of our childhood and continues to be written throughout our lives. The pattern of your life story is different from other people—these stories are the focus of our developmental psychology.

Contribution of Nature Verses Nurture

Psychologist look at several different things when looking at human development one of these is called Contribution of Nature Verses Nurture, nature meaning heredity or genes and how they effect our development, and also nurture which is the environment or experiences and how this effect our development.

One of the things developmental psychologists have noticed through studying children is that they are born with predispositions that cause them to behave and react in a particular way, this is called Temperament.

Temperament

Temperament is to do with inborn differences in children, their reactivity, how they respond to the environment, how easily soothed they are and how intense they are emotionally. This temperament appears early enough in life and with clear enough differences between infants that it is thought to be mostly biological. But it's how the parents react to that temperament later on that makes it come to life.

Most infants fall into one of three different temperaments, these being easy, difficult and slow to warm up.

Easy category—infants in this category are calm and consistently easy to soothe

Difficult category—babies in this category are fussy and hard to comfort

Slow to warm up category—these babies are shy and wary of new experiences.

But most psychologists agree that temperament isn't based on heredity, research has shown that the temperament of all three types of babies can be affected in both positive and negative ways by their environment. Psychologists have also found that our temperament is generally persistent throughout our lives, so that for example if you were a 'slow to warm up' baby then in your adolescent years you are most likely be a shy and calm person, which also means that you would likely be held back from society. However a persons temperament can also be changed by the environment around them, so you could for example, change from a slow to warm up person to an easy person, based on the environment and how you are treated in later life.

Attachment

Another important factor in a child development is the bond between the child and its [parents], this bond being referred to as attachment. Attachments form the basis of emotional relationships later in life, for example a securely attached child feels that their needs are going to be met appropriately and quickly. This means the child feels free to explore, but on the other hand an insecure attachment is where a parent may be neglectful, insensitive or inconstant in meeting a child's needs. This results in the child having an ambivalent attitude towards the parents. A child can also have different attachment levels with different people, for example the mother and father. The differences between the levels of attachment with different people depend on the childs relationships with them. The childs attachments with both mother and father affect the outcome of their active and academic lives later in life. Research shows that an insecure child will suffer difficulties later in life whereas a secure child will perform better in school and form better relationships with peers.

Cognitive Development

Another area of childhood that parents are concerned about is called Cognitive development, which is the ability to think, remember and process information. One of the most renowned psychologist in this area is a Swiss man called Jean Piaget. Piaget was not concerned if children were able to see the world accurately, but how they came to see the world. His basic theory is that there are four stages of cognitive development.

The first stage of Cognitive development is called the Sensorimotor stage. This is the infant and children at a young ages of 0—2 years old. This is where an infant or child will use their sense of touch and taste to identify the differences between objects.

The second stage is called the Preoperational stage. This stage appears between the ages of 2—5. In this stage, children are just beginning to develop their thinking skills. Children at this stage/age use words, symbols and images to represent the world.

The third stage starts at about the ages of 6—7. This is called the Concrete Operational Stage. This is where the child becomes logical, but is only tied to concrete activities and tasks, meaning they can produce relationships and think in a sequence.

Then when the child comes into adolescence, they move in to the final stage called Formal Operation Stage. This is where the child can think abstractly–understanding algebra, for example.

Unfortunately, Piaget's theory is nowhere near perfect because recent test show some actions appear before predicted; for example, if you ask a child an illogical question you will get an illogical answer, but if you ask a question that they understand better you will get a logical answer, so a child can give a good logical answer to a question like "Why can't I walk through a wall?". Now Piaget's theory is crumbling and a new theory is appearing called the Ecological Systems Theory. This is based on the contextual influences in the child's life like his/her immediate family, school, society and the world, and how these impact the child's development.

UNDERSTANDING ADOLESCENCE

Adolescence (lat *adolescere,* (to) grow) is a transitional stage of physical and mental human development that occurs between childhood and adulthood. This transition involves biological (i.e., pubertal), social, and psychological changes, though the biological or physiological ones are the easiest to measure objectively. Historically, puberty has been heavily associated with teenagers and the onset of adolescent development. In recent years, however, the start of puberty has had somewhat of an increase in preadolescence (particularly females), and adolescence has had an occasional extension beyond the teenage years (typically males). This has made adolescence less simple to discern.

The end of adolescence and the beginning of adulthood varies by country and by function, and furthermore even within a single nation-state there can be different ages at which an individual is considered to be (chonologically and legally) mature enough to be entrusted by society with certain tasks. Such milestones include, but are not limited to, driving a vehicle, having legal sexual relations, serving in the armed forces or on a jury, purchasing and drinking alcohol, voting, entering into contracts, and marrying.

Adolescence is usually accompanied by an increased independence allowed by the parents or legal guardians and less supervision, contrary to the preadolescence stage.

Puberty

Puberty is a period of several years in which rapid physical growth and psychological changes occur, culminating in sexual maturity. The average onset of puberty is at 10 for girls and age 12 for boys. Every person's individual timetable for puberty is influenced primarily by heredity, although environmental factors, such as diet and exercise, also exert some influence.

Puberty begins with a surge in hormone production, which in turn, causes a number of physical changes. It is also the stage of the lifespan in which a child develops secondary sex characteristics (for example, a deeper voice and larger adam's apple in boys, and development of breasts and more curved and prominent hips in girls) as his or her hormonal balance shifts strongly towards an adult state. This is triggered by the pituitary gland, which secretes a surge of hormones, such as testosterone (boys) or estrogen and progesterone (girls) into the blood stream and begins the rapid maturation of the gonads: the girl's ovaries and the boy's testicles. Some boys may develop gynecomastia due to an imbalance of sex hormones, tissue responsiveness or obesity. Put simply, puberty is the time when a child's body starts changing into an adult's body.

Facial hair in males normally appears in a specific order during puberty: The first facial hair to appear tends to grow at the corners of the upper lip, typically between 14 to 16 years of age. It then spreads to form a moustache over the entire upper lip. This is followed by the appearance of hair on the upper part of the cheeks, and the area under the lower lip. The hair eventually spreads to the sides and lower border of the chin, and the rest of the lower face to form a full beard. As with most human biological processes, this specific order may vary among some individuals. Facial hair is often present in late adolescence, around ages 17 and 18, but may not appear until significantly later. Some men do not develop full facial hair for 10 years after puberty. Facial hair will continue to get coarser, darker and thicker for another 2-4 years after puberty.

The major landmark of puberty for males is the first ejaculation, which occurs, on average, at age 13. For females, it is menarche, the onset of menstruation, which occurs, on average, between ages 12 and 13. The age of menarche is influenced by heredity, but a girl's diet and lifestyle contribute as well. Regardless of genes, a girl must have certain proportion of body fat to attain menarche. Consequently, girls who eat high-fat diet and who are not physically active begin menstruating earlier, on average, than girls whose diet contains less fat and whose activities involve fat reducing exercise (e.g ballet and gymnastics). Girls who experience malnutrition or are in societies in which children are expected to perform physical labour also begin menstruating at later ages.

The timing of puberty can have important psychological and social consequences. Early maturing boys are usually taller and stronger than their friends. They have the advantage in capturing the attention of girls and in becoming hand-picked for sports. Pubescent boys often tend to have a good body image, are more confident, secure, and more independent. Late maturing boys can be less confident because of poor body image when comparing themselves to already developed friends and peers. However, early puberty is not always positive for boys; early sexual maturation in boys can be accompanied by increased aggressiveness due to the surge of hormones that affect them. Because they appear older than their peers, pubescent boys may face increased social pressure to conform to adult norms; society may view them as more emotionally advanced, despite the fact that their cognitive and social development may lag behind their appearance. Studies have shown that early maturing boys are more likely to be sexually active and are more likely to participate in risky behaviours.

For girls, early maturation can sometimes lead to increased self-consciousness, though a typical aspect in maturing females. Because of their bodies developing in advance, pubescent girls can become more insecure. Consequently, girls that reach sexual maturation early are more likely than their peers to develop eating disorders. Nearly half of all American high school girls diet to lose weight. In addition, girls may have to deal with sexual advances from older boys before they are emotionally and mentally mature. In addition to having earlier sexual experiences and more unwanted pregnancies than late maturing girls, early maturing girls are more exposed to alcohol and drug abuse. Those who have had such experiences tend to perform less well in school than their "inexperienced" age mates.

By age 16, girls have usually reached full physical development. At this age, boys are close to completing their physical growth, which is usually attained by age 17 or 18. Teenage and early adult males may continue to gain natural muscle growth even after puberty.

Psychology

Adolescent psychology is associated with notable changes in mood sometimes known as mood swings. Cognitive, emotional and attitudinal changes which are characteristic of adolescence, often take place during this period, and this can be a cause of conflict on one hand and positive personality development on the other.

Because the adolescents are experiencing various strong cognitive and physical changes, for the first time in their lives they may start to view their friends, their peer group, as more important and influential than their parents/guardians. Because of peer pressure, they may sometimes indulge in activities not deemed socially acceptable, although this may be more of a social phenomenon than a psychological one. This overlap is addressed within the study of psychosociology.

The home is an important aspect of adolescent psychology: home environment and family have a substantial impact on the developing minds of teenagers, and these developments may reach a climax during adolescence. For example, abusive parents may lead a child to "poke fun" at other classmates when he/she is seven years old or so, but during adolescence, it may become progressively worse, for example, the child may now be using drugs or becoming intolerably violent among other classmates. If the concepts and theory behind right or wrong were not established early on in a child's life, the lack of this knowledge may impair a teenager's ability to make beneficial decisions as well as allowing his/her impulses to control his/her decisions.

In the search for a unique social identity for themselves, adolescents are frequently confused about what is 'right' and what is 'wrong.' G. Stanley Hall denoted this period as one of "Storm and Stress" and, according to him, conflict at this developmental stage is normal and not unusual. Margaret Mead, on the other hand, attributed the behaviour of adolescents to their culture and upbringing. However, Piaget, attributed this stage in development with greatly increased cognitive abilities; at this stage of life the individual's thoughts start taking more of an abstract form and the egocentric thoughts decrease, hence the individual is able to think and reason in a wider perspective.

Positive psychology is sometimes brought up when addressing adolescent psychology as well. This approach towards adolescents refers to providing them with motivation to become socially acceptable and notable individuals, since many adolescents find themselves bored, indecisive and/or unmotivated.

Adolescents may be subject to peer pressure within their adolescent time span, consisting of the need to have sex, consume alcoholic beverages, use drugs, defy their parental figures, or commit any activity in which the person who is subjected to may not deem appropriate, among other things. Peer pressure is a common experience between adolescents and may result briefly or on a larger scale. If it results on a larger scale, the adolescent needs medical advice or treatment.

It should also be noted that adolescence is the stage of a psychological breakthrough in a person's life when the cognitive development is rapid and the thoughts, ideas and concepts developed at this period of life greatly influence the individual's future life, playing a major role in character and personality formation.

Struggles with adolescent identity and depression usually set in when an adolescent experiences a loss. The most important loss in their lives is the changing relationship between the adolescent and their parents. Adolescents may also experience strife in their relationships with friends. This may be due to the activities their friends take part in, such as smoking, which causes adolescents to feel as though participating in such activities themselves is likely essential to maintaining these friendships. Teen depression can be extremely intense at times because of physical and hormonal changes but emotional instability is part of being a teenager. Their changing mind, body and relationships often present themselves as stressful and that change, they assume, is something to be feared.

Views of family relationships during adolescence are changing. The old view of family relationships during adolescence put an emphasis on conflict and disengagement and thought storm and stress was normal and even inevitable. However, the new view puts emphasis on transformation or relationships and maintenance of connectedness.

Sexuality

Adolescent sexuality refers to sexual feelings, behaviour and development in adolescents and is a stage of human sexuality. Sexuality and sexual desire usually begins to intensify along with the onset of puberty. The expression of sexual desire among adolescents (or anyone, for that matter), might be influenced by family values and the culture and religion they have grown up in (or as a backlash to such), social engineering, social control, taboos, and other kinds of social mores.

In contemporary society, adolescents also face some risks as their sexuality begins to transform. Whilst some of these such as emotional distress (fear of abuse or exploitation) and sexually transmitted diseases (including HIV/AIDS) may not necessarily be inherent to adolescence, others such as pregnancy (through failure or non-use of contraceptives) are seen as social problems in most western societies. In terms of sexual identity, all sexual orientations found in adults are also represented among adolescents.

According to anthropologist Margaret Mead and psychologist Albert Bandura, the turmoil found in adolescence in Western society has a cultural rather than a physical cause; they reported that societies where young women engaged in free sexual activity had no such adolescent turmoil.

In a 2008 study conducted by YouGov for Channel 4, 20 per cent of 14-17-years-old surveyed revealed that they had their first sexual experience at 13 or under.

The age of consent to sexual activity varies widely between international jurisdictions, ranging from 12 to 21 years.

Culture

In commerce, this generation is seen as an important target. Mobile phones, contemporary popular music, movies, television programmes, websites, sports, video games and clothes are heavily marketed and often popular amongst adolescents.

In the past (and still in some cultures) there were ceremonies that celebrated adulthood, typically occurring during adolescence. *Seijin shiki* (literally "adult ceremony") is a Japanese example of this. Upanayanam is a coming of age ceremony for males in the Hindu world. In Judaism, 12-years-old girls and 13-years-old boys become Bat or Bar Mitzvah, respectively, and often have a celebration to mark this coming of age. Among some denominations of Christianity, the rite or sacrament of Confirmation is received by adolescents and may be considered the time at which adolescents become members of the church in their own right (there is also a Confirmation ceremony in some Reform Jewish temples, although the bar or bat mitzvah ceremony appears to have precedence). In United States, girls will often have a "sweet sixteen" party to celebrate turning the aforementioned age, a tradition similar to the quinceañera in Latin culture. In modern western society, events such as getting your first driver's licence, high school and later on college graduation and first career related job are thought of as being more significant markers in transition to adulthood.

Adolescents have also been an important factor in many movements for positive social change around the world. The popular history of adolescents participating in these movements may perhaps start with Joan of Arc, and extend to present times with popular youth activism, student activism, and other efforts to make the youth voice heard.

Legal Issues, Rights and Privileges

Internationally, those who reach a certain age (often 18, though this varies) are legally considered to have reached the age of majority and are regarded as adults and are held to be responsible for their actions. People below this age are considered minors or children. A person below the age of majority may gain adult rights through legal emancipation.

Those who are under the age of consent, or legal responsibility, may be considered too young to be held accountable for criminal action. This is called *doli incapax* or the defense of infancy. The age of criminal responsibility varies from 7 in India to 18 in Belgium. After reaching the initial age, there may be levels of responsibility dictated by age and type of offense, and crimes committed by minors may be tried in a juvenile court.

The legal working age in Western countries is usually 14 to 16, depending on the number of hours and type of employment. In the United Kingdom and Canada, for example, young people between 14 and 16 can work at certain types of light work with some restrictions to allow for schooling; while youths over 16 can work full-time (excluding night work). Many countries also specify a minimum school leaving age, ranging from 10 to 18, at which a person is legally allowed to leave compulsory education.

The age of consent to sexual activity varies widely between jurisdictions, ranging from 12 to 21 years, although 14 to 16 years is more usual. In a 2008 study of 14 to 17-years-old conducted by YouGov for Channel 4, it was revealed that one in three 15-years-old were sexually active.

Sexual intercourse with a person below the local age of consent is usually treated as the crime of statutory rape. Some jurisdictions allow an exemption where both partners are close in age; for example, a 16-years-old and an 18-years-old. The age at which people are allowed to marry also varies, from 17 in Yemen to 22 for males and 20 for females in China. In Western countries, people are typically allowed to marry at 18, although they are sometimes allowed to marry at a younger age with parental or court consent. In developing countries, the legal marriageable age does not always correspond with the age at which people actually marry; for example, the legal age for marriage in Ethiopia is 18 for both males and females, but in rural areas most girls are married by age 16.

In most democratic countries, a citizen is eligible to vote at 18. For example, in the United States, the Twenty-sixth amendment decreased the voting age from 21 to 18. In a minority of countries, the voting age is 17 (for example, Indonesia) or 16 (for example, Brazil). By contrast, some countries have a minimum voting age of 21 (for example, Singapore) whereas the minimum age in Uzbekistan is 25. Age of candidacy is the minimum age at which a person can legally qualify to hold certain elected government offices. In most countries, a person must be 18 or over to stand for elected office, but some countries such as the United States and Italy have further restrictions depending on the type of office.

The sale of selected items such as cigarettes, alcohol, and videos with violent or pornographic content is also restricted by age in most countries. In the U.S., the minimum age to buy an R-rated movie, M-rated game or an album with a parental advisory label is 17 (in some states 18 or even 21). In practice, it is common that young people engage in underage smoking or drinking, and in some cultures this is tolerated to a certain degree. In the United States, teenagers are allowed to drive between 14-18 (each state sets its own minimum driving age of which a curfew may be imposed), in the US, adolescents 17 years of age can serve in the military. In Europe it is more common for the driving age to be higher (usually 18) while the drinking age is lower than that of the US (usually 16 or 18). In Canada, the drinking age is 18 in some areas and 19 in other areas. In Australia, universally the minimum drinking age is 18, unless a person is in a private residence or is under parental supervision in a licenced premises. The driving age varies from state to state but the more common system is a graduated system of "L plates" (a learning licence that requires supervision from a licenced driver) from age 16, red "P plates" (probationary licence) at 17, green "P plates" at 18 and finally a full licence, i.e. for most people around the age of 20.

The legal gambling age also depends on the jurisdiction, although it is typically 18.

The minimum age for donating blood in the U.S. is 17 although it may be 16 with parental permission in some states such as New York and Pennsylvania.

A number of social scientists, including anthropologist Margaret Mead and sociologist Mike Males, have noted the contradictory treatment of laws affecting adolescents in the United States. As Males has noted, the US Supreme Court has, "explicitly ruled that policy-makers may impose adult responsibilities and punishments on individual youths as if they were adults at the same time laws and policies abrogate adolescents' rights en masse as if they were children."

The issue of youth activism affecting political, social, educational, and moral circumstances is of growing significance around the world. Youth-led organizations around the world have fought for social justice, the youth vote seeking to gain teenagers the right to vote, to secure more youth rights, and demanding better schools through student activism.

Since the advent of the Convention on the Rights of the Child in 1989 (children defined as under 18), almost every country (except the U.S. & Somalia) in the world has become voluntarily legally committed to advancing an anti-discriminatory stance towards young people of all ages. This is a legally binding document which secures youth participation throughout society while acting against unchecked child labour, child soldiers, child prostitution, and pornography.

TOWARDS UNDERSTANDING THE YOUNG ADULT PSYCHOLOGY

According to Erik Erikson's stages of human development, first enumerated in *Childhood and Society* (1950), a young adult is generally a person between the ages of 20 and 40, whereas an adolescent is a person between the ages of 13 and 19, although definitions and opinions can vary. The young adult stage in human development precedes middle adulthood. A person in the middle adulthood stage is between the ages of 40 and 65. In maturity, a person is 65 years old or older.

Health

Young adults are generally in good health, subject neither to disease nor the problems of senescence.

Biological function and physical performance reach their peak from 20-35 years of age, waning after 35. Strength peaks around 25 years of age, plateaus through 35 or 40 years of age, and then declines. Flexibility also decreases with age throughout adulthood. However, there are large individual differences and a fit 40-years-old may outcompete a sedentary 20-years-old.

Women reach their peak fertility in their early 20s. Assuming unprotected intercourse with a man of the same age, women aged 19-26 have about a 50 per cent chance of becoming pregnant during a given menstrual cycle, compared with 40 per cent in the 27-34 age group and below 30 per cent for women 35-39.

In developed countries, mortality rates for the 18-40 age group are typically very low. Men are more likely to die at this age than women, particularly in the 18-25 group: reasons include car accidents and suicide. Mortality statistics among men and women level off during the late twenties and thirties, due in part to good health and less risk-taking behaviour.

Cancer is much less common in young than in older adults. Exceptions are testicular cancer, cervical cancer, and Hodgkin's lymphoma.

In sub-Saharan Africa, HIV/AIDS has hit the early adult population particularly hard. According to a United Nations report, AIDS has significantly increased mortality of between ages 20 to 55 for African males and 20 to 45 for African females, reducing the life expectancy in South Africa by 18 years and in Botswana by 34 years.

Early Adulthood

According to Erikson, the young adult stage involves the personal need for intimacy and sex. Failure to achieve this need results in isolation, which is avoided, and as a result the young adult strives for love and compassion. The young adult learns that love and compassion may get him what he wants.

In modern societies, young adults in their late teens and early 20s encounter a number of issues as they finish school and begin to hold full-time jobs and take on other responsibilities of adulthood.

Settling Down

After the upheaval of the early 30s, the middle to late 30s (roughly ages 34-39) are often characterized by settling down. People in their 30s may increase the financial and emotional investments they make in their lives. Many have been employed long enough to gain promotions and raises. They often become more focused on advancing their careers and gaining stability in their personal lives. They may have started a family.

TOWARDS UNDERSTANDING NEUROPSYCHOLOGY

Neuropsychology is the basic scientific discipline that studies the structure and function of the brain related to specific psychological processes and overt behaviours. The term neuropsychology has been applied to lesion studies in humans and animals. It has also been applied to efforts to record electrical activity from individual cells (or groups of cells) in higher primates (including some studies of human patients).

It is scientific in its approach and shares an information processing view of the mind with cognitive psychology and cognitive science.

It is one of the more eclectic of the psychological disciplines, overlapping at times with areas such as neuroscience, philosophy (particularly philosophy of mind), neurology, psychiatry and computer science (particularly by making use of artificial neural networks).

In practice neuropsychologists tend to work in academia (involved in basic or clinical research), clinical settings (involved in assessing or treating patients with neuropsychological problems—see clinical neuropsychology), forensic settings (often assessing people for legal reasons or court cases or working with offenders, or appearing in court as expert witness) or industry (often as consultants where neuropsychological knowledge is applied to product design or in the management of pharmaceutical clinical-trials research for drugs that might have a potential impact on CNS functioning).

Approaches

Experimental neuropsychology is an approach which uses methods from experimental psychology to uncover the relationship between the nervous system and cognitive function. The majority of work involves studying healthy humans in a laboratory setting, although a minority of researchers may conduct animal experiments. Human work in this area often takes advantage of specific features of our nervous system (for example that visual information presented to a specific visual field is preferentially processed by the cortical hemisphere on the opposite side) to make links between neuroanatomy and psychological function.

Clinical neuropsychology is the application of neuropsychological knowledge to the assessment (see neuropsychological test and neuropsychological assessment), management and rehabilitation of people who have suffered illness or injury (particularly to the brain) which has caused neurocognitive problems. In particular they bring a psychological viewpoint to treatment, to understand how such illness and injury may affect and be affected by psychological factors. They also can offer an opinion as to whether a person is demonstrating difficulties due to brain pathology or as a consequence of emotional or other (potentially) reversible cause. Clinical neuropsychologists often work in hospital settings in an interdisciplinary medical team, others work in private practice and may provide expert input into medico-legal proceedings.

Cognitive neuropsychology is a relatively new development and has emerged as a distillation of the complementary approaches of both experimental and clinical neuropsychology. It seeks to understand the mind and brain by studying people who have suffered brain injury or neurological illness. One model of neuropsychological functioning is known as functional localization. This is based on the principle that if a specific cognitive problem can be found after an injury to a specific area of the brain, it is possible that this part of the brain is in some way involved. However, there may be reason to believe that the link between mental functions and neural regions is not so simple. An alternative model of the link between mind and brain, such as parallel processing, may have more explanatory power for the workings and dysfunction of the human brain. Yet another approach investigates how the pattern of errors produced by brain-damaged individuals can constrain our understanding of mental representations and processes without reference to the underlying neural structure. A more recent but related approach is cognitive neuropsychiatry which seeks to understand the normal function of mind and brain by studying psychiatric or mental illness.

Connectionism is the use of artificial neural networks to model specific cognitive processes using what are considered to be simplified but plausible models of how neurons operate. Once trained to perform a specific cognitive task these networks are often damaged or 'lesioned' to simulate brain injury or impairment in an attempt to understand and compare the results to the effects of brain injury in humans.

Functional neuroimaging uses specific neuroimaging technologies to take readings from the brain, usually when a person is doing a particular task, in an attempt to understand how the activation of particular brain areas is related to the task. In particular, the growth of methodologies to employ cognitive testing within established functional Magnetic Resonance Imaging (fMRI) techniques to study brain-behaviour relations is having a notable influence on neuropsychological research.

In practice these approaches are not mutually exclusive and most neuropsychologists select the best approach or approaches for the task to be completed.

Methods and Tools

- The use of standardized neuropsychological tests. These tasks have been designed so the performance on the task can be linked to specific neurocognitive processes. These tests are typically standardized, meaning that they have been administered to a specific group(s) of individuals before being used in individual clinical cases. The data resulting from standardization are known as normative data. After these data have been collected and analyzed, they are used as the comparative standard against which individual performances can be compared. Examples of neuropsychological tests include: the Wechsler Adult Memory Scale (WMS), the Wechsler Adult Intelligence Scale (WAIS), and the Wechsler Intelligence Scale for Children (WISC). Other tests include the Halstead-Reitan Neuropsychological Battery, the Boston Naming Test, the Wisconsin Card Sorting Test, the Benton Visual Retention Test, and the Controlled Oral Word Association. [The Woodcock Johnson and the Nelson-Denny are not neuropsychological tests *per se*. They are psycho-educational batteries of tests used to measure an individual's intra-disciplinary strengths and weakness in specific academic areas (writing, reading and arithmetic)].
- The use of brain scans to investigate the structure or function of the brain is common, either as simply a way of better assessing brain injury with high resolution pictures, or by examining the relative activations of different brain areas. Such technologies may include fMRI (functional Magnetic Resonance Imaging) and PET (Positron Emission Tomography), which yields data related to functioning, as well as MRI (Magnetic Resonance Imaging) and CAT (or CT) (Computed Axial Tomography), which yields structural data.

- The use of electrophysiological measures designed to measure the activation of the brain by measuring the electrical or magnetic field produced by the nervous system. This may include EEG (Electroencephalography) or MEG (Magneto-encephalography).
- The use of designed experimental tasks, often controlled by computer and typically measuring reaction time and accuracy on a particular tasks thought to be related to a specific neurocognitive process. An example of this is the Cambridge Neuropsychological Test Automated Battery (CANTAB).

4

Emotional, Behavioural and Mental Disorders: Towards Proper Understanding and Treatment

UNDERSTANDING EMOTIONAL AND BEHAVIOURAL DISORDERS

Emotional and Behavioural Disorders (EBD) is a broad category which is used commonly in educational settings, to group a range of more specific perceived difficulties of children and adolescents. Both general definitions as well as concrete diagnosis of EBD may be controversial as the observed behaviour may depend on many factors.

Often EBD students may have other disabilities such as: PDD, autism, Rett syndrome, PDD-NOS, Asperger syndrome and ADHD.

Strategies for Students Classified with EBD

1. *Routine:* Provide a structured routine with visual time clock. Auditory sound cues may be helpful in addition to visual cues to help students manage their time efficiently. Post schedule and refer to schedule on regular basis. Routines may take 6-8 weeks to establish or even more for this population of students.
2. *Changes in Routine:* Convey any changes of routine to students as soon as available. The sooner students are aware of changes the more time students have to adjust to the new routine.
3. *Classroom Jobs Chart/Classroom Order Chart:* Classroom jobs offer an opportunity for student to show responsibility. In order to ensure success, make sure students have an opportunity to experience every job. One suggestion is having a chart with each students name and according job. Every week rotate the jobs. The list can double as the order in which students line up or choose preferred activities. Students with EBD classification tend to be competitive and need specific procedures informing the order students line up and choose activities.
4. *Logical Consequences:* Students must fix what they break. If a student pushes over a desk, he or she must pick it up. If a student runs in the hall, she must practice walking the correct way. If the student talks during the lesson, student

must make up the work on his time. Be consistent with consequences so students know what is expected of them.

5. *Target Behaviours:* After taking data on students observable behaviour, determine which behaviour or behaviours to direct attention. Work with student to develop a plan to replace undesirable behaviour with a more suitable behaviour. If student throws desks and pencils when angry, have student work on communicating anger to an adult or trusted peer and how to be assertive without being aggressive.
6. *Small Flexible Grouping:* Students with EBD may have difficulty establishing relationships with peers. Abusive language and other behaviours may interfere with learning. Smaller groups decrease distractions and student-to-teacher ratio. Differentiation of instruction is more manageable with smaller groups.
7. *Audience:* During a serious behaviour episode, the most effective strategy may be to remove the audience. The audience typically is other peers but may be other adults. The audience can be removed by moving the student if he or she is willing. However, moving the audience may be necessary in some cases. Develop a procedure with your class which will function as an "everybody out" drill. Behaviours amplified with an audience may be reduced or complete stopped when an audience is removed.
8. *Calm Spot:* Have a designated area of the classroom for students to calm down. This spot can be used pro actively to prevent behaviours. Alternatively, the spot may be used after a behaviour occurs to give the student a chance to refocus.
9. *Choices:* Students may frustrate easily when doing work. Giving students an option of when to complete the work is a powerful tool. For example, a teacher may say, "You need to get this done today. Would you rather do it now or during your free time?"

UNDERSTANDING NEURODEVELOPMENTAL DISORDER

A neurodevelopmental disorder, or disorder of neural development, is an impairment of the growth and development of the brain or central nervous system. One narrower use of the term refers to a disorder of brain function which affects emotion, learning ability and memory and which unfolds as the individual grows. The term is sometimes erroneously used as an exclusive synonym for autism and autism spectrum disorders.

Disorders considered to be neurodevelopmental in origin or to have neurodevelopmental consequences when they occur in infancy and childhood includes autism and autism spectrum disorders such as Asperger syndrome, traumatic brain injury (including congenital injuries such as those which cause cerebral palsy), communication, speech and language disorders, genetic disorders such as fragile-X syndrome, Down syndrome and Rett syndrome, epilepsy, fetal alcohol syndrome, learning disorders, neurological and psychiatric disorders. Neurodevelopmental disorders are associated with widely varying degrees of mental, emotional, physical and economic burden to individuals, families and society in general.

Causes

Causes include deprivation, genetic and metabolic diseases, immune disorders, infectious diseases, nutritional factors, physical trauma, toxic and environmental factors.

Some neurodevelopmental disorders such as autism and other pervasive developmental disorders are considered to be multifactoral syndromes (with many causes but more specific neurodevelopmental manifestation). However other multifactoral syndromes such as Pediatric Autoimmune Neuropsychiatric Disorders Associated with Streptococcal infections PANDAS are presently thought to have a more specific primary causation as well as a specific neurodevelopmental manifestation.

Deprivation

Infants and children require loving emotional nurture from caregivers—there is a spectrum of problems arising from the lack of it. The most severe deprivation disorder, hospitalism, was described in 1897 as a wasting away to the point of death. A sublethal form, anaclitic depression was first described by René Spitz in the 1940s. It occurred in infants over the age of six months who suffered the loss of their mothers, who then became depressed and show behavioural retardation (delay in reaching developmental milestones, especially as relate to social behaviours). Behavioural retardation, as in the reactive attachment disorders, has been observed in emotionally deprived children living with their families. However, prominent modern thought attributes other causative mechanisms to autism and autistic spectrum disorders (see Autism).

However, nurture is not the only cause of deprivation that leads to neurodevelopmental sequellae. A common example of sensory deprivation due to biologic factors is blindness. Blind infants have risk of poor developmental outcomes which, left untreated, may lead to severe, autistic-like behaviours. Despite its biologic basis, caregivers can ameliorate blindness-related sensory deprivation. This can lead to positive neurodevelopmental outcome, as in the cases of author Helen Keller who was trained in the use of tactile sign language, and musicians such as Arthel "Doc" Watson and Ray Charles who remained emotionally connected to others via their sense of hearing.

Genetic Disorders

A prominent example of a genetically determined neurodevelopmental disorder is Trisomy 21, also known as Down syndrome. This disorder usually results from an extra chromosome 21, although in uncommon instances it is related to other chromosomal abnormalities such as translocation of the genetic material. It is characterized by short stature, epicanthal (eyelid) folds, abnormal fingerprints and palm prints, heart defects, poor muscle tone (delay of neurological development) and mental retardation (delay of intellectual development).

Less commonly known genetically determined neurodevelopmental disorders include Fragile X syndrome, Rett syndrome and Williams syndrome. Fragile X syndrome was first described in 1943 by J.P. Martin and J. Bell, studying persons with family history of sex-linked "mental defect." Rett syndrome, another X-linked disorder, produces severe functional limitations. Williams syndrome is caused by small deletions of genetic material from chromosome 7.

Immune Dysfunction

Immune reactions during pregnancy, both maternal and of the developing child can produce neurodevelopmental disorders. One typical immune reaction in infants and children is PANDAS, or *Pediatric Autoimmune Neuropsychiatric Disorders Associated with Streptococcal infection* produce abnormal movements of the body, emotional disturbance and obsessive compulsive disorder symptoms. Another disorder is Sydenham's chorea, which results in more abnormal movements of the body and fewer psychological sequellae. Both are immune reactions against brain tissue which follow infection by *Streptococcus* bacteria. (Susceptibility to these immune diseases may be genetically determined, so sometimes several family members may suffer from one or both of them following an epidemic of Strep infection.)

Infectious Diseases

There are a number of infectious diseases which can be transmitted either congenitally or in early childhood and which can cause serious neurodevelopmental disorders such as schizophrenia. Congenital toxoplasmosis may result in formation of cysts in the brain and other organs, causing a variety of neurological deficits. Congenital syphilis may progress to neurosyphilis if it remains untreated. Measles can progress to subacute sclerosing panencephalitis. Congenital rubella syndrome can produce schizophrenia in addition to multiple other symptoms.

Metabolic Disorders

Metabolic disorders, present in either the mother or the child, can cause neurodevelopmental disorders. Two examples are diabetes mellitus (a multifactoral disorder) and phenylketonuria (an inborn error of metabolism). There are many such inherited diseases which may directly affect the child's metabolism and neural development but less commonly they can indirectly affect the child during gestation. (See also teratology).

In the child type 1 diabetes can produce neurodevelopmental damage by the effects of excessive or insufficient glucose. The problems continue and may worsen throughout childhood if the diabetes is not well controlled. Type 2 diabetes may be preceded in its onset by impaired cognitive functioning.

However a non-diabetic fetus can also be subjected to glucose effects if its mother has undetected gestational diabetes. Maternal diabetes causes excessive birth size, making it harder for the infant to pass through the birth canal without injury or it can directly produce early neurodevelopmental deficits. However usually the neurodevelopmental symptoms decrease in later childhood.

Phenylketonuria, also known as PKU is an inborn error of metabolism which can induce neurodevelopmental disorders in the child. Children with PKU require a strict diet to prevent mental retardation and other disorders. In the maternal form of PKU, excessive maternal phenylalanine can be absorbed by the fetus even if the fetus has not inherited the disease. This can produce mental retardation and other disorders.

Nutrition

Nutritional deficits may cause neurodevelopmental disorders, such as spina bifida which is common and anencephaly which is rare. Both disorders are neural tube defects with malformation and dysfunction of the nervous system and its supporting structures, leading to serious physical disability as well as its emotional sequellae. The most common nutritional cause of neural tube defects is maternal deficiency of folic acid, a B vitamin usually found in fruits, vegetables, whole grains and milk products. (Neural tube defects are also caused by medications and other environmental causes, many of which interfere with folate metabolism, thus they are considered to have multifactoral causes.) Another deficiency, iodine deficiency, produces a spectrum of neurodevelopmental disorders from mild emotional disturbance to severe mental retardation.

Excesses in both maternal and infant diets may cause disorders as well, with foods or food supplements proving toxic in large amounts. For instance in 1973 K.L. Jones and D.W. Smith of the University of Washington Medical School in Seattle found a pattern of "craniofacial, limb, and cardiovascular defects associated with prenatal onset growth deficiency and developmental delay" in children of alcoholic mothers. This disorder, now called fetal alcohol syndrome, has significant symptom overlap with several other entirely unrelated neurodevelopmental disorders. It has been discovered that iron supplementation in baby formula is linked to lowered IQ and other neurodevelopmental delays.

Trauma

Brain trauma in the developing human is a common cause (over 400,000 injuries per year in the US alone, without clear information as to how many produce developmental sequellae) of neurodevelopmental syndromes. It may be subdivided into two major categories, congenital injury (including injury resulting from otherwise uncomplicated premature birth) and injury occurring in infancy or childhood. Common causes of congenital injury are asphyxia (obstruction of the trachea), hypoxia (lack of oxygen to the brain) and the mechanical trauma of the birth process itself.

Overwhelmingly, in industrial nations the most common causes of childhood brain trauma are falls and transportation-related incidents. Child maltreatment such as shaken baby syndrome can produce neurodevelopmental consequences including blindness, neuromotor deficits and cognitive impairment. According to information published by the American Association of Neurological Surgeons, Sports injuries account for 21 per cent of the US incidence, however their site includes transportation-related sports injuries. They assert that cycling produced 64,993 head injuries requiring emergency room visits in 2007 while the second most common cause, football, only produced 36,412.

Toxic and Environmental Factors

One well-known environmental toxic cause of neurodevelopmental disorders is heavy metal poisoning, with a prominent 20th century example being Minamata disease. Developmental mercury poisoning can cause a spectrum of problems from mild impairment of emotional development to the full blown syndrome of peripheral nerve damage, visual impairment, impaired coordination and ambulation, hallucinations, mental retardation, depression and death. However other metals such as lead, manganese, arsenic, cadmium and iron, as well as pesticides, tobacco and other environmental toxins are also implicated as causative factors.

TOWARDS A PROPER UNDERSTANDING OF CHILDREN AND ADOLESCENTS WITH MENTAL, EMOTIONAL AND BEHAVIOURAL DISORDERS

Mental, Emotional and Behavioural Disorders are Real

Young people can have mental, emotional, and behavioural problems that are real, painful, and costly. These problems, often called "disorders," are sources of stress for children and their families, schools, and communities.

The number of young people and their families who are affected by mental, emotional, and behavioural disorders is significant. It is estimated that as many as one in five children and adolescents may have a mental health disorder that can be identified and require treatment.

Mental health disorders in children and adolescents are caused by biology, environment, or a combination of the two. Examples of biological factors are genetics, chemical imbalances in the body, and damage to the central nervous system, such as a head injury. Many environmental factors also can affect mental health, including exposure to violence, extreme stress, and the loss of an important person.

Families and communities, working together, can help children and adolescents with mental disorders. A broad range of services is often necessary to meet the needs of these young people and their families.

The Disorders

Below are descriptions of particular mental, emotional, and behavioural disorders that may occur during childhood and adolescence. All can have a serious impact on a child's overall health. Some disorders are more common than others, and conditions range from mild to severe. Often, a child has more than one disorder (U.S. Department of Health and Human Services, 1999).

Anxiety Disorders

Young people who experience excessive fear, worry, or uneasiness may have an anxiety disorder. Anxiety disorders are among the most common of childhood disorders. According to one study of 9- to 17-year-olds, as many as 13 of every 100 young people have an anxiety disorder (U.S. Department of Health and Human Services, 1999). Anxiety disorders include:

- Phobias, which are unrealistic and overwhelming fears of objects or situations.
- Generalized anxiety disorder, which causes children to demonstrate a pattern of excessive, unrealistic worry that cannot be attributed to any recent experience.
- Panic disorder, which causes terrifying "panic attacks" that include physical symptoms, such as a rapid heartbeat and dizziness.
- Obsessive-compulsive disorder, which causes children to become "trapped" in a pattern of repeated thoughts and behaviours, such as counting or hand washing.
- Post-traumatic stress disorder, which causes a pattern of flashbacks and other symptoms and occurs in children who have experienced a psychologically distressing event, such as abuse, being a victim or witness of violence, or exposure to other types of trauma such as wars or natural disasters.

Severe Depression

Many people once believed that severe depression did not occur in childhood. Today, experts agree that severe depression can occur at any age. Studies show that two of every 100 children may have major depression, and as many as eight of every 100 adolescents may be affected (National Institutes of Health, 1999). The disorder is marked by changes in:

- *Emotions*—Children often feel sad, cry, or feel worthless.
- *Motivation*—Children lose interest in play activities, or schoolwork declines.
- *Physical well-being*—Children may experience changes in appetite or sleeping patterns and may have vague physical complaints.
- *Thoughts*—Children believe they are ugly, unable to do anything right, or that the world or life is hopeless.

It also is important for parents and caregivers to be aware that some children and adolescents with depression may not value their lives, which can put them at risk for suicide.

Bipolar Disorder

Children and adolescents who demonstrate exaggerated mood swings that range from extreme highs (excitedness or manic phases) to extreme lows (depression) may have bipolar disorder (sometimes called manic depression). Periods of moderate mood occur in between the extreme highs and lows. During manic phases, children or adolescents may talk nonstop, need very little sleep, and show unusually poor judgement. At the low end of the mood swing, children experience severe depression. Bipolar mood swings can recur throughout life. Adults with bipolar disorder (about one in 100) often experienced their first symptoms during their teenage years (National Institutes of Health, 2001).

Attention-deficit/Hyperactivity Disorder

Young people with attention-deficit/hyperactivity disorder are unable to focus their attention and are often impulsive and easily distracted. Attention-deficit/hyperactivity disorder occurs in up to five of every 100 children (U.S. Department of Health and Human Services, 1999). Most children with this disorder have great difficulty remaining still, taking turns, and keeping quiet. Symptoms must be evident in at least two settings, such as home and school, in order for attention-deficit/hyperactivity disorder to be diagnosed.

Learning Disorders

Difficulties that make it harder for children and adolescents to receive or express information could be a sign of learning disorders. Learning disorders can show up as problems with spoken and written language, coordination, attention, or self-control.

Conduct Disorder

Young people with conduct disorder usually have little concern for others and repeatedly violate the basic rights of others and the rules of society. Conduct disorder causes children and adolescents to act out their feelings or impulses in destructive ways. The offences these children and adolescents commit often grow more serious over time. Such offences may include lying, theft, aggression, truancy, the setting of fires, and vandalism. Current research has yielded varying estimates of the number of young people with this disorder, ranging from one to four of every 100 children 9 to 17 years of age (U.S. Department of Health and Human Services, 1999).

Eating Disorders

Children or adolescents who are intensely afraid of gaining weight and do not believe that they are underweight may have eating disorders. Eating disorders can be life threatening. Young people with anorexia nervosa, for example, have difficulty maintaining a minimum healthy body weight. Anorexia affects one in every 100 to 200 adolescent girls and a much smaller number of boys (National Institutes of Health, 1999).

Youngsters with bulimia nervosa feel compelled to binge (eat huge amounts of food in one sitting). After a binge, in order to prevent weight gain, they rid their bodies of the food by vomiting, abusing laxatives, taking enemas, or exercising obsessively. Reported rates of bulimia vary from one to three of every 100 young people (National Institutes of Health, 1999).

Autism

Children with autism, also called autistic disorder, have problems interacting and communicating with others. Autism appears before the third birthday, causing children to act inappropriately, often repeating behaviours over long periods of time. For example, some children bang their heads, rock, or spin objects. Symptoms of autism range from mild to severe. Children with autism may have a very limited awareness of others and are at increased risk for other mental disorders. Studies suggest that autism affects 10 to 12 of every 10,000 children (U.S. Department of Health and Human Services, 1999).

Schizophrenia

Young people with schizophrenia have psychotic periods that may involve hallucinations, withdrawal from others, and loss of contact with reality. Other symptoms include delusional or disordered thoughts and an inability to experience pleasure. Schizophrenia occurs in about five of every 1,000 children (National Institutes of Health, 1997).

Treatment, Support Services and Research: Sources of Hope

Now, more than ever before, there is hope for young people with mental, emotional, and behavioural disorders. Most of the symptoms and distress associated with childhood and adolescent mental, emotional, and behavioural disorders can be alleviated with timely and appropriate treatment and supports.

In addition, researchers are working to gain new scientific insights that will lead to better treatments and cures for mental, emotional, and behavioural disorders. Innovative studies also are exploring new ways of delivering services to prevent and treat these disorders. Research efforts are expected to lead to more effective use of existing treatments, so children and their families can live happier, healthier, and more fulfilling lives.

Many of these research studies are funded by Federal agencies within the Department of Health and Human Services, including the:

- National Institutes of Health

  - *National Institute of Mental Health*
  - *National Institute of Child Health and Human Development*
  - *National Institute on Drug Abuse*
  - *National Institute on Alcohol Abuse and Alcoholism.*
- Substance Abuse and Mental Health Services Administration
  - *Center for Mental Health Services*
  - *Center for Substance Abuse Prevention*
  - *Center for Substance Abuse Treatment.*
- Administration for Children and Families
- Health Resources and Services Administration

Related activities are taking place within the:

- Department of Education
- Department of Justice

Important Messages About Children's and Adolescents' Mental Health

- Every child's mental health is important.
- Many children have mental health problems.
- These problems are real and painful and can be severe.
- Mental health problems can be recognized and treated.
- Caring families and communities working together can help.

LIST OF MENTAL DISORDERS AS DEFINED BY THE DSM AND ICD

Following is a list of mental disorders as defined by the DSM and ICD.

The Diagnostic and Statistical Manual of Mental Disorders (DSM) is the American Psychiatric Association's standard reference for psychiatry which includes over 400 different definitions of mental disorders. The International Statistical Classification of Diseases and Related Health Problems (ICD) is published by the World Health Organization, and it contains a section on psychological and behavioural disorders. The diagnostic criteria and information in the DSM and ICD are revised and updated with each new version. This list contains conditions currently recognised descriptions of mental disorders as defined by these two documents.

There is disagreement in various fields of mental health care, including the field of psychiatry, over the definitions and criteria used to delineate various disorders. Of particular concern to some professionals is whether some of these conditions should be classified as 'mental illnesses' at all, or whether they would be better described as neurological disorders, or in other ways. Some items listed are ultimately removed: homosexuality was originally listed in the DSM, but was removed when the American Psychiatric Association officially recognized that "homosexuality per se implies no impairment in judgement, stability, reliability, or general social or vocational capabilities."

- Academic problem
- Acculturation problem
- Acute stress disorder
- Adjustment disorder
- Adolescent antisocial behaviour
- Adult antisocial behaviour
- Adverse effects of medication-not otherwise specified
- Age-related cognitive decline
- Agoraphobia without history of panic disorder
- Alcohol-related disorder
- Amnestic disorder
- Amphetamine (or amphetamine-like)-related disorder
- Anorexia nervosa
- Antisocial personality disorder
- Anxiety disorder
- Anxiolytic-related disorder
- Asperger syndrome
- Attention-deficit/hyperactivity disorder
- Atypical autism
- Autistic disorder
- Autophagia
- Avoidant personality disorder
- Bereavement
- Bibliomania
- Binge eating disorder
- Bipolar disorder
- Boanthropy
- Body dysmorphic disorder
- Borderline intellectual functioning
- Borderline personality disorder
- Breathing-related sleep disorder
- Brief psychotic disorder
- Bulimia nervosa
- Caffeine-related disorder
- Cannabis-related disorder
- Catatonic disorder
- Childhood antisocial behaviour
- Childhood disintegrative disorder
- Chronic motor or vocal tic disorder
- Circadian rhythm sleep disorder
- Cocaine-related disorder
- Cognitive disorder
- Communication disorder
- Conduct disorder

- Conversion disorder
- Delirium
- Delusional disorder
- Dementia
- Dependent personality disorder
- Depersonalization disorder
- Depression
- Depressive disorder
- Derealization
- Developmental coordination disorder
- Disorder of infancy, childhood, or adolescence-not otherwise specified
- Disorder of written expression
- Disruptive behaviour disorder
- Dissociative amnesia
- Dissociative disorder
- Dissociative fugue
- Diogenes syndrome
- Dissociative identity disorder (DID)
- Down Syndrome
- Dyspareunia
- Dyssomnia
- Dysthymic disorder
- Eating disorder-not otherwise specified
- Echolalia
- Echopraxia
- Emotional disorder
- Encopresis
- Enuresis (not due to a general medical condition)
- Erotomania
- Exhibitionism
- Expressive language disorder
- Factitious disorder
- Feeding disorder of infancy or early childhood
- Female and male orgasmic disorders
- Female sexual arousal disorder
- Fetishism
- Fregoli delusion
- Frotteurism
- Ganser syndrome
- Gender identity disorder
- Generalized anxiety disorder
- General adaptation syndrome
- Hallucinogen-related disorder
- Histrionic personality disorder

- Homosexuality
- Huntington's disease
- Hypoactive sexual desire disorder
- Hypomanic episode
- Impulse control disorder-not elsewhere classified
- Inhalant-related disorder
- Insomnia due to a general medical condition
- Intermittent explosive disorder
- Joubert syndrome
- Kleptomania
- Learning disorders
- Lima syndrome
- Major depressive disorder
- Major depressive episode
- Male erectile disorder
- Malingering
- Manic episode
- Mathematics disorder
- Medication-related disorder
- Mental disorder-not otherwise specified due to a general medical condition
- Mental Retardation
- Mixed episode
- Mixed receptive-expressive language disorder
- Mood disorder
- Mood episode
- Motor skills disorder
- Munchausen's syndrome
- Munchausen's syndrome by proxy
- Narcissistic personality disorder
- Narcolepsy
- Neglect of child
- Neuroleptic-related disorder
- Nicotine-related disorder
- Nightmare disorder
- Obsessive-compulsive disorder (OCD)
- Obsessive-compulsive personality disorder (OCPD)
- Occupational problem
- Oneirophrenia
- Opioid-related disorder
- Oppositional defiant disorder (ODD)
- Pain disorder
- Panic attack
- Panic disorder with agoraphobia
- Panic disorder without agoraphobia

- Paranoid personality disorder
- Paraphilia
- Parasomnia
- Parent-child relational problem
- Partner relational problem
- Pathological gambling
- Pedophilia
- Perfectionism
- Personality change due to a general medical condition
- Personality disorder
- Personality disorder-not otherwise specified
- Pervasive developmental disorder (PDD)
- Pervasive Developmental Disorder-Non Otherwise Specified (PDD-NOS)
- Phase of life problem
- Phencyclidine (or phencyclidine-like)-related disorder
- Phonological disorder
- Physical abuse
- Pica
- Polysubstance-related disorder
- Post-traumatic embitterment disorder (PTED)
- Posttraumatic stress disorder (PTSD)
- Premature ejaculation
- Primary hypersomnia
- Primary insomnia
- Psychological factor affecting medical condition
- Psychotic disorder
- Psychotic disorder-non otherwise specified
- Pyromania
- Racjicode
- Reactive Attachment Disorder of infancy or early childhood
- Reading disorder
- Relational disorder
- Relational problem
- Religious or spiritual problem
- Residual schizophrenia
- Rett's disorder
- Rumination syndrome
- Schizoaffective disorder
- Schizoid personality disorder
- Schizophrenia
- Schizophreniform disorder
- Schizotypal personality disorder
- Sedative-, hypnotic-, or anxiolytic-related disorder
- Selective mutism

- Separation anxiety disorder
- Severe mental retardation
- Sexual abuse of adult
- Sexual abuse of child
- Sexual arousal disorder
- Sexual aversion disorder
- Sexual desire disorder
- Sexual disorder
- Sexual dysfunction
- Sexual pain disorder
- Sexual sadism
- Shared psychotic disorder
- Sibling relational problem
- Sleep disorder
- Sleep terror disorder
- Sleepwalking disorder
- Social phobia (Social anxiety disorder)
- Somatization disorder
- Somatoform disorder
- Specific phobia
- Stereotypic movement disorder
- Stuttering
- Substance-related disorder
- Tardive dyskinesia
- Tic disorder
- Tourette's disorder
- Transient tic disorder
- Transvestic Fetishism
- Trichotillomania
- Vaginismus
- Vascular dementia
- Voyeurism.

TOWARDS A PROPER TREATMENT OF CHILDREN WITH MENTAL DISORDERS: AN AMERICAN APPROACH

Research shows that half of all lifetime cases of mental illness begin by age 14. Scientists are discovering that changes in the body leading to mental illness may start much earlier, before any symptoms appear.

Through greater understanding of when and how fast specific areas of children's brains develop, we are learning more about the early stages of a wide range of mental illnesses that appear later in life. Helping young children and their parents manage difficulties early in life may prevent the development of disorders. Once mental illness develops, it becomes a regular part of your child's behaviour and more difficult to treat. Even though we know how to treat (though not yet cure) many disorders, many? children with mental illnesses are not getting treatment.

This fact sheet addresses common questions about diagnosis and treatment options for children with mental illnesses. Disorders affecting children may include anxiety disorders, attention deficit hyperactivity disorder (ADHD), autism spectrum disorders, bipolar disorder, depression, eating disorders, and schizophrenia.

Q. What should I do if I am concerned about mental, behavioural, or emotional symptoms in my child?

A. Talk to your child's doctor or health care provider. Ask questions and learn everything you can about the behaviour or symptoms that worry you. If your child is in school ask the teacher if your child has been showing worrisome changes in behaviour. Share this with your child's doctor or health care provider. Keep in mind that every child is different. Even normal development, such as when children develop language, motor, and social skills, varies from child to child. Ask if your child needs further evaluation by a specialist with experience in child behavioural problems. Specialists may include psychiatrists, psychologists, social workers, psychiatric nurses, and behavioural therapists. Educators may also help evaluate your child.

If you take your child to a specialist, ask, "Do you have experience treating the problems I see in my child?" Don't be afraid to interview more than one specialist to find the right fit. Continue to learn everything you can about the problem or diagnosis. The more you learn, the better you can work with your child's doctor and make decisions that feel right for you, your child, and your family.

Q. How do I know if my child's problems are serious?

A. Not every problem is serious. In fact, many everyday stresses can cause changes in your child's behaviour. For example, the birth of a sibling may cause a child to temporarily act much younger than he or she is. It is important to be able to tell the difference between typical behaviour changes and those associated with more serious problems. Pay special attention to behaviours that include:

- Problems across a variety of settings, such as at school, at home, or with peers
- Changes in appetite or sleep
- Social withdrawal, or fearful behaviour toward things your child normally is not afraid of
- Returning to behaviours more common in younger children, such as bed-wetting, for a long time
- Signs of being upset, such as sadness or tearfulness

- Signs of self-destructive behaviour, such as head-banging, or a tendency to get hurt often
- Repeated thoughts of death.

Q. Can symptoms be caused by a death in the family, illness in a parent, family financial problems, divorce, or other events?

A. Yes. Every member of a family is affected by tragedy or extreme stress, even the youngest child. It's normal for stress to cause a child to be upset. Remember this if you see mental, emotional, or behavioural symptoms in your child. If it takes more than one month for your child to get used to a situation, or if your child has severe reactions, talk to your child's doctor.

Check your child's response to stress. Take note if he or she gets better with time or if professional care is needed. Stressful events are challenging, but they give you a chance to teach your child important ways to cope.

Q. How are mental illnesses diagnosed in young children?

A. Just like adults, children with mental illness are diagnosed after a doctor or mental health specialist carefully observes signs and symptoms. Some primary care physicians can diagnose your child themselves, but many will send you to a specialist who can diagnose and treat children.

Before diagnosing a mental illness, the doctor or specialist tries to rule out other possible causes for your child's behaviour. The doctor will:

- Take a history of any important medical problems
- Take a history of the problem—how long you have seen the problem—as well as a history of your child's development
- Take a family history of mental disorders
- Ask if the child has experienced physical or psychological traumas, such as a natural disaster, or situations that may cause stress, such as a death in the family
- Consider reports from parents and other caretakers or teachers.

Very young children often cannot express their thoughts and feelings, so making a diagnosis can be challenging. The signs of a mental illness in a young child may be quite different from those in an older child or adult.

As parents and caregivers know, children are constantly changing and growing. Diagnosis and treatment must be viewed with these changes in mind. While some problems are short-lived and don't need treatment, others are ongoing and may be very serious. In either case, more information will help you understand treatment choices and manage the disorder or problem most effectively.

While diagnosing mental health problems in young children can be challenging, it is important. A diagnosis can be used to guide treatment and link your child's care to research on children with similar problems.

Q. Will my child get better with time?

A. Some children get better with time. But other children need ongoing professional help. Talk to your child's doctor or specialist about problems that are severe, continuous, and affect daily activities. Also, don't delay seeking help. Treatment may produce better results if started early.

Q. Are there treatment options for children?

A. Yes. Once a diagnosis is made, your child's specialist will recommend a specific treatment. It is important to understand the various treatment choices, which often include psychotherapy or medication. Talk about the options with a health care professional who has experience treating the illness observed in your child. Some treatment choices have been studied experimentally, and other treatments are a part of health care practice. In addition, not every community has every type of service or programme.

Q. What are psychotropic medications?

A. Psychotropic medications are substances that affect brain chemicals related to mood and behaviour. In recent years, research has been conducted to understand the benefits and risks of using psychotropics in children. Still, more needs to be learned about the effects of psychotropics, especially in children under six years of age. While researchers are trying to clarify how early treatment affects a growing body, families and doctors should weigh the benefits and risks of medication. Each child has individual needs, and each child needs to be monitored closely while taking medications.

Q. Are there treatments other than medications?

A. Yes. Psychosocial therapies can be very effective alone and in combination with medications. Psychosocial therapies are also called "talk therapies" or "behavioural therapy," and they help people with mental illness change behaviour. Therapies that teach parents and children coping strategies can also be effective.

Cognitive behavioural therapy (CBT) is a type of psychotherapy that can be used with children. It has been widely studied and is an effective treatment for a number of conditions, such as depression, obsessive-compulsive disorder, and social anxiety. A person in CBT learns to change distorted thinking patterns and unhealthy behaviour. Children can receive CBT with or without their parents, as well as in a group setting. CBT can be adapted to fit the needs of each child. It is especially useful when treating anxiety disorders.

Additionally, therapies for ADHD are numerous and include behavioural parent training and behavioural classroom management. Visit the NIMH Website for more information about therapies for ADHD.

Some children benefit from a combination of different psychosocial approaches.

An example is behavioural parent management training in combination with CBT for the child. In other cases, a combination of medication and psychosocial therapies may be most effective. Psychosocial therapies often take time, effort, and patience. However, sometimes children learn new skills that may have positive long-term benefits.

More information about treatment choices can be found in the psychotherapies and medications sections of the NIMH Website.

Q. When is it a good idea to use psychotropic medications in young children?

A. When the benefits of treatment outweigh the risks, psychotropic medications may be prescribed. Some children need medication to manage severe and difficult problems. Without treatment, these children would suffer serious or dangerous consequences. In addition, psychosocial treatments may not always be effective by themselves. In some instances, however, they can be quite effective when combined with medication.

Ask your doctor questions about the risks of starting and continuing your child on these medications. Learn everything you can about the medications prescribed for your child. Learn about possible side effects, some of which may be harmful. Know what a particular treatment is supposed to do. For example, will it change a specific behaviour? If you do not see these changes while your child is taking the medication, talk to his or her doctor. Also, discuss the risks of stopping your child's medication with your doctor.

Q. Does medication affect young children differently than older children or adults?

A. Yes. Young children handle medications differently than older children and adults. The brains of young children change and develop rapidly. Studies have found that developing brains can be very sensitive to medications. There are also developmental differences in how children metabolize—how their bodies process—medications. Therefore, doctors should carefully consider the dosage or how much medication to give each child. Much more research is needed to determine the effects and benefits of medications in children of all ages. But keep in mind that serious untreated mental disorders themselves can harm brain development.

Also, it is important to avoid drug interactions. If your child takes medicine for asthma or cold symptoms, talk to your doctor or pharmacist. Drug interactions could cause medications to not work as intended or lead to serious side effects.

Q. How should medication be included in an overall treatment plan?

A. Medication should be used with other treatments. It should not be the only treatment. Consider other services, such as family therapy, family support services, educational classes, and behaviour management techniques. If your child's doctor prescribes medication, he or she should evaluate your child regularly to make sure the medication is working. Children need treatment plans tailored to their individual problems and needs.

Q. What medications are used for which kinds of childhood mental disorders?

A. Psychotropic medications include stimulants, antidepressants, anti-anxiety medications, antipsychotics, and mood stabilizers. Dosages approved by the U.S. Food and Drug Administration (FDA) for use in children depend on body weight and age. NIMH's medications booklet describes the types of psychotropic medications and includes a chart that lists the ages for which each medication is FDA-approved. See the FDA Website for the latest information on medication approvals, warnings, and patient information guides.

Q. What does it mean if a medication is specifically approved for use in children?

A. When the FDA approves a medication, it means the drug manufacturer provided the agency with information showing the medication is safe and effective in a particular group of people. Based on this information, the drug's label lists proper dosage, potential side effects, and approved age. Medications approved for children follow these guidelines.

Many psychotropic medications have not been studied in children, which means they have not been approved by the FDA for use in children. But doctors may prescribe medications as they feel appropriate, even if those uses are not included on the label. This is called "off-label" use. Research shows that off-label use of some medications works well in some children. Other medications need more study in children. In particular, the use of most psychotropic medications has not been adequately studied in preschoolers.

More studies in children are needed before we can fully know the appropriate dosages, how a medication works in children, and what effects a medication might have on learning and development.

Q. Why haven't many medications been tested in children?

A. In the past, medications were seldom studied in children because mental illness was not recognized in childhood. Also, there were ethical concerns about involving children in research. This led to a lack of knowledge about the best treatments for children. In clinical settings today, children with mental or behavioural disorders are being prescribed medications at increasingly early ages. The FDA has been urging that medications be appropriately studied in children, and Congress passed legislation in 1997 offering incentives to drug manufacturers to carry out such testing. These activities have helped increase research on the effects of medications in children.

There still are ethical concerns about testing medications in children. However, strict rules protect participants in research studies. Each study must go through many types of review before, and after it begins.

Q. How do I work with my child's school?

A. If your child is having problems in school, or if a teacher raises concerns, you can work with the school to find a solution. You may ask the school to conduct an evaluation to determine whether your child qualifies for special education services. However, not all children diagnosed with a mental illness qualify for these services.

Start by speaking with your child's teacher, school counselor, school nurse, or the school's parent organization. These professionals can help you get an evaluation started. Also, each state has a Parent Training and Information Center and a Protection and Advocacy Agency that can help you request the evaluation. The evaluation must be conducted by a team of professionals who assess all areas related to the suspected disability using a variety of tools and measures.

Q. What resources are available from the school?

A. Once your child has been evaluated, there are several options for him or her, depending on the specific needs. If special education services are needed, and if your child is eligible under the Individuals with Disabilities Education Act (IDEA), the school district must develop an "individualized education programme" specifically for your child within 30 days.

If your child is not eligible for special education services, he or she is still entitled to "free appropriate public education," available to all public school children with disabilities under Section 504 of the Rehabilitation Act of 1973. Your child is entitled to this regardless of the nature or severity of his or her disability.

The U.S. Department of Education's Office for Civil Rights enforces Section 504 in programmes and activities that receive Federal education funds. Visit programmes for children with disabilities for more information.

Q. What special challenges can school present?

A. Each school year brings a new teacher and new schoolwork. This change can be difficult for some children. Inform the teachers that your child has a mental illness when he or she starts school or moves to a new class. Additional support will help your child adjust to the change.

Q. What else can I do to help my child?

A. Children with mental illness need guidance and understanding from their parents and teachers. This support can help your child achieve his or her full potential and succeed in school. Before a child is diagnosed, frustration, blame, and anger may have built up within a family. Parents and children may need special help to undo these unhealthy interaction patterns. Mental health professionals can counsel the child and family to help everyone develop new skills, attitudes, and ways of relating to each other.

Parents can also help by taking part in parenting skills training. This helps parents learn how to handle difficult situations and behaviours. Training encourages parents to share a pleasant or relaxing activity with their child, to notice and point out what their child does well, and to praise their child's strengths and abilities. Parents may also learn to arrange family situations in more positive ways. Also, parents may benefit from learning stress-management techniques to help them deal with frustration and respond calmly to their child's behaviour.

Sometimes, the whole family may need counselling. Therapists can help family members find better ways to handle disruptive behaviours and encourage behaviour changes. Finally, support groups help parents and families connect with others who have similar problems and concerns. Groups often meet regularly to share frustrations and successes, to exchange information about recommended specialists and strategies, and to talk with experts.

Q. How can families of children with mental illness get support?

A. Like other serious illnesses, taking care of a child with mental illness is hard on the parents, family, and other caregivers. Caregivers often must tend to the medical needs of their loved ones, and also deal with how it affects their own health. The stress that caregivers are under may lead to missed work or lost free time. It can strain relationships with people who may not understand the situation and lead to physical and mental exhaustion.

Stress from caregiving can make it hard to cope with your child's symptoms. One study shows that if a caregiver is under enormous stress, his or her loved one has more difficulty sticking to the treatment plan. It is important to look after your own physical and mental health. You may also find it helpful to join a local support group.

Q. Where can I go for help?

A. If you are unsure where to go for help, ask your family doctor. Others who can help are listed below.

- Mental health specialists, such as psychiatrists, psychologists, social workers, or mental health counsellors
- Health maintenance organizations
- Community mental health centres
- Hospital psychiatry departments and outpatient clinics
- Mental health programmes at universities or medical schools
- State hospital outpatient clinics
- Family services, social agencies, or clergy
- Peer support groups
- Private clinics and facilities
- Employee assistance programmes
- Local medical and/or psychiatric societies.

You can also check the phone book under "mental health," "health," "social services," "hotlines," or "physicians" for phone numbers and addresses. An emergency room doctor can also provide temporary help and can tell you where and how to get further help.

5

Intervention, Occupational Therapy and Adapted Physical Education: Role in Disability Related Disorder Management and Treatment

UNDERSTANDING RESPONSE TO INTERVENTION

In education, Response To Intervention (commonly abbreviated RTI or RtI) is a method of academic intervention designed to provide early, effective assistance to children who are having difficulty learning. Response to intervention was also designed to function as a data-based process of diagnosing learning disabilities. This method can be used at the group and individual level. The RTI method has been developed by researchers as an alternative to identifying learning disabilities with the ability-achievement discrepancy model, which requires children to exhibit a severe discrepancy between their IQ and academic achievement as measured by standardized tests. Further, the RTI process brings more clarity to the Specific Learning Disability (SLD) category of the Individuals with Disabilities Education Improvement Act (IDEA 2004), which has been referred to as a residual category for children with moderate learning problems.

RTI seeks to prevent academic failure through early intervention, frequent progress measurement, and increasingly intensive research-based instructional interventions for children who continue to have difficulty. Students who do not show a response to effective interventions are likely (or, more likely than students who respond) to have biologically-based learning disabilities and to be in need of special education.

For children with learning disabilities, RTI may assist schools in avoiding the so-called "wait-to-fail" method by providing intervention as soon as children exhibit difficulty.

One criticism of the RTI method suggests that RTI is really a means for limiting access to special ed services. The intervention model puts the onus on individual teachers to prove that they have done everything possible in the classroom before the child can be assessed. Because the RTI model is often implemented across years, assessment and classification of a student can be unreasonably delayed or never provided when each new year the student has a new teacher and a new RTI. Critics charge that requiring an extensive and lengthy paper trail prior to evaluation of a child is primarily used as a bureaucratic means for delaying that evaluation. They point to the fact that the cost of special ed services is a powerful incentive for districts to systematically delay services to as many children as possible as long as possible. However, it should be noted that public schools tend to receive more federal and state dollars the more students they identify as qualifying for special education. That said, RTI would if anything delay receipt of funding at the school level. Therefore the above criticism may stem from misinformation.

An additional criticism of this programme is associated with the model that it replaces. Because the RTI model only results in evaluation of the most critical failures in the regular classroom, students in special ed classrooms are less likely to succeed generally. The previous model which addressed discrepancy cast a net to students who could be said to possess areas of relative strength and were more likely to benefit from services. However, the body of relavent research suggests that slow-learners likewise benefit from services.

Description

Response to Intervention (RTI) is a philosophy that encompasses alternative assessment which utilizes quality interventions matched to student needs, coupled with formative evaluation to obtain data over time to make critical educational decisions.

RTI follows the following core assumptions:

1. that the educational system can effectively teach all children
2. that early intervention is critical to preventing problems from getting out of control
3. that the implementation of a multi-tiered service delivery model is necessary
4. that a problem solving model should be used to make decisions between tiers
5. that research based interventions should be implemented to the extent possible
6. that progress monitoring must be implemented to inform instruction
7. that data should drive decision making.

In this regard, RTI is not simply a set of interventions but a systematic model within general education and special education areas. In addition, RTI should be viewed as a systematic process for providing preventive, supplementary instructional services to students who are having challenges meeting benchmark levels. RTI is superior to the mathematical discrepancy approach in that it takes the focus away from within-child deficits to issues relative to the context of instruction or the extent to which a student has had the opportunity to learn. The assumption that a student cannot learn is typically attributed to some neurological or processing disorder residing within the child. This assumption fails to account for the possibility that interacting variables such as the lack of good instruction, the lack of an opportunity to learn, cultural variables, and/or language proficiency levels in the second language, for example, might be reasons for the lack of academic progress. The literature is clear that the traditional psychometric discrepancy model does more harm to students and actually has created a special education system that serves a disproportionate number of minority students.

What follows is an opinion from a person with 30 years experience in the public school system: The statement above about disproportionality is questionable; there are many categories of disability that are recognized in IDEA legislation as making a student eligible for Special Education (for example—blindness, deafness, mental retardation, autism, emotional disturbance, speech/language impairments, orthopedic impairments, specific medical syndromes (such as ADHD), etc.), Learning Disabilities are only one of about a dozen such categories. No LD definition by itself could "create" a discriminatory Special Education system. The net effect of some actions to address the statistic that a higher proportion of minority students in some school districts are classified as eligible for Special Education can itself be discriminatory; that is, if minority students with similar educational profiles to non-minority students become less likely to be classified out of a misplaced concern about proportions, the minority students could actually be denied services that their tax dollars pay for. But what are the possible sources of disproportionate classification? That is the real question here. The discrepancy model of LD, even with its flaws, was not the culprit. In some school districts where pre-referral interventions are not an economic option, Special Ed has provided the most intensive and individualized services to students who are not making it. Whether this is a good thing or a bad thing is a matter of opinion, not fact. RTI has its own major limitations and perhaps unintended consequences as well. RTI as currently defined applies mainly to reading (decoding and comprehension). But there are writing LDs as well (encoding) and math LDs that affect some students. The RTI requirements for tiered services makes documenting non-reading LDs nearly impossible, because schools generally do not have staff to address writing and math with multiple levels of remedial services; the funding does not exist for such things, especially in urban and lower income areas. Remember how schools are funded (local property taxes). Until there is more government support for education, richer neighbourhoods will have better schools. However RTI is a subtle way for Special Education legislation to affect non-Special Ed (general ed) practices in a major way. Notice that the steps prior to classification affect the way every school must handle their general education remedial reading programmes. How prepared are lower income school districts to fund such services, which must be paid for out of local monies (because remedial programmes fall within general ed; additional state funding is available only for Special Ed programmes). An unintended consequence of RTI definitions of LD is that anyone at a below average IQ level could be considered LD if they have received the various tiers of instruction and fail to progress. Such traditional "slow learners" were previously ineligible for Special Ed when classification as LD was based on a discrepancy model. Be prepared for larger overall numbers of classified students once the slow learner population becomes eligible for Special Ed under RTI.

RTI is conceptualized as a multi-tiered service delivery model including primary, secondary, and tertiary levels of support. The primary, or first tier is focused specifically at the school core curriculum level, meaning that the target level of intervention is the core curriculum. In this tier approximately 80 per cent to 85 per cent of the general student body should be able to meet grade level norms without additional assistance. The 15 per cent to 20 per cent of students who consistently show a discrepancy between their current level of performance and that of the expected level of performance are then given Tier 2 or secondary, supplementary instruction services (not to be confused with special education) targeting the problems the student is having. Of the students who are provided with intervention services at Tier 2, approximately 3 to 6 per cent of them will continue to have difficulties and continue to show resistance to intervention. At this point in time, these students will then receive Tier 3 intervention services (not to be confused with special education at this point either). Hence, the intensity of intervention increases as the severity of the problem increases.

RTI has three basic components: School-wide screening, Progress monitoring and Tiered service delivery, and Fidelity of implementation.

School-wide Screening

For a screening measure to be useful, it should satisfy three criteria: (a) It needs to identify students who require further assessment (b) It needs to be practical (c) It needs to generate positive outcomes (accurately identifies students without consuming resources that could be put to better use) A screening procedure must be brief as well as simple enough to be implemented reliably by teachers. Screening measures can use either a criterion referenced or normative comparison standard of performance. In the former, a specific criterion level of skills is specified as indicating an acceptable level of proficiency or mastery. In the normative comparison, the screening results are compared to an appropriate peer group (e.g., other students in first grade). Criterion measures are preferred because they give more accurate information about performance on relevant skills. Screening is not a one-time process but an iterative system during the school year and across grade levels. During the course of primary instruction (Tier 1), the school uses school-wide screening (consistency) in essential academic areas to identify each student's level of proficiency (usually three times per year). The National Research Center on Learning Disabilities recommends that schools use school-wide screening in combination with at least five weeks of weekly progress monitoring in response to general education to identify students who require preventative intervention. Their rationale is that one-time universal screening at the beginning of the year can over-identify students who require preventative intervention.

Progress Monitoring and Tiered Service Delivery

Progress monitoring is a set of assessment procedures for determining the extent to which students are benefiting from classroom instruction and for monitoring effectiveness of curriculum. Progress monitoring is the scientifically based practice of assessing students' academic performance on a regular basis for three purposes:

- To determine whether children are profiting appropriately from the instructional programme, including the curriculum
- To build more effective programmes for the children who do not benefit
- To estimate rates of student improvement.

In Tier 1, progress monitoring procedures serve several functions. First, progress monitoring displays individual student growth over time, to determine whether the student is progressing as expected. The steps in Tier 1 are: data is collected, students are identified using benchmark scores, and measurable goals are set for next data collection point for the class and students displaying difficulties. Then, the team problem-solves to determine scientifically research-based interventions for at-risk students that will work in whole-class instructions. Observations are conducted to ensure the fidelity of the classroom instruction. The teacher implements the interventions and the team reviews progress of students.

In Tier 2, the main purpose of progress monitoring and beyond interventions is to determine whether the intervention is successful in helping the student learn at an appropriate rate. Decision rules need to be created to determine when a student might no longer require Tier 2 and beyond services and can be returned to the general classroom (Tier 1), when the intervention needs to be changed, or when a student might be identified for special education. The steps in Tier 2 are: see if the child has not met benchmarks in Tier 1, has significantly lower performance levels, exhibit significant deviation from their grade-level peers in academic or behavioural issues, and are learning at a much slower rate and falling farther behind.

Tier 2 and beyond consists of general education instruction plus specialized intervention that has the following features: Size of instructional group. Tier 2 and beyond instruction is provided in small groups (two to four students). Cut scores identified on screening measures and continued growth as demonstrated by routine progress monitoring are indicators of content mastery. Although recommendations vary, weekly to three times per week monitoring of progress is typical. Tier 2 and beyond interventions last for nine to 12 weeks and can be repeated as needed. Tier 2 and beyond provides for three to four intervention sessions per week, each lasting 30 to 60 minutes. Instruction is conducted by trained and supervised personnel.

Tier 3 demands more intense interventions. The steps are: see if the child is having marked difficulties and have not responded to Tier 2 interventions, requires more frequent, intense interventions and more frequent progress monitoring.

In Tier 3, special education instruction is provided to individual students or small groups. Special education programmes, strategies, and procedures are designed and employed to supplement, enhance, and support Tier 1 and Tier 2 and beyond instruction by remediation of the relevant area and development of compensatory strategies. Mastery is relative to the student's functioning and determined by individualized education programme (IEP) goal setting and through results of comprehensive evaluation. Continuous progress monitoring informs the teaching process. Special education instruction likely will be considerably longer than the 10 to 12 weeks of supplemental instruction delivered in Tier 2 and beyond. The frequency of special education instruction depends upon student need. Special education teachers deliver the instruction. Exit criteria are specified and monitored so that placement is flexible.

Fidelity of Implementation

In an RTI model, fidelity is important at both the school level (e.g., implementation of the process) and the teacher level (e.g., implementation of instruction). Although both common sense and research support the concept of fidelity of implementation to ensure an intervention's successful outcome, the practical challenges associated with achieving high levels of fidelity are well documented. Factors that reduce fidelity of implementation are:

- *Complexity*. The more complex the intervention, the lower the fidelity because of the level of difficulty. (This factor includes time needed for instruction in the intervention).
- *Materials and resources required*. If new or substantial resources are required, they need to be readily accessible.
- *Perceived and actual effectiveness (credibility)*. Even with a solid research base, if teachers believe the approach will not be effective, or if it is inconsistent with their teaching style, they will not implement it well.
- *Interventionists*. The number, expertise, and motivation of individuals who deliver the intervention are factors in the level of fidelity of implementation.

Classification of RTI

In the educational literature, RTI is either referred to as a *Standard Protocol Approach* or as a *Problem Solving Model*. Both models incorporate problem solving to identify the academic problem the student is having. The main difference among these approaches is that the former uses a systematic, universal screening procedure during Tier 1 to determine which students are having difficulties meeting age or grade level benchmarks for a specific skill. Typically, Curriculum Based Measurement (CBM), or other methods are used to flag the students who are not meeting expected levels of performance. In the problem solving model approach, the teacher typically refers the student to the student success team or multidisciplinary team to ascertain the challenges a student is having within the classroom. Using information collected from the classroom teacher, observations, etc. the team determines what additional supports the student might need to address the learning gap.

Response To Intervention (RTI) is a method, or process, of educational intervention which includes, but is not limited to: reading tutoring, peer tutoring, phonological awareness, and phonics interventions. Key to the RTI method is the application of scientifically-based interventions that have been demonstrated to work in randomized controlled trials. The RTI method assumes accountability to the consumers of an educational programme by ensuring the application of programmes that work rather than programmes that simply look, sound, or feel good. In terms of its methods, after the intervention, collecting of data on change in student performance is undertaken. Curriculum Based Measurement (CBM) is often used to collect data on interventions and their effectiveness. CBM has over 30 years of scientific support. Response to intervention is based on discovering what works best for an individual student, not what might be the 'best' intervention for everyone. Additional methods are tried until students 'respond' to the intervention and improve their skills. Students that do not respond, or respond at significantly low rates, are deemed to have biologically-based learning disabilities, not simply learning difficulties.

RTI provides an alternative or additional means of gathering information to be used when classifying students for special education. When a student is identified as having difficulties in school, a team provides interventions of increasing intensity to help the child catch up with the rest of his or her peers. After interventions have been tried and proven ineffective, the child may then be referred for additional, special education services (IDEA). RTI is a way to ensure each student is afforded the opportunity to learn.

When interventions work, fewer children, particularly minority children, are referred for special education. The RTI model acts as a safeguard, insuring that a child is not given a label of a disability inappropriately. RTI also helps school districts by eliminating unnecessary referrals, which drain time and resources.

Relationship between IDEA and RTI

IDEA (Individuals with Disabilities Education Act) was revised and signed into law in 2004 and became effective in July, 2005. The 2004 reauthorization of IDEA makes mention of Response to Intervention as a pre-referral intervention model and encourages its implementation in three significant ways:

1. In diagnosing learning disabilities, LEAs are no longer required to use the discrepancy model. The Act states that, "a local educational agency shall not be required to take into consideration whether a child has a severe discrepancy between achievement and intellectual ability..."
2. Response to Intervention is specifically mentioned in the regulations in conjunction with the identification of a specific learning disability.
3. Early Intervening Services (EIS) are prominently mentioned in IDEA for the first time. These services are directed at interventions for students prior to referral in an attempt to avoid classification, such as in an RTI model. IDEA now authorizes the use of up to 15 per cent of IDEA allocated funds for EIS.

RTI was included in the regulations due to considerable concerns raised by both the House and Senate Committees regarding the use of IQ tests to identify learning disabled students. There was also recognition in these committees of a growing body of scientific research supporting methods of pre-referral interventions that resolved learning difficulties short of classification.

The IDEA Committee Conference Report (CCR) discusses the use of scientifically based early intervention programmes, describes a model Response to Intervention programme, and recommends the development of the most effective implementation of responsiveness to intervention models. The report describes such a model as an essential service for reducing the need to label children as disabled.

Response to RTI

As RTI has recently entered U.S. schools, some teachers believe that it has brought about tension between regular education teachers and special education teachers. In other schools, RTI has led to increased cooperation and understanding between regular education teachers and special education teachers. Regardless of teachers' responses, students are benefiting from the RTI process.

RTI has brought more than tension into the regular education teacher's classroom. It is a whole new way of doing things, including evidence-based instructional practices and more focus on students individual needs (which ultimately create more stress for today's teachers). Most teachers are used to referring students to special education who they 'can't get through to.' RTI forces teachers to keep these students in their classrooms and to search for research-based ways to help them. All in all, it requires more work from teachers than the old discrepancy model; this change in the status quo represents perhaps the greatest resistance towards RTI.

Among the school psychologists, multi-tiered progress monitoring approaches have been around as early as 1977 (Kovaleski, 2007). For school psychology, RTI is not so much a revolution as a return to the problem-solving that should have been going on all along.

KNOWING OCCUPATIONAL THERAPY AND ITS TYPES

Occupational Therapy, often abbreviated as "OT", incorporates meaningful and purposeful occupation to enable people with limitations or impairments to participate in everyday life. Occupational therapists work with individuals, families, groups and populations to facilitate health and well-being through engagement or re-engagement in occupation. Occupational therapists are becoming increasingly involved in addressing the impact of social and environmental factors that contribute to exclusion and occupational deprivation.

Defining Occupational Therapy

The World Federation of Occupational Therapists defines occupational therapy as a profession concerned with promoting health and well-being through occupation. The primary goal of occupational therapy is to enable people to participate in the activities of everyday life. Occupational therapists achieve this outcome by enhancing the individual's ability to participate, by modifying the environment, or by adapting the activity to better support participation.

Occupational therapy relies on understanding the importance of an activity to an individual, being able to analyze the physical, mental and social components of the activity, and then adapting the activity, the environment, and/or the person to enable them to resume the activity. Occupational therapists address the question, "Why does this person have difficulties managing his or her daily activities (or occupations), and what can we adapt to make it possible for him or her to manage better and how will this then impact his or her health and well-being?"

Occupational therapy gives people the "skills for the job of living" necessary for "living life to its fullest."

The College of Occupational Therapists (2004) describes OT as follows: Occupational Therapy enables people to achieve health, well-being and life satisfaction through participation in occupation.

Occupational therapy draws from the field of occupational science to provide an evidence base to practice and develop academic and practice links to other related disciplines such as social science and anthropology, and also utilizes a range of generic models to guide the practice of OT.

History of Occupational Therapy

The earliest evidence of using occupations as a therapeutic modality can be found in ancient times. One-hundred years before the birth of Christ, Greek physician Asclepiades initiated humane treatment of patients with mental illness via the use of therapeutic baths, massage, exercise, and music. Later, the Roman Celsus prescribed music, travel, conversation and exercise to his patients. Unfortunately, by medieval times, the concept of humane treatment of people considered to be insane was rare, if not nonexistent.

In eighteenth century Europe, revolutionaries such as Philippe Pinel and Johann Christian Reil reformed the hospital system. Instead of the use of metal chains and restraint, their institutions utilized rigorous work and leisure activities in the late 1700s. Although it was thriving abroad, interest in the reform movement waxed and waned in the United States throughout the nineteenth century. At the turn of the 20th century, as physicians became increasingly interested in chronic disease, enthusiasm for the reform of the mental healthcare system was revived in the states. Work therapy found its way to America.

The health profession of occupational therapy as we know it was conceived in the early 1910s. Focus was on promoting health in "invalids." Early professionals merged highly valued ideals, such as having a strong work ethic and the importance of crafting with one's own hands, with scientific and medical principles. Early adversaries viewed wood carving and crafting by ill patients trivial.

The emergence of occupational therapy challenged the views of mainstream scientific medicine. Instead of focusing on purely physical etiologies, they argued that a complex combination of social, economic, and biological reasons cause dysfunction. Principles and techniques were borrowed from many disciplines—including but not limited to nursing, psychiatry, rehabilitation, self-help, orthopedics, and social work—to enrich the profession's scope. Between 1900 and 1930, the founders defined the realm of practice and developed theories of practice. In a short 20-year span, they successfully convinced the public and medical world of the value of occupational therapy and established standards for the profession.

A substantial lack of primary sources of information has left today's occupational therapists with many questions concerning the founders of the field. Information is collected from early training institutions and hospitals, professional writings of practitioners, World War I records from government agencies, newspaper articles, and personal testimonials.

One of the most notable figures in the infancy of occupational therapy was Eleanor Clark Slagle. Slagle was part of the generation of women who challenged women's "rightful" place as a volunteer and strived for females to have a place in the professional world. At age forty, she was trained in curative occupations and recreations at the Chicago School of Civics and Philanthropy and later took a position at Hull House, where crafts were used to promote mental health.

It is speculated that Slagle's interest in healthcare stemmed from her personal life, as her father, brother, and nephew all suffered from various disabilities. Seeing the daily struggles of people with disabilities and illnesses may have sparked Slagle to enroll in the Chicago School in 1911. In 1912, renowned psychiatrist Adolph Meyer appointed Slagle to direct a new department of occupational therapy at John Hopkins Hospital. There, she learned habit training—a method of re-educating patients on decent habits of living via substituting healthful habits for bad habits.

Another psychiatrist, William Rush Dunton, Jr., worked diligently to raise the status of psychiatry in medicine in the first decades of the 20th century. He viewed occupational therapy as complementary to psychiatry, as it had the promise of meshing humanitarian values with science. Dunton became interested in the work of European moral therapy advocates. He accepted a position at the Sheppard Asylum, where it was standard practice in the early 1900s for patients to participate in activities such as bowling, gymnastics, art, etc. Dunton and his contemporaries called for the development of a theory to underlie the treatment known as "moral therapy" and "diversional occupation," among other names. He called for therapists to devise outcome measures so that the neophyte profession would be given the attention and respect he felt it deserved.

Another important figure in the early days of occupational therapy was Susan Tracy, a nurse by trade, who organized activity-oriented classes for nurses at the Adams Nervine Asylum. In 1910, she published a textbook that was widely used for over 30 years. She is credited with expanding the realm of occupational therapy from psychiatric institutions to the homes of patients, which is an important setting in which today's occupational therapists work. Upon breaking ties with the asylum, she set up her own institution, entitled the Experiment Station for the Study of Invalid Occupations. This training center educated nurses so they could gain control over their practice and not default to being dominated by physicians. By practising privately in patients' homes, this batch of occupational therapists expanded the domain of occupational therapy and began using OT to treat physical ailments as well as mental illness.

Herbert J. Hall was a physician with a strong work ethic and practical vision. He believed we could retract social ills by adapting the arts and crafts movement for medical purposes. A graduate of Harvard Medical School, he advised the government on wartime standards for occupational therapy during World War I. He introduced the concept of grading activities—now a hallmark of occupational therapy—to avoid exacerbating patient's frustration and fatigue.

George Edward Barton, an architect, also aided in promoting the occupational therapy profession. Diagnosed with tuberculosis in 1901, Barton later contracted gangrene and had a partial amputation, after which he was left paralyzed on his left side. He opened Consolation House, a sanctuary for people with physical disabilities, in 1914. There, intensive self-administered occupational therapy "cured" his ailments. He played an integral part in gathering the profession's leaders and forming the first national society.

The first meeting of the National Society for the Promotion of Occupational Therapy was held in March 1917. Barton (along with his secretary), Eleanor Clark Slagle, William Rush Dunton Jr., Thomas B. Kinder, and Susan Cox Johnson were the only six in attendance. In the fall of 1919, at the third meeting, 300 attendees participated. In 1921, the name of the organization was changed to the American Occupational Therapy Association and the Archives of Occupational Therapy, the first professional journal, began publication.

World War I forced the new profession to clarify its role in the medical domain and to standardize training and practice. In addition to clarifying its public image, OT also established clinics, workshops, and training schools nationwide. Due to the overwhelming number of wartime injuries, "reconstruction aides" (an umbrella term for physical therapists and occupational therapists) were recruited by the Surgeon General. Between 1917 and 1920, nearly 148,000 wounded men were placed in hospitals upon their return to the states. This number does not account for those wounded abroad. The success of the reconstruction aides, largely made up of women trying to "do their bit" to help with the war effort, was a great accomplishment. Post-war, however, there was a struggle to keep people in the profession. Emphasis was shifted from the altruistic war-time mentality to the financial, professional, and personal satisfaction that comes with being a therapist. To make the profession more appealing, practice was standardized, as was the curriculum. Entry and exit criterion were established, and AOTA advocated for steady employment, decent wages, and fair working conditions. Via these methods, occupational therapy sought and obtained medical legitimacy in the 1920s. By the time Slagle retired from the profession in 1937, the profession's medical identity was well on its way to being established.

Evolution of the Philosophy of Occupational Therapy

The philosophy of occupational therapy has evolved over the history of the profession. The philosophy articulated by the founders that have owed much to the ideals of romanticism, pragmatism and humanism which are collectively considered the fundamental ideologies of the past century.

William Rush Dunton, the creator of the National Society for the Promotion of Occupational Therapy, now the American Occupational Therapy Association, sought to promote the ideas that occupation is a basic human need, and that occupation was therapeutic. From his statements, came some of the basic assumptions of occupational therapy, which include:

- Occupation has an effect on health and well-being.
- Occupation creates structure and organizes time.
- Occupation brings meaning to life, culturally and personally.
- Occupations are individual. People value different occupations.

These have been elaborated over time to form the values which underpin the Codes of Ethics issued by each national association. However, the relevance of occupation to health and well-being remains the central theme. Influenced by criticism from medicine and the multitude of physical disabilities resulting from World War II, occupational therapy adopted a more reductionistic philosophy for a time. While this approach lead to developments in technical knowledge about occupational performance, clinicians became increasingly disillusioned and re-considered these beliefs. As a result, client centeredness and occupation are re-emerging as dominant themes in the profession, perhaps indicating growing maturity and self confidence. Over the past century, the underlying philosophy of occupational therapy has evolved from being a diversion from illness, to treatment, to enablement through meaningful occupation. This became evident through the development and widespread adoption of the Canadian Model of Occupational Performance.

The two most commonly mentioned values are that occupation is essential for health and the concept of holism. However, there have been some dissenting voices. Mocellin in particular advocated abandoning the notion of health through occupation as obsolete in the modern world and questioned the appropriateness of advocating holism when practice rarely supports it. The values formulated by the American Association of Occupational Therapists have also been critiqued as being therapist centred and not reflecting the modern reality of multicultural practice.

Central to the philosophy of occupational therapy is the concept of occupational performance. In considering occupational performance the therapist must consider the many factors which comprise overall performance. This concept is made more tangible using models such as the person-environment-occupation model proposed by Law *et al.* (1996). This approach highlights the importance of satisfactions in one's occupations, broadening the aim of occupational therapy beyond the mere completion of tasks to the holistic achievement of personal well-being.

In recent times occupational therapists have challenged themselves to think more broadly about the potential scope of the profession, and expanded it to include working with groups experiencing occupational deprivation which stems from sources other than disability. Examples of new and emerging practice areas would include therapists working with refugees, and with people experiencing homelessness.

Occupation, Occupational Form and Performance

Occupation

Occupation is the dynamic relationship between the occupational form and occupational performance.

Many people see the term occupation as a job one does. However, the meaning of occupation is seen in a much wider context by an Occupational Therapist. A human being can be engaged in a wide range of occupations: leisure, self-care or educational activities are just a few examples of occupation.

Occupational Form

Wu and Lin (1999) stated that the occupational form was the "... objective pre-existing structure or environmental context that elicits or guides subsequent human performance." The occupational form consists of objective features. These may include materials, human context and socio-cultural dimensions.

Occupational Performance

Occupational performance is the active voluntary human doing of the occupational form.

Occupational Therapy Process

An Occupational Therapist works systematically through a sequence of actions known as the occupational therapy process. There are several versions of this process as described by numerous writers. Creek (2003) has sought to provide a comprehensive version based on extensive research. This version has 11 stages, which for the experienced therapist may not be linear in nature. The stages are:

- Referral
- Information gathering
- Initial assessment
- Needs identification/problem formation
- Goal setting
- Action planning
- Action
- Ongoing assessment and revision of action
- Outcome and outcome measurement
- End of intervention or discharge
- Review.

Areas of Practice in Occupational Therapy

The role of Occupational Therapy allows OT's to work in many different settings, work with many different populations and acquire many different specialties. This broad spectrum of practice lends itself to difficulty categorizing the areas of practice that exist, especially because each country, each with a different healthcare system. In this section, the categorization from the American Occupational Therapy Association is used. However there are other ways to categorize areas of practice in OT, such as physical, mental, and community practice (AOTA, 2009). These divisions occur when the setting is defined by the population it serves for example acute physical or mental health settings (e.g.: hospitals), sub-acute settings (e.g.: aged care facilities), outpatient clinics and community settings.

In each area of practice below, OT can work with different populations, diagnosis, specialities, and in different settings.

Physical Health

- *Pediatrics—Schools, Community, inpatient hospital based child OT*: Often, children need OT services for the same reasons an adult needs OT services. However, OTs approach intervention in a different way with children. OT delivers approaches treatment through occupation, and the occupations of a child are different from those of an adult; and include play, chores, self-care and schoolwork. Common conditions that are specific to or more common in the pediatric population creating a need for OT services include: developmental disorders, sensory regulation or sensory processing deficits, fine motor developmental delays or deficits, autism, emotional and behavioural disturbances (Lambert, 2005), among others. In addition, children are seen for every injury, illness or chronic condition that may cause a person of any age to have performance deficits in their daily life and thus benefit from OT services.
- *Acute care hospitals:* Acute care is an inpatient hospital setting for individuals with a serious medical condition(s) usually due to a traumatic event, such as a traumatic brain injury, spinal cord injury, etc. The primary goal of acute care is to stabilize the patient's medical status and address any threats to his or her life and loss of function. Occupational therapy plays an important role in facilitating early mobilization, restoring function, preventing further decline, and coordinating care, including transition and discharge planning. Furthermore, occupational therapy's role focuses on addressing deficits and barriers that limit the patient's ability to perform activities that they need or want to do related to independence in self-care, home management, work-related tasks, and participating in leisure and community pursuits.
- *Inpatient rehabilitation (e.g., Spinal Cord Injuries):* People with disabilities have the right and the privilege to live meaningful purposeful lives. When a disability occurs it is sometimes possible to recover—when it is not it is important to learn the skills to adapt capacity and environmental supports to be able to participate. OTs use their knowledge to help both with recovery and adaptation.

- Rehabilitation centres (e.g., Traumatic Brain Injury (TBI), Stroke (CVA), Spinal Cord Injuries, Head Injuries).
- *Skilled nursing facilities:* An occupational therapists role in a skilled nursing facility is centered on each client's individual needs. Many of the skills an OT works on are known as activities of daily living or self-care such as feeding or dressing. OTs can provide equipment to assist with activities or offer expertise in modifying the environment to maximize independence and facilitate independence. Other OT roles include education in adaptive equipment (shower bench), energy conservation, or task simplification (Hofmann, 2008).
- *Home Health*: Occupational therapists who work in this area of practice generally work with client's in the geriatric population who have one or more of the following diagnoses: Alzheimer's disease, arthritis, depression, CVA, generalized weakness, COPD, or Parkinson's disease. Occupational therapists working with these client's evaluate their level of independence, cognition, and safety. Moreover, occupational therapists provide intervention to maximize independence and function through remedial and compensatory strategies, with the ultimate goal of the client's regaining the ability to live independently at home (Swanson Anderson & Malaski, 1999).
- Outpatient clinics (e.g., Hand Therapy, orthopaedics) Hand therapy is a specialty practice area of occupational therapy that is mainly concerned with treating orthopedic-based upper extremity conditions to optimize the functional use of the hand and arm. Diagnoses seen by this practice area include: fractures of the hand or arm, lacerations and amputations, burns, and surgical repairs of tendons and nerves. Additionally, hand therapists treat acquired conditions such as tendonitis, rheumatoid arthritis and osteoarthritis, and carpal tunnel syndrome. Occupational therapists who work in this field address biomechanical issues underlying upper-extremity conditions. In addition, occupational therapists use an occupation-based and client-centered approach by identifying participation needs of the client, then tailoring intervention to improve performance in desired activities. *(link for a picture of hand therapy)*
- Specialist assessment centres (e.g., Electronic assistive technology, Posture and Mobility services).
- *Hospices:* An occupational therapists common role in hospice care is modifying and preventing. Modifying the demands of the activity to fit with the abilities of the client. The intervention may be directly with the client or with the client and the client's caregivers. OT can offer the caregivers support an education. Progress is defined as improved quality of life in hospice care. (Hasselkaus, 1998)
- *Assisted Living Facilities:* In an assisted living facility OT services are provided by a home health agency, rehab agency, or a private practice. Medicare and some private insurance plans cover OT services in ALFs. Areas of treatment intervention often include: bathing, dressing, grooming, toileting, mobility,

money management, laundry, and community participation. Can treat persons with occupational performance decline or at risk for a decline. Increase quality of life so less residents need the services of a long-term SNF. Special areas include mobility device assessment (scooter), continence training, psychosocial needs and low vision programmes (Fagan, 2001).

- *Productive Aging*: An OT practising in this area would provide skills and services to older adults to maximize independence, participation, and quality of life. Typical issues addressed: Any impairment or condition that would limit their ability to carry out meaningful occupations and tasks that are necessary for daily life. Skills taught include: energy conservation, education in adaptive equipment (such as a shower bench), task simplification, adapting and modifying activities to progress with a client's changing abilities (Opp Hoffman, 2008), caregiver education and support (AOTA, 2004), safety, social interactions and communication, memory skills training, mobility device assessment and training (i.e. scooters, wheelchairs, walkers), low vision interventions, continence training, and facilitating performance in basic ADL and IADL (Fagan, 2001).
- Work hardening is essentially a specialized programme designed to enable people with physical, psychological, and psychosocial issues inhibiting a person's ability, to successfully return to work. The National Advisory Committee on Work Hardening best describes work hardening:
  "Work hardening is a highly structured, goal oriented, individualized treatment programme designed to maximize the individual's ability to return to work. Work hardening programmes, which are interdisciplinary in nature, use real or simulated work activities in conjunction with conditioning tasks that are graded to progressively improve the biomechanical, neuromuscular, cardiovascular/metabolic and psychosocial functions of the individual. Work hardening provides a transition between acute care and return to work while addressing the issues of productivity, safety, physical tolerances, and worker behaviours" (Ogden-Niemeyer & Jacobs, 1989, p. 1).
- Work conditioning is similar to work hardening, except work conditioning purely involves improving physical capacities, whereas work hardening improves physical, psychological, and psychosocial factors.

Mental Health

According to Medicare (2005) guidance, "Only a qualified occupational therapist has the knowledge, training, and experience required to evaluate and, as necessary, re-evaluate a patient's level of function, determine whether an occupational therapy programme could reasonably be expected to improve, restore, or compensate for lost function, and where appropriate, recommend to the physician a plan of treatment."

According to the American Occupational Therapy Association (AOTA), occupational therapists work with the Mental Health population throughout the life span and across many treatment settings where mental health services and psychiatric rehabilitation are provided (AOTA, 2009). Just as with other clients, the OT facilitates maximum independence in activities of daily living (dressing, grooming, etc.) and instrumental activities of daily living (medication management, grocery shopping, etc.). According to the American Occupational Therapy Association, OT improves functional capacity and quality of life for people with mental illness in the areas of employment, education, community living, and home and personal care through the use of real life activities in therapy treatments (AOTA, 2005).

Geriatric, Adult, Adolescents, and Children with any kind of mental illness or mental health issues. These conditions include but are not limited to: Schizophrenia, substance abuse, addiction, dementia, Alzheimer's, mood disorders, personality disorders, psychoses, eating disorders, anxiety disorders (including post-traumatic stress disorder, separation anxiety disorder) (Cara & MacRae, 2005), and reactive attachment disorder (children only) (Lambert, 2005).

Typical issues that are addressed are as follows: Helping people acquire the skills to care for themselves or others including; keeping a schedule, medication management, employment, education, increasing community participation, community access (grocery store, library, bank, etc.), money management skills, engaging in productive activities to fill the day, coping skills, routine building, building social skills, and childcare (Cara & MacRae, 2005).

Areas that Mental Health OT's could work in are as follows:

- Mental health inpatient units
  - Adolescent, adult and older people's acute mental health wards
  - Adult and older people's rehabilitation wards
  - Prisons/secure units (Forensic psychiatry)
  - Psychiatric intensive care unit
  - Specialist units for Eating Disorders, Learning disabilities.
- Community based mental health teams
  - Child and adolescent mental health teams
  - Adult and older people's community mental health teams
  - Rehabilitation and recovery and Assertive Outreach community teams
  - Primary care services in GP practices
  - Home treatment teams
  - Early psychosis teams
  - Specialist learning disability, eating disorder community services
  - Day services
  - Vocational Services
  - Dementia & Alzheimer Care: OTs focus on adapting activities as the client progresses through the illness (Hofmann, 2008) OT also works with caregivers to teach them how to grade activities to the client's ability. Interventions are based on using the client's strengths to increase their quality of life and their relationships with caregivers. Use of social interactions, communication, memory, safety and self maintenance.

Community

Community based practice involves working with people in their own environment rather than in a hospital setting. It often combines the knowledge and skills related to physical and mental health. It can also involve working with atypical populations such as the homeless or at-risk populations. Examples of community-based practice settings are:

- Health promotion and lifestyle change: Remaining healthy is the goal of all people in a society, including people with chronic disabling or health conditions. Achieving health requires skills to self-manage conditions that might limit their ability to function in daily life. The occupational therapist helps people acquire these skills (Wilcock, 2005).
- Private Practice.
- Aging in place: Occupational therapists implement environmental modifications in senior housing, assisted living, long-term-care facilities, and homes (Yamkovenko, 2008) Environmental modifications can include rearranging furniture, building ramps, widening doorways, grab bars, special toilet seats, and other safety equipment to use performance capabilities to their fullest (Moyers & Christiansen, 2004).
- Low Vision: Occupational therapists help clients use their remaining vision to complete their daily routines with compensation, remediation, disability prevention and health promotion. Compensations or that modifications to the environment may include proper lighting, colour contrast, reducing clutter and education on adaptive equipment (Golembiewski, 2004).
- Intermediate care services.
- Driving Centres: Driving is an instrumental activity of daily living and an occupational therapist may evaluate and treat skills needed to drive such as vision, executive function or memory. If a client needs more skilled assessment and training they would refer them to an OT Driver Rehabilitation Specialist which could do on the road assessment, training in adaptive equipment and make more specific recommendations.
- Day centres.
- Schools.
- Child development centres.
- People's own homes, carrying out therapy and providing equipment and adaptations.
- Work and Industry: To be a healthy successful worker there must be a person environment fit between the task, the equipment, and the person's skills. Occupational therapists work to achieve that fit (Ellexson, 2000; Clinger, Dodson, Maltchev, & Page, 2007).
- Populations, conditions, and diagnoses: People of working age and ability who have been born with or developed a condition, injury, or illness that compromises their abilitv to work (Ellexson, 2000; Clinger, Dodson, Maltchev, & Page, 2007).

- Settings: Return to work programmes, large organizations, consultants to large organizations, work hardening programmes, work conditioning programmes, transitional return to work programmes (Ellexson, 2000; Clinger, Dodson, Maltchev, & Page, 2007).
- Typical issues addressed: assessment of ability to work, interventions to enhancing work performance by means of work hardening, work conditioning, and improvement of ergonomics in the workplace, identification of accommodations necessary to return-to-work following illness or injury, prevention of work related injury, illness, or disability (Ellexson, 2000; Clinger, Dodson, Maltchev, & Page, 2007).
- Homeless Shelters.
- Educational Settings.
- Refugee Camps.

New Emerging Practice Areas for Therapy

- Children & Youth:
  - Psychosocial Needs of Children & Youth
- Health & Wellness:
  - Health & Wellness Consulting
  - Design & Accessibility Consulting & Home Modification
  - Ergonomic Consulting
  - Private Practice Community Health Services
- Productive Aging:
  - Driver Rehabilitation & Training
  - Low Vision Services
- Rehabilitation, Disability, & Participation:
  - Technology & Assistive Device Development & Consulting
- Work & Industry:
  - Ticket to Work Services
  - Welfare to Work Services.

Occupational Therapy Approaches

Services typically include:

- Teaching new ways of approaching tasks.
- How to break down activities into achievable components e.g. sequencing a complex task like cooking a complex meal.
- Comprehensive home and job site evaluations with adaptation recommendations.
- Performance skills assessments and treatment.
- Adaptive equipment recommendations and usage training.
- Environmental adaptation including provision of equipment or designing adaptations to remove obstacles or make them manageable.

- Guidance to family members and caregivers.
- The use of creative media as therapeutic activity.

Activity Analysis

Activity analysis has been defined as a process of dissecting an activity into its component parts and task sequence in order to identify its inherent properties and the skills required for its performance, thus allowing the therapist to evaluate its therapeutic potential.

Therapeutic Activity

Occupational therapists use therapeutic activity or therapeutic occupation to improve an individual's occupational performance and increase function in activities of daily living (ADLs).

A core and unique feature of occupational therapy practice is the use of occupation as a therapeutic medium. An occupational therapy core skill as defined by the College of Occupational Therapists (COT) is the use of activity as a therapeutic tool.

Occupational therapists have utilized activities, such as crafts, since the profession was founded. The arts and crafts movement in the very early 20th century had ascertained that goal directed activity had a curative effect on the social problems inherent in the newly industrialized societies. The founders of the occupational therapy profession extended this thinking to the treatment of individuals' with mental health problems and as a consequence between 1920 and 1940 much of occupational therapy practice concentrated around the use of crafts as purposeful activities. The emergence of occupational therapy in physical medicine began during World War II and craft activities were utilized to rehabilitate injured soldiers. This method of practice was later termed by Mosey as activity synthesis.

Activity synthesis or occupational synthesis is the core of occupational therapy practice; occupational therapists, in collaboration with clients, design occupational forms to produce a therapeutic occupation or activity, that is meaningful and purposeful to the client. The therapeutic activity or occupation may be used to assess the client's occupational needs or to achieve a therapeutic goal. The component parts of an activity or occupation are matched with the required occupational performance outcomes. For example, the muscle movements elicited by pottery may address fine motor and gross motor skills to improve shoulder flexion and extension, range of movement and elbow extension and flexion.

Other therapeutic activities or occupations may include cookery activities, such as making a smoothie or a healthy soup. The components of this activity such as planning and following a recipe may address cognitive components of occupational performance such as problem solving, sequencing and learning. Health may be promoted through this occupation, enabling clients to consider healthy eating issues. Occupational therapists may further use therapeutic activities or occupations to assess occupational performance. For example, an occupational therapist may ask a client to make a cup of tea or prepare a simple meal to assess performance in activities of daily living (ADLs). An occupational therapist may use a board or card game to assess cognitive components of occupational performance. This application of therapeutic activity/occupation involves use of the core skills of the occupational therapist, chiefly assessment and problem solving.

Theoretical Frameworks

Occupational Therapists use a number of theoretical frameworks to frame their practice. Note that terminology has differed between scholars. Theoretical bases for framing a human and their occupation being include the following:

Frames of Reference/Generic Models

Frames of reference or generic models are the overarching title given to a collation of compatible knowledge, research and theories that form conceptual practice. More generally they can be defined as "those aspects which influence our perceptions, decisions and practice."

Occupational Therapy Frame of References/Models:

- Person Environment Occupation Performance Model (PEOP)
- Model of Human Occupation (MOHO)
- Canadian Model of Occupational Performance (CMOP)
- Biomechanical
- Rehabilitative (compensatory)
- Cognitive Disabilities
- Sensory Integration
- Lifestyle Performance Model (Fidler).

Approaches/Intervention Models

These are the methods of carrying out the Frames of Reference. Again, terminology differs depending on your viewpoint and literature base. Using the above author, approaches can include the Adaptive (based on the compensatory Frame of Reference).

United States

Education Requirements

In many countries, occupational therapists are educated at the baccalaureate level. However, currently in United States and Canada, entry level is at the master's level. This change occurred in 2007, requiring all occupational therapists who started their educational programme after 2007 to continue their education beyond a four-year degree. Currently, six schools in the US offer a clinical doctorate for those who would like to further their education past the Master's level.

All occupational therapists have a well-rounded knowledge of biomedical, behavioural, environmental and occupational scientists. Occupational therapist base their interventions on the knowledge based on neuroscience, anatomy, applied technology, policy and environmental strategies.

These schools are currently accredited for Master's level education and Doctoral level education.

Employment

According to the Bureau of Labour Statistics, occupational therapists held 99,000 positions in 2006 (2009). States with the most licensed and employed occupational therapists are California, New York, Pennsylvania and Ohio. In 2006, 52.6 per cent of occupational therapists worked in hospitals, early intervention facilities and schools (American Occupational Therapy Association, 2006). The Bureau of Labour statistics reported that 78 per cent of occupational therapists worked full-time in 2006 (Bureau of Labour Statistics, 2009). In addition, the median number of years of experience for occupational therapists was 13 years (American Occupational Therapy Association, 2006). Occupational therapists can work in many different settings, some examples include:

- Hospitals
- Schools
- Early intervention facilities
- Skilled nursing facilities
- Home health care services
- Outpatient care centers
- Government agencies
- Private practice.

The field of occupational therapy is projected to see faster growth than other careers. The Bureau of Labour Statistics estimates that the number of jobs will grow to 122,000 in 2016 (2009). Areas of occupational therapy that involve helping older adults will see the most growth. This expansion is due to the large need to provide health care services to the aging baby boom generation (American Occupational Therapy Association, n.d.; Bureau of Labour Statistics, 2009). In addition, the area of school-based occupational therapy will see growth as well.

Earnings

According to the Bureau of Labour Statistics, in 2006 the average salary was $60,470 for occupational therapists (2009). The average starting entry-level salary for occupational therapists was $46,300 (American Occupational Therapy Association, n.d.). In 2006, the salaries of occupational therapists in the 50 per cent percentile ranged from $50,450 to $73,710 (Bureau of Labour Statistics, n.d.). Salary varies according to the setting and the following represents average salaries for some practice areas:

Hospitals	$61,610
School setting	$54,260
Nursing care services	$64,750
Home Health care	$67,600
Facilities of physical, occupational Speech therapists	$62,290
(Bureau of Labour Statistics, 2009)	

In addition, according to the Work Force Survey conducted by the American Occupational Therapy Association in 2006, average salaries for some other areas include:

Mental Health	$53,750
Academic	$66,000
(American Occupational Therapy Association, 2006)	

Challenges for Occupational Therapy

A key challenge for occupational therapy is to develop and maintain a definition of its nature and scope assert that while this presents a challenge, it also results in a unique flexibility which allows the discipline to move with the flow of social, cultural and environmental change. This difficulty in definition may be a cause of chronic strain for practitioners and may also contribute to a lack of role definition and subsequent blurring.

Recent literature has also called for occupational therapy to address the political nature of who occupational therapists are and what they do (Kronenberg & Pollard, 2005).

Occupational Therapy and ICF

The International Classification of Functioning, Disability and Health (ICF) is an outcome measure for health and occupation and illustrates how these components impact one's function. This relates very closely to the Occupational Therapy Practice Framework as it is stated, "The profession's core beliefs are in the positive relationship between occupation and health and its view of people as occupational beings" (2008). The ICF is also built into the 2nd edition of the practice framework. Activities and participation examples from the ICF overlap Areas of Occupation, Performance Skills, and Performance Patterns in the framework. The ICF also includes contextual factors (environmental and personal factors) that relate to the context in the framework. In addition, Body functions and structures classified within the ICF help describe the client factors as described in the OT framework (AOTA, 2002).

Further exploration of the relationship between occupational therapy and the components of the ICIDH-2 (revision of the original International Classification of Impairments, Disabilities, and Handicaps (ICIDH); later becoming the ICF) was conducted by McLaughlin Gray (2001). First, the ICF is an international framework and provides an opportunity for the occupational therapy field to become better known across the globe. Second, the ICF provides occupational therapists with a global language to describe their expertise to the larger international health care community. The ICF uses a positive, holistic language emphasizing skills, capacities, and strengths of an individual rather than focusing on one's deficits and disabilities. This is similar to the outlook of occupational therapists. Third, the ICF includes environmental and personal contextual factors which are incorporated into the theory behind occupational therapy. It is important to take into consideration an individual's personal, environmental, and occupational factors to develop an effective intervention (Christiansen & Baum, 2005). The last notable application of the ICF to occupational therapy is the recognition of cultural patterns in occupation. Culture has significance on an individual's activities and participation and it is important to keep this in mind when treating an individual.

Although the ICF can be very useful for occupational therapists, it is noted in the literature that occupational therapists should use specific occupational therapy vocabulary along with the ICF in order to ensure correct communication about specific concepts (Stamm, Cieza, Machold, Smolen, & Stucki, 2006). The ICF might lack certain categories to describe what occupational therapists need to communicate to clients and colleagues. It also may not be possible to exactly match the connotations of the ICF categories to occupational therapy terms. The ICF is not an assessment and specialized occupational therapy vocabulary should not be replaced with ICF terminology. (Haglund & Henriksson, 2003). The ICF is an overarching framework on which to hang current therapy practices.

Research Resources for Occupational Therapy

- American Journal of Occupational Therapy (AJOT)
- OT Search database (AOTA)
- World Federations of Occupational Therapists (WFOT)
- Australian Occupational Therapy Journal (AOTJ)
- New Zealand Journal of Occupational Therapy (NZJOT)
- Scandinavian Journal of Occupational Therapy (SJOT).

UNDERSTANDING ADAPTED PHYSICAL EDUCATION AND ITS ROLE

Adapted Physical Education (APE) is a sub-discipline of physical education. It is an individualized programme created for students who require a specially designed programme for more than 30 days. The programme involves physical fitness, motor fitness, fundamental motor skills and patterns, aquatics skills, dance skills, individual, group games, and sports (including lifetime sports). For people with disabilities, adapted physical education provides safe, personally satisfying, and successful experiences related to physical activity, rather than a sedentary alternative programme. Adapted Physical Education is a direct service, not a related service.

Students Who Receive Services

Students who qualify for adapted physical education include people with disabilities as specified in the Individuals with Disabilities Education Act (IDEA). This includes children who have:

Autism

Developmental disability significantly affecting verbal and non-verbal communication and social interaction, generally evident before age 3, that adversely affects a child's education performance. Other characteristics often associated with autism are engagement in repetitive activities and stereotyped movements, resistance to environmental change or change in daily routines, and unusual responses to sensory experiences.

Blindness

Concomitant hearing and visual impairments, the combination of which causes such severe communication and other developmental and educational needs that they cannot be accommodated in special education programmes solely for children with deafness or children with blindness.

Deafness

Hearing impairment that is so severe that the child is impaired in processing linguistic information through hearing, with or without amplification, that adversely affects a child's educational performance.

Emotional Disturbance

Condition exhibiting one or more of the following characteristics over a long period of time and to a marked degree that adversely affects a child's educational performance: inability to learn that cannot be explained by intellectual, sensory, or health factors; inability to build or maintain satisfactory interpersonal relationships with peers and teachers; inappropriate types of behaviour or feelings under normal circumstances; general pervasive mood of unhappiness or depression; and a tendency to develop physical symptoms or fears associated with personal or school problems.

This term also includes *schizophrenia*. Hearing Impairment. Impairment in hearing, whether permanent or fluctuating, that adversely affects a child's educational performance but that is not included under the definition of deafness in this section.

Mental Retardation. Significantly subaverge general intellectual functioning, existing concurrently with deficits in adaptive behaviour and manifested during the developmental period, that adversely affects a child's education performance.

Multiple Disabilities. Concomitant impairments (such as mental retardation-blindness, mental retardation- orthopedic impairment, etc.), the combination of which causes such severe educational needs that they cannot be accommodated in special education programmes solely for one of the impairments. The term does not include deaf-blindness.

Orthopedic Impairment. Severe orthopedic impairment that adversely affects a child's educational performance. The term includes impairments caused by congenital anomaly (e.g., clubfoot, absence of some member, etc.), impairments caused by disease (e.g., poliomyelitis, bone tuberculosis, etc.), and impairments from other causes (e.g., cerebral palsy, amputations, and fractures or burns that cause contractures).

Other Health Impairment having limited strength, vitality or alertness, including heightened alertness to environmental stimuli, that results in limited alertness with respect to the educational environment, that is due to chronic or acute health problems such as asthma, attention deficit disorder or attention hyperactivity disorder, diabetes, epilepsy, a heart condition, hemophilia, lead poisoning, leukemia, nephritis, rheumatic fever, and sickle cell anemia; and adversely affects a child's educational performance.

Specific Learning Disability. General disorder in one or more of the basic psychological processes involved in understanding or in using language, spoken or written, that may manifest itself in an imperfect ability to listen, think, speak, read, write, spell, or to do mathematical calculations, including conditions such as perceptual disabilities, brain injury, minimal brain dysfunction, dyslexia, and developmental aphasia. Disorders not include: learning problems that are primarily the result of visual, hearing, or motor disabilities, of mental retardation, of emotional disturbance, or of environmental, cultural, or economic disadvantage.

Speech or Language Impairment. Communication disorder, such as stuttering, impaired articulation, a language impairment, or a voice impairment, that adversely affects a child's educational performance.

Traumatic Brain Injury. An acquired injury to the brain caused by an external physical force, resulting in total or partial functional disability or psychosocial impairment, or both, that adversely affects a child's educational performance. The term applies to open or closed head injuries resulting in impairments in one or more areas, such as cognition; language; memory; attention; reasoning; abstract thinking; judgement; problem-solving; sensory; perceptual, and motor abilities; psychosocial behaviour; physical functions; information processing; and speech. The term does not apply to brain injuries that are congenital or degenerative, or to brain injuries induced by birth trauma. Do all students with disabilities need an IEP for physical education? If not, who qualifies for an IEP in physical education?

No federal law mandates that each individual with a disability only under IDEA (13 disabilities) have an IEP developed for him/her.

Autism Blindness Deafness Emotional Disturbance Hearing Impairment Mental Retardation Multiple Disabilities Orthopedic Impairment Other Health Impairment

Specific Learning Disability Speech or Language Impairment Traumatic Brain Injury Visual Impairment Including Blindness Also, if the students Least Restrictive Environment, or LRE, is general physical education, then they do not need an IEP either.

Visual Impairment Including Blindness

An impairment in vision that, even with correction, adversely affects a child's educational performance. This term includes both partial sight and blindness.

Infants and toddlers who need early intervention services because of developmental delays in cognitive, physical, communication, social, emotional or adaptive development can also qualify for adapted physical education. The state can chose to include infants and toddlers who are under three-years old who are "at risk" for experiencing a developmental delay if early intervention services are not provided.

Students who qualify under Section 504 of the Rehabilitation Act of 1973 can also receive adapted physical education. In Section 504, a person with a disability is anyone who has a physical or mental impairment that limits one or more major life activities, has a record of impairment, or is regarded as having an impairment.

A fourth group of students who might qualify for adapted physical education are students who are recuperating from injuries, accidents, recovering from non-communicable diseases, are overweight, have low skill levels, or have low levels of physical fitness. This group is not covered by legislation, but a school district can decide to develop a plan to meet these students' physical education needs.

Examples of the impairments highlighted in the above two paragraphs include, but are not limited to AIDS, alcoholism, blindess or visual impairment, cancer, deafness or hearing impairment, diabetes, drug addiction, heart disease, mental illness, and ADD/ADHD.

Adapted physical education serves people of all ages.

Laws

Some key laws that have been influential in the advancement of APE.

No Child Left Behind

Created in 2001, this Act puts significant federal support behind the improvement of reading and mathematics scores and compromises other critical curricular areas, including physical education, health, history, art, computer science, and music.

American with Disabilities Act (P.L. 101-336)

Created in 1990, the Act expanded civil rights protections for individual with disabilities in the public and private sectors. ADA outlaws discrimination against a person with a disability in employment, public services and transportation, public accommodations, and telecommunications.

Individuals with Disabilities Education Act (IDEA)

First created in 1990, but has been updated several times. In 1990, IDEA continued the emphasis upon FAPE, IEP, LRE, and physical education as a direct, educational service. In 1999, IDEA was reauthorized, the reauthorization emphasized education for learners with disabilities in the general education programme and increased the emphasis on parental participation in the assessment and IEP process.

Education for All Handicapped Children Act (P.L. 94-142)

Created in 1975, the Act mandated: (a) free appropriate public education (FAPE) for all children with disabilities between the ages of 3 and 21 years; (b) Individualized Education Plan; (c) education in the Least Restrictive Environment; and (d) physical education as a direct, educational service.

The Rehabilitation Act (P.L. 93-112, Section 504)

Created in 1973, the Act mandated that individuals with disabilities cannot be excluded from any programme or activity receiving federal funds solely on the basis of the disability.

Individual Education Programme or IEP

IEP stands for Individual Education Programme.

Purpose–Federal law mandates that each individual with a disability under IDEA have an IEP developed for him/her.

An IEP is a written statement for each SWD developed by a meeting with representatives from the local educational agency, the teacher, the parents or guardian, and the student, if appropriate, for the purpose of establishing an appropriate educational placement. Some consider the IEP to be a "management" programme to guide appropriate service delivery, which includes the area of physical education. An IEP should include a statement of:

- present level of performance
- annual goals
- short term objectives
- needed transition services
- projected dates of services
- appropriate evaluation procedures.

What are the steps in the assessment and IEP processes—include timeliness?

1. Referral—Student can be referred by several sources, for example, teacher, parent, or administrator
2. Obtain consent

3. Screening/checklist (preliminary), check history/background, (formal testing)
4. Talk with PT, OT, Special Ed teacher, (have conversations)
5. Observations (natural setting, 3 times, interviews with teachers and student)
6. Test
7. Strengths and Weaknesses
8. Develop IEP/Goals
9. Decide Placement
10. Implement IEP
11. Revisit every year/Test every 3 years.

Who must be present at an IEP for physical education meeting? Does the regular physical educator have to attend?

- The student when appropriate
- The parent(s) or guardian(s), or a designated representative
- A representative of the school administration, other than the child's teacher, who is qualified to provide or supervise the provision of special education
- The student's special educator
- At least one general educator, if the child will receive any services in the general education programme
- A member of the evaluation team or a professional able to interpret assessment data
- Any direct or related service personnel who have assessed the student
- The school nurse, particularly if the student has a chronic and/or serious medical condition and/or requires special medical procedures in order to function in the school environment
- An interpreter as required
- Representatives of community agencies that will be responsible for implementing individual transition plans
- The regular physical educator does not have to attend unless there is a case where a student's present level of performance is needed from the regular physical educator and they are against the student needing an IEP.

What is the regular physical educator's role in maintaining the IEP?

- Be sure to document progress and achievement of IEP goals.
- Assess the student in the areas of motor skills, sports skills, and physical fitness and give that information to the IEP team so appropriate IEP goals can be written for the student.
- Work closely with the related service providers, such as the physical therapist, occupational therapist, and speech therapist.
- Talk with your administrator and make sure he/she understands the importance of your participation in all phases of the IEP process (assessment, team meetings, goal writing, updates, etc.).

IEP Tips

1. State the positive first
2. State strengths and progress first
3. State needs as areas for growth, not weaknesses
4. Make parents feel comfortable (chat, eye-contact, smile, care)
5. Bring documentation of results and progress
6. Allow conversation, but move forward if needed
7. Propose pertinent, measurable, and attainable goals
8. Don't expect perfection
9. Communicate well
10. Explain the results of the test
11. Bring video documentation to back up your data.

Do all students with disabilities need an IEP for physical education? If not, who qualifies for an IEP in physical education?

No, federal law mandates that each individual with a disability only under IDEA (13 disabilities) have an IEP developed for him/her.

1. Autism
2. Blindness
3. Deafness
4. Emotional Disturbance
5. Hearing Impairment
6. Mental Retardation
7. Multiple Disabilities
8. Orthopedic Impairment
9. Other Health Impairment
10. Specific Learning Disability
11. Speech or Language Impairment
12. Traumatic Brain Injury
13. Visual Impairment Including Blindness.

Also, if the students Least Restrictive Environment, or LRE, is general physical education, then they do not need an IEP either.

Adaptations

There are four basic ways to adapt or modify any activity for a student with a disability. By adapting any area or multiple areas, a student will have more success in class and the teacher will be able to provide a better learning experience for the student. The four modification areas are:

1. *Equipment*—Easiest area to modify, options are almost unlimited. Objects should vary in size, shape, colour, weight, and texture. Equipment should represent the present skill level of a student. A student with a visual impairment should use a brightly coloured ball or other object during a striking unit. For some students, especially students with autism, it is important to have equipment which can be weight-bearing. Some students will need to wear backpacks to help with the stimulation process.
2. *Environment*—Limiting play area when movement capabilities are limited or restricted. Having a designated area for equipment when the activity is done (usually behind a mat) so students are not distracted during instruction or during the next activity. Having a certain area in the gymnasium, for students who have autism, helps if they need time to relax. Lighting and sound also play a vital role in the environmental setting for students with autism. Students with autism can observe minute changes which may be extremely distracting.
3. *Instructions*—Permitting the substitution or interchange of game and/or activity duties by determining positions in games that work with the abilities of the student. Using a variety of different instructional strategies such as verbal, visual, guided discovery and peer teaching are great ways to adapt instruction in APE. Using a variety of instructional strategies can give the students the opportunity to start learning on their own and to become more independent. Picture books are also very important in terms of instruction. Some students need to hear and see what they are supposed to do throughout the day. Students rely heavily on picture books and are thrown off if activities do not occur how they should.
4. *Rules*—Rule changes will help to equalize competition. Rules can also be modified to challenge different skill levels within an APE class. If a student with a disability is in an inclusion class, adapting and modifying rules is important for the students' success. Changing rules for a game in an inclusion class can also help a student with a disability become more involved. For example, during game play the team scores one point if the student with a disability is not involved in the scoring process, two points if they help score the point. Another example for rule modification to create success for a student with a disability would be to give them extra attempt at a skill where general students have only a limited number of attempts, i.e. strikes in baseball.

Another option for modification can be time; providing extra time or allowing a student additional rest. In each area a number of changes can be made for almost any activity.

APE teachers do not need to reinvent the wheel when looking for activities or games for students with disabilities. APE teachers can take activities used in general physical education and modify or adapt these activities for students with disabilities. If the APE teacher makes the proper modifications, the inclusion or APE experience for the student with a disability and the students without disabilities will be more enjoyable and productive. Making these modifications will hopefully increase practice time and success in an inclusion or APE setting.

Equipment such as standing frames and other assistive technology can make the environment more inclusive for children who ambulate with a wheelchair.

For throwing and catching balls it will be helpful to use a variety of balls. For throwing and shooting at a target smaller balls work best. For striking, kicking, and catching, bigger balls will create more success for students. These include yarn balls that do not bounce away and are easy to catch because students can grab onto the yarn. Wiffle balls are recommended because they are lightweight. Beach balls are useful because they are large and soft to catch. Giving the students the option of which ball to choose allows them the opportunity to create their own level of skill development. If a student seems to be struggling with a certain ball or a certain ball is not challenging enough, just suggest a different ball that you would like to see them try to use. For students with visual impairments, use multicoloured balls and balls with bells in them that make sound as they roll. Placing a ball in a plastic grocery bag, placing a bell inside of a balloon, and attaching bells to student's shoes are simple ways to accommodate students with visual impairments. A catapult works great for students who may have cerebral palsy or limb limitations during throwing and aiming activities. This can help involve the students in activities they may have been limited in. Catapults are also great for arm and hand strength development for students who have cerebral palsy or limited mobility of their arms and hands.

For kicking a variety of balls can also be used to benefit the students. For students who ambulate with a wheelchair, large balls bigger than soccer balls will be helpful. For students with cerebral palsy, a stationary ball can be used.

ADAPT-A-BAG

Adapted Physical Education (APE) teachers are always on the go and may be pressed for time to adapt an activity during APE, this is why it is important to develop or make an adapt-a-bag for these circumstances. An adapt-a-bag, is a bag an APE teacher can bring to each of his or her teaching areas, which can help modify or adapt an activity for a variety of disabilities.

> Some simple items to put in an adapt-a-bag are duck tape, velcro, string, dry erase board, bells (jiggling bells inside a balloon), shiny objects, pvc pipe (large and small—one for guide line and one for ramp), plastic shopping bag, and straws. Other objects which may cost little money are blinking balls, bubbles, bubble wrap, horns, jinggling bells inside a balloon, beep balls, and stimulating balls. It is important to remember there can never be too many items in an adapt-a-bag. Household items are great for making modifications in APE, it is important to always be looking and searching for items which can be put into an adapt-a-bag.

Along with these adaptations it is important to understand the individual's disability. For instance if a student has a Vestibular disability they may need an object that is easier to track. A balloon or a larger ball would be a great adaptation for this student. These students may also be very unstable, so something as simple as a mat beneath them while performing an activity could be a valuable adaptation.

Different variety. Another suggestion for the Adapt-A-bag would be to have a variety of colours for the items in the bag. Students with Autism may prefer and perform better with a certain coloured item.

Autism

Autism is the most common condition in a group of developmental disorders known as the Autism Spectrum Disorders (ASDs). Autism is characterized by impaired social interaction, problems with verbal and non-verbal communication, and unusual, repetitive, or severely limited activities and interests. When teaching students with Autism it is good to be aware of the student's sensory triggers. For example some students have overly sensitive senses. For a student with overly sensitive hearing being in a gym with a stereo playing loud music and peers running around and screaming must be the sensory trigger that causes a negative reaction in class. Another example or sensory issues would be students who are hypersensitive in their propreoceptors. This means that these students are overly sensitive in their joints. So someone giving them a high five could trigger a negative response. There could also be the opposite effect where students are hyposensitive which means there are under stimulated in their joints and may need weighted objects to even feel them. Knowing how each students senses works will help determine the type of equipment, instruction, and placement each student with autism needs. Other ASDs include Asperger syndrome, Rett syndrome, childhood disintegrative disorder, and pervasive developmental disorder not otherwise specified (usually referred to as PDD-NOS). It is estimated that three to six children out of every 1,000 will have autism. Males are four times more likely to have autism than females.

Common Characteristics

Hard to function within the school environment and they may struggle with expressive and receptive language.

Display Unusual Gross and Fine Motor Behaviours

Here are some examples that you might see in....

- Striking
- Hands flapping
- Pacing
- Spinning
- Running in circles
- Twirling a string
- Tearing paper
- Drumming
- Flipping light switches
- A slight shaking of the hand in front of the face.

A Typical Ways of Students with Autism Communicate

- Have temper tantrums
- Grabbing teachers hand (taking teacher where he/she wants to be)
- Performing self and other aggression.

Teaching Tips

- Use visuals
- Avoid long strings of verbal instruction
- Encourage development of child's special talents
- Use child's fixations to motivate school work
- Use concrete, visual methods to teach number concepts
- Protect child from sounds that hurt his/her ears
- Use weighted vests to calm nervous system
- Interact with child while he/she is swinging or rolled in a mat
- Don't ask child to look and listen at the same time
- Teach with tactile learning materials
- Use printed words and pictures on a flashcard
- Use a consistent beginning and ending to an activity.

Spina Bifida

Some tips for an individual with Spina Bifida could be adapting activities that can be played with the use of crutches, braces, or wheelchairs. The use of a helmet may also be necessary in case the student has a shunt. This will help to prevent further head injuries. This may also be done with the use of a soft foam ball or balloons, but be sure the student is not allergic to latex, because this is a common problem with individual with this disability. Individuals with Spina Bifida do make great athletes, so it is important to modify and develop an assortment of games and activities for these individuals. These individuals can become very mobile and skilled in wheelchairs, so introducing these individuals to games such as tennis, basketball, swimming, and even racquetball can be great for this skill development and also social interaction in the community.

Cerebral Palsy

Some suggestions for an individual with Cerebral Palsy (CP) are to do more stretching exercises. [Make sure that you consult the students PT (physical therapist before you do the stretches)]. The disease causes their muscles to have tendency to become very tight so a slow stretch can be helpful to reduce the tone. You can also work on body positioning, and strength exercises to help the student gain enough strength to support their own body weight.

Some adaptations for students with CP:

- Student in wheelchair—Can hold one handle on the parachute with the edge of his/her chair.

- Child with Quadriplegic spastic—If in dance session child can hold bells or some type of instrument.
- Child with Ataxia—Teacher can hold student in lap if doing a circle game.
- Aquatics—Vital part of curriculum for students with CP. The buoyancy of the water frees the child from the pull of gravity, allows for greater range of motion.

Some exercises for students with CP:

- Gravity Exercises—Exercise the involves lifting the weight of the body or body part.
- Gait Training—To teach or re-teach walking patterns.
- Body Mechanics—Lifting techniques to obtain maximum use of the large muscle groups of the body.

Visual Impairments

Individuals with a visual impairment may be more successful in a well-lit room. It may also help to keep objects in a routine place so they can become accustomed to knowing were they are. The use of audio devices in equipment and different textured equipment may also be very beneficial. Using of guidelines, and brightly coloured boundaries can also help these individuals to be more successful in the physical education setting. Some safety concerns for these individual would be to let them were protective goggles and keep the floor clear of any tripping hazards.

Also with students that have a visual impairment they might also be more successful with a certain colour. Some students who can partially see maybe able to see a certain colour better than another and you should use this type of colour for the activity that is going on to make them more successful.

Hearing Impairments

Individuals with a hearing impairment may need to use a guide in class. It is also important to keep their learning environment free of excessive noise to include music while giving instruction. They may need a shorter more direct instruction when it comes to activities. Visual indicators are also more important for these students to understand the beginning and end of game play. Students with a hearing impairment also tend to perform better in small groups and understand better if the instructor speaks clearly.

Here are some behavioural characteristics of a student hearing impaired might show:

- lack of attention
- imitates others
- responds to noises instead of words
- lack of speech development

- turns or cocks head
- acts out
- preoccupied with things and not people
- works best in small groups
- uses gestures
- reluctant to participate orally
- monotone quality in voice
- difficulty in following directions.

These are just a few that a student might show in the classroom that could be noticed very easily.

Some more characteristics of an individual with a hearing impaired might be: The impairment of the semi-circular canals, vestibule of the inner ear, and/or vestibular portion of the eighth cranial nerve which has a negative effect on balance. Congenitally deaf/hearing impaired individuals have poorer balance than those with acquired deafness. This means that if an individual was born with a hearing impairment that their balance is poorer than an individual that has acquired the deafness through some sort of means like: Excessive exposure to loud noise which can damage the tiny hairs in the cochlea and lead to hearing loss. This condition is known as noise-induced hearing loss. This individual was able to learn how to walk and balance before the hearing loss.

Muscular Dystrophy

Individuals with Muscular Dystrophy may tire quickly, are almost always in a wheel-chair. Lifetime activities these individuals can perform in their chair can be beneficial to them. Activities that involve breathing practices can also be beneficial for these students. Remember these students will be losing strength increasingly as they grow older.

Transition

In 1990, Congress passed the Individuals with Disabilities Education Act (IDEA), in order to make significant alterations to the Education of All Handicapped Act of 1975. For example, IDEA redefined the purpose and process of the Individualized Education Plan (IEP). One significant change to the IEP was a newly required transition statement, which was to be developed no later than a student's 16th birthday (Modell & Megginson, 2001).

Transition is the successful movement from a student in school to a productive, quality, and meaningful adult life. Effective transition is based on the individuals' needs, and consists of coordinated activities in the following areas: Education, Career, Community, Communication, Social Interaction, Recreation and Leisure. Not every transition programme will be the same; it is dependent upon the individual. Transition, as defined by IDEA 1997, is "...a coordinated set of activities for a student, designed within an outcome-oriented process which promotes movement form school to post-school activities, including post secondary education, vocational training, integrated employment (including supported employment), continuing and adult education, adult services, independent living, or community participation. (IDEA, 1997, Section 602.30) Furthermore, according to federal legislation, students 14 years and older are required to attain planning methods provided by the Adapted Physical Education Transition Model (Strategies for Success Transition, 2003, 98). All methods provide greater opportunity for students to transition into a more productive, and meaningful adult life.

Given their ever-expanding role, adapted physical educators must pay attention to this issue. As adapted physical educators it is important to provide students with experiences and resources during their time in an educational setting so the students have a better chance of staying physically active during and after the transition period. Expanding and exploring students ideas and knowledge about physical activity is essential for success outside of the education setting.

Transition in adapted physical education helps students with disabilities move towards community involvement through healthy and independent lifestyles. The first crucial element in a successful transition is for the student's IEP team to have a well developed and defined vision based on the students strengths, needs, and preferences. (Savage, 2005, 46)

It is essential for transition to be part of the school's curriculum. Without transitioning a student into real life situations he or she may have a difficult time taking part in some of the lifetime activities they learned throughout their time in school and thus have a more sedentary lifestyle leading to more health risks and issues. By putting transitioning into a schools curriculum it will increase the overall learning experience for students in adapted physical education. The curriculum for APE in the school setting should focus on developing the students' fitness, motor skills, sport skills, social-skill training, community adjustment, and take part in a recreation and leisure survey. During the transition period more focus should be put on fitness, sport, disability sport, friendships, community participation, and recreation and leisure (Modell & Megginson, 2001). If more focus is put in the curriculum during the years students with disabilities are in the school, the smoother the transition process with go.

Transitioning prepares students for life outside of school. Participation and experiences in leisure activities provides opportunities for skill and competency development needed to successfully participate in a variety of activities upon leaving school (Modell & Megginson, 2001, 45). As an adapted physical educator it is important to talk with the family and find some physical activities the family enjoys so you can help your student learn the knowledge and skills to participate with their family. Leisure activities may include, but are not limited to, the following:

- Aquatics
- Bowling
- Rock Climbing
- Water Skiing
- Gymnastics

- Golf
- Water Polo
- Canoeing
- Track and Field
- Horseshoes.

While teaching students leisure activities, it is critical to provide information of appropriate facilities. Community clubs, organizations, and parks provide many opportunities for students to remain active. Many community resources have programmes specifically designed for individuals with disabilities. The adapted physical education teacher should be familiar with these programmes and utilize them as a regular part of the students' transition programme. The APE teacher should also stress functional transition skills, such as the proper use of fitness equipment or how to use an electronic identification card to sign in at a fitness centre. Individuals with disabilities who have greater access to, and actively participate in recreation and leisure activities are more satisfied with their lives (Harner & Heal, 1993). In addition, when engaged in recreation and leisure activities, opportunities of success in communities increases for individuals with disabilities (Modell & Megginson, 2001, 45). The formation of a reverse mainstreaming physical education programme will also help in the transition of the student with a disability. This programme can benefit both the student with a disability and the peer mentor as together they will attempt to achieve better physical fitness skills, improved social skills, and higher standards of social and personal responsibilities.

Transition related to the adapted physical education curricular area focuses on most of the previously listed areas. Students will not only learn how to do an activity, but the progressive skills it takes to have the opportunity to complete the activity in a community based setting. Such skills can include the following:

- Finding the information about the activity
- Finding time of operation for places
- Figuring out transportation
- Know how to perform the activity independently
- Finding a way to fit the activity into the individual's weekly schedule.

These all include social interaction and various means of communication. Students will need to be taught many skills beyond the normal adapted physical education curriculum in order to achieve lifetime physical activity.

Some ideas for the student to find what interests him/her to help with transition 4—5 years prior to graduation:

- Take a community education class.
- Attend events to learn spectator or audience member skills.
- Learn how to plan recreation and leisure activities (where, when, cost, transportation).

- Establish exercise routines.
- Join a club or an organization in your community.

3 years prior to graduation:

- Explore new ways to use your free time.
- Identify supports needed to participate in activities of interest.

2 years prior to graduation:

- Try additional recreation and leisure activities.

1 year prior to graduation:

- Continue to take part in activities of interest.

1–2 years after graduation:

- Join and participate in adult recreation activities. (Auxter, Pyfer & Huettig, 2005, 97).

The process of transition can work very well with students, however this process does not happen overnight. Students will need the appropriate amount of time to learn all of the necessary skills. Transition services become a part of a student's education at the age of 14 or 16 depending on the school district and continue until the student is 22 years of age. At this time, an Individual Transition Plan is developed with goals and objectives written in person first language, specific to the individual student to ensure their abilities to function in the community when they graduate. The members involved in developing the Individual Transition Plan should be the IEP team members. The IEP team members should have the following questions in mind:

1. What interests or hobbies do the students and his or her family enjoy doing?
2. What knowledge and competencies does the student need in order to move from school-based to community based living in their particular community?
3. What knowledge and prior experience does the student already have?
4. What knowledge and experience will the student need to be successful?
5. What will the student's living situation be like after high school?
6. Will the student be employed in the area? Will working interfere with recreation/leisure time? If so, how will the student stay active?

As is true in most aspects of adapted physical education, the skills practiced during the transition process tend to be most successful when the students have an opportunity to contribute to the decision making process. Also, providing sufficient amounts of repeated trials will drastically improve the students' level of success.

Example of a Transition Plan

Making a Leisure Transition Plan (LTP) is a great way to help and aid an individual with a disability during the transition process. The purpose of the LTP is to develop the student's ability to select and participate in activities in the community during his or her free time. Specialists from the APE field must be aware of physical recreation opportunities available in the community; determine the student's activity interests, preferences, and needs and then include these activities in the student's physical education curricula and LTP. Here is an example of a LTP (Krueger & DiRocoo, 2000):

Transition Goal #1

Cindy will increase her awareness and use of public transportation.

Transition Activities

- Cindy will meet with a representative from Valley Transit to discuss bus routes.
- Cindy will experience getting on and off a bus with the use of a lift, while in her wheelchair.
- Cindy will verbally demonstrate her understanding of the proper way to anchor a wheelchair inside the bus.
- Cindy will map out a schedule to and from a destination (field trip), identifying bus routes, departure, and arrival times.
- Cindy will use Valley Transit as a means of transportation for a field trip.
- Cindy will meet with a representative of Medi-Vans to receive information on rules and regulations, cost, and how to schedule trips.
- Cindy will experience getting in and out of a Medi-Van while in her wheelchair.
- Cindy will receive information to share with her parents on the procedure for obtaining an ADA card (use with Medi-Van).
- Cindy will call to schedule transportation for a field trip using Medi-Vans.
- Cindy will travel on a field trip using Medi-Vans for transportation.
- Cindy will meet with a representative from Valley Cabs to discuss how to schedule trips.
- Cindy will schedule transportation for a field trip with Valley Cabs.
- Cindy will use Valley Cab as a means of transportation for a field trip.

Transition Goal #2

Cindy will increase her awareness of federal legislation (ADA and IDEA).

Transition Activities

- Cindy will do searches on the internet to locate five sites that give information on federal (disability) legislation, then print the first page of each to put in her transition portfolio for future reference.
- Cindy will locate "ADA Accessibility Guidelines For Buildings and Facilities" on the internet, then print the Table of Contents to put in transition portfolio for future reference.
- Cindy will locate three accessibility guidelines in ADA, record minimum requirements/measurements, and then check to see if her school building is in compliance.
- Cindy will locate three advocacy sites (for persons with disabilities) on the internet, print a document from each relating to federal legislation, and study and dictate a summary of each on audio tape. Cindy will share this audiotape with her parents.

Transition Goal #3

Cindy will plan and take field trips into the community to visit sites that offer physical activities that she has indicated are of interest to her. She will observe or participate in these activities while on the field trip. Cindy will evaluate each experience.

Transition Activities

- Cindy will identify locations and activities she would like to explore in the community.
- Cindy will discuss with the APE specialist and/or community resource person what preparations and arrangements need to be made prior to going on the field trip (i.e. time schedules, transportation, clothing, equipment, accommodations/adaptations, and money).
- Cindy will make arrangements for the field trip with the APE specialist and/ or community resource personnel.
- Cindy will fill out a critique form after each community experience. Critique will address accessibility, effectiveness of accommodations/adaptations, atmosphere of community setting (i.e. friendly, helpful), and personal reactions on enjoyment and possible future participation.

Many of the activities done in adapted physical education are also done in competition. As part of transitioning to life after school an adapted physical education teacher can let the students know about athletic competitions and associations for the activities done in adapted physical education. Some organizations include: the National Beep Baseball Association, the National Disability Sports Alliance (NDSA), Special Olympics International (SOI), the American Wheelchair Bowling Association (AWBA), the United States Association of Blind Athletes (USABA), and the Disabled Sports USA (DSUSA). These and other organizations like them can also introduce the students to new activities such as beep baseball, which is a baseball game played by individuals with visual impairments and others using blindfolds. As the name suggests they use a ball that beeps as well as bases that beep. These organizations and competitions can help students get interested in an activity that will keep them active for a lifetime.

People Involved in Individual Transition Plan

These people may be involved—

Direct Service Providers

- Special Educators
- Hospital/Home bound Instructors
- Instructors in Institutions and other settings
- Adapted Physical Educators
- General Physical Educators
- Vision, Orientation and Mobility Specialists.

Related Service Providers

- Audiologists
- Counselling Services
- Medical Diagnostic Service Personnel
- Occupational, Speech, Recreation and Physical Therapists
- Parent Counsellors and Trainers
- Psychologists
- Rehabilitation Counsellors
- Assistive Technology Service Personnel
- School Health Service Personnel
- Social Workers
- Transportation Specialists
- Transition Service Personnel (Auxter, Pyfer & Huettig, 2005, 103-12).

Advocacy for Transition

With respect to transition, adapted physical educators should first and foremost advocate that their own involvement in the post-school transition process be indicated on their students' Individualized Education Programme (IEP) (Modell & Megginson, 2001). Some other areas in transition which should be brought to the attention of administrators and community officials are implementing ways in which physical activity sites can become more accessible, advocating that students with disabilities be able to participate in the entire continuum of sports programmes (integrate and segregated) sponsored by the school and community; and helping parents rally for appropriate community recreation and sport opportunities for their children with disabilities (Modell & Megginson, 2001).

Barriers to Transition

- *Facilities:*

- *Transportation:* Transportation can become a problem during transition. Many students who have a disability cannot drive a car, so it is important to teach students, during their educational process, other means of transportation. This may mean teaching students routines on how to use the city bus system, or finding a group to car pool with, or even finding an older adult who may not mind picking up a student when they are going to the local YMCA.
- *Money:* Many fitness clubs are increasing prices for membership and with increasing gas prices it may be difficult for students with disabilities to afford a membership somewhere and have the means of getting there if they are not within walking distance.
- *Planning:* For many students with disabilities planning a trip to the YMCA or any facility will be difficult task. In school their schedule was planned for them and they didn't have to worry about how and when things were going to happen. As a result, planning is one of the biggest barriers to transition. Students with disabilities may need to be taught what to wear, what transportation to use, how to set up plans with friends, and how to figure out how much money they may need.
- *Lack of programmes:* There may be a lack of programmes in a community, who have the knowledge and ability to assist individuals with disabilities. This may mean individuals with disabilities may have to participate in programmes with individuals without disabilities. This may help with the socialization aspect of development, but may limit their practice and participation time. The individual may also be intimidated by the other individuals, which may push them away from that activity or programme.
- Lack of Support i.e., school, organizations, public, families...
- Staff/employee knowledge i.e. at local businesses, teacher assistants.
- Strange "New" places.
- *Lack of Motivation:* Students with a disability have received motivation by teachers, paraprofessionals, and classmates during their education process. When their education process is done these individuals may not be there to motivate and push them to become physically active. Finding out activities and sports during the education process which the student enjoys participating in can help intrisically motivate these students when they are in the transition period.
- Limited Community Recreation Activities.

Overcoming Barriers and Improving a Transition Programme

Many times teachers don't know how to help students transition from high school. There are many barriers students face once out of high school. However, there are things teachers, parents, and students can do to ensure their ability to function in the community when leaving the school setting. A big barrier is the knowledge of parents. A good way to help them is to hold parent workshops. Not only are they able to talk with other parents, but also learn about different ways they can help their child transition into the community. Another thing that can be helpful is to have parent mentors. Parents who have already had their child graduate can mentor a parent whose child hasn't graduated yet. Another mentoring option is to have students who have graduated mentor a student who hasn't graduated yet. This gives them a companion and a responsibility and a feeling of importance in another child's life. Activity newsletters are also wonderful tools for parents and students to receive information about different activities and programmes that go on in the community for them to get involved in.

Use of Technology

With the development of new and improved technology with physical education and especially adapted physical education it is important for the APE teacher to know and understand different ways to implement technology for a successful transitional period for his or her students. APE teachers can develop an updated website regarding a fitness workout plan, in which students, who may need to stay at home half of the day, can download and follow at home with a sibling or parents. Video files can also be used to demonstrate proper technique, and appropriate music for aerobic activities could be downloaded as well. With technology growing and becoming better each day, APE teachers need to continue to grow as professionals and try to use this to benefit and enhance their students physical development.

Adapted physical education teachers are not only required to teach students with disabilities how to stay and become physically active, but also how, when and where. APE teachers are responsible for recognizing and teaching students with disabilities how to overcome the barriers for transition. In order to achieve this APE teachers need to concentrate on activities in the community that promote a physically active lifestyle while enhancing the health and wellness of students with disabilities (Krueger, DiRocco, Felix, 2000, pg. 222). Upon graduation, students with disabilities should know how to plan their activity, perform their activity and become personally responsible for participating in recreational activities on a regular basis.

University Partnerships for Transition:

- Create Friendships.
- Introduce students to transportation system.
- Provide students with an opportunity to use facilities not available at high school level.
- Provide education for both university students and students with disabilities.
- Great stepping stone into the transition process.

TOWARDS ATTENTION-DEFICIT HYPERACTIVITY DISORDER MANAGEMENT

Attention-deficit/hyperactivity disorder management refers to the treatment options available to people with attention-deficit/hyperactivity disorder (ADHD).

There are several effective and clinically proven options to treat people with ADHD. Combined medical management and behavioural treatment is the most effective ADHD management strategy, followed by medication alone, and then behavioural treatment. The individually most effective and cost efficient way is with stimulant medication. The most common stimulant medications are methylphenidate (Ritalin), dextroamphetamine (Dexedrine), and mixed amphetamine salts (Adderall). Atomoxetine (Strattera) is currently the only non-stimulant drug approved for the treatment of ADHD. Other medications which may be prescribed off-label include certain antidepressants such as tricyclic antidepressants, SNRIs or MAOIs. The presence of comorbid (relating to two diseases that occur together, e.g. depression and ADHD) disorders make finding the right treatment and diagnosis much more costly and time consuming.

A variety of psychotherapeutic and behavioural approaches to managing ADHD are employed by psychologists and psychiatrists. These include psychotherapy and working memory therapy. Improving the surrounding home and school environment with parent management training and classroom management can improve the behaviour of children with ADHD. Specialized ADHD coaches provide services and strategies to improve functioning, like time management or organizational suggestions.

Experimental and alternative treatments include nutritional supplements, specialized diets, and biofeedback.

A 2006 meta-analysis of ADHD research concluded that there was a shortage of data regarding ADHD drugs' potential adverse effects, with very few studies assessing the safety or efficacy of treatments beyond four months, and no randomized controlled trials assessing for periods of usage longer than two years. Treatment of preschool children is not recommended. The FDA found that a large number of the controlled trials required subjects who were known to respond to stimulants or who had no history of intolerance to stimulants, and this limits assumed generalizability of the trials' results.

Attention-deficit/Hyperactivity Disorder

Attention-deficit/Hyperactivity disorder (ADHD) is a neurobehavioural developmental disorder characterized by a persistent pattern of inattention and/or hyperactivity, as well as forgetfulness, poor impulse control or impulsivity, and distractibility. The most common symptoms of ADHD include, but are not limited to, distractibility, difficulty with concentration and focus, short term memory slippage, procrastination, problems organizing ideas and belongings, tardiness, impulsivity, and weak planning and execution. ADHD has three sub-types: predominantly inattentive, predominantly hyperactive, and combined.

ADHD is most likely a heterogeneous disorder caused by a combination of both genetics and environmental conditions. Researchers believe that a large majority of ADHD arises from a combination of various genes, many of which affect dopamine transporters. It appears to be highly heritable. The estimated contribution of non-genetic factors in 20 per cent, the majority of which are trauma or toxic exposure.

ADHD has a high rate of comorbidity (relating to two diseases that occur together, i.e. ADHD and depression). Oppositional defiant disorder, conduct disorder, anxiety, depression, bipolar disorder, and substance abuse can be comorbid conditions. Treating ADHD is much more difficult when comorbidities are present.

In the USA the usual criteria for diagnosis are those of the American Psychiatric Association in their Diagnostic and Statistical Manual of Mental Disorders (DSM-IV), 4th edition.

Cost Effectiveness

Combined medical management and behavioural treatment is the most effective ADHD management strategy, followed by medication alone, and then behavioural treatment. In terms of cost-effectiveness, management with medication has been shown to be the most cost-effective, followed by behavioural treatment, and combined treatment. The individually most effective and cost efficient way is with stimulant medication. Additionally, long-acting medications for ADHD, in comparison to short-acting varieties, generally seem to be cost effective. Comorbid (relating to two diseases that occur together, e.g. depression and ADHD) disorders make finding the right treatment and diagnosis much more costly than when comorbid disorders are absent.

Psychotherapeutic Approaches

There are a variety of psychotherapy approaches employed by psychologists and psychiatrists, the one used depends on the patient and the patient's symptoms. The approaches include psychotherapy, cognitive-behaviour therapy, support groups, parent training, meditation, and social skills training. If psychotherapy fails to bring improvement medications can be considered as an add-on or alternative.

Psychotherapy

Psychotherapy is another option, with or without medication, that has been shown to be effective.

Parent Education and Classroom Management

Improving the surrounding home and school environment can improve the behaviour of children with ADHD. Parents of children with ADHD often show similar deficits themselves, and thus may not be able to sufficiently help the child with his or her difficulties. Improving the parents' understanding of the child's behaviour and teaching them strategies to improve functioning and communication and discourage unwanted behaviour has measurable affect on the children with ADHD. The different educational interventions for the parents are jointly called Parent Management Training. Techniques include operant conditioning: a consistent application of rewards for meeting goals and good behaviour (positive reinforcement) and punishments such as time-outs or revocation or privileges for failing to meet goals or poor behaviour. Classroom management is similar to parent management training; educators learn about ADHD and techniques to improve behaviour applied to a classroom setting. Strategies utilized include increased structuring of classroom activities, daily feedback, and token economy.

Working Memory Training

Many of the problems shown by children with ADHD can be traced back to deficits in working memory (or short-term memory). By training and improving this memory some of the other symptoms may diminish as well. In a study by Klingberg *et al.*, a computerized training programme has shown good results in working memory, even if the generalized effect to behavioural symptoms was not as clear.

Coaching

ADHD Coaching is a specialized type of life coaching that uses specific techniques geared toward working with the unique brain wiring of individuals with attention-deficit/hyperactivity disorder. Professional coaching is not a substitute for traditional, multimodal treatment for ADHD such as medication, diet, exercise, and therapy.

Medications

FDA Approved Medicines

Stimulants are the most effective medications available for the treatment of ADHD. Five different formulations of stimulants have been approved by the FDA for the treatment of ADHD: three derived from amphetamine and two derived from methylphenidate. Atomoxetine is the only non-controlled, non-stimulant Food and Drug Administration (FDA) approved drug for the treatment of ADHD. There are no differences in effectiveness between medications used for ADHD.

Short-term clinical trials have shown medications to be effective for ADHD but the trials usually use exclusion criteria means knowledge on medications for ADHD is limited to a small subset of typical patients seen in clinical practice. They have not been found to improve school performance and data is lacking on long-term effectiveness and the severity of side effects. This class of medicines is generally regarded as one unit; however, they affect the brain differently. Some investigations are dedicated to finding the similarities of children who respond to a specific medicine. The behavioural response to stimulants in children is similar regardless of whether they have ADHD or not.

Stimulant medication is an effective treatment for Adult Attention-deficit hyperactivity disorder although the response rate may be lower for adults than children. Some physicians may recommend antidepressant drugs as the first line treatment instead of stimulants although antidepressants have lower treatment effect sizes than stimulant medication.

Amphetamine Based Medications

Three different medicines derived from amphetamine are used in ADHD treatment. Their trade names are *Adderall* (a mixture of 72% dextroamphetamine and 28% levoamphetamine), *Dexedrine* (pure dextroamphetamine), and *Desoxyn* (pure dextromethamphetamine). The differences in these three Amphetamine based medications' active compounds and mixture ratios results in each medications' slightly different activities.

Levoamphetamine and Dextroamphetamine: Levoamphetamine and dextroamphetamine have the same chemical formula but are mirror images of each other, the same way that a person's hands are the same but are mirror images of each other. This mirror difference is enough to cause the two compounds to be metabolized differently. Adderall begins to work before dextroamphetamine because of levoamphetamine. Levoamphetamine also provides Adderall with a longer clinical effect than dextroamphetamine. However, the brain's preference for dextroamphetamine over levoamphetamine shows that the clinical value of Adderall is, for the most part, due to dextroamphetamine. A few children with ADHD and comorbid disorders have helpful responses to levoamphetamine.

Dextromethamphetamine: The body metabolizes dextromethamphetamine into dextroamphetamine (in addition to less important chemicals). A quarter of dextromethamphetamine will ultimately become dextroamphetamine. After comparing only the common ground between dextroamphetamine and dextromethamphetamine, the latter is said to be the stronger stimulant. In theory and in practice a larger dose of dextroamphetamine is needed to achieve dextromethamphetamine's clinical potency. In fact, when dextroamphetamine and methylphenidate are unhelpful, some doctors may prescribe dextromethamphetamine. Although more rarely prescribed, anecdotal reports suggest dextromethamphetamine is very helpful in cases where the other two are ineffective, or cause limiting side effects.

Methylphenidate Based Medications

There are two different medicines derived from methylphenidate: *Ritalin,* which is half dextrothreomethylphenidate and half levothreomethylphenidate, and *Focalin,* which is pure dextrothreomethylphenidate. Dextrothreomethylphenidate has a higher pharmocological activity than its mirror handed levo-form. The levothreomethylphenidate if orally taken Ritalin has no useful activity and therefore does not improve child's symptoms; however, if *Daytrana* (Ritalin in transdermal patch form) is used, then levothreomethylphenidate accounts for about a thirteenth of the total clinical value.

Controlled Release of Drugs

Doctors may prescribe a controlled release pharmaceutical so that patients only have to take medication in the morning, or at a time more convenient for the patient. This is especially helpful for children who do not like taking their medication in the middle of the school day. Several controlled release methods are used in the FDA approved medications for ADHD. Each way provides makes the FDA drugs pharmaceutically different.

Multiple beads: Adderall and Dexedrine Spansules are examples of pharmaceuticals that use a system of two beads to achieve a controlled release. The beads are contained in a gelatin capsule that quickly dissolves in water, thus releasing the beads. The two different types of beads dissolve at different rates, thus extending the effects of the amphetamines. The company that markets Adderall is developing a new version of Adderall with three different kinds of beads that would be effective for up to 16 hours.

Osmosis: The only ADHD medication that currently utilizes osmotic pressure to achieve a controlled release of medicine is Concerta. A tablet of Concerta is actually a coated capsule. The coating is a mix of methylphenidate hydrochloride and binders such as lactose, povidone, and carnauba wax. Under that coating is a hollow filled capsule made of a semipermeable rigid membrane. The actual capsule is insoluble in water, but some of the ingredients that fill the capsule are water-soluble and others react in special ways with water. At one end of the capsule there is a laser drilled small hole, big enough for methylphenidate particles to pass through. The capsule's volume is partitioned into three sections. At the end closest to the hole is the first partition, which is a mixture containing a small concentration of methylphenidate. In the middle is the second partition is a different mixture that contains a higher concentration of methylphenidate. Occupying the third of the capsules volume that is furthest away from the small hole is triacetin, cellulose acetate, hypromellose, polyethylene glycol and polyethylene oxides.

Once swallowed, the capsule's shell quickly disintegrates and the methylphenidate that was contained in the shell is released. When water sweeps through the semipermeable membrane, the third partition that is furthest away from the capsule's hole will grow because the hypromellose absorbs water and swells up and the polyethylene glycol will increase the osmotic pressure. This partition will slowly push the contents of the other two partitions out the small hole, starting with the lower concentrations of methylphenidate, once the lower concentration of methylphenidate has mostly left the capsule the higher concentration of methylphenidate will begin to be pushed out of the capsule's hole. The capsule will be pharmacologically inactive once all the methylphenidate is expelled.

Transdermal: This is a patch applied to the skin that allows the drug to diffuse through the skin layers and enter the bloodstream. Unlike oral drugs, it may be removed and replaced conveniently, so it is flexible around the patient's schedule. Daytrana is the brand name of a transdermal patch which is essentially the same formulation as Ritalin. Daytrana is applied to the skin in the morning and the drug is evenly absorbed throughout the day, the patient should expect to feel the effects of the methylphenidate until two hours after the patch was removed, so patients should expect to take the patch off a few hours before bedtime. The collaborators that developed Daytrana are developing a transdermal patch version of dextroamphetamine and have completed phase 1 FDA human studies. This medicinal patch is code named SPD483 (a.k.a., ATS; Amphetamine Transdermal System; Amphetamine patch).

Prodrug: A prodrug is a compound which is itself inactive, but when metabolized becomes pharmacologically active. Prodrugs are usually designed to improve oral bioavailability as the chemical properties of the active compound may cause it to be poorly absorbed from the gastrointestinal tract. Lisdexamfetamine (Sold as Vyvanse) is a prodrug of dextroamphetamine. Vyvanse is a gelatin capsule that quickly dissolves once swallowed releasing lisdexamfetamine dimesylate.

Non Stimulants

Atomoxetine (Strattera) is a non-stimulant drug approved for the treatment of attention-deficit hyperactivity disorder (ADHD). It is less effective than stimulants for ADHD, is associated with individual cases of liver damage, carries an FDA black box warning regarding suicidal idealization, and controlled studies show increases in heart rate, decreases of body weight, decreased appetite and treatment-emergent nausea.

Certain antidepressants such as tricyclic antidepressants, SNRIs or MAOIs are sometimes prescribed and are also effective in the treatment of ADHD.

FDA Non-Approved Medications

Off-label Medications

Some medications used to treat ADHD are prescribed off-label, outside the scope of their FDA approved indications for various reasons. The Food and Drug Administration (FDA) requires numerous clinical trials to prove a potential drug's safety and efficacy in treating ADHD. The drugs below have not been through these tests, so the efficacy is unproven (however these drugs have been licenced for other indications, so have been proven to be safe in those populations), however proper dosage and usage instructions are not as well characterized.

- *Amantadine (Symmetrel)*—An antiviral drug and dopamine agonist. There have been reports of low-dose amantadine having been successfully used off-label to treat ADHD.
- *Amineptine (Survector/Maneon)*—A tricyclic antidepressant now illegal in many countries for being thought to have a small potential for abuse. It is still legal in some parts of the EU, such as Spain and Italy; it is no longer available in the U.S., Canada, France or the UK.
- *Benzphetamine (Didrex)*—A less powerful stimulant. It has little psychoactive effects until the liver metabolizes it into amphetamine and methamphetamine. Since this acts as a sustained release mechanism, it has lower abuse potential and is schedule 3.
- *Bupropion (Wellbutrin)* is classified as an antidepressant. It is the most common of off-label prescription for ADHD. It inhibits the reuptake of norepinephrine, and to a lesser extent, dopamine, in neuronal synapses, and has little or no effect on serotonergic re-uptake. Bupropion is not a controlled substance. It is commonly prescribed as a timed release formulation to decrease the risk of side effects. Bupropion is not particularly known for its stimulant properties because at high doses it tends to cause seizures in a large portion of the population.
- *Clonidine*—Initially developed as a treatment for high blood pressure, low

doses in evenings and/or afternoons are sometimes used in conjunction with stimulants to help with sleep and because Clonidine sometimes helps moderate impulsive and oppositional behaviour and may reduce tics. It may be more useful for comorbid Tourette syndrome.

- *Milnacipran*, an anti-depressant drug, is currently being investigated for potential to alleviate the symptoms of ADHD in adults.
- *Modafinil (Provigil/Alertec/Sparlon)*—In the U.S., it is currently off-label pending decision by the FDA on August 22, 2006. It was originally pending marketing on-label as Alertec but denied for a reported incidence of Stevens-Johnson Syndrome.
- *Pemoline* (*Cylert*)—A stimulant used with great success until the late 1980s when it was discovered that this medication could cause liver damage. In March 2005, the makers of Cylert announced that it would discontinue the medication's production. It is no longer available in the United States.
- *Reboxetine* (*Edronax*) is a selective norepinephrine reuptake inhibitor which is mainly used as an antidepressant. Studies outside the USA have found it to be an effective treatment for ADHD, and it is prescribed off-label for this purpose in Israel and some European countries, however reboxetine has never been approved by the FDA in the United States.
- *Selegiline*—An MAOI currently being investigated for ADHD.
    - Emsam is a version of Selegiline delivered via transdermal patch.

Tricyclic anti-depressants are also occasionally prescribed, but they seem to only treat the hyperactive part of the condition. There is research on the selective serotonin reuptake enhancer class of medications (SSREs); currently, the only one available is tianeptine (trade name Stablon); this is an atypical tricyclic anti-depressant which is inconclusive in its efficacy and hence not approved. Tianeptine is not available in North America.

Experimental and Alternative Medicine Treatments

Alternative therapies are often sought out due to concerns of the long-term effects of stimulants on children. Parents, children, consumer advocacy organizations and some physicians are increasingly looking for alternatives to stimulant drugs. There is a large body of evidence of effectiveness of some alternative therapies including supplementation with certain nutrients, elimination diets, avoidance of food additives or dyes, allergy treatment, family counseling and behaviour therapy. Some advocate that alternative therapies should be tried before ADHD medications although not all ADHD children will have an effective response.

Aerobic Fitness

Aerobic fitness may improve cognitive functioning and neural organization related to executive control during pre-adolescent development, though more studies are needed in this area. One study suggests that athletic performance in boys with ADHD may increase peer acceptance when accompanied by fewer negative behaviours.

Biofeedback

EEG biofeedback also sometimes referred to as neurofeedback is effective in treating attention, impulsivity and hyperactivity. There are no known side effects from biofeedback therapy although research into biofeedback has been limited and further research has been recommended.

Dietary Supplements

There are indications that children with ADHD are metabolically different from others.

- *Zinc*–Although the role of zinc in ADHD has not be elucidated, "numerous controlled studies report cross-sectional evidence of lower zinc tissue levels."
- *Omega-3 fatty acids*–Some studies suggest that a lack of omega-3 fatty acids is associated with certain ADHD symptoms. And it has therefore been suggested that diet modification may play a role in the management of ADHD. People with ADHD were found to have significantly lower plasma phospholipids and erythrocytes omega-3 fatty acids. Their intake of saturated fat was found to be 30 per cent higher than in controls, while the intake of many other nutrients was not different. In support of the idea that it is not the intake of essential fatty acids that causes low tissue levels, a preliminary study showed that exhaled ethane, a marker of omega-3 fatty acids peroxidation, was higher in children with ADHD relative to controls. Researchers from Australia's national science agency showed polyunsaturated fatty acids to provide "medium to strong positive treatment effects" in ADHD. Another double blind study conducted by the University of Oxford, where children were given omega-3 fatty acids concluded that "significant improvements for active treatment versus placebo were found in reading, spelling, and behaviour over 3 months of treatment in parallel groups." A 2008 study also concludes that Omega-3/Omega-6 supplementation reduces ADHD-symptoms for some. Thus it increasingly is documented in clinical studies that omega-3 fatty acids provide a safe way to treat hyperactivity.
- *Magnesium and vitamin B6 (pyridoxine)*—In 2006, a study demonstrated that children with autism had significantly lower magnesium than controls, and that the correction of this deficit was therapeutic: Mousain-Bosc *et al.* showed that children with ADHD (n = 46) had significantly lower red blood cell magnesium levels than controls (n = 30). Intervention with magnesium and vitamin B6 reduced hyperactivity, hyperemotivity/aggressiveness and improved school attention.
- *Iron supplements*—In 2005, the official journal of the American Academy of Pediatrics, Pediatrics, published the case report of a child with ADHD with

low ferritin who showed "considerable behavioural improvement" after his ferritin was normalized by iron supplementation. Based on earlier studies on iron deficiency and attentional function (notably the dopamine synthesis aspect), the screening of ferritin levels in children with ADHD was suggested.

- *Potassium*—In 2007, Harvard-associated researchers described a form of ADHD that was well treated with over-the-counter potassium supplements. The molecular mechanism suggested by the authors was one producing sensory overstimulation, often triggered by ingesting carbohydrates, suggesting that people with ADHD who have sensitivity to sugar may be particularly likely to have this variant.
- *Medical cannabis*—Medical cannabis is used by many people with ADHD, most often self-medicated, or occasionally, supervised by a doctor.
- In the 1980s vitamin B_6 was promoted as a helpful remedy for children with learning difficulties including inattentiveness; however, a study of large doses of vitamins with ADHD children showed that they were ineffective in changing behaviour.
- Mild stimulants such as caffeine, theobromine, and nicotine may improve the function of some children suffering from ADHD.

Diets

Perhaps the best known of the dietary alternatives is the Feingold diet which involves removing salicylates, artificial colours and flavours, and certain synthetic preservatives from children's diets. However, studies have shown little if any effect of the Feingold diet on the behaviour of children with ADHD.

A meta-analysis has found that dietary elimination of artificial food colouring and preservatives provides a statistically significant benefit in children with ADHD. Other more recent studies agree with these conclusions. The UK Food Standards Agency (FSA) has called for a ban on the use of six artificial food colourings and the European Union (EU) has ruled that some food dyes must be labeled with the relevant E number as well as this warning: *"may have an adverse effect on activity and attention in children."*

Treatment of ADHD with Comorbid Disorders

Because ADHD comorbidities are diverse and the rate of comorbidity is high, special care must dedicated to certain comorbidities. The FDA is not set up to address this issue, and does not approve medications for comorbidities, nonetheless certain such topics have been extensively researched.

Tic Disorders

Patients with Tourette syndrome who are referred to specialty clinics have a high rate of comorbid ADHD. Patients who have ADHD along with tics or tic disorders may also have problems with disruptive behaviours, overall functioning, and cognitive function, accounted for by the comorbid ADHD.

The treatment of ADHD in the presence of tic disorders has long been a controversial topic. Past medical practice held that stimulants (such as Ritalin) could not be used in the presence of tics, due to concern that their use might worsen tics; however, multiple lines of research have shown that stimulants can be cautiously used in the presence of tic disorders. Several studies have shown that stimulants do not exacerbate tics any more than placebo does, and suggest that stimulants may even reduce tic severity. Controversy remains, and the PDR continues to carry a warning that stimulants should not be used in the presence of tic disorders, so physicians may be reluctant to use them. Others are comfortable using them and even advocate for a stimulant trial when ADHD co-occurs with tics, because the symptoms of ADHD can be more impairing than tics.

The stimulants are the first line of treatment for ADHD, with proven efficacy, but they do fail in up to 20 per cent of cases, even in patients without tic disorders. Current prescribed stimulant medications include: methylphenidate (brand names Ritalin, Metadate, Concerta), dextroamphetamine (Dexedrine), and mixed amphetamine salts (Adderall). Other medications can be used when stimulants are not an option. These include the alpha-2 agonists (clonidine and guanfacine), tricyclic antidepressants (desipramine and nortriptyline), and newer antidepressants (bupropion and venlafaxine). There have been case reports of tics worsening with bupropion (brand name Wellbutrin). There is good empirical evidence for short-term safety and efficacy for the use of desipramine, bupropion and atomoxetine (Strattera).

Concerns about the Use of Stimulant Medication

The National Institute of Mental Health states that, "stimulant drugs, when used with medical supervision, are usually considered quite safe." Still, some parents and professionals have raised questions about the side effects of drugs and their long- term use. A recent review states that ADHD studies "have major methodological deficiencies which are compounded by their restriction to school-age children, relatively short follow-up, and few data on adverse effects."

The American Heart Association feel that it is prudent to carefully assess children for heart conditions before treating them with stimulant medications.

Increase in Use of Stimulant Medication in Children

Outpatient treatment rates have held steady in the US recently. Prior to this, outpatient treatment for ADHD in the US grew from 0.9 children per 100 in 1987 to 3.4 per 100 in 1997. There is concern about the rising use of methylphenidate (Ritalin), mainly to treat ADHD and similar disorders, in the UK. The incidence of ADHD is estimated at three to five per cent of the population, while the number of children in the United States taking Ritalin is estimated at one to two per cent. In a small study of four American communities, the reported incidence of ADHD varied from 1.6 per cent to

9.4 per cent. The study also found that only 12.5 per cent of the children reportedly meeting the DSM-III-R ADHD criteria for ADHD had been treated with stimulants during the past year.

Stimulant Misuse

There is non-medical prescription stimulant use. A 2003 study found that non-prescription use by college students in the US was 6.9 per cent with 4.1 per cent using them within the last year. A 2006 study with teens in Grades 7 to Grade 12 found that 2 per cent reported non-medical use of prescription stimulant medication in the past 12 months, with 2 per cent also reporting non-medical use of prescribed sedatives/ and or anxiety medications, 3 per cent using sleeping medications, and 12 per cent reporting non-medical use of prescribed pain medications.

Use of Medication in Preschoolers

It is believed that ADHD affects seven per cent of the preschool-aged population. Michael J. Manos of the Cleveland hospital for Children states, "Severe ADHD in children 2—4 years of age is especially problematic. Young children do not have the ability to use or respond to language to moderate behaviour that older children have." Evidence indicates that forty per cent of children who show signs of ADHD are suspended from preschool, while approximately sixteen per cent are eventually expelled. The disorder, which makes it difficult for children to control their behaviour and pay attention, affects about 7 per cent of the school-aged population. Parents of children with ADHD note that they usually display their symptoms at an early age. Dr. John Van Brakle has stated, "pediatricians have long questioned whether such children can accurately be identified, given the overlap with normal behaviours in young children." The use of stimulant medication has not been approved by the FDA for children under the age of six. A growing trend is the diagnosis of younger children with ADHD. Prescriptions for children under the age of 5 rose nearly 50 per cent from 2000 to 2003. Research on this issue has indicated that stimulant medication can help younger children with "severe ADHD symptoms" but typically at a lower dose then older children. It was also found that children at this age are more sensitive to side effects and should be closely monitored. Manos states, "it is prudent for physicians to be cautious," with medications. Evidence suggests that careful assessment and highly individualized behavioural interventions significantly improve both social and academic skills while medication only treats the symptoms of the disorder. Manos suggests that, "one of the primary reasons cited for the growing use of psychotropic interventions was that many physicians realize that psychological interventions are costly and difficult to sustain."

A study published in the November 2006 *Journal of the American Academy of Child and Adolescent Psychiatry* followed 300 three- to five-years-old with severe ADHD (hyperactive/impulsive, inattentive, or combined type). One-third of those children experienced reduced ADHD symptoms after engaging in 10 weeks of behaviour modification techniques wherein parents offered consistent praise, ignored negative behaviour, and used time-outs. The remaining two-thirds showed improvement with a combination of behaviour therapy and low doses of Ritalin. 11 per cent of the children stopped treatment due to side effects including appetite reduction, insomnia, and anxiety.

Adverse Side Effects

A number of possible side effects are of concern with respect to ADHD medications.

Tics

The emergence or worsening of tics have been thought to occur. Despite belief to the contrary, no significant effects have been observed on the emergence of tics.

Weight Loss

The stunting of growth in children has been a concern. Past studies suggested that "long-term use of the drugs could stunt children's growth." However, more recent studies suggest that children eventually do reach normal height and weight. According to Wilens (2004), treated children with ADHD tend to grow at a slower rate but catch up during adolescence and adulthood. One notion is that psychostimulant medication can decrease appetite which may result in loss of weight and may be a factor in stunted growth.

Cardiovascular Side Effects

There is concern that stimulants and Atomoxetine, which increase the heart rate and blood pressure, might cause serious cardiovascular problems.

In 2007 the FDA requires all ADHD drug manufacturers to notify patients about serious cardiovascular side effects. This was due to reports of sudden death in children taking these medications who had underlying heart problems and of high risk adults who suffered heart attacks and strokes.

Studies indicated that, "the rate of sudden death of children taking ADHD medications do not appear to exceed the base rate of sudden death in the general population." Matthew Smith is purported to have died at age 14 after long-term use of Ritalin. The medical examiner determined that Smith died from Ritalin usage, but medical experts dispute this. The examiner also argued that it was likely that diabetic children were at higher risk for cardiac problems.

Psychiatric Side Effects

In 2006 the FDA examined the occurrence of psychiatric side effects in ADHD medication. They found increased rates of psychosis and or mania with all drug treatments examined, including: Concerta, Ritalin LA, d-MPH, Atomoxetine, Adderall XR, Modafinil, MTS, and Metadate.

Sleep problems may occur.

Many of these drugs are associated with physical and psychological dependence.

Issues with Long-term Use of Stimulant Medication

The short-term use of stimulant medication has been shown to be effective yet its long-term effects are yet to be determined. The Multimodal Treatment Study of Children with ADHD study concluded that while drugs such as Ritalin and Concerta (a delayed release form of Ritalin) worked in the short-term, there was no demonstrable improvement in children's behaviour after three years of medication."

Wilens and other professionals have shown that the controlled use of medication can reduce the likelihood of substance abuse later on. Biederman and colleagues reported on a longitudinal study in which it was found that unmedicated children with ADHD were at greater risk of later substance use. Children who received medication for their ADHD were less likely to later use substances. A 2007 study from the Mayo clinic found that, "treatment with stimulant medication during childhood was associated with more favourable long-term school outcomes."

Long-term Use and Schizophrenia and Drug Induced Psychosis

Although the safety profile of short-term methylphenidate therapy in clinical trials has been well established, repeated use of psychostimulants such as methylphenidate is less clear. The long-term effects of methylphenidate such as drug addiction, withdrawal reactions, psychosis and depression and effects in pregnancy has received very little research and thus the long-term effects of using stimulants for ADHD are largely unknown. There are no well defined withdrawal schedules for discontinuing long-term use of stimulants. Short-term clinical trials have shown an incidence of psychosis of 0.1 per cent. Psychosis occurs more commonly as a result of chronic use effecting about 6 per cent of children on long-term methylphenidate. The long-term effects on mental health disorders in later life of chronic use of methylphenidate is unknown. Concerns have been raised that long-term therapy might cause drug dependence, paranoia, schizophrenia and behavioural sensitisation, similar to other stimulants. Psychotic symptoms from methylphenidate can include, hearing voices, visual hallucinations, urges to harm oneself, severe anxiety, euphoria, grandiosity, paranoid delusions, confusion, increased aggression and irritability. Methylphenidate psychosis is unpredictable in who it will occur. Family history of mental illness does not predict the incidence of stimulant toxicosis in ADHD children. High rates of childhood stimulant use are found in ADHD patients who will eventually be diagnosed with comorbid schizophrenia and bipolar disorder. Individuals with a diagnosis of bipolar or schizophrenia who were prescribed stimulants during childhood typically have a significantly earlier onset of the psychotic disorder and suffer a more severe clinical course of psychotic disorder.

Stimulant Withdrawal and Rebound Effects

Stimulant withdrawal or rebound reactions can occur and should be minimised in intensity, i.e. via a gradual tapering off of medication over a period of weeks or months. A very small study of abrupt withdrawal of stimulants did suggest that withdrawal reactions are not typical. Nonetheless withdrawal reactions may still occur in susceptible individuals. The withdrawal or rebound symptoms of methylphenidate can include psychosis, irritability and depression and a return of ADHD symptoms in an exagerated form. Methylphenidate may be worse for causing rebound and withdrawal effects due to its very short half life. Amphetamine may cause less severe rebound or withdrawal effects due to its somewhat longer half life. Up to a third of ADHD children experience a rebound effect in ADHD symptoms when the methylphenidate dose wears off.

Questions about the Possibility of Stimulant Medication Causing Cancer

A small-scale 2005 Texas study indicated that methylphenidate might cause chromosome aberrations. At the time this study caused concern because of the link between chromosome aberrations and cancer. The authors of the study stated that all the children in this study showed suspicious DNA changes within a very short time and suggested that further research was warranted. A team from the Food and Drug Administration (FDA), the National Institutes of Health (NIH) and the Environmental Protection Agency (EPA) went to Texas in 2005 to evaluate the methodology of the study. Dr. David Jacobson-Kram of the FDA said that the study had flaws in its methods but that its results could not be dismissed. Flaws cited are (1) that the study did not include a control group on placebo, and (2) that it is too small. A follow up study led by a team of six scientists from the Department of Child and Adolescent Psychiatry and Psychotherapy and the Department of Toxicology, University of Würzburg, Würzburg, Germany looked at this issue with an in-depth study. They sought to respond to the challenge noted above to attempt to replicate the results of El-Zein *et al.* in a larger study. Their paper was completed in 2006 and published in 2007 in Environmental Health Perspectives (EHP), the peer-reviewed journal of the United States' National Institute of Environmental Health Sciences. This study used a larger cohort and a longer period of follow-up and included a small group of long-term users, but otherwise used what researchers believed to be an identical methodology to that used by El-Zein *et al.* (They note that El-Zein *et al.* published a short study report and did not publish detailed descriptions of methodology.) After follow-ups at six months, the researchers found no evidence that methylphenidate might cause cancer, stating "the concern regarding a potential increase in the risk of developing cancer later in life after long-term MPH treatment is not supported."

History

Medication Use

The first reported evidence of stimulant medication used to treat children with concentration and hyperactivity problems came in 1937. Dr. Charles Bradley in Providence, RI reported that a group of children with behavioural problems improved after being treated with the stimulant Benzedrine. In 1957, the stimulant methylphenidate (Ritalin, which was first produced in 1950) became available under various names (including Focalin, Concerta, Metadate, and Methylin); it remains one of the most widely prescribed medications for ADHD. Initially the drug was used to treat narcolepsy, chronic fatigue, depression, and to counter the sedating effects of other medications. The drug began to be used for ADHD in the 1960s and steadily rose in use.

In 1975, pemoline (Cylert) was approved by the FDA for use in the treatment of ADHD. While an effective agent for managing the symptoms, the development of liver failure in 14 cases over the next 27 years would result in the manufacturer withdrawing this medication from the market. New delivery systems for medications were invented in 1999 that eliminated the need for multiple doses across the day or taking medication at school. These new systems include pellets of medication coated with various time-release substances to permit medications to dissolve hourly across an 8—12 hour period (Metadate CD, Adderall XR, Focalin XR) and an osmotic pump that extrudes a liquid methylphenidate sludge across an 8—12 hour period after ingestion (Concerta).

In 2003, atomoxetine (Strattera) received the first FDA approval for a nonstimulant drug to be used specifically for ADHD. In 2007, lisdexamfetamine (Vyvanse) becomes the first prodrug to receive FDA approval for ADHD.

In 1999 the largest study of treatment for ADHD was published in the *American Journal of Psychiatry*. Known as the *Multimodal Treatment Study of ADHD* (MTA Study), it involved more than 570 children with ADHD at 6 sites in the United States and Canada randomly assigned to 4 treatment groups. All 4 treatment groups showed marked improvement from the time of baseline measurements to completion of the study 14 months later. Behavioural treatment was as effective as medication alone on 16 of 19 outcome measures.

ANALYZING ALTERNATIVE THERAPIES FOR DEVELOPMENTAL AND LEARNING DISABILITIES

Alternative therapies for developmental and learning disabilities include a range of practices used in the treatment of dyslexia, ADHD, Asperger syndrome, autism, Down syndrome and other developmental and learning disabilities. Treatments include changes in diet, dietary supplements, biofeedback, chelation therapy, homeopathy, massage and yoga. These therapies generally rely on theories that have little scientific basis, lacking well-controlled, large, randomized trials to demonstrate safety and efficacy; small trials that have reported beneficial effects can be generally explained by the ordinary waxing and waning of the underlying conditions.

Treatment Needs

There are a number of non-standard treatments for developmental and learning disabilities. There is a call for alternative therapies particularly when a condition lacks a reliable remediation. For example, there is no cure for autism; the main goals of mainstream behavioural and medical management are to lessen associated deficits and family distress, and to increase quality of life and functional independence. Some alternative therapies, such as gluten-free, casein-free diets, may be appealing to some parents because the treatment recommended by most experts is thought to be "cold and manipulative." Parents may also consider a drug treatment for attention deficit as avoidable. Alternative treatments to a stimulant medication range from natural products to psychotherapeutic techniques and highly technological interventions. It has been argued that although texts that promote alternative therapies do not directly accuse parents of inadequacy, the claims that the disability is caused by certain factors, such as poor nutrition, supports the culture of mother-blame.

Prevalence

From 12 per cent to 64 per cent of families of a child with ADHD use an alternative therapy, with the lower estimates likely come from narrower definitions of complementary and alternative medicine (CAM). School teachers, family and friends are the most common source of suggestion of alternative therapies for ADHD. In 2003, 64 per cent of families of a child with special health care needs reported that they use alternative therapies. These therapies included spiritual healing, massage, chiropractic, herbs and special diets, homeopathy, self hypnosis and other methods of complementary and alternative medicine. The need for an alternative therapy was related to the child's condition and to its evaluation as repairable or not. A 2008 study found that about 40 per cent of Hong Kong children with autism spectrum disorder were treated with CAM, with the most popular therapies being acupuncture, sensory integration therapy, and Chinese herbology; the 40 per cent is a lower prevalence than in Canada and the U.S., where biological-based therapies such as special diets predominate. In the U.S. CAM is used by an estimated 20-40 per cent of healthy children, 30-70 per cent of children with special health care needs, and 52-95 per cent of children with autism, and a 2009 survey of U.S. primary care physicians found that more of them recommended than discouraged multivitamins, essential fatty acids, melatonin, and probiotics as CAM treatments for autism.

Evidence Basis

Complementary and alternative medicine often lacks support in scientific evidence, so its safety and efficacy are often questionable. Some therapists who advocate CAM may claim to cure many conditions or disabilities that are not diseases and therefore cannot be "cured."

While some experts encourage parents to be open-minded, others argue that treatments and services with no proven efficacy have *opportunity costs* because they displace the opportunity to participate in efficient treatments and services. According to Scott O. Lilienfeld, many individuals who spend large amounts of time and money on ineffective treatments may be left with precious little of either. As a result, they may forfeit the opportunity to obtain treatments that could be more helpful. Thus, even ineffective treatments that are by themselves innocuous can indirectly produce negative consequences.

There is often little or no scientific evidence for effectiveness of alternative therapies. It may be difficult to separate the success of a specific treatment from natural development or from the benefits of the individual's positive attitude. Some phenomena to be considered when evaluating studies are the placebo effect, the Hawthorne effect and different types of attentional and motivational effects. However, there is no doubt that people with disabilities may benefit from some alternative therapies, at least for relaxation, social interaction, personal development and self-esteem. This can be important because many children with learning difficulties suffer from low self-esteem.

For instance, a randomised controlled trial with dyslexic children was undertaken to evaluate the efficiency of Sunflower therapy which includes applied kinesiology, physical manipulation, massage, homeopathy, herbal remedies and neuro-linguistic programming. There were no significant improvements in cognitive nor literacy test performance associated with the treatment, but there were significant improvements in self-esteem for the treatment group. This study did not control for the placebo effect.

Precautions

Because many alternative therapies have not been evaluated in scientific studies there may be no guarantee for their safety. In most countries, with the exception of osteopathy and chiropractic, complementary medical disciplines have not been state registered. This means there is no law to forbid anyone from setting up as a practitioner even with no qualification nor experience. There are also a lot of 'universities' offering all kinds of alternative medicine degrees for a fee, and their certificates can look very real. These organisations may, on the other hand, offer ongoing training and an insurance to their registered members.

Experts of alternative therapies advice customers to be careful when choosing a therapist. Before taking a therapy, it is wise to find out whether or not previous customers recommend it, the therapist has a qualification and is a registered practitioner, whether the therapy could be dangerous, how much the treatment costs, and whether money will be refunded if the therapy does not work.

TOWARDS LISTING THE ALTERNATIVE THERAPIES FOR DEVELOPMENTAL AND LEARNING DISABILITIES

This list covers alternative therapies for developmental and learning disabilities. Many of the treatments—including physiotherapy, massage and others—are neither generally considered as 'alternative therapies' nor as standard treatments for developmental and learning disabilities. They are, however, sometimes given or recommended as treatments specifically for these disabilities and therefore included in the list.

Bioenergy Therapies

- Bi-Aura therapy
- Craniosacral therapy
- Distant healing
- Electromagnetic Field (EMF) Balancing Technique
- Magnetic field therapy
- Therapeutic Touch (TT)
- Thought Field Therapy (TFT).

Bodyworks

- Alexander technique
- Chiropractic
- Feldenkreis
- Osteopathy
- Physiotherapy and occupational therapy for learning disabilities
- Pilates
- Yoga
- Zero Balancing.

Dietary Treatments

- Additive-free diets
- Antifungal medication
- Ayurvedic medicine
- B6-magnesium treatment
- Chelation therapy
- Fatty acids
- Feingold Diet
- Food allergies, multiple chemical sensitivities (diet base)
- Gluten-free, casein-free diet (GFCF)
- Glyconutritional supplement
- Herbal medicine
- Iron
- Lutein-free Diet
- Megavitamins
- Refined sugar-free diet
- Secretin treatment
- Trace minerals, trace elements
- Vaccination (avoidance)
- Zinc.

Eclectic Approaches

- Educational kinesiology (Edu-K)
- Sunflower therapy.

Hearing Therapies

- Auditory integration training (AIT), auditory processing training
- Interactive Metronome
- Lexiphone
- Mozart Effect
- Music therapy
- Spectral Activated Music of Optimal Natural Structure (SAMONAS)
- The Tomatis Method.

Holistic Healing

- Applied Kinesiology
- Crystal therapy
- Flower remedies
- Homeopathy
- Naturopathy.

Medical Interventions

- Anti-motion sickness medication and other types for Vestibular Dysfunction.

Movement-based Therapies

- Brain Gym
- Doman method
- Brushing technique
- DDAT or the Dore Treatment; Balance Remediation Exercise Training Programme
- Developmental Exercise Programme (inhibition of primitive reflexes)
- Learning Breakthrough
- (Psychomotor) patterning
- Primary Movement.

Pedagogical Approaches and Policies

- Full inclusion
- Gentle Teaching
- Person Centered Approach (PCA).

Psychosocial Interventions

- Floortime (aka DIR)
- Holding therapy
- TEACCH.

Stress Management

- Caffeine-free diet
- Laughter therapy
- Meditation
- Positive thinking
- Stress management.

Student Profiling

- Brain Organisation Profile (BOP)
- Learning styles.

Technological Interventions

- Biofeedback
- Facilitated Communication
- Fast ForWord.

Touch Therapies

- Acupressure
- Acupuncture
- Aromatherapy
- Bowen Technique
- Brushing and joint compression
- Emotional Freedom Technique
- Massage
- Reflexology
- Reiki.

Training Methods

- Davis Dyslexia Correction
- Positive Behaviour Support (PBS)
- Sensory Integration Training (SIT)
- Whole Language.

Visual Approaches

- Asfedic Tuning (TintaVision)
- Coloured overlays
- Dunlop test
- Harris Filters

- Intuitive Colorimeter
- Irlen Syndrome
- Optim-Eyes
- Optometric evaluation and optometric visual training
- Prism glasses
- Tinted lenses, ChromaGen lenses
- Visual Tracking Magnifier.

Emerging Therapies

- Dolphin Assisted Therapy
- Hypnotherapy
- Light and Colour Therapy.

6

Dyslexia and Autism: Select Case Studies

TOWARDS UNDERSTANDING DYSLEXIA AND CREATING AN AWARENESS

Dyslexia is a learning disorder that manifests itself primarily as a difficulty with reading and spelling. It is separate and distinct from reading difficulties resulting from other causes, such as a non-neurological deficiency with vision or hearing, or from poor or inadequate reading instruction. It is estimated that dyslexia affects between 5 per cent to 17 per cent of the U.S. population.

Although dyslexia is thought to be the result of a neurological difference, it is not an intellectual disability. Dyslexia is diagnosed in people of all levels of intelligence, average, above average, and highly gifted.

Definition

There are many definitions of the disorder called *dyslexia* but no consensus. The World Federation of Neurology defined dyslexia as follows:

> *Specific developmental dyslexia is a disorder manifested by difficulty learning to read despite conventional instruction, adequate intelligence, and adequate socio-cultural opportunity. It is dependent upon fundamental cognitive disabilities that are frequently of constitutional origin.*

Some of the other published definitions are purely descriptive, while still others embody causal theories. From the varying definitions used by dyslexia researchers and organizations around the world, it appears that dyslexia is not one thing but many, in so far as it serves as a conceptual clearing-house for a number of reading skills deficits and difficulties, with a number of causes.

Castles and Coltheart, 1993, described phonological and surface types of developmental dyslexia by analogy to classical subtypes of acquired dyslexia (alexia) which are classified according to the rate of errors in reading non-words. However the distinction between surface and phonlogical dyslexia has not replaced the old empirical terminology of dysphonetic versus dyseidetic types of dyslexia. The surface/ phonological distinction is only descriptive, and devoid of any aetiological assumption as to the underlying brain mechanisms, in contrast the dysphonetic/dyseidetic distinction refers to two different mechanisms one relates to a speech discrimination deficit, and the other to a visual preception impairment. (Most people with dyslexia who have Boder's Dysiedetic type, have attentional and spatial difficulties which interfere with the reading acquisition process.

Signs and Symptoms

Dyslexia symptoms vary according to the severity of the disorder as well as the age of the individual.

Pre-school Age Children

It is difficult to obtain a certain diagnosis of dyslexia before a child begins school, but many dyslexic individuals have a history of difficulties that began well before kindergarten. Children who exhibit these symptoms have a higher risk of being diagnosed as dyslexic than other children. Some of these symptoms are:

- Delay in learning to speak
- Learns new words slowly
- Has difficulty rhyming words, as in nursery rhymes
- Late in establishing a dominant hand.

Early Elementary School-Age Children

- Difficulty in learning the alphabet
- Difficulty with associating sounds with the letters that represent them (sound-symbol correspondence)
- Difficulty in identifying or generating rhyming words, or counting syllables in words (phonological awareness)
- Difficulty in segmenting words into individual sounds, or blending sounds to make words (phonemic awareness)
- Difficulty with word retrieval or naming problems
- Difficulty in learning to decode words
- Confusion with before/after, right/left, over/under, and so on
- Difficulty in distinguishing between similar sounds in words; mixing up sounds in multisyllable words (auditory discrimination) (for example, "aminal" for animal, "bisghetti" for spaghetti).

Older Elementary School Children

- Slow or inaccurate reading
- Very poor spelling
- Difficulty in associating individual words with their correct meanings

- Difficulty with time keeping and concept of time
- Difficulty with organization skills
- Due to fear of speaking incorrectly, some children become withdrawn and shy or become bullies out of their inability to understand the social cues in their environment
- Difficulty in comprehending rapid instructions, following more than one command at a time or remembering the sequence of things
- Reversals of letters (b for d) and a reversal of words (saw for was) are typical among children who have dyslexia. Reversals are also common for children age 6 and younger who don't have dyslexia. But with dyslexia, the reversals persist
- Children with dyslexia may fail to see (and occasionally to hear) similarities and differences in letters and words, may not recognize the spacing that organizes letters into separate words, and may be unable to sound out the pronunciation of an unfamiliar word.

Diagnosis

Formal diagnosis of dyslexia is made by a qualified professional, such as a neurologist, neuropsychologist, developmental pediatrician, or educational psychologist and qualified specialist dyslexia teachers. Evaluation generally includes testing of reading ability together with measures of underlying skills such as tests of rapid naming to evaluate short-term memory and sequencing skills, and nonword reading to evaluate phonological coding skills. Evaluation will usually also include an IQ test to establish a profile of learning strengths and weaknesses. While such "discrepancy" tests between full scale IQ and reading level have, on their own, been shown to be flawed, the tests often include interdisciplinary testing to exclude other possible causes for reading difficulties, such as a more generalized cognitive impairment or physical causes such as problems with vision or hearing.

Leppänen PH *et al.*, investigated whether children born to families with a history of dyslexia are at an elevated risk for the disorder. They studied 6-month-old infants with and without a high risk of familial dyslexia and measured differences in electrical activation in the brain generated by changes in the temporal structure of speech sounds, a critical cuing feature in speech. The infants at risk differed from control infants in both their initial responsiveness to sounds and in their change-detection responses dependent on the stimulus context. This indicates that infants at risk due to a familial background of reading problems process auditory temporal cues of speech sounds differently than infants without such risk even before they learn to speak, and that incidence of familial dyslexia may assist in diagnosis.

Recent dyslexia research using neuroimaging suggests that it may one day be possible to identify children with dyslexia before they learn to read.

Currently, lack of access to neuroimaging makes it impractical for diagnosing dyslexia; however, there are testing instruments that can be used to assess the specific manifestations of these neurobiological differences. These instruments assess accurate and/or fluent word recognition, single real word and pseudoword reading fluency, phonological processing, and for older students, spelling deficits and general language competence. There are screening instruments that can be used to identify children at high risk for dyslexia as young as 6 years of age.

In UK, the identification of symptoms from the study of patterns across many clinical observations of dyslexic children led researcher Thomas Richard Miles to develop the Bangor Dyslexia Diagnostic Test.

Disagreement exists in dyslexia research as to whether dyslexia exists as a disorder, or whether it simply reflects individual differences among different readers.

Conditions that often Co-occur with Dyslexia

The following conditions often occur with dyslexia in the same individual. It is unclear whether these conditions share underlying neurological causes with dyslexia.

- Dysgraphia is a disorder which expresses itself primarily during writing or typing, although in some cases it may also affect eye-hand coordination in such direction or sequence oriented processes as tying knots or carrying out a repetitive task. Dysgraphia is distinct from Dyspraxia in that the person may have the word to be written or the proper order of steps in mind clearly, but carries the sequence out in the wrong order.
- Dyscalculia is a neurological condition characterized by a problem with learning fundamentals and one or more of the basic numerical skills. Often people with this condition can understand very complex mathematical concepts and principles but have difficulty in processing formulas and even basic addition and subtraction.
- Developmental dyspraxia is a neurological condition characterized by a marked difficulty in carrying out routine tasks involving balance, fine-motor control, kinesthetic coordination, difficulty in the use of speech sounds, problems with short-term memory and organization are typical of dyspraxics.
- Specific Language Impairment is a developmental language disorder that can affect both expressive and receptive language. SLI is defined as a "pure" language impairment, meaning that is not related to or caused by other developmental disorders, hearing loss or acquired brain injury. A study by the Universities of Maastricht and Utrecht examined speech perception and speech production in 3-year-old Dutch children at familial risk of developing dyslexia. Their performance in speech sound categorisation and their production of words was compared to that of age-matched children with specific language impairment (SLI) and typically developing controls. The results of the at-risk and SLI-group were highly similar. Analysis of the individual data revealed that both groups contained subgroups with good and poorly performing children. Their impaired expressive phonology seemed to be related to a deficit in speech perception. The findings indicate that both dyslexia and SLI can be explained by a multi-risk model which includes cognitive processes as well as genetic factors.

- Cluttering is a speech fluency disorder involving both the rate and rhythm of speech, and resulting in impaired speech intelligibility. Speech is erratic and dysrhythmic, consisting of rapid and jerky spurts that usually involve faulty phrasing. The personality of the clutterer bears striking resemblance to the personalities of those with learning disabilities.

Exacerbating Conditions

Dyslexia is believed to be a neurological condition that influences the individual's ability to read and spell written language.

The following conditions may be contributory or overlapping factors, similar to dyslexia as they can lead to difficulty in reading:

- Auditory processing disorder is a condition that affects the ability to process auditory information. Auditory Processing Disorder is a Listening Disability. It can lead to problems with auditory memory and auditory sequencing. Many people with dyslexia have auditory processing problems including history of auditory reversals, and may develop their own Logographic cues to compensate for this type of deficit. Auditory processing disorder is recognized as one of the major causes of dyslexia. Some children can acquire auditory processing disorder as a result of experiencing otitis media with effusion (Glue Ear, Sticky Ear, Grommits) and other severe ear conditions.
- Scotopic sensitivity syndrome, also known as Irlen Syndrome, is a term used to describe sensitivity to certain wavelengths of light which interfere with visual processing.
- Attention deficit hyperactivity disorder. Occurs in between 12 per cent and 24 per cent of those with dyslexia.
- Dysphasia.

Experience of speech acquisition delays, and speech and language problems can be due to problems processing and decoding auditory input prior to reproducing their own version of speech, and may be observed as stuttering, cluttering or hesitant speech.

Dyslexia Research

The majority of currently available dyslexia research relates to the alphabetic writing system, and especially languages of European origin. However, more research is becoming available regarding dyslexia in speakers of Hebrew and Chinese.

History of Dyslexia Research

- Identified by Oswald Berkhan in 1881, the term 'dyslexia' was later coined in 1887 by Rudolf Berlin, an ophthalmologist practicing in Stuttgart, Germany.

- In 1896, W. Pringle Morgan published a description of a reading-specific learning disorder in the British Medical Journal "Congenital Word Blindness."
- During the 1890s and early 1900s, James Hinshelwood published a series of articles in medical journals describing similar cases of congenital word blindness. In his 1917 book *Congenital Word Blindness,* Hinshelwood asserted that the primary disability was in visual memory for words and letters, and described symptoms including letter reversals, and difficulties with spelling and reading comprehension.
- In 1925 Samuel T. Orton determined that there was a syndrome unrelated to brain damage that made learning to read difficult. Orton's theory strephosymbolia described individuals with dyslexia having difficulty associating the visual forms of words with their spoken forms. Orton observed that reading deficits in dyslexia did not seem to stem from strictly visual deficits. He believed the condition was caused by the failure to establish hemispheric dominance in the brain. Orton later worked with psychologist and educator Anna Gillingham to develop an educational intervention that pioneered the use of simultaneous multisensory instruction.
- In contrast, Dearborn, Gates, Bennet and Blau considered a faulty guidance of the seeing mechanism to be the cause. They sought to discover if a conflict between spontaneous orientation of the scanning action of the eyes from right to left and training aimed at the acquisition of an opposite direction would allow an interpretation of the facts observed in the dyslexic disorder and especially of the ability to mirror-read.
- In 1949 research conducted under (thesis G. Mahec Paris 1951) went further. The phenomenon is clearly linked to the dynamics of sight as it disappears when the space between letters is increased, transforming the reading into spelling. This experience also explains the ability to mirror-read.
- In the 1970s, a new hypothesis emerged that dyslexia stems from a deficit in phonological processing or difficulty in recognizing that spoken words are formed by discrete phonemes affected individuals have difficulty associating these sounds with the visual letters that make up written words. Key studies suggested the importance of phonological awareness.
- In 1979 Galaburda and Kemper, and Galaburda *et al.* 1985, from the examination of post autopsy brains of people with dyslexia. Observed anatomical differences in the language center in a dyslexic brain, these studies and those of Cohen *et al.* 1989, suggested abnormal cortical development which was presumed to occur before or during the sixth month of foetal brain development.
- In 1993 Castles and Coltheart describe developmental dyslexia as two prevalent and distinct varieties using the subtypes of Alexia, Surface and Phonological Dyslexia. Manis *et al.* 1996, concluded that there were probably more than two subtypes of dyslexia, which would be related to multiple underlying deficits.
- In 1994 from post autopsy specimens Galaburda *et al.,* reported: Abnormal auditory processing in people with dyslexia suggests that accompanying

anatomical abnormalities might be present in the auditory system. Supported the reported behavioural findings of a left hemisphere-based phonological defect in dyslexic individuals.

- The development of neuroimaging technologies during the 1980s and 1990s enabled dyslexia research to make significant advances. Positron emission tomography (PET) and functional magnetic resonance imaging (fMRI) studies have revealed the neural signature of adult normal reading (e.g. Fiez and Petersen, 1998; Turkeltaub *et al.*, 2002) and phonological processing (e.g., Gelfand and Bookheimer, 2003; Poldrack *et al.*, 1999). Employing various experimental approaches and paradigms (e.g., the detection or judgement of rhymes, nonword reading, and implicit reading), these studies have localized dysfunctional phonological processing in dyslexia to left-hemisphere perisylvian regions, especially for the alphabetic writing system (Paulesu *et al.*, 2001; for review, see Eden and Zeffiro, 1998). However, it has been demonstrated that in non-alphabetic scripts, where reading places less demands on phonemic processing and the integration of visual-orthographic information is crucial, dyslexia is associated with under activity of the left middle frontal gyrus (Siok *et al.*, 2004).
- In 1999 Wydell and Butterworth reported the case study of an English-Japanese bilingual with monolingual dyslexia. Suggesting that any language where orthography-to-phonology mapping is transparent, or even opaque, or any language whose orthographic unit representing sound is coarse (i.e. at a whole character or word level) should not produce a high incidence of developmental phonological dyslexia, and that orthography can influence dyslexic symptoms.
- In 2003, A review by Collins and Rourke concluded that the current models of the relation between the brain and dyslexia generally focus on some form of defective or delayed brain maturation.
- 2007 Lyytinen *et al.* Researchers are seeking a link between the neurological and genetic findings, and the reading disorder.
- In 2008 S. Heim *et al.* in a paper "Cognitive subtypes of dyslexia" described how they compared different sub-groups of dyslexics in comparison with a control group. This is one of the first studies not to just compare dyslexics with a non-dyslexic control, but to go further and compare the different cognitive sub-groups with a non-dyslexic control group.

Theories of Developmental Dyslexia

The following theories should not be viewed as competing, but viewed as theories trying to explain the underlying causes of a similar set of symptoms from a variety of research perspectives and background.

Cerebellar Theory

Another view is represented by the automaticity/cerebellar theory of dyslexia. Here the biological claim is that the cerebellum of people with dyslexia is mildly dysfunctional and that a number of cognitive difficulties ensue.

Evolutionary Hypothesis

This theory posits that reading is an unnatural act, and carried out by humans for an exceedingly brief period in our evolutionary history (Dalby, 1986). It has been less than a hundred years that most western societies promoted reading by the mass population and therefore the forces that shape our behaviour have been weak. Many areas of the world still do not have access to reading for the majority of the population. There is no evidence that "pathology" underlies dyslexia but much evidence for cerebral variation or differences. It is these essential differences that are taxed with the artificial task of reading.

Magnocellular Theory

There is a unifying theory that attempts to integrate all the findings mentioned above. A generalization of the visual theory, the magnocellular theory postulates that the magnocellular dysfunction is not restricted to the visual pathways but is generalized to all modalities (visual and auditory as well as tactile).

Naming Speed Deficit and Double Deficit Theories

The speed with which an individual can name familiar objects or letters is a strong predictor of dyslexia. Slow naming speed can be identified as early as kindergarten; slow naming speed persists in adults with dyslexia.

A deficit in naming speed is hypothesized to represent a deficit that is separate from phonological processing deficit. Wolf identified four types of readers: readers with no deficits, readers with phonological processing deficit, readers with naming speed deficit, and readers with double deficit, that is, problems both with phonological processing and naming speed. Students with double deficits are most likely to have severe reading impairments.

Distinguishing among these deficits has important implications for instructional intervention. If students with double deficits receive instruction only in phonological processing, they are only receiving part of what they need.

Perceptual Visual-noise Exclusion Hypothesis

The concept of a perceptual noise exclusion (Impaired filtering of behaviourally irrelevant visual information in dyslexia or Visual-Noise) deficit is an emerging hypothesis, supported by research showing that subjects with dyslexia experience difficulty in performing visual tasks such as motion detection in the presence of perceptual distractions, but do not show the same impairment when the distracting factors are removed in an experimental setting. The researchers have analogized their findings concerning visual discrimination tasks to findings in other research related to auditory discrimination tasks. They assert that dyslexic symptoms arise because of an impaired ability to filter out both visual and auditory distractions, and to categorize information so as to distinguish the important sensory data from the irrelevant.

Phonological Deficit Theory

The phonological deficit theory postulates that people with dyslexia have a specific impairment in the representation, storage and/or retrieval of speech sounds. It explains the reading impairment of people with dyslexia on the basis that learning to read an alphabetic system requires learning the grapheme/phoneme correspondence, i.e. the correspondence between letters and constituent sounds of speech.

Rapid Auditory Processing Theory

The rapid auditory processing theory is an alternative to the phonological deficit theory, which specifies that the primary deficit lies in the perception of short or rapidly varying sounds. Support for this theory arises from evidence that people with dyslexia show poor performance on a number of auditory tasks, including frequency discrimination and temporal order judgement.

Visual Theory

The visual theory reflects another long standing tradition in the study of dyslexia, that of considering it as a visual impairment giving rise to difficulties with the processing of letters and words on a page of text. This may take the form of unstable binocular fixations, poor vergence, or increased visual crowding. The visual theory does not exclude a phonological deficit.

Research Using Functional Brain Imaging

Modern neuroimaging techniques such as functional Magnetic Resonance Imaging (fMRI) and Positron Emission Tomography (PET) have produced clear evidence of structural differences in the brains of children with reading difficulties. It has been found that people with dyslexia have a deficit in parts of the left hemisphere of the brain involved in reading, which includes the inferior frontal gyrus, inferior parietal lobule, and middle and ventral temporal cortex.

That dyslexia is neurobiological in origin is supported by what Lyon *et al.* proclaimed as "overwhelming and converging data from functional brain imaging investigations" (2003, p. 3). The results of these studies suggest that there are observable differences in how the dyslexic brain functions when compared to the brain of a typical reader. Using fMRI, Shaywitz found that good readers show a consistent pattern of strong activation in the back of the brain with weaker activation in the front of the brain during reading tasks. In contrast, the brain activation pattern in dyslexics is the opposite during reading tasks—the frontal part of the brain becomes overactive with weaker activation in the back. Shaywitz points out "It is as if these struggling readers are using the systems in the front of the brain to try to compensate for the disruption in the back of the brain."

Shaywitz has also conducted studies of dyslexic students both before and after a year-long reading remediation using an effective programme for dyslexics. Before the remedial programme, the students' brain activation patterns were the same as the patterns typical in dyslexics. After going through the programme, the students' brain activation patterns were comparable to those of students who had always been good readers. This demonstrates that, with early and effective intervention, the dyslexic brain can be rewired and dyslexic children can become good readers.

Brain activation studies using PET to study language have produced a breakthrough in our understanding of the neural basis of language over the past decade. A neural basis for the visual lexicon and for auditory verbal short-term memory components have been proposed. With some implication that the observed neural manifestation of developmental dyslexia is task-specific (i.e., functional rather than structural).

A University of Hong Kong study argues that dyslexia affects different structural parts of children's brains depending on the language which the children read. The study focused on comparing children that were raised reading English and children raised reading Chinese.

A University of Maastricht (Netherlands) study revealed that adult dyslexic readers underactivate superior temporal cortex for the integration of letters and speech sounds.

Genetic Research

Molecular studies have linked several forms of dyslexia to genetic markers for dyslexia. Several candidate genes have been identified, including at the two regions first related to dyslexia: DCDC2 and KIAA0319 on chromosome 6, and DYX1C1 on chromosome 15.

A 2007 review reported that no specific cognitive processes are known to be influenced by the proposed susceptibility genes.

A unifying theoretical framework of three working memory components provides a systems perspective for discussing past and new findings in a 12-year research programme that point to heterogeneity in the genetic and brain basis and behavioural expression of dyslexia.

Contributing Factors

Effect of Language Orthography

The complexity of a language's orthography, or writing and spelling system, has a direct impact on how difficult it is to learn to read in that language. Although English has an alphabetic orthography, it is a complex orthography that employs spelling patterns at several levels. The major structural categories that make up English spelling are letter-sound correspondences, syllables, and morphemes. Some other languages, such as Spanish, have alphabetic orthographies that employ only letter-sound correspondences. It is relatively easy to learn to read in languages like Spanish; it is much more difficult to learn to read in languages that have more complex orthographies, as in English.

From a neurological perspective, different types of writing, for example, alphabetic as compared to pictographic, require different neurological pathways in order to read, write and spell. Because different writing systems require different parts of the brain to process the visual notation of speech, children with reading problems in one language might not have a reading problem in a language with a different orthography. The neurological skills required to perform the tasks of reading, writing, and spelling can vary between different writing systems and as a result different neurological skill deficits can cause dyslexic problems in relation to different orthographies.

Inexpert Teaching

Controversy

Distinguishing between categories of 'dyslexia' and 'poor reader' or 'reading disabled' are scientifically unsupportable, arbitrary and therefore potentially discriminatory. Reading ability is on a spectrum, and dyslexia merely represents the low end of the spectrum. While the potential of genetics and neuroscience for guiding assessment and educational practice at some stage in the future, there is a mistaken belief that current knowledge in these fields is sufficient to justify a category of dyslexia as a subset of those who encounter reading difficulties.

Managing Dyslexia Symptoms

There is no cure for dyslexia, but dyslexic individuals can learn to read and write with appropriate educational support.

For alphabet writing systems, the fundamental aim is to increase a child's awareness of correspondences between graphemes and phonemes, and to relate these to reading and spelling. It has been found that training focused towards visual language and orthographic issues yields longer-lasting gains than mere oral phonological training.

The best approach is determined by the underlying neurological cause(s) of the dyslexic symptom.

Incidence

It is estimated that dyslexia affects 5 per cent to 17 per cent of the U.S. population.

Dyslexia and Education Law

There are many different national legal statutes and different national special education support structures with regard to special education provision which relate to the management of dyslexia.

ANALYZING DYSLEXIA INTERVENTIONS

Most teaching is geared to remediating specific areas of weakness, such as addressing difficulties with phonetic decoding by providing phonics-based tutoring. Some teaching is geared to specific reading skill areas, such as phonetic decoding; whereas other approaches are more comprehensive in scope, combining techniques to address basic skills along with strategies to improve comprehension and literary appreciation. Many programmes are multisensory in design, meaning that instruction includes visual, auditory, and kinesthetic or tactile elements; as it is generally believed that such forms of instruction are more effective for dyslexic learners.

Research Findings for Academic Interventions

There is little empirical or quantitative research supporting the use of any particular programme for reading instruction when used with dyslexic children. However, a committee of prominent researchers formed by the National Academy of Sciences reviewed the research on how to prevent reading difficulties. The report, *Preventing Reading Difficulties in Young Children,* concluded that systematic phonics combined with many opportunities to practice new words in meaningful text and opportunities to write in the classroom helped to prevent reading problems in the general population. The report further concluded that for struggling readers, the same type of instruction is successful when used in small group or one-to-one settings.

In addition, the researchers Joseph Torgesen and Richard Wagner have shown that, when teaching children with reading disabilities, programmes including systematic and explicit instruction in phoneme awareness and grapheme-phoneme correspondence are far more successful than programmes that do not.

Academic Remediations

With appropriate instruction, dyslexics can become skilled readers. Appropriate remedial instruction includes using:

- Direct, explicit and comprehensive instruction in the structure of language
- A systematic sequence for teaching individual skills
- Structured information from the simple to the complex
- Simultaneous multisensory approaches, including combinations of visual, auditory, and kinesthetic modalities
- Interaction between student and teacher during instruction of new skills
- Reinforcement throughout the day of newly learned skills
- Integrated spelling and handwriting instruction sequence with reading instruction, so that they are mutually reinforcing
- Extended practice for each skill until the student overlearns the skill (see Overlearning and Automaticity)
- Ongoing review of previously learned skills
- Careful pacing to avoid information overload
- Intensive instruction until reading, spelling and writing skills are at grade level
- Repeated reading to help develop fluency and reading rate
- Paired reading to help develop fluency and enhance comprehension.

Classroom Accommodations

Although there are no treatments or quick cures for dyslexia there are many techniques that can be used to assist dyslexic students in the classroom while reading skills are being remediated. These include such things as:

- Oral testing
- Untimed tests
- Eliminate or reduce spelling tests
- Minimizing the need to read out loud
- Accept dictated homework
- Reduce homework load
- Grade on content, not spelling nor handwriting
- Reduce copying tasks
- Avoid or reduce essay tests
- Using books on tape
- Providing teacher handouts to supplement the notes taken
- Using materials that are not visually overcrowded
- Using appropriate font type and size. It is suggested that Sassoon and Comic Sans may be the easiest to read; Times New Roman may be one of the most difficult to read. The font should not be too small.
- To increase motivation, giving assignments in areas in which the student has a strong interest, for example, sports stories, biographies of inventors or rock musicians, or fiction about teenage issues.
- Experimenting with coloured paper to see if this makes it easier for the student to read.

Recent Developments

Accessible publishing works to make reading easier for all that struggle with the standard one-size-fits-all method of book publishing. Accessible publishing works with publishers and Print on Demand technology which allows the reader to choose how the books will be published. Available format variations include choosing the font size (from 11 point font through to 28 point font), whether the font is bold, italic or regular, and choosing the amount of line spacing. There are also a variety of special fonts being developed for dyslexia, eye tracking problems and other conditions. Accessible publishers, such as ReadHowYouWant, also work to make books available in Braille, e-books, audiobooks and DAISY. Context sensitive spell checkers combined with text-to-speech and aimed for dyslexia assistance, such as Ghotit Dyslexia Spellchecker, are the new directions in making writing easier.

Teachers are also using audiobooks as a way of teaching textbooks in an engaging way to those with dyslexia. In the UK, one of the biggest charities is Listening Books, offering members a streaming service over the internet. www.listening-books.org.uk An Australian company, ReadHowYouWant is working to make all published books available in audiobook form. These audiobooks work well for those who do not have the neurological auditory processing problems that can cause dyslexia.

Effective training is given by teachers at school or kindergarten. Meta-analysis evaluating the effects of phonological awareness instruction has shown that word reading skills of all children, those with a risk for reading problems as well as those developing typically, improved their reading in systematic phonics instruction, a method that encourages a word to be recognised through the building of its constituent sounds. Basic phonemic awareness instruction did not, however, improve spelling in disabled readers.

Individuals with dyslexia require more practice to master skills in their areas of deficit. In the circumstances where typically developing children need 30 to 60 hours training, the number of hours that has resulted in optimistic conclusions concerning the treatability of dyslexia is between 80 and 100 hours, or less if the intervention is started sufficiently early. Only approximately 20 per cent of adults with early reading difficulties have acquired fluent reading skills in adulthood.

Functional MRI (fMRI) studies have shown changes in the brains of dyslexic children and adults with phonics tutoring, along with improved performance on tests of phonemic awareness and text decoding. fMRI studies have also shown changes in the brain and spelling improvement of dyslexic children taught spelling phonetically in an orthographic manner.

Alternative Therapies

There are many alternative therapies for developmental and learning disabilities, including nutritional supplements, special diets, homeopathy, and osteopathy/chiropractic manipulation.

RECORDING FOR THE BLIND AND DYSLEXIC: A CASE STUDY

Recording for the Blind & Dyslexic (RFB&D) is a non-profit volunteer organization operating nationwide in the United States. It produces and maintains a library of educational accessible audiobooks to people who cannot effectively read standard print because of visual impairment, dyslexia or other disability.

History

RFB&D was founded in 1948 by Anne T. Macdonald, a member of the New York Public Library's Women's Auxiliary, in response to an influx of inquiries from soldiers who had lost their sight in combat during World War II. The newly-passed *GI Bill of Rights* guaranteed a college education to all veterans, but texts were mostly inaccessible to the recently-blinded veterans, who did not read Braille and had little access to live readers. Macdonald mobilized the women of the Auxiliary under the motto "Education is a right, not a privilege."

Members of the Auxiliary formed Recording for the Blind and transformed the attic of the New York Public Library into a studio, recording textbooks using then state-of-the-art six-inch vinyl SoundScriber phonograph discs that played approximately 12 minutes of material per side. In 1952, Macdonald established recording studios in seven additional cities across the United States; as of 2008 there were 30 studios in addition to the National Headquarters in Princeton, New Jersey.

By 1970, the organization found itself serving an increasing number of people who had learning disabilities, including dyslexia. To acknowledge this growing member population, the organization's name was changed in 1995 to Recording for the Blind & Dyslexic. More than 70 per cent of RFB&D's membership, including children and adults, are certified as having learning disabilities.

The SoundScriber discs were eventually replaced by four-track cassettes; since 2007, all titles have been distributed on CD in a specialized format which facilitates accessing the audio recording by chapter or by a given page number from the printed material. As of August 2008, titles have been converted into downloadable audio files.

Services

A volunteer force of approximately 7,000 people records over 6,000 titles annually into RFB&D's library, which in 2007 contained over 37,000 titles in a broad variety of specialty and academic subjects, from kindergarten through post-graduate and professional. In addition to general interest titles, RFB&D records specific titles requested by member borrowers, provided that the title is educational in nature and supports a formal academic curriculum, and that the member can provide two copies of the book to RFB&D, which are necessary for the recording and editing process.

Borrowers must provide a certification of their disability, and may borrow titles through an individual membership, through their association with a member institution such as a school, or both.

Titles are digitally recorded onto CD or downloadable audio file in a specialized format which allows RFB&D to respect copyright and allows borrowers to access the audio recordings by chapter or page number. Titles must be played back by a specially adapted CD player, available from RFB&D. Downloadable audio textbooks can be played back using portable media players or Microsoft Windows-compatible computers.

AUTISM SPECTRUM DISORDERS AND PERVASIVE DEVELOPMENTAL DISORDERS: AN OVERVIEW

Autism Spectrum Disorders (ASD), also known as Pervasive Developmental Disorders (PDDs), cause severe and pervasive impairment in thinking, feeling, language, and the ability to relate to others. These disorders are usually first diagnosed in early childhood and range from a severe form, called autistic disorder, through pervasive development disorder not otherwise specified (PDD-NOS), to a much milder form, Asperger syndrome. They also include two rare disorders, Rett syndrome and Childhood disintegrative disorder.

Signs and Symptoms

Parents are usually the first to notice unusual behaviours in their child. In some cases, the baby seemed "different" from birth, unresponsive to people or focusing intently on one item for long periods of time. The first signs of an autism spectrum disorder can also appear in children who had been developing normally. When an affectionate, babbling toddler suddenly becomes silent, withdrawn, self-abusive, or indifferent to social overtures, something is wrong.

Treatment

There is no single best treatment package for all children with ASD. Decisions about the best treatment, or combination of treatments, should be made by the parents with the assistance of a trusted expert diagnostic team.

Getting Help: Locate Services

Locate mental health services in your area, affordable healthcare, NIMH clinical trials, and listings of professionals and organizations.

TOWARDS A BROADER UNDERSTANDING OF AUTISM AND AUTISTIC PERSONS

Autism is a brain development disorder characterized by impaired social interaction and communication, and by restricted and repetitive behaviour. These signs all begin before a child is three years old. Autism involves many parts of the brain; how this occurs is not well understood. The two other autism spectrum disorders (ASD) are Asperger syndrome, which lacks delays in cognitive development and language, and PDD-NOS, diagnosed when full criteria for the other two disorders are not met.

Autism has a strong genetic basis, although the genetics of autism are complex and it is unclear whether ASD is explained more by rare mutations, or by rare combinations of common genetic variants. In rare cases, autism is strongly associated with agents that cause birth defects. Controversies surround other proposed environmental causes, such as heavy metals, pesticides or childhood vaccines; the vaccine hypotheses are biologically implausible and lack convincing scientific evidence. The prevalence of ASD is about 6 per 1,000 people, with about four times as many males as females. The number of people known to have autism has increased dramatically since the 1980s, partly due to changes in diagnostic practice; the question of whether actual prevalence has increased is unresolved.

Parents usually notice signs in the first two years of their child's life. The signs usually develop gradually, but some autistic children first develop more normally and then regress. Although early behavioural or cognitive intervention can help children gain self-care, social, and communication skills, there is no known cure. Not many children with autism live independently after reaching adulthood, though some become successful. An autistic culture has developed, with some individuals seeking a cure and others believing autism should be tolerated as a difference and not treated as a disorder.

Characteristics

Autism is a highly variable brain development disorder that first appears during infancy or childhood, and generally follows a steady course without remission. Overt symptoms gradually begin after the age of six months, become established by age two or three years, and tend to continue through adulthood, although often in more muted form. It is distinguished not by a single symptom, but by a characteristic triad of symptoms: impairments in social interaction; impairments in communication; and restricted interests and repetitive behaviour. Other aspects, such as atypical eating, are also common but are not essential for diagnosis. Autism's individual symptoms occur in the general population and appear not to associate highly, without a sharp line separating pathologically severe from common traits.

Social Development

Social deficits distinguish autism and the related autism spectrum disorders (ASD; see *Classification*) from other developmental disorders. People with autism have social impairments and often lack the intuition about others that many people take for granted. Noted autistic Temple Grandin described her inability to understand the social communication of neurotypicals, or people with normal neural development, as leaving her feeling "like an anthropologist on Mars."

Unusual social development becomes apparent early in childhood. Autistic infants show less attention to social stimuli, smile and look at others less often, and respond less to their own name. Autistic toddlers differ more strikingly from social norms; for example, they have less eye contact and turn taking, and are more likely to communicate by manipulating another person's hand. Three- to five-year-old autistic children are less likely to exhibit social understanding, approach others spontaneously, imitate and respond to emotions, communicate nonverbally, and take turns with others. However, they do form attachments to their primary caregivers. They display moderately less attachment security than usual, although this feature disappears in children with higher mental development or less severe ASD. Older children and adults with ASD perform worse on tests of face and emotion recognition.

Contrary to common beliefs, autistic children do not prefer being alone. Making and maintaining friendships often proves to be difficult for those with autism. For them, the quality of friendships, not the number of friends, predicts how lonely they feel. Functional friendships, such as those resulting in invitations to parties, may affect their quality of life more deeply.

There are many anecdotal reports, but few systematic studies, of aggression and violence in individuals with ASD. The limited data suggest that, in children with mental retardation, autism is associated with aggression, destruction of property, and tantrums. A 2007 study interviewed parents of 67 children with ASD and reported that about two-thirds of the children had periods of severe tantrums and about one-third had a history of aggression, with tantrums significantly more common than in children with a history of language impairment. A 2008 Swedish study found that, of individuals aged 15 or older discharged from hospital with a diagnosis of ASD, those who committed violent crimes were significantly more likely to have other psychopathological conditions such as psychosis.

Communication

About a third to a half of individuals with autism do not develop enough natural speech to meet their daily communication needs. Differences in communication may be present from the first year of life, and may include delayed onset of babbling, unusual gestures, diminished responsiveness, and vocal patterns that are not synchronized with the caregiver. In the second and third years, autistic children have less frequent and less diverse babbling, consonants, words, and word combinations; their gestures are less often integrated with words. Autistic children are less likely to make requests or share experiences, and are more likely to simply repeat others' words (echolalia) or reverse pronouns. Joint attention seems to be necessary for functional speech, and deficits in joint attention seem to distinguish infants with ASD: for example, they may look at a pointing hand instead of the pointed-at object, and they consistently fail to point at objects in order to comment on or share an experience. Autistic children may have difficulty with imaginative play and with developing symbols into language.

In a pair of studies, high-functioning autistic children aged 8—15 performed equally well, and adults better than individually matched controls at basic language tasks involving vocabulary and spelling. Both autistic groups performed worse than controls at complex language tasks such as figurative language, comprehension and inference. As people are often sized up initially from their basic language skills, these studies suggest that people speaking to autistic individuals are more likely to overestimate what their audience comprehends.

Repetitive Behaviour

Autistic individuals display many forms of repetitive or restricted behaviour, which the Repetitive Behaviour Scale-Revised (RBS-R) categorizes as follows.

- *Stereotypy* is repetitive movement, such as hand flapping, making sounds, head rolling, or body rocking.
- *Compulsive behaviour* is intended and appears to follow rules, such as arranging objects in a stacks or lines.
- *Sameness* is resistance to change; for example, insisting that the furniture not be moved or refusing to be interrupted.
- *Ritualistic behaviour* involves an unvarying pattern of daily activities, such as an unchanging menu or a dressing ritual. This is closely associated with sameness and an independent validation has suggested combining the two factors.

- *Restricted behaviour* is limited in focus, interest, or activity, such as preoccupation with a single television programme, toy, or game.
- *Self-injury* includes movements that injure or can injure the person, such as eye poking, skin picking, hand biting, and head banging. A 2007 study reported that self-injury at some point affected about 30 per cent of children with ASD.

No single repetitive behaviour seems to be specific to autism, but only autism appears to have an elevated pattern of occurrence and severity of these behaviours.

Other Symptoms

Autistic individuals may have symptoms that are independent of the diagnosis, but that can affect the individual or the family. An estimated 0.5 per cent to 10 per cent of individuals with ASD show unusual abilities, ranging from splinter skills such as the memorization of trivia to the extraordinarily rare talents of prodigious autistic savants. Many individuals with ASD show superior skills in perception and attention, relative to the general population. Sensory abnormalities are found in over 90 per cent of those with autism, and are considered core features by some, although there is no good evidence that sensory symptoms differentiate autism from other developmental disorders. Differences are greater for under-responsivity (for example, walking into things) than for over-responsivity (for example, distress from loud noises) or for sensation seeking (for example, rhythmic movements). Several studies have reported associated motor problems that include poor muscle tone, poor motor planning, and toe walking; ASD is not associated with severe motor disturbances.

Unusual eating behaviour occurs in about three-quarters of children with ASD, to the extent that it was formerly a diagnostic indicator. Selectivity is the most common problem, although eating rituals and food refusal also occur; this does not appear to result in malnutrition. Although some children with autism also have gastrointestinal (GI) symptoms, there is a lack of published rigorous data to support the theory that autistic children have more or different GI symptoms than usual; studies report conflicting results, and the relationship between GI problems and ASD is unclear.

At some point in childhood, about two-thirds of individuals with ASD are affected by sleep problems; these most commonly include symptoms of insomnia such as difficulty in falling asleep, frequent nocturnal awakenings, and early morning awakenings. Sleep problems are associated with difficult behaviours and family stress, and are often a focus of clinical attention over and above the primary ASD diagnosis.

Parents of children with ASD have higher levels of stress. Siblings of children with ASD report greater admiration of and less conflict with the affected sibling than siblings of unaffected children or those with Down syndrome; siblings of individuals with ASD have greater risk of negative well-being and poorer sibling relationships as adults.

Classification

Autism is one of the five pervasive developmental disorders (PDD), which are characterized by widespread abnormalities of social interactions and communication, and severely restricted interests and highly repetitive behaviour. These symptoms do not imply sickness, fragility, or emotional disturbance.

Of the five PDD forms, Asperger syndrome is closest to autism in signs and likely causes; Rett syndrome and childhood disintegrative disorder share several signs with autism, but may have unrelated causes; PDD not otherwise specified (PDD-NOS; also called *atypical autism*) is diagnosed when the criteria are not met for a more specific disorder. Unlike with autism, people with Asperger syndrome have no substantial delay in language development. The terminology of autism can be bewildering, with autism, Asperger syndrome and PDD-NOS often called the *autism spectrum disorders* (ASD) or sometimes the *autistic disorders*, whereas autism itself is often called *autistic disorder, childhood autism*, or *infantile autism*. In this article, *autism* refers to the classic autistic disorder; in clinical practice, though, *autism*, *ASD*, and *PDD* are often used interchangeably. ASD, in turn, is a subset of the broader autism phenotype (BAP), which describes individuals who may not have ASD but do have autistic-like traits, such as avoiding eye contact.

The manifestations of autism cover a wide spectrum, ranging from individuals with severe impairments—who may be silent, mentally disabled, and locked into hand flapping and rocking—to high functioning individuals who may have active but distinctly odd social approaches, narrowly focused interests, and verbose, pedantic communication. Sometimes the syndrome is divided into low-, medium- or high-functioning autism (LFA, MFA, and HFA), based on IQ thresholds, or on how much support the individual requires in daily life; these subdivisions are not standardized and are controversial. Autism can also be divided into syndromal and non-syndromal autism; the syndromal autism is associated with severe or profound mental retardation or a congenital syndrome with physical symptoms, such as tuberous sclerosis. Although individuals with Asperger syndrome tend to perform better cognitively than those with autism, the extent of the overlap between Asperger syndrome, HFA, and non-syndromal autism is unclear.

Some studies have reported diagnoses of autism in children due to a loss of language or social skills, as opposed to a failure to make progress, typically from 15 to 30 months of age. The validity of this distinction remains controversial; it is possible that regressive autism is a specific subtype, or that there is a continuum of behaviours between autism with and without regression.

Research into causes has been hampered by the inability to identify biologically meaningful subpopulations and by the traditional boundaries between the disciplines of psychiatry, psychology, neurology and pediatrics. Newer technologies such as fMRI can help identify biologically-relevant phenotypes (observable traits) that can be viewed on brain scans, to help further neurogenetic studies of autism. It has been proposed to classify autism using genetics as well as behaviour, with the name *Type 1 autism* denoting rare autism cases that test positive for a mutation in the CNTNAP2 gene.

Causes

It has long been presumed that there is a common cause at the genetic, cognitive, and neural levels for autism's characteristic triad of symptoms. However, there is increasing suspicion that autism is instead a complex disorder whose core aspects have distinct causes that often co-occur.

Autism has a strong genetic basis, although the genetics of autism are complex and it is unclear whether ASD is explained more by rare mutations with major effects, or by rare multigene interactions of common genetic variants. Complexity arises due to interactions among multiple genes, the environment, and epigenetic factors which do not change DNA but are heritable and influence gene expression. Early studies of twins estimated heritability explains more than 90 per cent of the risk of autism, assuming a shared environment and no other genetic or medical syndromes. However, most of the mutations that increase autism risk have not been identified. Typically, autism cannot be traced to a Mendelian (single-gene) mutation or to a single chromosome abnormality like fragile X syndrome, and none of the genetic syndromes associated with ASDs has been shown to selectively cause ASD. Numerous candidate genes have been located, with only small effects attributable to any particular gene. The large number of autistic individuals with unaffected family members may result from copy number variations—spontaneous deletions or duplications in genetic material during meiosis. Hence, a substantial fraction of autism cases may be traceable to genetic causes that are highly heritable but not inherited, that is, the mutation that causes the autism is not present in the parental genome.

Autism caused by some rare mutations may disrupt some synaptic pathways, such as those involved with cell adhesion. Gene replacement studies in mice suggest that autistic symptoms are closely related to later developmental steps that depend on activity in synapses and on activity-dependent changes. All known teratogens (agents that cause birth defects) related to the risk of autism appear to act during the first eight weeks from conception, and though this does not exclude the possibility that autism can be initiated or affected later, it is strong evidence that autism arises very early in development. Although evidence for other environmental causes is anecdotal and has not been confirmed by reliable studies, extensive searches are underway. Environmental factors that have been claimed to contribute to or exacerbate autism, or may be important in future research, include certain foods, infectious disease, heavy metals, solvents, diesel exhaust, PCBs, phthalates and phenols used in plastic products, pesticides, brominated flame retardants, alcohol, smoking, illicit drugs, vaccines, and prenatal stress. Parents may first become aware of autistic symptoms in their child around the time of a routine vaccination, and this has given rise to theories that vaccines or their preservatives cause autism. Although these theories lack convincing scientific evidence and are biologically implausible, parental concern about autism has led to lower rates of childhood immunizations and higher likelihood of measles outbreaks.

Mechanism

Autism's symptoms result from maturation-related changes in various systems of the brain. Despite extensive investigation, how autism occurs is not well understood. Its mechanism can be divided into two areas: the pathophysiology of brain structures and processes associated with autism, and the neuropsychological linkages between brain structures and behaviours. The behaviours appear to have multiple pathophysiologies.

Pathophysiology

Unlike many other brain disorders such as Parkinson's, autism does not have a clear unifying mechanism at either the molecular, cellular, or systems level; it is not known whether autism is a few disorders caused by mutations converging on a few common molecular pathways, or is (like intellectual disability) a large set of disorders with diverse mechanisms. Autism appears to result from developmental factors that affect many or all functional brain systems, and to disturb the timing of brain development more than the final product. Neuroanatomical studies and the associations with teratogens strongly suggest that autism's mechanism includes alteration of brain development soon after conception. This anomaly appears to start a cascade of pathological events in the brain that are significantly influenced by environmental factors. Although many major structures of the human brain have been implicated, almost all postmortem studies have been of individuals who also had mental retardation, making it difficult to draw conclusions. Brain weight and volume and head circumference tend to be greater in autistic children. The cellular and molecular bases of pathological early overgrowth are not known, nor is it known whether the overgrown neural systems cause autism's characteristic signs. Current hypotheses include:

- An excess of neurons that causes local overconnectivity in key brain regions.
- Disturbed neuronal migration during early gestation.
- Unbalanced excitatory—inhibitory networks.
- Abnormal formation of synapses and dendritic spines, for example, by modulation of the neurexin—neuroligin cell-adhesion system, or by poorly regulated synthesis of synaptic protein. Disrupted synaptic development may also contribute to epilepsy, which may explain why the two conditions are associated.

Interactions between the immune system and the nervous system begin early during the embryonic stage of life, and successful neurodevelopment depends on a balanced immune response. Several symptoms consistent with a poorly regulated immune response have been reported in autistic children. It is possible that aberrant immune activity during critical periods of neurodevelopment is part of the mechanism of some forms of ASD. As autoantibodies have not been associated with pathology, are found in conditions other than ASD, and are not always present in ASD, the relationship between immune disturbances and autism remains unclear and controversial.

Several neurotransmitter abnormalities have been detected in autism, notably increased blood levels of serotonin. Whether these cause structural or behavioural abnormalities is unclear. Some data suggest an increase in several growth hormones; other data argue for diminished growth factors. Also, some inborn errors of metabolism are associated with autism but probably account for less than 5 per cent of cases.

The mirror neuron system (MNS) theory of autism hypothesizes that distortion in the development of the MNS interferes with imitation and leads to autism's core features of social impairment and communication difficulties. The MNS operates when an animal performs an action or observes another animal perform the same action. The MNS may contribute to an individual's understanding of other people by enabling the modeling of their behaviour via embodied simulation of their actions, intentions, and emotions. Several studies have tested this hypothesis by demonstrating structural abnormalities in MNS regions of individuals with ASD, delay in the activation in the core circuit for imitation in individuals with Asperger syndrome, and a correlation between reduced MNS activity and severity of the syndrome in children with ASD. However, individuals with autism also have abnormal brain activation in many circuits outside the MNS and the MNS theory does not explain the normal performance of autistic children on imitation tasks that involve a goal or object.

ASD-related patterns of low function and aberrant activation in the brain differ depending on whether the brain is doing social or nonsocial tasks. In autism there is evidence for reduced functional connectivity of the default network, a large-scale brain network involved in social and emotional processing, with intact connectivity of the task-positive network, used in sustained attention and goal-directed thinking. In people with autism the two networks are not negatively correlated in time, suggesting an imbalance in toggling between the two networks, possibly reflecting a disturbance of self-referential thought. A 2008 brain-imaging study found a specific pattern of signals in the cingulate cortex which differs in individuals with ASD.

The underconnectivity theory of autism hypothesizes that autism is marked by underfunctioning high-level neural connections and synchronization, along with an excess of low-level processes. Evidence for this theory has been found in functional neuroimaging studies on autistic individuals and by a brain wave study that suggested that adults with ASD have local overconnectivity in the cortex and weak functional connections between the frontal lobe and the rest of the cortex. Other evidence suggests the underconnectivity is mainly within each hemisphere of the cortex and that autism is a disorder of the association cortex.

From studies based on event-related potentials, transient changes to the brain's electrical activity in response to stimuli, there is considerable evidence for differences in autistic individuals with respect to attention, orientiation to auditory and visual stimuli, novelty detection, language and face processing, and information storage;

several studies have found a preference for non-social stimuli. For example, magnetoencephalography studies have found evidence in autistic children of delayed responses in the brain's processing of auditory signals.

Neuropsychology

Two major categories of cognitive theories have been proposed about the links between autistic brains and behaviour.

The first category focuses on deficits in social cognition. The empathizing—systemizing theory postulates that autistic individuals can systemize—that is, they can develop internal rules of operation to handle events inside the brain—but are less effective at empathizing by handling events generated by other agents. An extension, the extreme male brain theory, hypothesizes that autism is an extreme case of the male brain, defined psychometrically as individuals in whom systemizing is better than empathizing; this extension is controversial, as many studies contradict the idea that baby boys and girls respond differently to people and objects.

These theories are somewhat related to the earlier theory of mind approach, which hypothesizes that autistic behaviour arises from an inability to ascribe mental states to oneself and others. The theory of mind hypothesis is supported by autistic children's atypical responses to the Sally—Anne test for reasoning about others' motivations, and the mirror neuron system theory of autism described in *Pathophysiology* maps well to the hypothesis. However, most studies have found no evidence of impairment in autistic individuals' ability to understand other people's basic emotions or goals; instead, data suggests that impairments are found in understanding more complex social emotions or in considering others' viewpoints.

The second category focuses on nonsocial or general processing. Executive dysfunction hypothesizes that autistic behaviour results in part from deficits in working memory, planning, inhibition, and other forms of executive function. Tests of core executive processes such as eye movement tasks indicate improvement from late childhood to adolescence, but performance never reaches typical adult levels. A strength of the theory is predicting stereotyped behaviour and narrow interests; two weaknesses are that executive function is hard to measure and that executive function deficits have not been found in young autistic children.

Weak central coherence theory hypothesizes that a limited ability to see the big picture underlies the central disturbance in autism. One strength of this theory is predicting special talents and peaks in performance in autistic people. A related theory—enhanced perceptual functioning—focuses more on the superiority of locally oriented and perceptual operations in autistic individuals. These theories map well from the underconnectivity theory of autism.

Neither category is satisfactory on its own; social cognition theories poorly address autism's rigid and repetitive behaviours, while the nonsocial theories have difficulty explaining social impairment and communication difficulties. A combined theory based on multiple deficits may prove to be more useful.

Screening

About half of parents of children with ASD notice their child's unusual behaviours by age 18 months, and about four-fifths notice by age 24 months. As postponing treatment may affect long-term outcome, any of the following signs is reason to have a child evaluated by a specialist without delay:

- No babbling by 12 months.
- No gesturing (pointing, waving goodbye, etc.) by 12 months.
- No single words by 16 months.
- No two-word spontaneous phrases (other than instances of echolalia) by 24 months.
- Any loss of any language or social skills, at any age.

The American Academy of Pediatrics recommends that all children be screened for ASD at the 18- and 24-month well-child doctor visits, using autism-specific formal screening tests. In contrast, the UK National Screening Committee recommends against screening for ASD in the general population, because screening tools have not been fully validated and interventions lack sufficient evidence for effectiveness. Screening tools include the Modified Checklist for Autism in Toddlers (M-CHAT), the Early Screening of Autistic Traits Questionnaire, and the First Year Inventory; initial data on M-CHAT and its predecessor CHAT on children aged 18—30 months suggests that it is best used in a clinical setting and that it has low sensitivity (many false-negatives) but good specificity (few false-positives). It may be more accurate to precede these tests with a broadband screener that does not distinguish ASD from other developmental disorders. Screening tools designed for one culture's norms for behaviours like eye contact may be inappropriate for a different culture. Genetic screening for autism is generally still impractical.

Diagnosis

Diagnosis is based on behaviour, not cause or mechanism. Autism is defined in the DSM-IV-TR as exhibiting at least six symptoms total, including at least two symptoms of qualitative impairment in social interaction, at least one symptom of qualitative impairment in communication, and at least one symptom of restricted and repetitive behaviour. Sample symptoms include lack of social or emotional reciprocity, stereotyped and repetitive use of language or idiosyncratic language, and persistent preoccupation with parts of objects. Onset must be prior to age three years, with delays or abnormal functioning in either social interaction, language as used in social communication, or symbolic or imaginative play. The disturbance must not be better accounted for by Rett syndrome or childhood disintegrative disorder. ICD-10 uses essentially the same definition.

Several diagnostic instruments are available. Two are commonly used in autism research: the Autism Diagnostic Interview-Revised (ADI-R) is a semistructured parent interview, and the Autism Diagnostic Observation Schedule (ADOS) uses observation and interaction with the child. The Childhood Autism Rating Scale (CARS) is used widely in clinical environments to assess severity of autism based on observation of children.

A pediatrician commonly performs a preliminary investigation by taking developmental history and physically examining the child. If warranted, diagnosis and evaluations are conducted with help from ASD specialists, observing and assessing cognitive, communication, family, and other factors using standardized tools, and taking into account any associated medical conditions. A pediatric neuropsychologist is often asked to assess behaviour and cognitive skills, both to aid diagnosis and to help recommend educational interventions. A differential diagnosis for ASD at this stage might also consider mental retardation, hearing impairment, and a specific language impairment such as Landau—Kleffner syndrome. The presence of autism can make it harder to diagnose coexisting psychiatric disorders such as depression.

Clinical genetics evaluations are often done once ASD is diagnosed, particularly when other symptoms already suggest a genetic cause. Although genetic technology allows clinical geneticists to link an estimated 40 per cent of cases to genetic causes, consensus guidelines in the U.S. and UK are limited to high-resolution chromosome and fragile X testing. A genotype-first model of diagnosis has been proposed, which would routinely assess the genome's copy number variations. As new genetic tests are developed several ethical, legal, and social issues will emerge. Commercial availability of tests may precede adequate understanding of how to use test results, given the complexity of autism's genetics. Metabolic and neuroimaging tests are sometimes helpful, but are not routine.

ASD can sometimes be diagnosed by age 14 months, although diagnosis becomes increasingly stable over the first three years of life: for example, a one-year-old who meets diagnostic criteria for ASD is less likely than a three-year-old to continue to do so a few years later. In the UK the National Autism Plan for Children recommends at most 30 weeks from first concern to completed diagnosis and assessment, though few cases are handled that quickly in practice. A 2009 U.S. study found the average age of formal ASD diagnosis was 5.7 years, far above recommendations, and that 27 per cent of children remained undiagnosed at age 8 years. Although the symptoms of autism and ASD begin early in childhood, they are sometimes missed; years later, adults may seek diagnoses to help them or their friends and family understand themselves, to help their employers make adjustments, or in some locations to claim disability living allowances or other benefits.

Underdiagnosis and overdiagnosis are problems in marginal cases, and much of the recent increase in the number of reported ASD cases is likely due to changes in diagnostic practices. The increasing popularity of drug treatment options and the expansion of benefits has given providers incentives to diagnose ASD, resulting in some overdiagnosis of children with uncertain symptoms. Conversely, the cost of screening and diagnosis and the challenge of obtaining payment can inhibit or delay diagnosis. It is particularly hard to diagnose autism among the visually impaired, partly because some of its diagnostic criteria depend on vision, and partly because autistic symptoms overlap with those of common blindness syndromes.

Management

The main goals of treatment are to lessen associated deficits and family distress, and to increase quality of life and functional independence. No single treatment is best and treatment is typically tailored to the child's needs. Studies of interventions have methodological problems that prevent definitive conclusions about efficacy. Although many psychosocial interventions have some positive evidence, suggesting that some form of treatment is preferable to no treatment, the methodological quality of systematic reviews of these studies has generally been poor, their clinical results are mostly tentative, and there is little evidence for the relative effectiveness of treatment options. Intensive, sustained special education programmes and behaviour therapy early in life can help children acquire self-care, social, and job skills, and often improve functioning and decrease symptom severity and maladaptive behaviours; claims that intervention by around age three years is crucial are not substantiated. Available approaches include applied behaviour analysis (ABA), developmental models, structured teaching, speech and language therapy, social skills therapy, and occupational therapy. Educational interventions have some effectiveness in children: intensive ABA treatment has demonstrated effectiveness in enhancing global functioning in preschool children and is well-established for improving intellectual performance of young children. Neuropsychological reports are often poorly communicated to educators, resulting in a gap between what a report recommends and what education is provided. It is not known whether treatment programmes for children lead to significant improvements after the children grow up, and the limited research on the effectiveness of adult residential programmes shows mixed results.

Many medications are used to treat ASD symptoms that interfere with integrating a child into home or school when behavioural treatment fails. More than half of U.S. children diagnosed with ASD are prescribed psychoactive drugs or anticonvulsants, with the most common drug classes being antidepressants, stimulants, and antipsychotics. Aside from antipsychotics, there is scant reliable research about the effectiveness or safety of drug treatments for adolescents and adults with ASD. A person with ASD may respond atypically to medications, the medications can have adverse effects, and no known medication relieves autism's core symptoms of social and communication impairments. Experiments in mice have reversed or reduced some symptoms related to autism by replacing or modulating gene function after birth, suggesting the possibility of targeting therapies to specific rare mutations known to cause autism.

Although many alternative therapies and interventions are available, few are supported by scientific studies. Treatment approaches have little empirical support in quality-of-life contexts, and many programmes focus on success measures that lack predictive validity and real-world relevance. Scientific evidence appears to matter less to service providers than programme marketing, training availability, and parent requests. Though most alternative treatments, such as melatonin, have only mild adverse effects some may place the child at risk. A 2008 study found that compared to their peers, autistic boys have significantly thinner bones if on casein-free diets; in 2005, botched chelation therapy killed a five-year-old child with autism.

Treatment is expensive; indirect costs are more so. For someone born in 2000, a U.S. study estimated an average lifetime cost of $3.66 million (net present value in 2009 dollars, inflation-adjusted from 2003 estimate), with about 10 per cent medical care, 30 per cent extra education and other care, and 60 per cent lost economic productivity. Publicly supported programmes are often inadequate or inappropriate for a given child, and unreimbursed out-of-pocket medical or therapy expenses are associated with likelihood of family financial problems; one 2008 U.S. study found a 14 per cent average loss of annual income in families of children with ASD, and a related study found that ASD is associated with higher probability that child care problems will greatly affect parental employment. U.S. states increasingly require private health insurance to cover autism services, shifting costs from publicly-funded education programmes to privately-funded health insurance. After childhood, key treatment issues include residential care, job training and placement, sexuality, social skills, and estate planning.

Prognosis

There is no known cure. Children recover occasionally, so that they lose their diagnosis of ASD; this occurs sometimes after intensive treatment and sometimes not. It is not known how often recovery happens; reported rates in unselected samples of children with ASD have ranged from 3 per cent to 25 per cent. A few autistic children have acquired speech at age 5 or older. Most children with autism lack social support, meaningful relationships, future employment opportunities or self-determination. Although core difficulties tend to persist, symptoms often become less severe with age. Few high-quality studies address long-term prognosis. Some adults show modest improvement in communication skills, but a few decline; no study has focused on autism after midlife. Acquiring language before age six, having an IQ above 50, and having a marketable skill all predict better outcomes; independent living is unlikely with severe autism. A 2004 British study of 68 adults who were diagnosed before 1980 as autistic children with IQ above 50 found that 12 per cent achieved a high level of independence as adults, 10 per cent had some friends and were generally in work but required some support, 19 per cent had some independence but were generally living at home and needed considerable support and supervision in daily living, 46 per cent needed specialist residential provision from facilities specializing in ASD with a high level of support and very limited autonomy, and 12 per cent needed high-level hospital care. A 2005 Swedish study of 78 adults that did not exclude low IQ found worse prognosis; for example, only 4 per cent achieved independence. A 2008 Canadian study of 48 young adults diagnosed with ASD as preschoolers found outcomes ranging through poor (46%), fair (32%), good (17%), and very good (4%); 56 per cent of these young adults had been employed at some point during their lives, mostly in volunteer, sheltered or part-time work. Changes in diagnostic practice and increased availability of effective early intervention make it unclear whether these findings can be generalized to recently diagnosed children.

Epidemiology

Most recent reviews tend to estimate a prevalence of 1—2 per 1,000 for autism and close to 6 per 1,000 for ASD; because of inadequate data, these numbers may underestimate ASD's true prevalence. PDD-NOSs prevalence has been estimated at 3.7 per 1,000, Asperger syndrome at roughly 0.6 per 1,000, and childhood disintegrative disorder at 0.02 per 1,000. The number of reported cases of autism increased dramatically in the 1990s and early 2000s. This increase is largely attributable to changes in diagnostic practices, referral patterns, availability of services, age at diagnosis, and public awareness, though unidentified environmental risk factors cannot be ruled out. The available evidence does not rule out the possibility that autism's true prevalence has increased; a real increase would suggest directing more attention and funding toward changing environmental factors instead of continuing to focus on genetics.

Boys are at higher risk for ASD than girls. The sex ratio averages 4.3:1 and is greatly modified by cognitive impairment: it may be close to 2:1 with mental retardation and more than 5.5:1 without. Although the evidence does not implicate any single pregnancy-related risk factor as a cause of autism, the risk of autism is associated with advanced age in either parent, and with diabetes, bleeding, and use of psychiatric drugs in the mother during pregnancy. Most professionals believe that race, ethnicity, and socio-economic background do not affect the occurrence of autism.

Autism is associated with several other conditions:

- *Genetic disorders*. About 10—15 per cent of autism cases have an identifiable Mendelian (single-gene) condition, chromosome abnormality, or other genetic syndrome, and ASD is associated with several genetic disorders.
- *Mental retardation*. The fraction of autistic individuals who also meet criteria for mental retardation has been reported as anywhere from 25 per cent to 70 per cent, a wide variation illustrating the difficulty of assessing autistic intelligence. For ASD other than autism, the association with mental retardation is much weaker.
- *Anxiety disorders* are common among children with ASD; there are no firm data, but studies have reported prevalences ranging from 11 per cent to 84 per cent. Many anxiety disorders have symptoms that are better explained by ASD itself, or are hard to distinguish from ASD's symptoms.
- *Epilepsy*, with variations in risk of epilepsy due to age, cognitive level, and type of language disorder.

- Several *metabolic defects*, such as phenylketonuria, are associated with autistic symptoms.
- *Minor physical anomalies* are significantly increased in the autistic population.
- *Pre-empted diagnoses*. Although the DSM-IV rules out concurrent diagnosis of many other conditions along with autism, the full criteria for ADHD, Tourette syndrome, and other of these conditions are often present and these comorbid diagnoses are increasingly accepted.

History

A few examples of autistic symptoms and treatments were described long before autism was named. The *Table Talk* of Martin Luther contains the story of a 12-year-old boy who may have been severely autistic. According to Luther's notetaker Mathesius, Luther thought the boy was a soulless mass of flesh possessed by the devil, and suggested that he be suffocated. The earliest well-documented case of autism is that of Hugh Blair of Borgue, as detailed in a 1747 court case in which his brother successfully petitioned to annul Blair's marriage to gain Blair's inheritance. The Wild Boy of Aveyron, a feral child caught in 1798, showed several signs of autism; the medical student Jean Itard treated him with a behavioural programme designed to help him form social attachments and to induce speech via imitation.

The New Latin word *autismus* (English translation *autism*) was coined by the Swiss psychiatrist Eugen Bleuler in 1910 as he was defining symptoms of schizophrenia. He derived it from the Greek word *autós* (αὐτός, meaning *self*), and used it to mean morbid self-admiration, referring to "autistic withdrawal of the patient to his fantasies, against which any influence from outside becomes an intolerable disturbance."

The word *autism* first took its modern sense in 1938 when Hans Asperger of the Vienna University Hospital adopted Bleuler's terminology *autistic psychopaths* in a lecture in German about child psychology. Asperger was investigating an ASD now known as Asperger syndrome, though for various reasons it was not widely recognized as a separate diagnosis until 1981. Leo Kanner of the Johns Hopkins Hospital first used *autism* in its modern sense in English when he introduced the label *early infantile autism* in a 1943 report of 11 children with striking behavioural similarities. Almost all the characteristics described in Kanner's first paper on the subject, notably "autistic aloneness" and "insistence on sameness", are still regarded as typical of the autistic spectrum of disorders. It is not known whether Kanner derived the term independently of Asperger.

Kanner's reuse of *autism* led to decades of confused terminology like *infantile schizophrenia,* and child psychiatry's focus on maternal deprivation led to misconceptions of autism as an infant's response to "refrigerator mothers." Starting in the late 1960s autism was established as a separate syndrome by demonstrating that it is lifelong, distinguishing it from mental retardation and schizophrenia and from other developmental disorders, and demonstrating the benefits of involving parents in active programmes of therapy. As late as the mid-1970s there was little evidence of a genetic role in autism; now it is thought to be one of the most heritable of all psychiatric conditions. Although the rise of parent organizations and the destigmatization of childhood ASD have deeply affected how we view ASD, parents continue to feel social stigma in situations where their autistic children's behaviours are perceived negatively by others, and many primary care physicians and medical specialists still express some beliefs consistent with outdated autism research. The Internet has helped autistic individuals bypass nonverbal cues and emotional sharing that they find so hard to deal with, and has given them a way to form online communities and work remotely. Sociological and cultural aspects of autism have developed: some in the community seek a cure, while others believe that autism is simply another way of being.

SELECT CONTROVERSIES IN AUTISM

Controversies in autism encompass the disagreement over the exact nature of autism, its causes and manifestations. Autism is considered to be a neurodevelopmental condition which manifests itself in markedly abnormal social interaction, communication ability, and patterns of interests.

The cause(s) of autism and the spectrum of pervasive developmental disorders (PDDs) are either unknown or unclear.

Epidemiology

There is uncertainty and controversy over whether the incidence of autism spectrum disorders (ASD) is actually increasing or if there simply is an increase in the number of reported cases and better diagnosis.

Genetics

There is evidence that autism has a genetic component, and ongoing research focuses on finding the biomarkers that determine autistic phenotypes. One, as yet unproven theory is that there may be genes which contribute to a vulnerability to environmental triggers or have another role in the etiology of autism.

Genetics is viewed as an underlying factor. However, while some parents of those with autism are progressively also being diagnosed on the autism spectrum, at least some autistic children have apparently neurotypical parents. This suggests to some that genetics are either not a necessary cause or that they don't play a part in all cases of ASD, although it could also mean that the gene(s) responsible may be recessive or a spontaneous mutation. The spectrum of autistic disorders is notable for its significant gender disparity, with the incidence of autism in males greatly exceeding the incidence in females. Whilst this could argue against a genetic theory, it has also been argued that male brains may be more vulnerable during early development.

Vaccines

Several controversial claims have been made with regard to autism and vaccinations, leading notably to the MMR vaccine controversy, the thiomersal controversy, and the theory of vaccine overload. These theories lack scientific evidence and are biologically implausible.

Intelligence

A 2007 study suggested that Raven's Progressive Matrices (RPM), a test of abstract reasoning, may be a better indicator of intelligence for autistic children than the more commonly used Wechsler Intelligence Scale for Children (WISC). Researchers suspected that the WISC relied too heavily on language to be an accurate measure of intelligence for autistics. The neurotypical children scored similarly on both tests, but the autistic children fared far better on the RPM than on the WISC. The RPM measures abstract, general and fluid reasoning, an ability autistics have been presumed to lack. A 2008 study found a similar effect, but to a much lesser degree and only for individuals with Wechsler IQs less than 85.

A 2006 review questioned the validity of IQ testing of autistic people.

Joint Attention

Joint attention refers to a cluster of behaviours in one of two classes: a child's response to someone else pointing or shifting eye gaze, and a child seeking another's attention. Many joint-attention Behaviours differ in children with autism, for example, eye contact is relatively absent or atypical. These joint attention skills seem to be prerequisites for functional language development. It has also been hypothesized that autistic children initiate joint attention perhaps even as often as their neurotypical peers, albeit in atypical ways, and that a parent should join an autistic child's focus of attention and try harder to notice the child's atypical requests for attention rather than insist on typical Behaviour from the child. The empirical data supporting the latter hypothesis has been questioned.

7

Inclusive Education, Ableism, Universal Design and Assistive Technology: Evaluating Roles in Special Needs Education

UNDERSTANDING INCLUSION IN TERMS OF EDUCATION

Inclusion in the context of education is a term that refers to the practice of educating students with special needs in regular classes for all or nearly all of the day instead of in special education classes.

There are two types of inclusion:

One model is often referred to as *regular inclusion* or *partial inclusion*. In this model, students with special needs are educated in regular classes for nearly all of the day or at least half of the day. In a partial inclusion model, specialized services are provided outside a regular classroom. In this case, the student occasionally leaves the regular classroom to attend smaller, more intensive instructional sessions, or to receive other related service such as speech and language therapy, occupational and/or physical therapy, and social work. Sometimes, students with more intensive needs are educated within the regular classroom with the service providers coming into the regular classroom. This is often referred as *integrated classroom*. It is however, different from an inclusive classroom.

The second model is referred to as "full inclusion." Full inclusion is the integration of all students, even those with the most severe educational disabilities, into regular classes and an avoidance of special, segregated special education classes. Consequently, special education services are delivered within the normal classroom. Teacher aides are assigned to help the children with special needs progress. Schools with full inclusion have no separate special education classes. However, full inclusion is a controversial practice, and it is not widely applied.

Inclusion Compared to "Full" Inclusion

Some authors, such as Frank Bowe, distinguish between regular *inclusion* and *full inclusion*.

Under regular inclusion, students with disabilities may spend two-thirds or more of the school week in general classrooms. They need not be physically located there all of the time. Rather, they may be pulled out for occupational or physical therapy, speech/language pathology, or other related services. This is very similar to many mainstreaming practices.

Under full inclusion, by contrast, students classified as disabled remain in general classrooms virtually all the time. Related services are provided via "push in," meaning that professionals enter the classroom and deliver assistance there.

Bowe argues that inclusion, but not full inclusion, is a reasonable approach for most students with special needs. He also cautions that for some students, notably those with severe autism spectrum disorders or mental retardation, as well as many who are deaf or have multiple disabilities, even regular inclusion may not offer an appropriate education.

Other authors, such as Stainback and Stainback, by contrast, propose that placement in general classrooms is a civil right. These advocates believe that schools should be restructured so that full inclusion can be provided for all students with special needs, including those with the most severe disabilities.

Necessary Resources

Although once hailed as a way to increase achievement while decreasing costs, full inclusion does not save money, reduce students' needs or improve academic outcomes; in most cases, it merely moves the special education professionals out of their own classroom and into a corner of the general classroom. To avoid harm to the academic education of students with disabilities, a full panoply of services and resources is required, including:

- Adequate supports and services for the student
- Well-designed individualized education programmes
- Professional development for all teachers involved, general and special educators alike
- Time for teachers to plan, meet, create, and evaluate the students together
- Reduced class size based on the severity of the student needs
- Professional skill development in the areas of cooperative learning, peer tutoring, adaptive curriculum
- Collaboration between parents, teachers and administrators
- Sufficient funding so that schools will be able to develop programmes for students based on student need instead of the availability of funding.

Classroom

The setting for inclusive education is the general classroom, emphasizing the students' role in the broader community. Whenever possible, the students receive any additional help or special instruction in the general classroom.

Selection of Students for Regular Inclusion

Some students with special needs are not good candidates for inclusion. Many schools expect a fully included student to be working at or near grade level, but more fundamental requirements exist: First, being included requires that the student is able to attend school. Students that are entirely excluded from school (for example, due to long-term hospitalization), or who are educated outside of schools (for example, due to enrollment in a distance education programme) cannot attempt inclusion.

Additionally, some students with special needs are poor candidates for inclusion because of their effect on other students. For example, students with severe behavioural problems, such that they represent a serious physical danger to others, are poor candidates for inclusion, because the school has a duty to provide a safe environment to all students and staff. Students whose behaviour is seriously disruptive to other students (for example, a student that unconsciously makes loud, continuous noises throughout the day) are also poor candidates for inclusion, because the school has a duty to provide an environment in which all students are able to learn.

Finally, some students are not good candidates for inclusion because the normal activities in a general education classroom will prevent them from learning. For example, a student with severe attention difficulties or extreme sensory processing disorders might be highly distracted or distressed by the presence of other students working at their desks. Inclusion needs to be appropriate to the child's unique needs.

Most students with special needs do not fall into these extreme categories, as most do attend school, are not violent, do not have severe sensory processing disorders, etc. In fact, the majority of students with a specific learning disability are included in the general classroom, rising to 99 per cent of students with learning disabilities in Denmark.

Relationship to Progressive Education

Some advocates of inclusion promote the adoption of progressive education practices. In the progressive education or inclusive classroom, everyone is exposed to a "rich set of activities," and each student does what he or she can do, or what he or she wishes to do and learns whatever comes from that experience. Maria Montessori's schools are one example of inclusive schools.

Arguments for Full Inclusion

The key argument in favour of inclusion is that some people believe that even partial non-inclusion is morally unacceptable. Even if the purpose behind exclusion is to improve academic achievement by the non-included students, proponents believe that the non-inclusion reduces the disabled students' social importance. In the long-term, proponents believe, society comes to treat disabled students as less worthy because they are less visible in general education classrooms. Some advocates assert that even if typical students are harmed by inclusion of some special needs students, that the non-inclusion of these students would still be morally unacceptable, as advocates believe that the harm to typical students' education is always less important than the social harm caused by making people with disabilities less visible in society.

A second key argument is that everybody benefits from inclusion. Advocates suggest that there are many children and young people who don't fit in (or feel as though they don't), and that an inclusive school feels welcoming to all. However, in a public school this philosophy is viewed as impractical. Studies on the long-term impact of inclusion have not conclusively shown any benefit either academically nor socially to students with disabilities.

Advocates for inclusion say that the long-term effects of typical students who are included with special needs students at a very young age have a heightened sensitivity to the challenges that others face, increased empathy and compassion, and improved leadership skills, which benefits all of society.

Disability advocacy groups like Kids Together, Inc., say that the principal goal for inclusion is to make non-disabled children understand and value diversity. Kids Together, Inc., says that "Meeting all their needs together increases their [students with disabilities'] ability to achieve academic and physical growth to reach their potential, which also enhances their quality of life [for students with disabilities]." Through inclusive education, educators place children with disabilities on a path that teaches them how to be a participating member of their community. Another goal is to promote teamwork and how to function and interact with people with different disabilities.

Another advocacy group, Consortium, says that the three goals for inclusion are "to establish a change process in multiple states focused on systematic form, to translate research and policy information into implementable educational practices, [and] to develop the capacity of state and local agencies to provide inclusive educational services."

Criticism

Critics of full and partial inclusion include both educators, administrators and parents. Full and partial inclusion approaches neglect to acknowledge the fact most students with special needs require individualized instruction or highly controlled environments. Thus, general education classroom teachers often are teaching a curriculum while the special education teacher is remediating instruction at the same time. Similarly, a child with serious inattention problems may be unable to focus in a classroom that contains twenty or more active children. The approach is viewed by some as a practice philosophically attractive yet impractical, and studies have not corroborated the proposed advantages of full or partial inclusion. Moreover, "push in" servicing does not allow students with moderate to severe disabilities individualized instruction in special classrooms, from which many show considerable benefit in both learning and emotional development.

Parents may be cautious about placing their children in an inclusion programme because of fears that the children will be ridiculed by other students, or be unable to develop regular life skills in an academic classroom.

KNOWING ABOUT INCLUSIVE SCHOOLS AND INCLUSIVE EDUCATION

Inclusive school is a term used to describe an educational institution that practises full inclusion or the narrower term inclusive education. Some educators argue that an alternative to mainstreaming, called full inclusion, might be more effective. Full inclusion is the integration of all students, even those with the most severe educational disabilities, into regular classes and an avoidance of special, segregated special education classes. Teacher aides are assigned to help the children with special needs progress. Schools with full inclusion have no separate special education classes. However, full inclusion is a controversial practice, and it is not widely applied. Full inclusion educates special needs students in regular classes for all of the day instead of in special education classes.

Inclusive education is about the education of all children in mainstream schools and classrooms and the recent drive toward inclusive education is about more than disability or 'special educational needs'. It reflects changes in the social and political climate wherein a new approach characterizes thinking about difference. In recent debate about inclusion, a premium is placed upon full participation by all and respect for the rights of others. Discussion about the benefits of an inclusive society assumes that a society which can nurture, develop and use the skills, talents and strengths of all its members will enlarge its collective resources and ultimately is likely to be more at ease with itself. These changes in thinking are espoused in much recent discourse about education. Increasingly, this discourse emphasises learners' rights as well as their needs, and stresses the importance of an education free from discrimination and segregation.

LEGISLATION: The new anti-discriminatory climate has provided the basis for much change in policy and statute, nationally and internationally. Inclusion has been enshrined as segregation and discrimination have been rejected and outlawed. Articulations of the new developments in ways of thinking, in policy and in law include:

- The UN Convention on the Rights of the Child (1989) which sets out children's rights in respect of freedom from discrimination and in respect of the representation of their wishes and views.
- The UNESCO Salamanca Statement (1994) which calls on all governments to give the highest priority to inclusive education.

What is Inclusive Education?

Inclusive education differs from previously held notions of 'integration' and 'mainstreaming', which tended to be concerned principally with disability and 'special educational needs' and implied learners changing or becoming 'ready for' accommodation by the mainstream. By contrast, inclusion is about the child's right to participate and the school's duty to accept. It is about...

- rejecting segregation or exclusion of learners for whatever reason—ability, gender, language, care status, family income, disability, sexuality, colour, religion or ethnic origin;

- maximising the participation of all learners in the community schools of their choice;
- making learning more meaningful and relevant for all, particularly those learners most vulnerable to exclusionary pressures;
- rethinking and restructuring policies, curricula, cultures and practices in schools and learning environments so that diverse learning needs can be met, whatever the origin or nature of those needs.

Inclusion is about school change to improve the educational system for all students. It means changes in the curriculum, changes in how teachers teach and how students learn, as well as changes in how students with and without special needs interact with and relate to one another. Inclusive education practices reflect the changing culture of contemporary schools with emphasis on active learning, authentic assessment practices, applied curriculum, multi-level instructional approaches, and increased attention to diverse student needs and individualization. The claim is that schools, centres of learning and educational systems must change so that they become caring, nurturing, and supportive educational communities where the needs of all students and teachers are truly met. Inclusive schools no longer provide "regular education" and "special education." Instead, inclusive schools provide an inclusive education and as a result students will be able to learn together. In other words, it is open to all students, and that ensure that all students learn and participate. For this to happen, teachers, schools and systems may need to change so that they can better accommodate the diversity of needs that pupils have and that they are included in all aspects of school-life. It also means identifying any barriers within and around the school that hinder learning and participation, and reducing or removing these barriers. Inclusive education is a process of enabling all students, including previously excluded groups, to learn and participate effectively within mainstream school systems. Placing excluded students within a mainstream setting does not of itself achieve inclusion.

Principles

- Every student has an inherent right to education on basis of equality of opportunity.
- No student is excluded from, or discriminated within education on grounds of race, colour, sex, language, religion, political or other opinion, national, ethnic or social origin, disability, birth, poverty or other status.
- All students can learn and benefit from education.
- Schools adapt to the needs of students, rather than students adapting to the needs of the school.
- The student's views are listened to and taken seriously.
- Individual differences between students are a source of richness and diversity, and not a problem.
- The diversity of needs and pace of development of students are addressed through a wide and flexible range of responses.

Practice

The practice of developing inclusive schools involves:

- Understanding inclusion as a continuing process, not a one-time event.
- Strengthening and sustaining the participation of all students, teachers, parents and community members in the work of the school.
- Restructuring the cultures, policies and practices in schools to respond to the diversity of pupils within their locality. Inclusive settings focus on identifying and then reducing the barriers to learning and participation, rather than on what is "special" about the individual student or group of students, and targeting services to address the "problem."
- Providing an accessible curriculum, appropriate training programmes for teachers, and for all students, the provision of fully accessible information, environments and support.
- Identifying and providing support for staff as well as students.

A somewhat different model is implemented by Hands On Learning Australia wherein disengaged students, as well as some students with special needs, are taken out of class one day per week and put into an alternative cross-age peer group to develop strong relationships and enable them to better cope with mainstream classes.

Teaching/Programming

It is general practice that students in an inclusive classroom are with their chronological age-mates. Also, to encourage a sense of belonging, emphasis is placed on the value of friendships. Teachers often nurture a relationship between a student with special needs and a peer without need. Another common practice is the assignment of a buddy to accompany a student with special needs at all times (for example in the cafeteria, on the playground, on the bus and so on).

In principle, several factors can determine the success of inclusive classrooms:

- Family-school partnerships
- Collaboration between general and special educators
- Well-constructed Individualized Education Programme plans
- Team planning and communication
- Integrated service delivery
- Ongoing training and staff development.

Teachers use a number of techniques to help build classroom communities:

- Games designed to build community
- Involving students in solving problems
- Songs and books that teach community

- Openly dealing with individual differences
- Assigning classroom jobs that build community
- Teaching students to look for ways to help each other
- Utilizing physical therapy equipment such as standing frames, so students who typically use wheelchairs can stand when the other students are standing and more actively participate in activities.

Benefits

Inclusive education is claimed by its advocates to have many benefits for the students. Instructional time with peers without need helps the learners to learn strategies taught by the teacher. Teachers bring in different ways to teach a lesson for special needs students and peers without need. All of the students in the classroom benefit from this. The students can now learn from the lesson how to help each other. Socialization in the school allows the students to learn communication skills and interaction skills from each other. Students can build friendships from these interactions. The students can also learn about hobbies from each other. A friendship in school is important for the development of learning. When a student has a friend the student can relate to a member of the classroom. Students' being able to relate to each other gives them a better learning environment. Involving peers without need with special needs peers gives the students a positive attitude towards each other. The students are the next generation to be in the workforce; the time in the classroom with the special needs and peers without need will allow them to communicate in the real world someday. Special needs students are included in all aspects of school-life. For example, homeroom, specials such as art and gym, lunch, recess, assemblies, and electives. Special needs students involved in these classrooms will give them the time they need to participate in activities with their peers without need. Awareness should be taught to students that will be in the classroom with the special needs peers. The teacher can do a puppet show, show a movie, or have the student talk to the class. The teacher could also read a book to help the student describe his or her special needs. The class can ask questions about what they learned and what they want to know. This will help when the students are together in the classroom. Positive modelling is important for the students in the classroom. Positive modelling is the teacher showing a good example towards both special needs and peers without need this will help the students to get along more.

Criticism

Opponents of inclusive schools believe that individual differences will slow the progress of students without special needs. Therefore, this will create problems for teachers. Some argue that inclusive schools are not a cost-effective response when compared to cheaper or more effective interventions, such as special education. They argue that special education helps "fix" the special needs students by providing individualized and personalized instruction to meet their unique needs. This is to help students with special needs adjust as quickly as possible to the mainstream of the school and community. Proponents counter that students with special needs are not fully into the mainstream of student life because they are secluded to special education. Some argue that isolating students with special needs may lower their self-esteem and may reduce their ability to deal with other people. In keeping these students in separate classrooms they aren't going to see the struggles and achievements that they can make together.

More recently, post-modern and post-structuralist approaches have also led to critiques of mainstream thinking on inclusion. Broadly, these have explored the exclusionary influence of the language that is characteristic of most current debates on inclusion, going on to challenge the relations of power and hierarchy that operate in much inclusive education. Julie Allan, for example, examines the ideas of the 'philosophers of difference'—Gilles Deleuze, Michael Foucault and Jacques Derrida—and puts them to work on inclusion (Allan 2008). She argues that these ideas allow the task of including children to be reframed, and offer not solutions, but different ways of working which involve altering adult-child relationships—subverting, subtracting, and inventing and restructuring teacher education—recognition, rupture and repair. She also advocates making greater use of the arts to challenge exclusion, disrupt boundaries, and establish more inclusive practices.

UNDERSTANDING ABLEISM

Ableism is used to describe effective discrimination against people with disabilities in favour of people who are not disabled. An *ableist* society is said to be one that treats non-disabled individuals as the standard of 'normal living', which results in public and private places and services, education, and social work that are built to serve 'standard' people, thereby inherently excluding those with various disabilities. By contrast with the US, United Kingdom usage favours 'Disablism' to describe the same processes. Other English-speaking nations may use either term or both.

The 'Traditional Model' in Myths, Literature, Theatre, Folklore, Biography and History

The Traditional-Model

Traditionally, in many cultures around the world, people with physical, sensory or mental impairments were thought of as under the spell of witchcraft, possessed by demons, or as penitent sinners, being punished by God for wrong-doing by themselves or their parents. Ancient societies used to place deformed or otherwise disabled babies upon concrete slabs outdoors exposed to storms and other harsh elements, thus killing them gradually over the course of a few days.

With the Age of Enlightenment in the 18th century, came a more scientific understanding of the causes of impairment and, with it, a sense of confidence in medical science's ability to cure, or at least rehabilitate, disabled people. Some disabled people (often for social or political reasons) were deemed incurable and placed in long-stay institutions and special schools (or, today, in day-care centres). A notion of 'normality' was invested with great pseudo-scientific significance. It was based on assessments of impairments from a deficit point of view against normality: what one cannot do, instead of what one can do. This has been called 'medical model' (or 'individual model') thinking by the Disabled People's Movement over the last 30 years. This is not to deny the very necessary role of medical science in keeping many disabled people alive, and reducing their pain and discomfort, but it is to argue that disabled people should not be reduced to just their impairments.

The 'medical model' sees disabled people as the problem. They need to be adapted to fit into the world as it is. If this isn't possible, then they should be shut away in a specialised institution or isolated at home, where only their most basic needs are met. The emphasis is on dependence, backed up by the stereotypes of disability that bring out pity, fear and patronising attitudes. Usually, the impairment is focused on, rather than the needs of the person. The power to change disabled people seems to lie with the medical and associated professions, with their talk of cures, normalisation and science. Often, disabled people's lives are handed over to these professionals. Their decisions affect where disabled people go to school; what support they get; where they live; what benefits they are entitled to; whether they can work; and even, at times, whether they are born at all, or allowed to have children themselves.

In addition, the Disability Movement points out how the built environment imposes further limitations on disabled people. Medical model thinking would say these problems are due to the disabled person's lack of rehabilitation. The Disability Movement perceives the difficulties disabled people experience as the barriers that disable them and curtail their life chances. These difficulties include in school and higher education, in finding work and suitable work environments, accessing leisure and entertainment facilities, using private and public transport, obtaining suitable housing, or in their personal, family and social life.

Powerful and pervasive medical model views are reinforced in the media, books, films, comics, art and language. Many disabled people internalise negative views of themselves and develop feelings of low self-esteem and underachievement, which reinforce non-disabled people's assessments of their worth. The medical model, plus the built environment and social attitudes it creates, lead to a cycle of dependency and exclusion which is difficult to break. This thinking predominates in filmmaking, leisure, work and education. In schools, for instance, special educational needs are considered the problem of the individual, who is seen as different, faulty and needing to be assessed and made as 'normal' as possible.

Disablism

As noted above, 'disablism' rather than 'ableism' is the term favoured in the United Kingdom, this usage flows out of a perspective driven by the Social model of disability which regards 'disability' as the discrimination experienced by a person as a response to their impairment, making 'disablist' or 'disablism' the logical terms to describe discrimination on the grounds of disability.

Discrimination

The presumption that everyone is non-disabled is said to encourage environments that are inaccessible to disabled people. It is a system by which mainstream society denigrates, devalues, and thus oppresses those with disabilities, while privileging those without disabilities, according to those who describe ableist circumstances.

In extreme cases, morality, worth and intelligence may even be equated to being able-bodied or able-minded, while disability is conflated with immorality, stupidity, and worthlessness, and disabled lives may be devalued to the point that many in the society believe that one is better off dead than living with disability. The eugenics movement of the 19th and 20th centuries, which took its most extreme form in Nazi Germany with Action T4, was a product of this belief, and some believe the 'right to die' movement is also an outgrowth of ableist beliefs.

Laws Against Discrimination

In the US, Section 504 of the Rehabilitation Act of 1973 and the Americans with Disabilities Act of 1990 (ADA) enacted into law certain civil penalties for failing to make a public places comply with access codes known as the ADA Access Guidelines (ADAAG); this law also helped expand the use of certain adaptive devices, such as TTYs (phone systems for the deaf/speech impaired), some computer-related hardware and software, and ramps or lifts on public transportation buses and private automobiles.

In the UK, meanwhile, the 1995 Disability Discrimination Act and Disability Discrimination Act 2005 attempts the same.

These laws often concentrate mainly on the civil or legal aspect of disability discrimination and neglect the cultural dimensions that are integral to the social model of disability.

Inclusion

Inclusion, comparatively, means that all products, services, and societal opportunities and resources are fully accessible, welcoming, functional and usable for as many different types of abilities as reasonably possible. An *ableist* society tends towards isolation, pity, paternalism and low self-esteem among people with disabilities, whereas an *inclusive* society tends toward sociability and interdependency between the able-bodied and disabled.

TOWARDS MAINSTREAMING EDUCATION: AN AMERICAN APPROACH

Mainstreaming in the context of education is a term that refers to the practice of educating students with special needs in regular classes during specific time periods based on their skills. This means regular education classes is combined with special education classes. Schools that practice mainstreaming believe that special needs students who cannot function in a regular classroom to a certain extent "belong" to the special education environment.

Access to a special education classroom, often called a "self-contained classroom or special classroom", is valuable to the student with a disability. Students have the ability to work one-on-one with special education teachers, addressing any need for remediation during the school day. Many parents have advocated the importance of these classrooms amongst political environments that favour their elimination.

Proponents of both mainstreaming and inclusion assert that educating children with disabilities alongside their non-disabled peers fosters understanding and tolerance, better preparing students of all abilities to function in the world beyond school.

Advantages

Benefits to students with disabilities: It is believed that educating children with disabilities alongside their non-disabled peers facilitates access to the general curriculum for children with disabilities. Studies show that students with disabilities who are mainstreamed have:

- *Higher academic achievement:* Mainstreaming has shown to be more academically effective than exclusion practices. For instance, The National Research Center on Learning Disabilities found that graduation rates of all students with disabilities in the U.S. increased by 14 per cent from 1984 to 1997, although this report does not differentiate between students enrolled in mainstreaming, inclusive, or segregated programmes.
- *Higher self-esteem:* By being included in a regular-paced education setting, students with disabilities have shown to be more confident and display qualities of raised self-efficacy. All students in California who went to a different school prior to attending a mainstreaming programme were asked to fill out an assessment of their old school as compared to inclusion programme. The assessments showed that out of all students with disabilities 96 per cent felt they were more confident, 3 per cent thought they had the same experience as an excluded student, and 1 per cent felt they had less self-esteem. Overall, students felt that they were equal to their peers and felt that they should not be treated any differently.
- *Better social skills:* Any kind of inclusion practice, including mainstreaming, allows students with disabilities to learn social skills through observation, gain a better understanding of the world around them, and become a part of the "regular" community. Mainstreaming is particularly beneficial for children with autism. By interacting with same-aged "normal" children, children with autism were observed to be six times more likely to engage in social relations outside of the classroom. Because children with autism spectrum disorders have severely restricted interests and abnormalities in communication and social interaction, the increased interaction with typical

children may be beneficial to them. The same 1999 study showed that students with Down's syndrome were three times more likely to communicate with other people.

Mainstreaming also benefits other children. It opens the lines of communication between those students with disabilities and their peers. If they are included into classroom activities, all students become more sensitive to the fact that these students may need extra assistance.

Benefits to non-disabled students: Many people believe that educating non-disabled students and students with disabilities together creates an atmosphere of understanding and tolerance that better prepares students of all abilities to function in the world beyond school. Students without disabilities who engaged in an inclusive physical education programme reported increases in self-concept, tolerance, self worth, and a better understanding of other people. The students also reported that the inclusion programme was important because it prepared them to deal with disability in their own lives. Positive aspects that come from inclusion are often attributed to contact theory. Contact theory asserts that frequent, meaningful, and pleasant interactions between people with differences tend to produce changes in attitude.

Disadvantages

Although mainstreaming in education has been shown to provide benefits, there are also disadvantages to the system.

Harm to non-disabled students' academic education: One potentially serious disadvantage to mainstreaming, is that a mainstreamed student may require much more attention from the teacher than non-disabled students in a general class. Time and attention may thus be taken away from the rest of the class to meet the needs of a single student with special needs. The effect that a mainstreamed student has on the whole class depends strongly on the particular disabilities in question and the resources available for support. In many cases, this problem can be mitigated by placing an aide in the classroom to assist the student with special needs, although this raises the costs associated with educating this child.

Some parents also fear that general education standards will be lowered to the level of the least able students.

Harm to advanced students' academic education: It can be difficult or even impossible to simultaneously accommodate students with significant intellectual disabilities while also adequately challenging very advanced students. Beyond the lost opportunities to learn advanced academic skills, gifted students are typically bored by or even angry about being subjected to the constant repetition of basic skills which the least able students require. Many advanced students in mainstreaming classes are drafted as informal, unpaid tutors for classmates with academic deficits and often resent this imposition on their time and energy. Advanced students will also lose the opportunity to develop persistence on difficult tasks, because they are never faced with tasks which they find difficult. In some cases, this situation will lead to classroom disruption, behavioural problems, and an inflated sense of self-importance.

Harm to students with disabilities' academic education: Parents fear that general education teachers do not have the training and skills to accommodate special needs students in a general education classroom setting. However, professional training and supportive services can usually address these concerns.

Social issues: Compared to fully included students with disabilities, those who are mainstreamed for only certain classes or certain times may feel conspicuous or socially rejected by their classmates. They may become targets for bullying. Mainstreamed students may feel embarrassed by the additional services they receive in a regular classroom, such as an aide to help with written work or to help the student manage behaviours. Some students with disabilities may feel more comfortable in an environment where most students are working at the same level or with the same supports.

Costs: Schools are required to provide special education services but may not be given additional financial resources. The per-student cost of special education is high. The U.S.'s 2005 Special Education Expenditures Programme (SEEP) indicates that the cost per student in special education ranges from a low of $10,558 for students with learning disabilities to a high of $20,095 for students with multiple disabilities. The average cost per pupil for a regular education with no special education services is $6,556. Therefore, the average expenditure for students with learning disabilities is 1.6 times that of a general education student. However, the cost of mainstreaming a student is generally much less than the cost of keeping that student in a special classroom.

Careful attention must be given as well to combinations of students with disabilities in a mainstreamed classroom. For example, a student with conduct disorder may not combine well with a student with autism, while putting many children with dyslexia in the same class may prove to be particularly efficient.

Alternatives: What Mainstreaming is Not

The alternatives to mainstreaming for special needs students are segregation, inclusion, and excluding the student from school. Normally, the student's individual needs are the driving force behind selecting mainstreaming or another style of education.

Mainstreaming does not involve putting a child full-time in a special school or a self-contained classroom which only serves students with disabilities. A student who does not spend any part of the day with non-disabled students is not mainstreamed; that student is segregated.

Mainstreaming does not involve placing a child full-time in a regular classroom. A student who spends the entire day in a regular classroom with non-disabled peers is considered fully included. Most students with mild levels of disabilities such as dyslexia or attention deficit disorder, or with non-cognitive disabilities such as diabetes are fully included.

Mainstreaming does not involve teaching the child outside of school. A student who is taught in an institution (such as a hospital) or at home (such as while recovering from a serious illness) is excluded. Such a student may receive one-on-one instruction or may attend small group instruction. A student who is excluded from school may or may not have been expelled from the school.

History of Mainstreaming in US Schools

Before the Education for All Handicapped Children Act (EHA) was enacted in 1975, U.S. public schools educated only 1 out of 5 children with disabilities. Approximately 200,000 children with disabilities such as deafness or mental retardation lived in state institutions that provided limited or no educational or rehabilitation services, and more than one million children were excluded from school. Another 3.5 million children with disabilities attended school but did not receive the educational services they needed. Many of these children were segregated in special buildings or programmes that neither allowed them to interact with non-disabled students nor provided them with even basic academic skills.

The EHA, later renamed the Individuals with Disabilities Education Act (IDEA), required schools to provide specialized educational services children with disabilities. The ultimate goal was to help these students live more independent lives in their communities, primarily by mandating access to the general education standards of the public school system.

Initially, children with disabilities were often placed in heterogeneous "special education" classrooms, making it difficult for any of their difficulties to be addressed appropriately. In the 1980s, the mainstreaming model began to be used more often as a result of the requirement to place children in the least restrictive environment (Clearinghouse, E. 2003). Students with relatively minor disabilities were integrated into regular classrooms, while students with major disabilities remained in segregated special classrooms, with the opportunity to be among normal students for up to a few hours each day. Many parents and educators favoured allowing students with disabilities to be in classrooms along with their non-disabled peers.

In 1997, IDEA was modified to strengthen requirements for properly integrating students with disabilities. The IEPs must more clearly relate to the general-education curriculum, children with disabilities must be included in most state and local assessments, such as high school exit exams, and regular progress reports must be made to parents. All public schools in the U.S. are responsible for the costs of providing a Free Appropriate Public Education as required by federal law. Mainstreaming or inclusion in the regular education classrooms, with supplementary aids and services if needed, are now the preferred placement for all children. Children with disabilities may be placed in a more restricted environment only if the nature or severity of the disability makes it impossible to provide an appropriate education in the regular classroom.

UNDERSTANDING THE LEAST RESTRICTIVE ENVIRONMENT

As part of the U.S. Individuals with Disabilities Education Act, the least restrictive environment is identified as one of the six principles that govern the education of students with disabilities. By law, schools are required to provide a Free Appropriate Public Education (FAPE) in the least restrictive environment for students who have disabilities.

"Least restrictive environment" means that a student who has a disability should have the opportunity to be educated with non-disabled peers, to the greatest extent possible. They should have access to the general education curriculum, extracurricular activities, or any other programme that non-disabled peers would be able to access. The student should be provided with supplementary aids and services necessary to achieve educational goals if placed in a setting with non-disabled peers. Should the nature or severity of his or her disability prevent the student from achieving these goals in a regular education setting, then the student would be placed in a more restrictive environment, such as a special classroom or a hospital programme. Generally, the less opportunity a student has to interact and learn with non-disabled peers, the more that the setting is considered to be restricted.

To determine what an appropriate setting is for a student, a team will review the student's needs and interests. The types of educational settings for students with disabilities will vary. With the differences in needs and interests among students with disabilities, there is no single definition of what an LRE will be for all students.

Least Restrictive Environment and the Courts

Because the law does not clearly state to what degree the least restrictive environment is, courts have had to interpret the LRE principle. In a landmark case interpreting IDEA's predecessor statute (EHA), Daniel R. *v. State Board of Education* (1989), it was determined that students with disabilities have a right to be included in both academic and extracurricular programmes of general education. But, the Court stated, IDEA does not contemplate an all-or-nothing educational system in which [disabled] children attend either regular or special education. Rather, the Act and its regulations require schools to offer a continuum of services. Thus, the school must take intermediate steps where appropriate, such as placing the child in regular education for some academic classes and in special education for others, mainstreaming the child for non-academic classes only, or providing interaction with non-disabled children during lunch and recess. The appropriate mix will vary from child to child and, it may be hoped, from school year to school year as the child develops. If the school officials have provided the maximum appropriate exposure to non-disabled students, they have fulfilled their obligation under IDEA. *Daniel R.R. v. State Bd. of Educ.,* 874 F.2d 1036, 1050 (5th Cir.1989).

In Board of Education, Sacramento City Unified School District v. Holland (1994), four factors were identified as things needed to be taken into consideration when determining if the student's LRE is appropriate. They are:

- the educational benefits of integrated settings versus segregated settings,
- non-academic benefits (primarily social interaction with non-disabled peers),
- the effect the student with a disability can have on the teacher and his or her peers, and

- the cost of supplementary services that will be required for that student to stay in the integrated setting.

Simply stated, the student should receive an appropriate version of the educational and social benefits which non-disabled students routinely receive in school. In broad theory, the court does not allow the education of the student's non-disabled peers to be negatively affected, although applying this test fairly to all the facts and circumstances of a specific situation may be very difficult. The final factor, cost of supplementary services, provides a safeguard for schools so that they do not exceed spending on one particular student.

KNOWING ABOUT TECHNOLOGY ENHANCED LEARNING ENVIRONMENT

A Technology Enhanced Learning Environment (TELE) enables students to not only use educational material available but to optimize and enhance their learning in all aspects of education.

TELE challenges students through interaction, which in turn helps them learn at their own pace/abilities. It allows for an interactive environment, and facilitates higher learning and critical thinking.

TELE can refer to any setting where technology is used to enhance the learning of a user or observer.

Technology helps to maximize learning by challenging students to be creative with the learning process and also produces a thought-provoking environment.

It's important to acquire proficiency skills on the computer, but more important to realize its significance for the future.

A level, degree, means, or environment of learning, one typically more accelerated than the classroom without the integration of technologies, that may only be reached with the implementation of technology.

INDIVIDUALIZED EDUCATION PROGRAMME: TOWARDS UNDERSTANDING AN APPROACH

In the United States an Individualized Education Plan, commonly referred to as an IEP, is mandated by the Individuals with Disabilities Education Act (IDEA). In Canada and the United Kingdom, an equivalent document is called an Individual Education Plan.

In the US, the IDEA requires public schools to develop an IEP for every student with a disability who is found to meet the federal and state requirements for special education. The IEP must be designed to provide the child with a Free Appropriate Public Education (FAPE). The IEP refers both to the educational programme to be provided to a child with a disability and to the written document that describes that educational programme.

Key considerations in developin, an IEP include assessing students in all areas related to the suspected disability(ies), considering access to the general curriculum, considering how the disability affects the student's learning, developing goals and objectives that make the biggest difference for the student, and ultimately choosing a placement in the least restrictive environment.

Definition

An individualized educational plan means one that is designed to meet the unique educational needs of one child, as defined by federal regulations. 34 CFR 300.320 The IEP must be tailored to the individual student's needs as identified by the evaluation process and must help teachers and related service providers understand the student's disability and how the disability affects the learning process. In other words, the IEP should describe how the student learns, how the student best demonstrates that learning and what teachers and service providers will do to help the student learn more effectively.

Components

The IDEA 2004 requires that an IEP must be written according to the needs of one student, and it must include the following:

- The child's present levels of academic and functional performance
- Measurable annual goals, including academic and functional goals
- How the child's progress toward meeting the annual goals are to be measured and reported to the parents
- Special education services, related services, and supplementary aids to be provided to the child
- Schedule of services to be provided, including when the services are to begin, the frequency, duration and location for the provision of services
- Programme modifications or supports provided to school personnel on behalf of the child
- Explanation of any time the child will not participate along with non-disabled children
- Accommodations to be provided during state and district assessments that are necessary to the measuring child's academic and functional performance.

Additionally, when the student is 24 years old, a statement of post-secondary goals and a plan for providing what the student needs to make a successful transition is required. This transitional plan can be created at an earlier age if desired.

IEPs also include other pertinent information found necessary by the team, such as a health plan or a behaviour plan for some students.

Procedural Requirements for Development

The outcome of the IEP development process is an official document that describes the education plan designed to meet the unique needs of one child with a disability.

Determination of Eligibility for Special Education

Before an IEP is written for a child with a disability, the school must first determine whether the child qualifies for special education services. To qualify, the child's disability must have an adverse effect on the child's educational progress. Merely having a disability is not sufficient for eligibility.

To determine eligibility, the school must conduct a full evaluation of the child in all areas of suspected disability. Based in part on the results of the evaluation, the school along with the parents meet to review the results and the child's current level of performance and to determine whether special education services are needed.

If the child is found eligible for services, the school is required to convene an IEP team and develop an appropriate educational plan for the child. The IEP should be implemented as soon as possible after the child is determined eligible. IDEA does not state specific timeframes for each step. However, some states have added specific timelines that schools must follow for the eligibility, IEP development, and IEP implementation milestones.

Members of the IEP Team

The IEP team must include the student's parent(s) or guardian(s), a special education teacher, at least one regular education teacher, a representative of the school or district who is knowledgeable about the availability of school resources, and an individual who can interpret the instructional implications of the child's evaluation results (such as the school psychologist).

The parent or school may also bring other individuals who have knowledge or special expertise regarding the child. For example, the school may invite related service providers such as speech and occupational therapists. The parent may invite professionals who have worked with or assessed the child, or someone to assist the parent in advocating for their child's needs, such as a parent advocate or attorney. Many parents choose to bring at least one other person with them to IEP meetings because meeting with such a large group of school personnel can be intimidating to parents.

If appropriate, the child may also participate in IEP team meetings. For example, some children begin participating in their IEP meetings when they reach middle school age.

A typical IEP team meeting includes:

- One or both of the child's parents. Consistent with the IDEA's stated policy, parents should expect to be treated as equal participants with school personnel in developing the IEP.
- A representative of the school district (not the child's teacher) who is qualified to provide or supervise special education.
- The child's teacher(s). If the child has more than one teacher, then all teachers are required to attend.

- If the programme to be recommended includes activities with general education students, even if the child is in a special education class in the school, a general education teacher is required to attend.
- Professionals who are qualified to explain the results of the testing. Usually this requires at least the presence of a psychologist and educational evaluator.
- Parents may bring with them any others involved with the child who they feel are important for the IEP team to hear; for example, the child's psychologist or tutor.
- Parents may elect to bring an educational advocate, social workers and/or lawyer knowledgeable in the IEP process.
- Although not required, if the child is receiving related services (such as speech therapy or occupational therapy), it is valuable for related service personnel to attend the meeting or at least provide written recommendations concerning the services in their area of speciality.

In some localities additional members are required. For example, New York State requires the presence of a parent member. A parent member is the parent of a child with a disability (not the parent of the child for whom the IEP is being developed) who has had special training in the workings of the IEP process.

Role of the Parents

Parents are considered to be full and equal members of the IEP team, along with school personnel. Parents are crucial members of the team because they have unique knowledge of their child's strengths and needs. Parents have the right to be involved in meetings that discuss the identification, evaluation, IEP development and educational placement of their children. They also have the right to ask questions, dispute points, and request modifications to the plan, as do all members of the IEP team.

Although IEP teams are required to work toward consensus, school personnel ultimately are responsible for ensuring that the IEP includes the services that the student needs. By law, schools districts are obligated to make a proposal for services to the parent. If agreement cannot be reached, the school district cannot delay in providing the services that it believes are the best services to ensure that the student receives an effective educational programme.

An IEP meeting is not to be confused with a Parent/Teacher conference in which the parent sits and listens as the teacher reports the student's progress and performance. In order to fully participate in developing their child's IEP, parents must be knowledgeable about their child's specific disabilities, their rights under federal and state law, and the policies and procedures of the local education agency. Few parents have this knowledge when their child is initially identified as having a disability. Under IDEA Part D, the U.S. Department of Education funds at least one parent training and information center in each state and most territories to provide parents the information they need to advocate effectively for their child. Some centres may also provide a knowledgeable person to accompany a parent to IEP meetings to assist the parent in participating more fully in the process.

The school must make a significant effort to ensure that one or both of the parents are present at each IEP team meeting. If parents are unable to attend, the school must be able to show that due diligence was made to enable the parents to attend, including notifying the parents early enough that they have an opportunity to attend, scheduling the meeting at a mutually agreed on time and place, and offering alternative means of participation, such as a phone conference. Grades may not be discussed during the IEP to the parent unless he or she is having a problem stated on the IEP.

The school must also take whatever action is necessary to ensure that the parent understands the proceedings of IEP team meetings, including arranging for an interpreter for parents who are deaf or whose native language is not English.

Developing the Child's Education Plan

After the child is determined to be eligible for special education services, the IEP team must develop an individual education plan to be implemented as soon as possible after eligibility is determined. Using the results of the Full Individual Evaluation (FIE), the IEP team works together to identify the child's present level of educational performance, the child's specific academic, and any related or special services that the child needs in order to benefit from their education.

When developing an IEP, the team must consider the strengths of the child, the concerns of the parent for their child's education, results of the initial or most recent evaluation of the child (including private evaluations conducted by the parents), and the academic, developmental, and functional needs of the child. In the case of a child whose behaviour impedes the child's learning or that of other children, the team must consider the use of positive behavioural interventions and supports to address the behaviour.

The IEP team must also consider the communication needs of the child. For example, if a child is blind or visually impaired, the IEP must provide for instruction in Braille and the use of Braille unless an evaluation of the child's reading and writing skills, needs, and future needs indicate that this instruction is not appropriate for the child. If a child is deaf or hard of hearing, the team must consider the child's language and communication needs, including the need to communicate with school personnel and peers, and the child's need for direct instruction in the child's language and communication mode. In the case of a child with limited English proficiency, the team must consider the language needs of the child as those needs relate to the child's IEP.

A matrix is then drafted containing the student's present level of performance, indicators about ways the student's disability influences participation and progress in the general curriculum, a statement of measurable goals; including benchmarks or short-terms objectives, the specific educational services to be provided; including programme modifications or supports, an explanation of the extent that the child will not participate in general education, a description of all modifications in statewide or district-wide assessments, the projected date for initiation of the services and the expected duration of those services, the annual statement of transition service needs (beginning at age 14), and a statement of interagency responsibilities to ensure continuity of services when the student leaves school (by age 16), a statement regarding how the student's progress will be measured and how the parents will be informed in the process.

IDEA requires a child's IEP be developed solely based on the child's needs, and not based on pre-existing programmes or services available in the district. Whether particular services are available in the district should not be considered when identifying the services a child needs to receive an appropriate education.

Determining the Appropriate Placement

After the IEP is developed, the IEP team then determines placement, that is, the environment in which the child's IEP can most readily be implemented. IDEA requires that the IEP be complete before placement decisions are made so that the child's educational needs drive the IEP development process. Schools may not develop a child's IEP to fit into a pre-existing programme for a particular classification of disability. The IEP is written to fit the student. The placement is chosen to fit the IEP.

IDEA requires state and local education agencies to educate children with disabilities with their non-disabled peers to the maximum extent appropriate. A child can only be placed in a separate school or special classes if the severity or nature of the disability is such that appropriate education cannot be provided to the child in the regular classroom, even with the use of supplementary aids and services.

Implementation

Schools must have an IEP in effect at the beginning of the school year. Initial IEPs must be developed within 30 days of the determination of eligibility, and the services specified in the child's IEP must be provided as soon as possible after the IEP is developed.

Annual Review

After the IEP is developed and placement is determined, the child's teachers are responsible for implementing all educational services, programme modifications or supports as indicated by the individual education plan.

Acceptance and Amendments

An initial IEP must be accepted and signed by a parent or guardian before any of the outlined services may begin. However, parents/guardians need not sign any paper work when it is initially proposed. Formerly, they had 30 calendar days to take the paper work home for their consideration. Recent changes have instituted the 11th day rule. The IEP must be signed or appealed after 10 days, or the school can implement the most recent version.

The IEP is never set in stone; any member of the team may call a meeting at any time to edit the IEP.

Procedural Safeguards

School personnel have an obligation to provide parents with a Procedural Safeguards Notice, which must include an explanation of all of the procedural safeguards built into IDEA. In addition, the information must be in understandable language and in the native language of the parent. A copy of the Procedural Safeguards Notice must be presented at the IEP meeting. Parents must sign that they were given a copy. Schools must give parents a copy of the child's IEP at no cost to the parent.

An extensive system of conflict resolution procedures is set out in the statutory provisions. They include, the right to examine records, advance notification of intent to change the educational programme, the right to engage in mediation, and a right to an impartial due process hearing.

Services that may be Provided to a Child with a Disability

- Specially designed instruction
- Related services
- Programme modifications
- Classroom accommodations
- Supplementary aids and services.

Specially Designed Instruction

Specially designed instruction affects the instructional content, method of instructional delivery, and the performance methods and criteria that are necessary to assist the student make meaningful educational progress. This instruction is designed by or with an appropriately credentialled special education teacher or related service provider.

For some students, teachers may need to present information through the use of manipulatives. For other students, teachers may need to select and teach only important key concepts and then alter evaluation activities and criteria to match this content change.

The IEP team should determine whether a specific type of instruction should be included in a student's IEP. Generally, if the methodology is an essential part of what is required to meet the individualized needs of the student, the methodology should be included. For instance, if a student has a learning disability and has not learned to read using traditional methods, then another method may be required. When including such an IEP recommendation, the Team should describe the components of the appropriate type of methodology as opposed to naming a specific programme.

Related Services

If the child needs additional services in order to access or benefit from special education, schools are to provide the services as related services.

Services specified in IDEA include, but are not limited to, speech therapy, occupational or physical therapy, interpreters, medical services (such as a nurse to perform procedures the child needs during the day, for example, catheterization), orientation and mobility services, parent counselling and training to help parents support the implementation of their childs IEP, psychological or counselling services, recreation services, rehabilitation, social work services, and transportation.

Programme Modifications

- Modifications to the content of the programme
- Lowered success criteria for academic success
- Increased emphasis on daily living skills and decrease
- Alternative state assessments, such as off-grade level assessments.

Classroom Accommodations

Some of the student's educational needs may be met using accommodations. Accommodations are typically provided by general educators within the general education environment. Accommodations do not involve modifying the material content but do allow students to receive information or to demonstrate what they have learned in ways that work around their disabilities.

Accommodations may include such provisions as preferential seating, providing photocopies of teacher notes, giving oral rather than written quizzes, alternative or modified assignments, extended time for tests and assignments, use of a word processor or laptop, and taking tests in a quiet room.

The IEP team must reflect on the affect the disability(ies) has on educational progress and then identify accommodations, if any are needed, for the student to make effective progress.

Supplementary Aids and Services

- Assistive technology
- Teacher's aide in classroom that provide additional support for one or more specific students

UNDERSTANDING POST SECONDARY TRANSITION FOR HIGH SCHOOL STUDENTS WITH DISABILITIES: CASE STUDY OF AN APPROACH

The Post Secondary Transition For High School Students with Disabilities refers to the ordinance that every public school district in the United States must provide all students with disabilities ages 3 through 21 with an individualized and free appropriate public education in the least restrictive environment. President Gerald R. Ford established this right when in 1975 he signed Public Law 94-142, the Education of All Handicapped Children Act (EAHCA). Parents of children with disabilities and other advocates hailed EAHCA as the "education civil rights act" for their children.

History

The Act was reauthorized in 1983, 1990, 1997, and 2004. In 1997 the Act was renamed The Individuals with Disabilities Education Act. Most recently, President George W. Bush signed the Act into law on December 3, 2004 (Public Law 108-446).

Public Law 108-446, the Individuals with Disabilities Education Act of 2004, is most commonly called IDEA 2004. Following enactment, the U.S. Department of Education took nearly two years to develop the federal regulations to answer common questions about critical parts of the law. The final draft of the federal regulations were published August 14, 2006, and took effect 60 days later, October 13, 2006. To some extent, the federal regulations clarify how the law should be put into practice. In some areas the final implementation of the law is up to the state educational agencies (SEAs) and local educational agencies (LEAs)—the public school districts.

IDEA 2004 continues granting to students with disabilities the right to a public education. IDEA 2004 continues regulating the special education services provided to these students through the SEAs and the public schools. Most notably, IDEA 2004 emphasizes preparing students with disabilities, ages 16 (or younger) through 21, for life beyond high school.

From "Get'em in"—to "Get'em through"—and now "Get'em Ready!"

An Act in Three Stages

The intent of the law changed over time in keeping with increasingly improved understandings of the needs of students with disabilities. PL 94-142, 'stage one,' purposed to "Get'em in"—opening the doors of public schools to students with disabilities.

The informal 'second stage' seeks to "Get'em through." This phase continues and overlaps with 'stage three.' Educators, related services staff, personnel from non-LEA agencies and parents alike work to keep students with disabilities from dropping out. In the best of situations, all are working together to enable the students to graduate with well-deserved general education diplomas.

In the informal 'third stage,' IDEA 2004 most practically directs special education service providers to "Get'em ready," preparing students for further education, employment, and independent living.

Further Underscores Transition

IDEA 2004 builds upon the amendments and reauthorizations of 1983, 1990, and 1997, clarifies the concept and position of transition, and strengthens the future-focus of special education services. IDEA 2004 indicates one of its purposes is "...to ensure that all children with disabilities have available to them a free appropriate publ education that emphasizes special education and related services designed to me their unique needs and prepare them for *further* education, employment and independent living..." (author emphasis). The key word "further" emphasizes the direction and purpose and expected results of this special education legislation.

From Breaking Down the Walls to Looking Beyond the Walls

Educational Near-sightedness no Longer

No longer will teachers be permitted to restrict their vision of education to the four walls of the classroom and the four years of high school. The focus is on the future. One constraining influence is the 'other' education legislation—the No Child Left Behind Act of 2001 (NCLB). NCLB constantly pulls special education services and resources towards standardized testing and improving test scores. IDEA 2004 continuously counteracts by emphasizing individualized education and individualized preparation of individual children with disabilities for their individual lives in their individual communities beyond high school.

IDEA 2004 and the accompanying regulations most clearly reflect the focus on the future through the many uses of the word "transition" when it comes to directing the high school education and activities of children with disabilities: transition, transition planning, transition assessments, transition services, transition service providers.

An effective transition plan, in the eyes of many, drives middle school students' and high school students' IEPs Individualized Education Programmes (IEPs). IDEA 2004 highlights post secondary goals and putting in place transition services, including courses of study, to facilitate the students' movement from high school to post high school life.

EI to ECE Transition in IDEA 2004

Within IDEA 2004, the word "transition" has several different definitions according to its context in the Act.

In IDEA 2004, transition describes the process of a young child moving from early intervention services (EI) to early childhood education (ECE). In this EI to ECE process, transition indicates moving young children from one environment, set of services, and service personnel to another: "...the steps to be taken to support the transition of the toddler with a disability to preschool or other appropriate services." It also indicates moving from one set of entitlements to another, "...a child who is transitioning from Part C of the Act to Part B and is no longer eligible for Part C services because the child has turned 3..."

Post-secondary Transition in IDEA 2004

When talking about post-secondary transition the context is "...services and activities for older students (e.g., transition services, post-secondary goals)." But unlike the EI services to ECE transition, the high school students only start in the position of receiving entitlements—entitlements to services. The students who leave, whether by graduation, aging out, or dropping out, leave to a condition of possible eligibility for services, with no absolute guarantee by law that they will continue to receive services.

One of the consequences, then, is an urgency to help students with disabilities make the most of the time they are in high school, while some funding, at least, is available, to prepare for post high school life.

IDEA 2004 Citations Related to Post-secondary Transition

References to the Act and the corresponding regulations within this article on post secondary transition are from FR Doc 06-6656 [Federal Register: August 14, 2006 (Volume 71, Number 156)] [Rules and Regulations [Page 46539-46845] From the Federal Register Online via GPO Access.

Transition Services, Post-secondary Goals, and Transition Assessments

These include: "(b) Transition services. Beginning not later than the first IEP to be in effect when the child turns 16, or younger if determined appropriate by the IEP Team, and updated annually, thereafter, the IEP must include–

> "(aa) appropriate measurable postsecondary goals based upon age appropriate transition assessments related to training, education, employment, and where appropriate independent living skills;
> "(bb) the transition services (including courses of study) needed to assist the child in reaching those goals..."

Transition Services

Section 300.43 Transition services include:
(*a*) Transition services means a coordinated set of activities for a child with a disability that—

"(1) Is designed to be within a results-oriented process, that is focused on improving the academic and functional achievement of the child with a disability to facilitate the child's movement from school to post-school activities, including postsecondary education, vocational education, integrated employment (including supported employment), continuing and adult education, adult services, independent living, or community participation;

"(2) Is based on the individual child's needs, taking into account the child's strengths, preferences, and interests; and includes—

"(*i*) Instruction;
"(*ii*) Related services;

"*(iii)* Community experiences;

"*(iv)* The development of employment and other post-school adult living objectives; and

"*(v)* If appropriate, acquisition of daily living skills and provision of a functional vocational evaluation.

(b) Transition services for children with disabilities may be special education, if provided as specially designed instruction, or a related service, if required to assist a child with a disability to benefit from special education. "[(Authority: 20 U.S.C. 1401(34)]"

Transition—IEP Participants

"*(b)* Transition services participants.

"(1) In accordance with paragraph (a)(7) of this section, the public agency must invite a child with a disability to attend the child's IEP Team meeting if a purpose of the meeting will be the consideration of the postsecondary goals for the child and the transition services needed to assist the child in reaching those goals under Sec. 300.320(b).

"(2) If the child does not attend the IEP Team meeting, the public agency must take other steps to ensure that the child's preferences and interests are considered.

"(3) To the extent appropriate, with the consent of the parents or a child who has reached the age of majority, in implementing the requirements of paragraph (b)(1) of this section, the public agency must invite a representative of any participating agency that is likely to be responsible for providing or paying for transition services."

Parental Consent and Notification

"(2) For a child with a disability beginning not later than the first IEP to be in effect when the child turns 16, or younger if determined appropriate by the IEP Team, the notice also must–

"*(i)* Indicate–

"*(A)* That a purpose of the meeting will be the consideration of the postsecondary goals and transition services for the child, in accordance with Sec. 300.320(b); and

"*(B)* That the agency will invite the student; and

"*(ii)* Identify any other agency that will be invited to send a representative.

"(2) Parental consent, or the consent of an eligible child who has reached the age of majority under State law, must be obtained before personally identifiable information is released to officials of participating agencies providing or paying for transition services in accordance with Sec. 300.321(b)(3)."

Non-LEA Agencies not Meeting Transition Commitments

"*(c)* Failure to meet transition objectives—

"(1) Participating agency failure. If a participating agency, other than the public agency, fails to provide the transition services described in the IEP in accordance with Sec. 300.320(b), the public agency must reconvene the IEP Team to identify alternative strategies to meet the transition objectives for the child set out in the IEP.

"(2) Construction. Nothing in this part relieves any participating agency, including a State vocational rehabilitation agency, of the responsibility to provide or pay for any transition service that the agency would otherwise provide to children with disabilities who meet the eligibility criteria of that agency."

State Performance Plans Put "Teeth" into IDEA 2004 Transition Requirements

Where's the teeth? As of 2005, the federal government will monitor transition plans for students with disabilities. The anticipated results of the monitoring will be improvements in the post school results for students with disabilities, made possible through the improvement of in-school educational programmes.

Monitoring

The monitoring will happen through three related vehicles.

- State Performance Plan (SPP) (and especially Indicators 1, 2, 13 and 14)
- Annual Performance Report (APR)
- Continuous Improvement Focused Monitoring Process (CIFMP).

Early years of the monitoring focus on establishing a baseline for transition plans, and beyond that the federal and state governments will be using the data collection and analysis results to approve, inform, direct, and assist local school districts in the improvement of their educational programmes.

Transition for Students Means a Transition for Teachers

Planning for the future of the individual student often requires a paradigm shift for everyone involved. With the IEP that is in effect the year the student turns 16, the IEPs often make a subtle change from overcoming deficits and approaching developmental norms to post secondary goals, transition plan activities and transition services that capitalize on the students' strengths, needs, preferences, and interests.

The special education professional community is working hard to catch up with this change in emphasis, and certainly many believe that it has a long way to go. At this point, nearly 6½ million children receive special education services. However, few college programmes, like those at the University of Wisconsin Whitewater are preparing the next generation of professional educators to become effective in the transition planning and preparation process.

An Electronic Checklist Simplifies Transition Planning

The Department of Education is working hard to clarify the content of IDEA 2004 to the state directors of special education, the state transition specialists, and the national secondary transition technical support staff. Meanwhile, LEA directors of special education and special education teachers across the country are working and periodically struggling to get their arms around post secondary transition, what it means, and how it affects the education of their students.

One of the promising means of guiding students and teachers through the maze of transition involves deploying corporate research-based technologies used for decades in private industry. In 1999, the Office of Special Education and Rehabilitative Services provided two grants to fund research into the feasibility of adapting existing technology. The research launched a web-based, commercially available product in use by teachers and parents primarily in Illinois and Minnesota but increasingly around the country.

UNDERSTANDING UNIVERSAL DESIGN AND ITS RELEVANCE

Universal design is a relatively new paradigm that emerged from "barrier-free" or "accessible design" and "assistive technology." Universal design strives to be a broad-spectrum solution that produces buildings, products and environments that are usable and effective for everyone, not just people with disabilities. Moreover, it recognizes the importance of how things look. For example, while built up handles are a way to make utensils more usable for people with gripping limitations, some companies introduced larger, easy to grip and attractive handles as feature of mass produced utensils. They appeal to a wide range of consumers.

As life expectancy rises and modern medicine has increased the survival rate of those with significant injuries, illnesses and birth defects, there is a growing interest in universal design. There are many industries in which universal design is having strong market penetration but there are many others in which it has not yet been adopted to any great extent.

Universal design is a part of everyday living and is all around us. The "undo" command in most software products is a good example. Colour-contrast dish ware with steep sides that assist those with visual problems as well as those with dexterity problems are another. Additional examples include cabinets with pull-out shelves, kitchen counters at several heights to accommodate different tasks and postures and low-floor buses that kneel and are equipped with ramps rather than lifts.

The Principles of Universal Design

"The authors, a working group of architects, product designers, engineers and environmental design researchers, collaborated to establish the following Principles of Universal Design to guide a wide range of design disciplines including environments, products, and communications."

1. Equitable use

2. Flexibility in use
3. Simple and intuitive
4. Perceptible information
5. Tolerance for error
6. Low physical effort
7. Size and space for approach and use.

These principles are broader than that of accessible design.

Examples

- Ramps at A-Tech
- Smooth ground surfaces of entranceways, without stairs
- Wide interior doors and hallways
- Lever handles for opening doors rather than twisting knobs
- Light switches with large flat panels rather than small toggle switches
- Buttons on control panels that can be distinguished by touch
- Bright and appropriate lighting, particularly task lighting
- Auditory output redundant with information on visual displays
- Visual output redundant with information in auditory output
- Contrast controls on visual output
- Use of meaningful icons as well as text labels
- Clear lines of sight (to reduce dependence on sound)
- Volume controls on auditory output
- Speed controls on auditory output
- Choice of language on speech output
- Ramp access in swimming pools
- Closed captioning on television networks.

Design Standards

In October 2003, representatives from China, Japan, and South Korea met in Beijing and agreed to set up a committee to define common design standards for a wide range of products and services that are easy to understand and use. Their goal is to publish a standard in 2004 which covers, among other areas, standards on containers and wrappings of household goods (based on a proposal from experts in Japan), and standardization of signs for public facilities, a subject which was of particular interest to China as prepared to host the 2008 Summer Olympics.

The International Organization for Standardization, the European Committee for Electrotechnical Standardization, and the International Electrotechnical Commission have developed:

- [1]; CEN/CENELEC Guide 6. Guidelines for standards developers to address the needs of older persons and persons with disabilities (Identical to ISO/IEC Guide 71, but free for download)

These standards are still under development:

- ISO 20282-1—Ease of operation of everyday products—Part 1: Context of use and user characteristics
- ISO 20282-2—Ease of operation of everyday products—Part 2: Test method.

UNDERSTANDING ACCESSIBILITY AND ITS IMPORTANCE

Accessibility is a general term used to describe the degree to which a product (e.g., device, service, environment) is accessible by as many people as possible. Accessibility can be viewed as the "ability to access" the functionality, and possible benefit, of some system or entity. Accessibility is often used to focus on people with disabilities and their right of access to entities, often through use of assistive technology. Several definitions of accessibility refer directly to access-based individual rights laws and regulations. Products or services designed to meet these regulations are often termed *Easy Access* or *Accessible.*

Accessibility is not to be confused with usability which is used to describe the extent to which a product (e.g., device, service, environment) can be used by specified users to achieve specified goals with effectiveness, efficiency and satisfaction in a specified context of use.

Accessibility is strongly related to universal design when the approach involves "direct access." This is about making things accessible to all people (whether they have a disability or not). However, products marketed as having benefited from a Universal Design process are often actually the same devices customized specifically for use by people with disabilities. An alternative is to provide "indirect access" by having the entity support the use of a person's assistive technology to achieve access (e.g., screen reader).

Disabilities

The disability rights movement advocates equal access to social, political, and economic life which includes not only physical access but access to the same tools, services, organizations and facilities which we all pay for.

While it is often used to describe facilities or amenities to assist people with disabilities, as in "wheelchair accessible", the term can extend to Braille signage, wheelchair ramps, elevators, audio signals at pedestrian crossings, walkway contours, website design, reading accessibility, and so on.

Various countries have legislation requiring physical accessibility which are (in order of enactment):

- In the US, under the Americans with Disabilities Act of 1990, new public and private business construction generally must be accessible. Existing private businesses are required to increase the accessibility of their facilities when making any other renovations in proportion to the cost of the other renovations. The U.S. Access Board is "A Federal Agency Committed to Accessible Design for People with Disabilities." The Job Accommodation Network discusses accommodations for people with disabilities in the workplace. Many states in the US have their own disability laws.

- In Australia, Disability Discrimination Act 1992 has numerous provisions for accessibility.
- In the UK, the Disability Discrimination Act 1995 has numerous provisions for accessibility.
- In South Africa The Promotion of Equality and the Prevention of Unfair Discrimination Act 2000 has numerous provisions for accessibility.
- In Ontario, Canada, the Ontarians with Disabilities Act of 2001 is meant to "improve the identification, removal and prevention of barriers faced by persons with disabilities..."

Transportation

In transportation, accessibility refers to the ease of reaching destinations. People who are in places that are highly accessible can reach many other activities or destinations quickly, people in inaccessible places can reach many fewer places in the same amount of time.

A measure that is often used is to measure accessibility in a traffic analysis zone *i* is:

$$Accessbility_i = \sum_j Opportunities_j \times f\,(C_{ij}) \text{ where:}$$

- i = index of origin zones
- j = index of destination zones
- $f\,(C_{ij})$ = function of generalized travel cost (so that nearer or less expensive places are weighted more than farther or more expensive places).

For a non-motorized mode of transport, such as walking or cycling, the generalized travel cost may include additional factors such as safety or gradient.

Automobile accessibility also refers to ease of use by disabled people.

Accessibility Planning

In the United Kingdom, the Department for Transport have mandated that each local authority produce an Accessibility Plan that is incorporated in their Local Transport Plan. An Accessibility Plan sets out how each local authority plans to improve access to employment, learning, health care, food shops and other services of local importance, particularly for disadvantaged groups and areas. Accessibility targets are defined in the accessibility plans, these are often the distance or time to access services by different modes of transport including walking, cycling and public transport.

Accessibility Planning was introduced as a result of the report "Making the Connections: Final Report on Transport and Social Exclusion." This report was the result of research carried out by the Social Exclusion Unit.

Low Floor

A significant development in transportation, and public transport in particular, to achieve accessibility, is the move to "low floor" vehicles. In a low floor vehicle, access to part or all of the passenger cabin is unobstructed from one or more entrances by the presence of steps, enabling easier access for the infirm or people with push chairs. A further aspect may be that the entrance and corridors are wide enough to accommodate a wheelchair. Low floor vehicles have been developed for buses, trolleybuses and trams.

Low floor in the vehicular sense is normally combined in a conceptual meaning with normal pedestrian access from a standard kerb height. However, the accessibility of a low floor vehicle can also be utilised from slightly raising portions of kerb at bus stops, or through use of level boarding bus rapid transit 'stations' or tram stops. The combination of access from a kerb was the technological development of the 1990s, as step free interior layouts for buses had existed in some cases for decades, with entrance steps being introduced as chassis designs and overall height regulations changed.

Low-floor buses may also be designed with special height adjustment controls that permit a stationary bus to temporarily lower itself to ground level, permitting wheelchair access. This is referred to as a kneeling bus.

Housing

Most existing and new housing, even in the wealthiest nations, lack basic accessibility features unless the designated, immediate occupant of a home currently has a disability. However, there are some initiatives to change typical residential practices so that new homes incorporate basic access features such as zero-step entries and door widths adequate for wheelchairs to pass through. Occupational Therapists are a professional group skilled in the assessment and making of recommendations to improve access to homes. They are involved in both the adaptation of existing housing to improve accessibility, and in the design of future housing.

Great Britain applies the most widespread application of home access to date. In 1999, Parliament passed Section M, an amendment to residential building regulations requiring basic access in all new homes. ("Doors to Be Swept Away in New Rules for Builders", Rachel Kelley, The Times, December 5, 1997.) In the United States, the 1988 Amendments to the Fair Housing Act added people with disabilities, as well as familial status, to the classes already protected by law from discrimination (race, colour, sex, religion and country of origin). Among the protection for people with disabilities in the 1988 Amendments are seven construction requirements for all multifamily buildings of more than four units first occupied after March 13, 1991. These seven requirements are as follows:

1. An accessible building entrance on an accessible route.
2. Accessible common and public use areas.
3. Doors usable by a person in a wheelchair.

4. Accessible route into and through the dwelling unit.
5. Light switches, electrical outlets, thermostats and other environmental controls in accessible locations.
6. Reinforced walls in bathrooms for later installation of grab bars.
7. Usable kitchens and bathrooms.

(From Fair Housing First, a website sponsored by the U.S. Department of Housing and Urban Development).

Access is typically defined within the limits of what a person sitting in a wheelchair is able to reach with arm movement only, with minimal shifting of the legs and torso. As such lighting and thermostat controls should not be above and power outlets should not be below the reach of a wheelchair bound person.

Sinks and cooking areas typically need to be designed without cupboards below them, to permit the legs of the wheelchair user to roll underneath, and countertops may be of reduced height to accommodate a sitting rather than standing user. In some cases two food preparation areas may be combined into a single kitchen to permit both standing and wheelchair users.

In spite of these advancements, the housing types where most people in the United States reside—single-family homes—are not covered by the Americans with Disabilities Act, the Fair Housing Act, or any other federal law with the exception of the small percentage of publicly-funded homes impacted by Section 504 of the Rehabilitation Act. As a result, the great majority of new single-family homes replicate the barriers in existing homes.

The broad concept of Universal Design is relevant to housing, as it is to all aspects of the built environment. Furthermore, a Visitability movement begun by grassroots disability advocates in the 1980s focuses specifically on changing construction practices in new housing. This movement, a network of interested people working in their locales, works on educating, passing laws, and spurring voluntary home access initiatives with the intention that basic access become a routine part of new home construction.

Adaptations and Accommodations

Many ranch style homes and manufactured homes utilize a main floor slightly raised above ground level, but have an overall flat layout with either a crawlspace or slightly raised basement below for plumbing, electrical, and heating systems. These homes can be relatively easily modified to accommodate wheelchairs and walkers, with the installation of a long low-rise ramp outside the buiding, up to the house entrance, placed over the existing stairway. This ramp can then be removed at a later time, reverting back to the stairway entrance if the handicapped access is no longer necessary.

Split level homes tend to be designed with multiple internal stairways and half-floor landings inside the building. There may be an entrance area inside the building at ground level, with stairs inside the entrance that immediately go up and down from the ground level. These homes are difficult to accommodate inexpensively since there is often no space available inside the structure to install long sloping wheelchair ramps to access the various floors. It may be possible to retrofit stair lifts into the stairwells or wheelchair lifts into balconies near the stairwell.

Multi-storey homes can sometimes be accommodated by installing a private residential elevator, which is usually much less expensive and has fewer design and layout requirements than a full commercial elevator. Homebuilders can in some cases plan for a future residential elevator by designing closet spaces in each floor stacked vertically with the same dimensions and location. At a later time the closet floors and ceilings are removed and the elevator equipment is installed into the open shaft.

Telecommunications and IT Access

Another dimension of accessibility is the ability to access information and services by minimizing the barriers of distance and cost as well as the usability of the interface. In many countries this has led to initiatives, laws and regulations that aim toward providing universal access to the internet and to phone systems at reasonable cost to citizens.

Currently there are a few major movements to coordinate a set of guidelines for accessibility for the web. The first and most well-known is The Web Accessibility Initiative (WAI), which is part of the World Wide Web Consortium (W3C). This organization developed the Web Content Accessibility Guidelines (WCAG) 1.0 which explains how to make Web content accessible to people with disabilities. Web "content" generally refers to the information in a Web page or Web application, including text, images, forms, sounds, and such. (More specific definitions are available in the WCAG documents.)

The WCAG is separated into 3 levels of compliance, A, AA and AAA. Each level requires a stricter set of conformance guidelines, such as different versions of HTML (Transitional *vs* Strict) and other techniques that need to be incorporated into your code before accomplishing validation. Online tools such as the Watchfire WebXACT engine or the imergo Web Compliance Manager will allow users to submit their website and automatically run it through the WCAG guidelines and produce a report, stating whether or not they conform to each level of compliance. Adobe Dreamweaver also offers plugins which allow web developers to test these guidelines on their work from within the programme.

Another source of web accessibility guidance comes from the US government. Section 508 of the US Rehabilitation Act is a comprehensive set of rules designed to help web designers make their sites accessible. They have also developed a website where you can take online training course for free to learn about these rules.

In general, for a website to comply with accessibility standards, they should at least have the following:

- (X) HTML Validation from the W3C for the pages content
- CSS Validation from the W3C for the pages layout

- At least WAI-AA (preferably AAA) compliance with the WAI's WCAG
- Compliance with all guidelines from Section 508 of the US Rehabilitation Act
- Access keys built into the HTML
- Semantic Web Markup
- A high contrast version of the site for individuals with low vision
- Alternative media for any multimedia used on the site (video, flash, audio, etc.)

Another good idea is for websites to include a web accessibility statement on the site. This page details the accessible status of the page, lists access keys and can display which validations have been achieved for the site as well as include their pledge for accessibility. Example of an accessibility statement.

Meeting and Conference Access

Meetings and conferences should consider the needs of all of their participants. Checklists such as this may make it easier to identify specific needs:

Mobility access:

- Wheelchair accessible transportation
- Reserved parking
- Barrier-free meeting rooms/restrooms/podium/speaker's platform
- Handicap accessible lodging.

Hearing access:

- Advance copies of papers
- An assistive listening system
- Sign language interpreters
- A quiet place to gather for social conversation (a quieter space that is still visible to others should be reserved at social events or dinners so that people who are hard of hearing may go there to talk with their colleagues.)
- TTY access or Internet-based TRS.

Sight access:

- Large print/braille copies of the programme and papers
- A student volunteer to guide and describe the artwork, computer work, etc.
- A tech to help with assistive devices and screen readers (e.g., JAWS reader)
- Gloves to touch three dimensional work (where permissible).

Other issues:

- Notification if social events include flashing lights and noises (these can cause seizures, so either avoid them or announce them ahead of time)

- Notices asking participants to refrain from allergy-producing problems (e.g., perfumes)
- Inform food providers of food allergies (e.g., peanuts, shellfish, etc.)
- Referral information for local personal care attendant agencies
- Referral information for veterinarian care for service animals
- Access to a place to rest during the day (if the conference venue is far from the lodgings).

Test Accessibility

With the passage of the No Child Left Behind Act of 2001, student accountability in essential content areas such as reading, mathematics, and science has become a major area of focus in educational reform. As a result, test developers have needed to create tests to ensure all students, including those with special needs (e.g., students identified with disabilities), are given the opportunity to demonstrate proficiency on state assessments. Currently, states are permitted to develop two different types of tests in addition to the standard grade-level assessments to target students with special needs. First, the alternate assessment may be used to report proficiency for up to 1 per cent of students in a state. Second, new regulations permit the use of alternate assessments based on modified academic achievement standards to report proficiency for up to 2 per cent of students in a state.

To ensure these new tests generate results that permit valid inferences about student performance, they must be accessible to as many individuals as possible. The Test Accessibility and Modification Inventory (TAMI) was developed for this purpose. Integrating principles of universal design, assessment accessibility, cognitive load theory, and research on item-writing and test development, the TAMI is a decision-making tool designed to facilitate a comprehensive analysis of tests and test items to enhance their accessibility for all students. The TAMI is a non-commercial instrument that has been made available to all state assessment directors and testing companies.

UNDERSTANDING BARRIER-FREE DESIGNS AND ITS IMPLICATIONS

Barrier-free building modification consists of modifying buildings or facilities so that they can be used by the physically disadvantaged or disabled. The term is used primarily in Japan, while in English-speaking countries, terms such as "accessibility" and "handicapped accessible" dominate in regular everyday use.

An example would be installing a ramp for wheelchairs alongside or in place of some steps. The idea of barrier free modification has largely been superseded by the concept of universal design, which seeks to design things from the outset to support easy access. This latter approach usually leads to lower total cost. However, with pre-existing structures, barrier free may be the most appropriate or only valid approach.

Freeing a Building of Barriers Means

- recognising the features that could form barriers for some people

- thinking inclusively about the whole range of impairments
- reviewing everything—from structure to smallest detail
- seeking feedback from users and learning from mistakes.

Barrier Free *vs.* ADA

Barrier free is also a term that applies to handicap accessibility in situations where legal codes such as the Americans with Disabilities Act of 1990 Guidelines don't make specifications.

UNDERSTANDING THE ROLE OF EDUCATIONAL TECHNOLOGY

Educational technology (also called learning technology) is the study and ethical practice of facilitating learning and improving performance by creating, using and managing appropriate technological processes and resources." The term educational technology is often associated with, and encompasses, instructional theory and learning theory. While instructional technology covers the processes and systems of learning and instruction, educational technology includes other systems used in the process of developing human capability. Educational Technology includes, but is not limited to, software, hardware, as well as Internet applications and activities.

Perspectives and Meaning

Educational technology is most simply and comfortably defined as an array of tools that might prove helpful in advancing student learning. Educational Technology relies on a broad definition of the word "technology." Technology can refer to material objects of use to humanity, such as machines or hardware, but it can also encompass broader themes, including systems, methods of organization, and techniques. Some modern tools include but are not limited to overhead projectors, laptop computers, and calculators. Newer tools such as "smartphones" and games (both online and offline) are beginning to draw serious attention for their learning potential.

Those who employ educational technologies to explore ideas and communicate meaning are learners or teachers.

Consider the *Handbook of Human Performance Technology*. The word technology for the sister fields of Educational and Human Performance Technology means "applied science." In other words, any valid and reliable process or procedure that is derived from basic research using the "scientific method" is considered a "technology." Educational or Human Performance Technology may be based purely on algorithmic or heuristic processes, but neither necessarily implies physical technology. The word technology, comes from the Greek "Techne" which means craft or art. Another word "technique", with the same origin, also may be used when considering the field Educational technology. So Educational technology may be extended to include the techniques of the educator.

A classic example of an Educational Psychology text is Bloom's 1956 book, *Taxonomy of Educational Objectives*. Bloom's taxonomy is helpful when designing learning activities to keep in mind what is expected of–and what are the learning goals for–learners. However, Bloom's work does not explicitly deal with educational technology *per se* and is more concerned with pedagogical strategies.

According to some, an Educational Technologist is someone who transforms basic educational and psychological research into an evidence-based applied science (or a technology) of learning or instruction. Educational Technologists typically have a graduate degree (Master's, Doctorate, Ph.D., or D.Phil.) in a field related to educational psychology, educational media, experimental psychology, cognitive psychology or, more purely, in the fields of Educational, Instructional or Human Performance Technology or Instructional (Systems) Design. But few of those listed below as theorists would ever use the term "educational technologist" as a term to describe themselves, preferring terms like "educator." The transformation of educational technology from a cottage industry to a profession is discussed by Shurville, Browne, and Whitaker.

History

One comprehensive history of the field is Saettler's *The evolution of American educational technology*. Another worthy title is Larry Cuban's *Oversold and Underused—Computers in the Classroom*.

For several decades, vendors of equipment such as laptop computers and interactive white boards have been claiming that their technologies would transform classrooms and learning in many positive ways, but there has been little evidence provided to substantiate these claims.

To some extent, the history of educational technology has been marked by a succession of innovations that arrive with much fanfare but often fade into the background once fully tested, as Cuban argues in the above title.

Theories and Practices

Three main theoretical schools or philosophical frameworks have been present in the educational technology literature. These are Behaviourism, Cognitivism and Constructivism. Each of these schools of thought are still present in today's literature but have evolved as the Psychology literature has evolved.

Behaviourism

This theoretical framework was developed in the early 20th century with the animal learning experiments of Ivan Pavlov, Edward Thorndike, Edward C. Tolman, Clark L. Hull, B.F. Skinner and many others. Many psychologists used these theories to describe and experiment with human learning. While still very useful this philosophy of learning has lost favour with many educators.

Skinner's Contributions

B.F. Skinner wrote extensively on improvements of teaching based on his functional analysis of Verbal Behaviour, and wrote "The Technology of Teaching", an attempt to dispel the myths underlying contemporary education, as well as promote his system he called programmed instruction. Ogden Lindsley also developed the Celeration learning system similarly based on behaviour analysis but quite different from Keller's and Skinner's models.

Cognitivism

Cognitive science has changed how educators view learning. Since the very early beginning of the Cognitive Revolution of the 1960s and 1970s, learning theory has undergone a great deal of change. Much of the empirical framework of Behaviourism was retained even though a new paradigm had begun. Cognitive theories look beyond behaviour to explain brain-based learning. Cognitivists consider how human memory works to promote learning.

After memory theories like the Atkinson-Shiffrin memory model and Baddeley's Working memory model were established as a theoretical framework in Cognitive Psychology, new cognitive frameworks of learning began to emerge during the 1970s, 80s, and 90s. It is important to note that Computer Science and Information Technology have had a major influence on Cognitive Science theory. The Cognitive concepts of working memory (formerly known as short-term memory) and long-term memory have been facilitated by research and technology from the field of Computer Science. Another major influence on the field of Cognitive Science is Noam Chomsky. Today researchers are concentrating on topics like Cognitive load and Information Processing Theory.

Constructivism

Constructivism is a learning theory or educational philosophy that many educators began to consider in the 1990s. One of the primary tenets of this philosophy is that learners construct their own meaning from new information, as they interact with reality or others with different perspectives.

Constructivist learning environments require students to utilize their prior knowledge and experiences to formulate new, related, and/or adaptive concepts in learning. Under this framework the role of the teacher becomes that of a facilitator, providing guidance so that learners can construct their own knowledge. Constructivist educators must make sure that the prior learning experiences are appropriate and related to the concepts being taught. Jonassen (1997) suggests "well-structured" learning environments are useful for novice learners and that "ill-structured" environments are only useful for more advanced learners. Educators utilizing technology when teaching with a constructivist perspective should choose technologies that reinforce prior learning perhaps in a problem-solving environment.

Connectivism

Connectivism is "a learning theory for the digital age," and has been developed by George Siemens and Stephen Downes based on their analysis of the limitations of behaviourism, cognitivism and constructivism to explain the effect technology has had on how we live, how we communicate, and how we learn. Donald G. Perrin, Executive Editor of the International Journal of Instructional Technology and Distance Learning says the theory "combines relevant elements of many learning theories, social structures, and technology to create a powerful theoretical construct for learning in the digital age."

Instructional Technique and Technologies

Problem Based Learning and Inquiry-based learning are active learning educational technologies used to facilitate learning. Technology which includes physical and process applied science can be incorporated into project, problem, inquiry-based learning as they all have a similar educational philosophy. All three are student centered, ideally involving real-world scenarios in which students are actively engaged in critical thinking activities. The process that students are encouraged to employ (as long as it is based on empirical research) is considered to be a technology. Classic examples of technologies used by teachers and Educational Technologists include Bloom's Taxonomy and Instructional Design.

Theorists

This is an area where new thinkers are coming to the forefront everyday. Many of the ideas spread from theorists, researchers, and experts through their blogs. Extensive lists of educational bloggers by area of interest are available at Steve Hargadon's "SupportBloggers" site or at the "movingforward" wiki started by Scott McLeod. Many of these blogs are recognized by their peers each year through the edublogger awards. Web 2.0 technologies have led to a huge increase in the amount of information available on this topic and the number of educators formally and informally discussing it. Most listed below have been around for more than a decade, however, and few new thinkers mentioned above are listed here.

- Hall Davidson
- Lawrence Tomei
- Karl Fisch
- Ian Jukes[
- Jamie McKenzie, Ed.D.
- Scott McLeod
- Jonathan Mott
- Frank Grimes
- Alan November

- Seymour Papert
- Will Richardson
- Gary Stager
- John Sweller
- Alex Jones
- Joyce Kazman Valenza
- David Warlick
- David Marcovitz
- George Siemens
- David Wiley.

Benefits

Educational technology is intended to improve education over what it would be without technology. Some of the claimed benefits are listed below:

- *Easy-to-access course materials.* Instructors can post the course material or important information on a course website, which means students can study at a time and location they prefer and can obtain the study material very quickly.
- *Student motivation.* Computer-based instruction can give instant feedback to students and explain correct answers. Moreover, computer is patient and non-judgemental, which can give the student motivation to continue learning. According to James Kulik, who studies effectiveness of computers used for instruction, students usually learn more in less time when receiving computer-based instruction and they like classes more and develop more positive attitudes toward computers in computer-based classes.
- *Wide participation.* Learning material can be used for long distance learning and are accessible.
- *Improved student writing.* It is convenient for students to edit their written work on word processors, which in turn improves the quality of their writing. According to some studies, the students are better at critiquing and editing written work that is exchanged over a computer network with students they know.
- *Subjects made easier to learn.* Many different types of educational software are designed and developed to help children or teenagers to learn specific subjects. Examples include pre-school software, computer simulators, and graphics software.
- A structure that is more amenable to measurement and improvement of outcomes.

Criticism

Similarly to learning a new task or trade, there is special training that is involved with adding elements of educational technology to the classroom. Without proper training, teachers and students cannot benefit from devices that will improve the quality of education. Devices are a waste of time and money if teachers are not receiving proper training. Another disadvantage is that if teachers plan on using educational technology, they must come to the classroom prior to start time and set everything up and make sure it is all working.

Educational Technology and the Humanities

Research from the Alberta Initiative for School Improvement (AISI) indicates that inquiry and project-based approaches, combined with a focus on curriculum, effectively supports the infusion of educational technologies into the learning and teaching process.

Technology in the Classroom

- *Computer in the Classroom:* Having a computer in the classroom is an asset to any teacher. With a computer in the classroom, teachers are able to demonstrate a new lesson, present new material, illustrate how to use new programmes, and show new websites.
- *Class Website:* What better way to display your student's work, than to create a web page designed just for your class. Once a web page is designed, teachers can post homework assignments, student work, famous quotes, trivia games, and so much more. In current day society, children know how to use the computer and navigate their way through a website, so why not give them one where they can be a published author.
- *Wireless Classroom Microphones:* Noisy classrooms are a daily occurrence, and with the help of microphones, students are able to hear their teachers clearer. Children learn better when they hear the teacher clearly. The benefit for teachers is that they no longer lose their voices at the end of the day.

Societies

Learned societies concerned with educational technology include:

- Association for the Advancement of Computing in Education (AACE)
- Association for Educational Communications and Technology
- Association for Learning Technology
- International Society for Technology in Education—(ISTE)
- Northwest Council for Computer Education
- Computer-Using Educators.

ROLE OF ASSISTIVE TECHNOLOGY

Assistive technology (AT) is a generic term that includes assistive, adaptive, and rehabilitative devices for people with disabilities and includes the process used in selecting, locating, and using them.

The Technology-Related Assistance for Individuals with Disabilities Act of 1988 (US Public Law 100-407) states that it is "technology designed to be utilized in an assistive technology device or assistive technology service."

AT promotes greater independence by enabling people to perform tasks that they were formerly unable to accomplish, or had great difficulty accomplishing, by providing enhancements to or changed methods of interacting with the technology needed to accomplish such tasks.

Likewise, disability advocates point out that technology is often created without regard to people with disabilities, creating unnecessary barriers to hundreds of millions of people.

Assistive Technology and Universal Accessibility

Universal (or broadened) accessibility, or universal design means greater usability, particularly for people with disabilities.

Universally accessible technology yields great rewards to the typical user as well; good accessible design *is* universal design. One example is the "curb cuts" (or dropped curbs) in the sidewalk at street crossings. While these curb cuts enable pedestrians with mobility impairments to cross the street, they also aid parents with carriages and strollers, shoppers with carts, and travellers and workers with pull-type bags.

As an example, the modern telephone is inaccessible to people who are deaf or hard of hearing. Combined with a text telephone (also known as a TDD Telecommunications device for the deaf and in the USA generally called a TTY[TeleTYpewriter]), which converts typed characters into tones that may be sent over the telephone line, a deaf person is able to communicate immediately at a distance. Together with "relay" services, in which an operator reads what the deaf person types and types what a hearing person says, the deaf person is then given access to everyone's telephone, not just those of people who possess text telephones. Many telephones now have volume controls, which are primarily intended for the benefit of people who are hard of hearing, but can be useful for all users at times and places where there is significant background noise. Some have larger keys well-spaced to facilitate accurate dialling.

Also, a person with a mobility impairment can have difficulty using calculators. Speech recognition software recognizes short commands and makes use of calculators easier.

People with learning disabilities like dyslexia or dysgraphia are using text-to-speech (TTS) software for reading and spelling programmes for assistance in writing texts.

Computers with their peripheral devices, editing, spellchecking and speech synthesis software are becoming the core-stones of the assistive technologies coming for relief to the people with learning disabilities and to the people with visual impairments. The assisting spelling programmes and voice facilities are bringing better and more convenient text reading and writing experience to the general public.

Toys which have been adapted to be used by children with disabilities may have advantages for non-disabled children as well. The Lekotek movement assists parents by lending assistive technology toys and expertise to families.

The following professionals may be certified by RESNA (RESNA.org) to serve the assistive technology needs of individuals: occupational therapists, physical therapists, speech language pathologists/audiologists, orthotists and prosthetists, educators, and a variety of other rehabilitation and health professionals.

Assistive Technology Products

Personal Emergency Response Systems

Personal Emergency Response Systems (PERS), or Telecare (UK term), are a particular sort of assistive technology that use electronic sensors connected to an alarm system to help caregivers manage risk and help vulnerable people stay independent at home longer. An example would be the systems being put in place for senior people such as fall detectors, thermometers (for hypothermia risk), flooding and unlit gas sensors (for people with mild dementia). Notably, these alerts can be customized to the particular person's risks. When the alert is triggered, a message is sent to a carer or contact centre who can respond appropriately.

Technology similar to PERS can also be used to act within a person's home rather than just to respond to a detected crisis. Using one of the examples above, gas sensors for people with dementia can be used to trigger a device that turns off the gas and tells someone what has happened.

Designing for people with dementia is a good example of how the design of the interface of a piece of AT is critical to its usefulness. People with dementia or any other identified user group must be involved in the design process to make sure that the design is accessible and usable. In the example above, a voice message could be used to remind the person with dementia to turn off the gas himself, but whose voice should be used, and what should the message say? Questions like these must be answered through user consultation, involvement and evaluation.

Accessible Computer Input

Sitting at a desk with a QWERTY keyboard and a mouse remains the dominant way of interacting with a personal computer. Some Assistive Technology reduces the strain of this way of work through ergonomic accessories with height-adjustable furniture, footrests, wrist rests, and arm supports to ensure correct posture. Keyguards fit over the keyboard to help prevent unintentional keypresses.

Alternatively, Assistive Technology may attempt to improve the ergonomics of the devices themselves:

- Ergonomic keyboards reduce the discomfort and strain of typing.
- Chorded keyboards have a handful of keys (one per digit per hand) to type by 'chords' which produce different letters and keys.
- Expanded keyboards with larger, more widely-spaced keys.
- Compact and miniature keyboards.

- Dvorak and other alternative layouts may offer more ergonomic layouts of the keys. There are also variants of Dvorak in which the most common keys are located at either the left or right side of the keyboard.

Input devices may be modified to make them easier to see and understand:

- Keyboards with lowercase keys.
- Keyboards with big keys.
- Large print keyboard with high contrast colours (such as white on black, black on white, and black on ivory).
- Large print adhesive keyboard stickers in high contrast colours (such as white on black, black on white, and black on yellow).
- Embossed locator dots help find the 'home' keys, F and J, on the keyboard.
- Scroll wheels on mice remove the need to locate the scrolling interface on the computer screen.
- Footmouse—Foot-operated mouse.

More ambitiously, and quite crucially when keyboard or mouse prove unusable, AT can also replace the keyboard and mouse with alternative devices such as the LOMAK keyboard, trackballs, joysticks, graphics tablets, touchpads, touch screens, foot mice, a microphone with speech recognition software, sip-and-puff input, switch access, and vision-based input devices.

Software can also make input devices easier to use:

- Keyboard shortcuts and MouseKeys allow the user to substitute keyboarding for mouse actions. Macro recorders can greatly extend the range and sophistication of keyboard shortcuts.
- Sticky keys allows characters or commands to be typed without having to hold down a modifier key (Shift, Ctrl, Alt) while pressing a second key. Similarly, ClickLock is a Microsoft Windows feature that remembers a mouse button is down so that items can be highlighted or dragged without holding the mouse button down throughout.
- Customization of mouse or mouse alternatives' responsiveness to movement, double-clicking, and so forth.
- ToggleKeys is a feature of Microsoft Windows 95 onwards. A high sound is heard when the CAPS LOCK, SCROLL LOCK, or NUM LOCK key is switched on and a low sound is heard when any of those keys are switched off.
- Customization of pointer appearance, such as size, colour and shape.
- Predictive text.
- Spell checkers and grammar checkers.

Durable Medical Equipment (DME)

- Seating products that assist people to sit comfortably and safely (seating systems, cushions, therapeutic seats).

- Standing products to support people with disabilities in the standing position while maintaining/improving their health (standing frame, standing wheelchair, active stander).
- Walking products to aid people with disabilities who are able to walk or stand with assistance (canes, crutches, walkers, gait trainers).
- Advanced technology walking products to aid people with disabilities, such as paraplegia or cerebral palsy, who would not at all able to walk or stand (exoskeletons).
- Wheeled mobility products that enable people with reduced mobility to move freely indoors and outdoors (wheelchairs/scooters).
- Vehicles modified with Height adjustable suspension, to allow wheelchair entry to the vehicle.
- Robot-aided rehabilitation is a sensory-motor rehabilitation technique based on the use of robots and mechatronic devices.

Learning Difficulties

- Age-appropriate software
- Cause and effect software
- Hand-eye co-ordination skills software
- Diagnostic assessment software
- Mind mapping software
- Study skills software
- Symbol-based software
- Text-to-speech
- Touch typing software.

Visual Impairment

Choice of appropriate hardware and software will depend on the user's level of functional vision.

- RIAS (Remote Infrared Audible Signage) has the potential to help both low vision and the blind navigate outside and indoors.

Hardware

- Large monitors.
- Adjustable task lamp, using a fluorescent bulb, shines directly onto the paper and can be adjusted to suit.
- Copyholder holds printed material in near vertical position for easier reading and can be adjusted to suit.
- Closed circuit television (CCTV) or video magnifiers. Printed materials and objects are placed under a camera and the magnified image is displayed onto a screen.

- Modified cassette recorder. To record a lecture, own thoughts, ideas, notes etc.
- Desktop compact cassette dictation system. To allow audio cassette playback with the aid of a foot pedal.
- Fusers produce tactile materials, for example diagrams and maps, by applying heat to special swell paper.
- Scanner. A device used in conjunction with OCR software. The printed document is scanned and converted into electronic text, which can then be displayed on screen as recognisable text.
- Standalone reading aids integrate a scanner, optical character recognition (OCR) software, and speech software in a single machine. These function together without a separate PC.
- Refreshable Braille display. An electronic tactile device which is placed below the computer keyboard. A line of cells which correspond to Braille text move up and down to represent a line of text on the computer screen.
- Electronic Notetaker. A portable computer with a Braille or QWERTY keyboard and synthetic speech. Some models have an integrated Braille display.
- Braille embosser. Embosses Braille output from a computer by punching dots onto paper. It connects to a computer in the same way as a text printer.
- Perkins Brailler. To manually emboss Grade 1 or 2 Braille.

Software

- Customization of graphical user interfaces to alter the colours and size of desktops, short-cut icons, menu bars and scroll bars.
- Screen magnifiers.
- Screen readers.
- Self-voicing applications.
- Optical character recognition. Converts the printed word into text, via a scanner.
- Braille translation. Converts the printed word into Braille, which can then be embossed via a Braille embosser.
- Text-to-speech and Speech-to-text.
- Spell checkers and Grammar checkers.

Augmentative and Alternative Communication (AAC)

Augmentative and alternative communication is a well defined specialty within AT. It involves ways of communication that either enhance or replace verbal language. When combined with Applied Behaviour Analysis (ABA) teaching methods, AAC has improved communication skills in children with Autism. AAC devices vary widely with respect to their technological sophistication:

- *Low-tech systems.* Simple paper or object based systems, i.e. do not require a battery (e.g., Talking Mats, Dry Erase Boards, Clipboards, 3-Ring Binders, Manila File Folders, Photo Albums, Laminated PCS/Photographs, Highlight tape).

- *Light-tech systems.* Typically consisting of a digitized speech recorder with a touch-sensitive display pad and sometimes switch access. Lite-tech systems require a battery (e.g., Tape Recorder, Language Master, Overhead Projector, Timers, Calculators).
- *High-tech systems.* Computerized VOCAs that vary from single purpose appliance-like systems to multipurpose computer-based communication aids. Typically high-tech systems require training and ongoing support to operate the devices (e.g., Video Cameras, Computers and Adaptive Hardware, Complex Voice Output Devices).

Deafness and Hearing Loss

- Audiometer.
- Fire alarm paging system.
- Loop system (portable and fixed).
- Radio aids.
- Telecommunications device for the deaf.
- Teletext.
- Video cassette recorders that can read and record subtitles (Closed Captioning).
- Vibrating fire alarm placed under pillow when asleep.
- Door bell lighting system.

Others

- Wakamaru provides companionship, reminds users to take medicine and calls for help if something is wrong.
- Telephone Reassurance: community based programme that calls seniors at home ensuring their well-being.
- Cosmobot is part of a play therapy system designed to motivate children to participate in therapy.
- General User Interface for Disorders of Execution (GUIDE) is an interactive verbal prompting system that talks people with cognitive impairment through daily routine tasks.

Bibliography

Aaron, P.G. (1995). *"Differential Diagnosis of Reading Disabilities."* School Psychology Review 24 (3): 345–60.

Arlinger, M., Stamm, T.A., Pisetsky, D.S., Yarboro, C.H., Cieza, A., Smolen, J.S., & Stucki, G. (2006). *"ICF core sets: how to specify impairment and function in systemic lupus erythematosus."* Lupus, 15, 248-253.

Armbrester, Margaret E. (1992). *"The Civilian Story"*. Birmingham, AL: Ebsco Media. pp. 74-75.

Auxter, David, Pyfer, Jean, Huettig, Carol. (2005). *"Principles and Methods of Adapted Physical Education and Recreation"*. Boston, MA: McGraw Hill.

Bandian, N.A. (1999). *"Reading disability defined as a discrepancy between listening and reading comprehension: A longitudinal study of stability, gender differences, and prevalence"*. Journal of Learning Disabilities, 32(2) 138-148.

Berk L. (2005). *"Infants, Children, and Adolescents"*. Boston: Allyn & Bacon.

Berk, Laura E. (2009). *"Child Development"*. 8th ed. United States of America: Pearson Education, Inc.

Bornman, J. (2004). *"The World Health Organization's terminology and classification: Application to severe disability"*. Disability and Rehabilitation, 26, 182-188.

Bowe, Frank. (2005). *"Making Inclusion Work"*. Merrill Education/Prentice Hall.

Breines, E. (1990). *"Genesis of occupation: A philosophical model for therapy and theory"*. Australian Occupational Therapy Journal, 37(1), 45-49.

Bronfenbrenner, U. (1979). *"The Ecology of Human Development: Experiments by Nature and Design"*. Cambridge, MA: Harvard University Press.

Bruner, J.S. (1990). *"Acts of Meaning"*. Cambridge MA: Harvard University Press.

Carrie Y. Nordlund, *"Art Experiences in Waldorf Education"*, Ph.D. Dissertation, University of Missouri-Columbia, May 2006.

Charlotte Pearson (2006). *"Direct Payments and Personalisation of Care"*, Edinburgh, Dunedin Academic Press.

Chi, M.T.H. (1997). *"Quantifying qualitative analyses of verbal data: A practical guide"*. Journal of the Learning Sciences, 6, 271-315.

Colangelo, N., & Davis, G. (2003). *"Handbook of Gifted Education"*. Boston: Pearson education, Inc.

COT (2006). *"COT/BAOT Briefings: Definitions and Core Skills for Occupational Therapists"*. London: College of Occupational Therapists.

Coutinho, M.J. & Oswald, D.P. (2005). *"State variation in gender disproportionally in special education: Finding and recommendations"*. Remedial and Special Education, 26(1), 7-15.

Creek (2003). *"Occupational Therapy Defined as a Complex Intervention"*, London COT.

Creek, J. (2003). *"Occupational therapy defined as a complex intervention"*. London: College of Occupational Therapists.

David Johnstone (2001). *"An Introduction to Disability Studies"*, 2nd edition.

David Johnstone, *"An Introduction to Disability Studies"*, David Fulton Publishers Ltd. 2001.

DePoy, E., & Gilson, S.F. (2004). *"Rethinking disability: Principles for professional and social change"*. Pacific Grove, CA: Wadsworth.

Donahue, Wong. (2002). *"The Social Dimensions of Learning Disabilities: Essays in Honour of Tanis Bryan"*.

Douglas, F.M. (2004). *"Occupational still matters: A tribute to a pioneer"*. British Journal of Occupational Therapy, 67(6), 239.

Elizabeth DePoy & Stephen Gilson, *"Rethinking Disability: Principles for Professional and Social Change"*. Pacific Grove, CA: Wadsworth 2004.

Elliot, A.J. (1999). *"Approach and avoidance motivation and achievement goals"*. Educational Psychologist, 34, 169–189.

Emerson, E. (1995). *"Challenging Behaviour: Analysis and Intervention with People with Learning Difficulties"*. Cambridge: Cambridge University Press.

Emmer, E.T., & Stough, L.M. (2001). *"Classroom management: A critical part of educational psychology with implications for teacher education"*. Educational Psychologist, 36, 103-112.

Ericsson, K.A., & Simon, H. (1993). *"Protocol analysis: Verbal reports as data"* (Rev. ed.). Cambridge, MA: MIT Press.

Evans, J., Hsieh, P.P., & Robinson, D.H. (2005). *"Women's Involvement in educational psychology journals from 1976 to 2004"*. Educational Psychology Review, 17, 263-271.

Everall, R.D., Bostik, K.E. & Paulson, B.L. (2005). *"I'm sick of being me: Developmental themes in a suicidal adolescent"*. Adolescence, 40, 693-708.

Finn, C.E., Rotherham A.J. & Hokanson C.R. (2001). *"Rethinking Special Education for a New Century"*, Progressive Policy Institute.

Folsom-Meek, Sherry L., Ruth J. Nearing, and Renae E. Bock. *"Transitioning Children, Youths, and Young Adults with Disabilities."* JOPERD 3 (2007): 38-45.

Foster, M. (2002). *"Theoretical Frameworks"*, In: Occupational Therapy and Physical Dysfunction, Eds. Turner, Foster & Johnson.

Frank Bowe, *"Handicapping America: Barriers to Disabled People"*, Harper & Row, 1978.

Gardner, Howard. (1983). *"Frames of Mind: The Theory of Multiple Intelligences."* New York: Basic Books.

Garn, S.M. *"Physical growth and development"*. In: Friedman S.B, Fisher M., Schonberg S.K., editors. Comprehensive Adolescent Health Care. St. Louis: Quality Medical Publishing; 1992. Retrieved on 2009-02-20.

Gary L. Albrecht, (ed.), *"Encyclopedia of Disability"*. Sage Publications, Thousand Oaks, Calif. 2006, 5 v., ill.

Gaylord-Ross, R. (Ed.) (1989). *"Integration strategies for students with handicaps"*. Baltimore: Paul H. Brookes.

Gerald Coles (1987). *"The Learning Mystique: A Critical Look at "Learning Disabilities."* Accessed April 4, 2008.

Glantz, C. & Richman, N. (2007). *"Occupation-based, ability-centered care for people with dementia"*. [Electronic Version]. OT Practice, 12(2), 10-16.

Glenn, Eddie. March 20, 1997. *"African American Women with Disabilities: An Overview."*

Golledge, J. (1998). *"Distinguishing between Occupation, Purposeful Activity and Activity, Part 2: Why is the Distinction Important?"* British Journal of Occupational Therapy, 61(4), pp. 157-160.

Goodman, Libby (1990). *"Time and Learning in the Special Education Classroom"*. Albany, N.Y: State University of New York Press, p. 122.

Greenberg, D. (1992). Education in America, A View from Sudbury Valley, *"Special Education" —A noble Cause Sacrificed to Standardization.*

Greenough W, Black J. and Wallace C. (1993), *"Experience and Brain Development"*, in Johnson M, *"Brain Development and Cognition"*, Oxford: Blackwell, pp. 319–322.

Gretchell, N., Pabreja, P., Neeld, K. & Carrio, V. (2007) *"Comparing children with and without dyslexia on the movement assessment battery for children and the test of gross motor development"*. Perceptual and Motor Skills, 105(1), 207-214.

Gronlund, N.E. (2000). *"How to Write and use Instructional Objectives"* (6th ed.). Columbus, OH, USA: Merrill.

Gross, Miraca U.M. (2004). *"Exceptionally Gifted Children"*. New York: RoutledgeFalmer. pp.

Harner, C., & Heal, L. (1993). *"The Multifaceted Lifestyle Satisfaction Scale (MLSS): Psychometric Properties of an Interview Schedule for Assessing Personal Satisfaction of Adults with Limited Intelligence"*. Research in Developmental Disabilities, 14, 221-236.

Hart, B. and Risley, T. (1995). *"Meaningful Differences in the Everyday Experience of Young American Children"*. Baltimore: P.H. Brookes.

Hattie, J., Biggs, J., & Purdie, N. (1996). *"Effects of learning skills interventions on student learning: A meta-analysis"*. Review of Educational Research, 66, 99-136.

Hemmingsson, H., & Jonsson, H. (2005). *"An occupational perspective on the concept of participation in the international classification of functioning, disability and health– Some critical remarks"*. The American Journal of Occupational Therapy, 59, 569-576.

Hocking, C. (2004). *"Making a difference: The romance of occupational therapy"*. South African Journal of Occupational Therapy, 34(2), 3-5.

Hocking, C. and Whiteford, G. (1995). *"Multiculturalism in occupational therapy: A time for reflection on core values"*. Australian Occupational Therapy Journal, 42(4), 172-175.

Ingram, D. (1999). *"Phonological acquisition"*, in Barrett M, *"The Development of Language"*, London: Psychology Press, pp. 73–97.

James, T. Webb, Elizabeth A. Mechstroth, Stephanie Tolan (March 1989). *"Guiding The Gifted Child"*. Great Potential Press.

Johnsen, S.K. (2004). *"Identifying Gifted Students: A Practical Guide."* Waco, Texas: Prufrock Press, Inc.

Kail, R.E. (2006). *"Children and their Development (4 ed.)"*. Prentice Hall.

Kaushik, R., 1999, *"Access Denied: Can we overcome disabling attitudes,"* Museum International (UNESCO) , Vol. 51, No. 3, pp. 48-52.

Kielhofner, G. (1997). *"Conceptual Foundations of Occupational Therapy"*. 2nd Ed. Philadelphia, F.A. Davis.

Kramer, P. and Hinojosa, J. and Royeen, C.R. (2003). *"Perspectives in Human Occupation: Participation in Life"*. Baltimore: Lippincott Williams and Wilkins.

Lemma A. (2007). *"Psychodynamic Therapy: The Freudian Approach"*, in Dryden W, *"Handbook of Individual Therapy"* (5 ed.), Sage publications.

Lennard Davis (ed.), *"Disability Studies Reader"*, Routledge 1997.

Lerner, Janet W. (2000). *"Learning Disabilities: Theories, Diagnosis, and Teaching Strategies"*. Boston: Houghton Mifflin.

Lipsey, M.W., & Wilson, D.B. (2001). *"Practical Meta-analysis."* London: Sage.

Lollar, D.J., & Simeonsson, R.J. (2005). *"Diagnosis to function: Classification for children and youths"*. Developmental and Behavioural Pediatrics, 26, 323-330.

Lovecky, Deirdre V., *"Different Minds: Gifted Children with Ad/Hd, Asperger Syndrome, and Other Learning Deficits"*. Jessica Kingsly Publishers. pp. 20–24.

Marcia A. Barnes; Fletcher, Jack; Fuchs, Lynn. (2007). *"Learning Disabilities: From Identification to Intervention"*. New York: The Guilford Press.

Margai, F. & Henry, N. (2003). *"A community-based assessment of learning disabilities using environmental and contextual risk factors"*. Social Science & Medicine, 56(5), 13.

Mayer, R.E. (2001). *"Multimedia learning"*. Cambridge, UK: Cambridge University Press.

Michael Oliver, *"The Politics of Disablement"*, St. Martin's Press 1997.

Mocellin, G. (1988). *"A perspective on the principles and practice of occupational therapy"*. Generally they need to eat loads of bananas and chocolate. British Journal of Occupational Therapy, 51(1), 4-7.

Mocellin, G. (1995). *"Occupational therapy: A critical overview, Part 1"*. British Journal of Occupational Therapy, 58(12), 502-506.

Mocellin, G. (1996). *"Occupational therapy: A critical overview, Part 2"*. British Journal of Occupational Therapy, 59(1), 11-16.

Modell, S.J., & Megginson, N.L. (February 2001). *"Life After School: A Transition Model for Adapted Physical Educators"*. JOPERD, 72(2), 45-48.

Moerk E.L. (1986). *"Environmental factors in early language acquisition"*, in Whitehurst GJ, Annals of Child Development, 3, CTJAI Press.

Mosey, A.C. (1985). *"Psychosocial Components of Occupational Therapy"*. New York: Raven Press.

National Council on Disability. (1994). *"Inclusionary education for students with disabilities: Keeping the promise"*. Washington, DC: Author.

National Dissemination Center for Children with Disabilities (NICHY), 2004. [1]. Accessed May 11, 2007.

National Institute for Direct Instruction [2]. Accessed May 23, 2007.

Nelson, D. (1996). *"Therapeutic Occupation: A Definition"*. American Journal of Occupational Therapy, 50(10), pp. 775-782.

Nelson, D., L. (1988). *"Occupation: Form and Performance"*. American Journal of Occupational Therapy. 42 (10) pp. 633-641.

Nikora, L.; Karapu, R.; Hickey, H.; & Awekotuku, N. "[5]" , *"Disabled Maori and Disability Support Options"*, 2004. Retrieved on April 19, 2009.

Ogden-Niemeyer, L. & Jacobs, K. (1989). *"Work Hardening: State of the Art."* Slack: Thorofare, N.J.

Ogonowski, J., Kronk, R., Rice, C., & Feldman, H. (2004). *"Inter-rater reliability in assigning ICF codes to children with disabilities"*. Disability and Rehabilitation, 26, 353-361.

Parker, W.D. & Mills, C.J. (1996). *"The Incidence of Perfectionism in Gifted Students"*. Gifted Child Quarterly, 40, 194-199.

Patti L. Harrison; Flanagan, Dawn P. (2005). *"Contemporary Intellectual Assessment: Theories, Tests, and Issues"*. New York: Guilford Press.

Pea, R.D. (1993). *"Learning scientific concepts through material and social activities: Conversational analysis meets conceptual change"*. Educational Psychologist, 28, 265-277.

Perkins, D.N., & Grotzer, T.A. (1997). *"Teaching intelligence"*. American Psychologist, 52, 1125-1133.

Peter Breggin (February 2001). *"Reclaiming Our Children"*. Perseus Publishing. pp. 21–22, 115–116, 159–162.

Pinker S. (1994). *"The Language Instinct"*. London: Allen Lane.

Punwar, A.J. (1994). *"Philosophy of Occupational Therapy in Occupational Therapy, Principles and practice"*. 2nd Ed. Williams and Wilkins, Baltimore, 7-20.

Rainforth, B., York, J., & Macdonald,C. (1992). *"Collaborative teams for students with severe disabilities"*. Baltimore: Paul H. Brookes.

Rauch, A., Cieza, A., & Stucki, G. (2008). *"How to apply the International Classification of Functioning Disability and Health (ICF) for rehabilitation management in clinical practice"*. European Journal of Physical and Rehabilitation Medicine, 44, 329-342.

Reed, G., Lux, J., Bufka, L., Peterson, D., Threats, T., Trask, C., Stark, S., Jacobson, J., & Hawley, J. (2005). *"Operationalizing the International Classification of Functioning, Disability, and Health: A model to guide clinical thinking, practice and research in the field of cerebral palsy"*. Seminars in Pediatric Neurology, 11, 5-10.

Richards, S. (2003). *"Occupational Therapy: Comment"*. The Independent.

Robert Holland (6/1/2002). *"Vouchers Help the Learning Disabled: Lesson from 22 countries: Special-education students thrive in private schools."* The Heartland Institute.

Rogers J.C. (1983). *"Eleanor Clarke Slagle Lecture. Clinical Reasoning; the ethics, science and art"*. American Journal of Occupational Therapy, 37(9):601-616.

Rourke, B.P. (1989). *"Non-verbal learning disabilities: The syndrome and the model"*. New York: Guilford Press.

Sameroff, A. (1983). *"Factors in predicting successful parenting."* In Sasserath, V. (Ed.), Minimizing High-Risk Parenting. Skilman, NJ: Johnson & Johnson.

Savage, R. 2005. *"The Great Leap Forward: Transition into the adult World"*. Preventing School Failure. Summer 2005. Vol. 49, (4) p. 46.

Simeonsson, R.J., Lollar, D., Hollowell, J., & Adams, M. (2000). *"Revision of the international classification of impairments, disabilities, and handicaps developmental issues"*. Journal of Clinical Epidemiology, 53, 113-124.

Simeonsson, R.J., Scarborough, A.A., & Hebbeler, K.M. (2006). *ICF and ICD codes provide a standard language of disability in young children*. Journal of Clinical Epidemiology, 59, 365-373.

Simi Linton, *"Claiming Disability: Knowledge and Identity"*, in series 'Cultural Front', Michael Berube (ed.), New York University Press 1998.

Smith P.K., Cowie H. and Blades M. *"Understanding Children's Development"*. Basic psychology (4 ed.). Oxford, England: Blackwell.

Southwest Educational Development Laboratory (SEDL), 2007. *"Southwest Educational Development Laboratory"*. Accessed September 15, 2007.

Spearman, C. (1904). *"General intelligence" objectively determined and measured*. American Journal of Psychology, 15, 201–293.

Stainback, W. & Stainback, S.(Eds.) (1990). *"Support networks for inclusive schooling: Interdependent integrated education"*. Baltimore: Paul H. Brookes.

Stern, D.N. (1990). *"Diary of a Baby"*. Harmondsworth: Penguin.

Sternberg, R.J., & Grigorenko, E.L. (1999). *"Our labelled children: What every parent and teacher needs to know about learning disabilities"*. Reading, MA: Perseus Publishing Group.

Strategies for Success Transition. (January 2003). Adapted Physical Activity Quartely, 20(1), 98.

Stucki, G., Ewert, T., & Cieza, A. (2002). *"Value and application of the ICF in rehabilitation medicine"*. Disability and Rehabilitation, 24, 932-938.

Swan, W.W., & Morgan, J.L. (1993). *"Collaborating for comprehensive services for young child and their families"*. Baltimore: Paul H. Brookes.

Swanson Anderson, L.L. & Malaski, C.K. (1999). *"Occupational Therapy as a Career: An Introduction to the Field and a Structured Method for Observation"*. F.A. Davis Company: USA.

Tanner J.M. (1978). *"Fetus into Man"*. Cambridge MA: Harvard University Press.

Taylor, E. and Manguno, J. (1990). *"Use of Treatment Activities in Occupational Therapy"*. American Journal of Occupational Therapy, 45(4), pp. 317-322.

Taylor, M.J. & Barusch, A.S. (2004). *"Personal, family, and multiple barriers of long-term welfare recipients"*. Social Work, 49(2), 175-183.

Thomas Kelly (2004). *"Positive psychology and adolescent mental health: False promise or true breakthrough?"*.

Thomas, G. and Loxley, A. (2007). *"Deconstructing Special Education and Constructing Inclusion"* (2nd Edition). Open University Press.

Thorndike, E.L. (1912). *"Education: A First Book"*. New York: MacMillan.

Tom Shakespeare, (1999). *"Genetic Politics: from Eugenics to Genome"*, with Anne Kerr, New Clarion Press.

Tubbs, C. and Drake, M. (2007). *"Crafts and Creative Media in Therapy"*. 3rd ed. Thorofare: Slack Incorporated.

Turner, A. (2002). *"History and Philosophy of Occupational Therapy"*, in Turner, A., Foster, M. and Johnson, S. (eds.). *"Occupational Therapy and Physical Dysfunction, Principles, Skills and Practice"*. 5th Edition. Edinburgh, Churchill Livingstone, 3-24.

Turner, A., Foster, M. and Johnson, S.E. (1997). *"Occupational Therapy and Physical Dysfunction: Principles, Skills and Practice"*. Edinburgh: Churchill Livingstone.

Ustun, B., Chatterji, S., & Kostanjsek, N. (2004). *"Comments from WHO for the Journal of Rehabilitation Medicine special supplement on ICF core sets"*. Journal of Rehabilitation Medicine, (Suppl. 44), 7-8.

Üstün, T.B., Chatterji, S., Bickenbach, J., Kostanjsek, N., & Schneider, M. (2003). *"The International Classification of Functioning, Disability and Health: A new tool for understanding disability and health"*. Disability and Rehabilitation, 25, 565–571.

Watson, J.B. (1926). *"What the nursery has to say about instincts"*. In C. Murchison (Eds.) Psychologies of 1925. Worchester, MA: Clark University Press.

Wechsler, D. (1949). *"The Wechsler Intelligence Scale for Children"*. New York: Psychological Corp.

White, S.H.(1968). *"The learning maturation controversy"*: Hall to Hull. Merrill-Palmer Quarterly, 14, 187-196.

Whiteford, G. and Fossey, E. (2002). *"Occupation: The essential nexus between philosophy, theory and practice"*. Australian Occupational Therapy Journal, 49(1), 1-2.

Winnick, Joseph, P. (2005). *"Adapted Physical Education and Sport, Fourth Edition"*. Champaign, IL: Human Kinetics.

Wolf Wolfensberger (January 10, 1969). *"The Origin and Nature of Our Institutional Models."* *Changing Patterns in Residential Services for the Mentally Retarded*. President's Committee on Mental Retardation, Washington, D.C.

Wood, S.E., Wood, C.E. and Boyd, D. (2006). *"Mastering the World of Psychology"* (2 ed.). Allyn & Bacon.

Woolfolk, A.E., Winne, P.H. & Perry, N.E. (2006). *"Educational Psychology (3rd Canadian ed.)"*. Toronto, Canada: Pearson.

World Health Organization. (2001). *"International Classification of Functioning, Disability and Health (ICF)"*. Geneva: Author.

Young Adults: *"A Psychiatrist's View"*. Journal of Secondary Gifted Education 17(4)199-210.

Zabel, R.H. & Nigro, F.A. (1999). *"Juvenile offenders with behavioural disorders, learning disabilities, and no disabilities: Self-reports of personal, family, and school characteristics"*. Behavioural Disorders, 25(1), 22-40.

Index